SHELDON JACOBS'

GUIDE TO
Successful No-Load Fund Investing

Also by the same author

**The Handbook for No-Load
Fund Investors**

The No-Load Fund Investor

SHELDON JACOBS'

GUIDE TO Successful No-Load Fund Investing

The No-Load Fund Investor, Inc.
Post Office Box 318, Irvington-on-Hudson, NY 10533
Telephone: 914-693-7420, 800-252-2042

The No-Load Fund Investor, Inc. publishes *Sheldon Jacobs' Guide to Successful No-Load Mutual Fund Investing*, the annual *Handbook for No-Load Fund Investors*, and the monthly *No-Load Fund Investor* newsletter. The *Handbook* is regularly $45; twelve monthly *No-Load Fund Investor* newsletter issues are $135. All three publications are available to new subscribers only at a special introductory rate of $129. Additional copies of the *Guide* are $25. A sample issue of the *Investor* newsletter can be obtained free from *The No-Load Fund Investor.*

Unless otherwise indicated, the mutual fund data in this book originate in *The No-Load Fund Investor* newsletter or *The Handbook for No-Load Fund Investors.* Where necessary, we will refer to these two publications as the *Investor* and the *Handbook.*

If you have any suggestions for future editions of this *Guide*, or have spotted any mistakes, I would be glad to hear from you. Please write me at *The No-Load Fund Investor.* SJ.

First Edition: May 1995
Second Edition: April 1998

The No-Load Fund Investor, Inc. is not associated with the management or sale of any mutual fund, nor with any mutual fund association. The *Investor*'s sole objective is to present unbiased information about funds. Readers desiring information about a particular fund should examine the fund's prospectus. Performance results quoted in this book do not take into account any tax consequences and are not, in or of themselves, predictive of future performance. This publication is designed to provide accurate and authoritative information in regard to the subject matter covered. It is sold with the understanding that neither the author nor the publisher renders legal or accounting advice. If legal advice or other expert assistance is required, the services of a competent professional person should be sought.

Library of Congress Catalog Card No. 95—796688

ISBN: 0-9664627-0-X

To my loving wife, Liz,
whose help and support I depend on.

CONTENTS

TABLES AND CHARTS

What you are about to read is the third incarnation of the first book ever written on how to invest in no-load funds. The first was called *Put Money in Your Pocket*, subtitled *The Art of Selecting No-Load Mutual Funds for Maximum Gain*. It was published by Simon & Schuster in 1974. *Put Money in Your Pocket* was an instant success. *Money* and *Financial World* magazines published chapters. The reviews were good. Even today—more than two decades later—people tell me how much the book influenced them.

I received the following letter in 1990, and it meant a lot to me.

> I feel compelled to write a note to you and send it with my application for a one year subscription to your *No-Load Fund Investor*.
>
> One day during 1975, I was drifting through the aisles of my local library. A book entitled *Put Money in Your Pocket* caught my eye. I checked it out, read it, and became fascinated by what you had written. That book planted the seed that was to change my outlook on investing. Through me, it also changed the outlook of quite a few of my friends and relatives.
>
> Five years later, I retired (4 years earlier than required) and with a philosophy of investing that began with the seed planted by your book, we have enjoyed seeing our investments grow at a compound rate in excess of 16%. So you see, subscribing to your service is really a small "Thank You" for what you started with *Put Money in Your Pocket*, more than 15 years ago. Thank you.

I wrote *Put Money In Your Pocket* when I was simply a private investor who believed that no-load funds were the best way for the individual to build a nestegg.

The popularity of *Put Money In Your Pocket* enabled me to become a professional investment advisor. I wrote for others for several years, and then in 1979 I started my own newsletter, *The No-Load Fund Investor*. Two years later I complemented the newsletter with a companion publication, *The Handbook For No-Load Fund Investors*.

The *Handbook* had three sections: 1) an editorial how-to section, 2) a statistical section with detailed 10-year performance data, and 3) a comprehensive Directory providing purchase and selection information for virtually all no-load mutual funds available to individual investors.

To write the editorial section, I thoroughly updated *Put Money in Your Pocket*, and made it the first section of *The Handbook For No-Load Fund Investors*, an annual book that is published by my company, The No-Load Fund Investor, Inc.

The *Handbook*'s first edition, published in 1981, was a 160-page book covering 291 funds. We're still publishing the *Handbook*, but with the thousands of funds now available, we made the decision to produce it in two volumes. The *Handbook* now includes the statistical and directory data only. The editorial how-to section is contained in this volume. Thus, *Sheldon Jacobs' Guide to Successful No-Load Fund Investing* is the third generation of my original book, *Put Money In Your Pocket*. This "new book" actually is the culmination of 25 years of study, advising, writing and rewriting.

The *Guide* can provide useful guidance to both beginning and expert investors. In addition, it is designed to enable subscribers of the *No-Load Fund Investor* newsletter to maximize their investing results from the newsletter's recommendations. Other newsletters provide little or no guidance to their subscribers, merely asking them to accept their newsletter's recommendations. You can accept our newsletter's recommendations too. But we believe you will be a better and more confident investor, and will make better use of the *Investor's* recommendations, if you really understand the art of no-load fund investing. Other newsletters offer at most a short pamphlet on the basics. We think the subject is so important that it deserves a whole book. I hope that you will find it worthwhile.

Sheldon Jacobs
Irvington-on-Hudson, NY

PART I

The Case For Mutual Funds

CHAPTER 1

Mutual funds — investments for the 1990s, and beyond

I began investing when I was 17 years old.

That was in 1948—before many readers of this book were born.

At first I bought individual stocks. That's what almost all investors did back then. If you went to a cocktail party in the '50s and '60s most people bragged about their winning stock selections. That was true even in the go-go era of the 1960s when the top-performing funds received much publicity. Back in 1967, at the height of the long-running bull market at that time, mutual funds had less than eight million shareholder accounts. With only 204 mutual funds in existence, only a few percent of Americans owned mutual funds. The prevailing opinion at the time was if you had any brains you bought stocks. Mutual funds were for dumbbells, people who couldn't pick their own stocks (or I suppose find a broker to do it for them).

I, too, bought individual stocks during those years. I made some money, but I wasn't satisfied. I knew that there had to be a better way.

Finally, I asked my broker "where do you put your own money?" His answer was both honest and astonishing. (He was honest because he was a relative.) He said "mutual funds."

I was shocked. Back then, I thought brokers knew it all, had the inside dope acted on the hottest tips. And yet here was my own broker—a man I respected—admitting that he relied on a mutual fund manager to pick his stocks.

At the time, investors didn't have the benefit of the vast financial marketplace that exists today. Most of the funds familiar to individuals were load funds, and their commissions were way to high—usually 8.5% and sometimes even more.

But then I learned about no-load funds. I bought my first one in 1965.

From then on, I seldom purchased another share of stock. Not only did I make more money in no-load funds, but I also received more enjoyment, more excitement, and a greater sense of accomplishment than I ever did from stocks.

I'm confident that the personal decision I made in 1965 was a good one then. In the 33 years since, the rationale for mutual funds has become even more sound. Why? Academic research has helped investors understand the reasons stock prices move in a market which has steadily grown more "efficient" as it has grown larger. Once you understand how and why stock prices move, you begin to see better how you can earn profits and reach your investment goals over the long haul. And in most cases, you will see why no-load mutual funds are the best vehicle to take you there.

Why stocks move

Stock prices fluctuate for many reasons. If you own just one stock, the value of your portfolio will be heavily influenced by events relating to the company and its industry. However, if you own a portfolio of many stocks, the picture changes. Astonishingly, research shows that *events pertaining to individual companies account for an almost insignificant percentage of the price movement of modern diversified portfolios.*

In a classic study, Gary Brinson, L. Randolph Hood and Gilbert L. Beebower evaluated 91 large pension plans over a ten-year period. They found that the selection of asset classes (e.g. stocks, bonds, cash) accounted for 94% of price variation of these portfolios. Market timing—i.e., shifting portfolio assets in and out of the market or between asset classes—accounted for another 2% of the variation. Finally, individual security selection, finding "underpriced" companies—what many individuals and brokers concentrate on—accounted for 4% of price variation. Another study, this one by Fama-French, found that by controlling for risk, capitalization size, and style (i.e., growth vs. value), explains 95% of a portfolio's return.

These two studies have come under criticism because they focused on institutional portfolios that didn't differ significantly from each other. However, in earlier editions of this book, I cited three studies from the 1950s and 1960s that showed that individual company selection accounted for only 12%, 20%, and 45% of the variation in common stock prices respectively. The majority of the price movement was due to the general market and the industry.

Whatever the exact numbers, it's obvious that specific stock selections are not very important at all unless you forego diversification altogether, a terrible idea. You can be a good investor simply by allocating your assets accurately among major asset classes, risk levels, styles, etc. These decisions are hugely important in producing superior returns over time, while the specific stock selections are not very important at all. And yet, too many investors still focus on evaluating individual stocks in an effort to determine which will be hottest.

The inevitable conclusion is that devoting hours to studying individual stocks is a waste of time. Over holding periods of a few years or more, you will do better by buying a diversified mutual fund portfolio and relying on the expertise of sophisticated fund managers who, with their skills, training, and research staffs, are much better equipped to deal successfully with the markets.

Mutual funds are pools of investors' dollars. The money is used to purchase a diversified portfolio of stocks, bonds or money market instruments under the continuous supervision of professional managers. Mutual funds seek to do for investors what they might do for themselves if they had the time, inclination, background, experience and resources to spread investments among many securities.

So just what are mutual funds?

Each investor shares in the fund's income, expenses, profits and losses in proportion to the number of shares owned. When a mutual fund provides joint ownership of securities—stocks and bonds—that can fluctuate in value, the fund cannot guarantee a specific return to its investors. It is thus fundamentally different from a bank savings account or certificate of deposit. Bank accounts do guarantee a fixed rate of return to depositors, who are lenders, rather than owners.

Technically, every mutual fund is owned by its shareholders. However, mutual funds are seldom managed along conventional corporate lines by their own officers and directors. A typical fund is "externally managed," meaning that most or all of its work is done for it by a separate company usually called the *investment adviser*, who presides over a fund's birth and generally remains in control throughout its life. Almost invariably, a fund's shareholders vote to renew the adviser's management contract.

Funds have been around since the 20s

Mutual funds evolved from investment trusts and investment companies that were founded toward the close of the nineteenth century in Boston, New York, Philadelphia, and other cities. The first mutual fund, or open-end investment company, was formed in 1924 when the Massachusetts Investors Trust (M.I.T.) granted its shareholders the right to redeem their shares at net asset value—total assets held by the fund divided by the number of shares outstanding—minus a discount of $2 per share. However, mutual funds did not achieve significant growth until after the passage of the Investment Company Act of 1940, which eliminated abuses of the 1920s and provided statutory safeguards for investors. This act provided the essential framework for the substantial growth of the mutual fund industry in the past six decades.

The term "mutual fund" seems to have arisen in the late '30s. Some think it was coined to take the onus off the word "Trust." Investors' faith in "trusts" was severely shaken by the 1929 crash.

While mutual funds initially were started for investors of moderate means, many wealthy individuals and institutions have found them to be a good way to achieve their investment objectives. In 1996, 26 per cent mutual fund assets were held in fiduciary, financial, business and other organizational accounts.

Both individual and institutional investors participate in mutual funds to take advantage of the following benefits:

- ■ Funds offer professional management.
- ■ Past performance records are readily available for systematic evaluation.
- ■ In their prospectuses, funds must disclose unfavorable facts, such as being sued.
- ■ Funds are diversified.

- They have low transaction costs.
- They can provide access to inaccessible markets.
- They can automatically reinvest your dividends and distributions.
- Funds' risk-reward ratios can be determined fairly accurately, and the ratios are generally acceptable.
- The entire field can be adequately researched and mastered by an individual who lacks formal training in finance.
- Purchasing and redeeming shares is easy.

Mutual fund shareholders receive *professional management* at rock-bottom fees. Years ago Bernard Baruch made the cogent comparison:

> It would never occur to anyone to open a department store in competition with Macy's or Gimbel's or to make motor cars against Ford and General Motors without prior training or preparation. Yet many people will cheerfully toss their savings into a market dominated by professionals who are as expert in their line as the department stores and auto makers are in theirs.

The second reason is by far the more important and bears emphasis. *Past performance records are easily available.* From the individual investor's point of view, this is unique and terribly important. There is no way to compare the performance of stockbrokers or, in most cases, even investment counselors. Only mutual funds publish industry-wide performance records that are readily accessible. With this indispensable data bank, the lay investor can make intelligent investment decisions.

When you buy a mutual fund you will always receive a *prospectus.* It will tell you in detail what the fund is all about. You can learn its objective—whether the fund seeks growth, income or a combination; what kinds of securities the fund will invest in; and the amount of risk the fund plans to take. In addition, the prospectus may give you unfavorable facts about the fund, as well as the favorable information that fund management would like to convey. The SEC requires information on pending lawsuits, management changes, etc. This makes the prospectus a valuable data source, one not available when you select an investment counselor or buy stock, unless it's a new issue. Chapter 23 shows you how to get the most out of a prospectus.

Diversification, owning a large portfolio of stocks, is another key benefit of buying funds. There are two basic risks in owning stocks:

1) that the market will go down; and 2) that an individual company will do poorly. Diversification can eliminate the latter risk. And since the wise investor is risk averse, it makes sense to avoid taking any risk that's unnecessary. In fact, academic studies have found that investors who don't diversify are *not* rewarded for taking on this additional risk. Every time a stock plummets, be happy that your investments are diversified in mutual funds.

The art of diversification is more complicated than it might appear. It is not enough to own a dozen or more stocks. Proper diversification demands investments in stocks of different industries that are unlikely to behave the same way at the same time. Some examples: cyclical industries versus industries that are relatively insensitive to business cycles. This distinction is lost on the average stock broker; most do not seem to understand the importance of diversifying across a range of industries. Their conventional "widows and orphans" portfolio—supposedly ultraconservative—tends to be heavily invested in bonds and utility stocks, all of which decline simultaneously when interest rates rise. In 1994, these portfolios did far worse than other portfolios invested more aggressively.

Diversity is a major advantage that mutual funds have over stock advisory letters or stockbrokers' recommended lists. There is always great variation in the performances of individual stocks. But with funds, it is the portfolio's overall performance that counts.

Mutual funds can provide *access* to foreign markets that you might find difficult to trade in yourself, and this also increases diversification.

With each mutual fund, you can determine its historic *risk* and *reward* level with simple, readily available measurements. Funds must stick to the objectives stated in their prospectuses, and these tend to be targeted to common investor needs. For example, a very popular fund category is growth-income, with a risk level about 60-70% of the stock market average? Why is this category popular? Huge numbers of investors want to participate in stocks without exposing their money to all the stock market's risk.

An average person can do the sort of analysis with funds that only professionals do well with stocks. The *entire field can be well researched and mastered,* even if the time you have for investing is very limited. Uniform data for most no-load funds are readily available from mutual fund advisory services, such as our companion publications, *The Handbook for No-Load Fund Investors* and *Investor* newsletter. Both contain performance computations, as well as rankings and comparisons of similar funds. So you can easily spot the best, virtually forcing you into an organized approach to investing. You look automatically for the best performers and eliminate the rest. You thus have an excellent chance to maximize your profits, and need to expend relatively little energy. The sizeable increase in the number of funds over the past few years has not altered this fact. In contrast, most investors don't compare the relative merits of stocks because data are seldom complete or uniform.

Until the late 40s, most mutual funds followed conservative investment policies. The funds that survived the Depression had names like Massachusetts Investors Trust, Investment Company of America, American Business Shares, Dividend Shares, Founders Mutual, Income Foundation, and Lexington Income Trust. As a result, they were considered stodgy, beneficial only to small investors who were incapable of understanding the basic principles of investing. In those days, "smart" investors bought stocks. In fact in 1952, the entire mutual fund industry had assets of only $3.9 billion. Today, scores of individual funds are larger.

How profitable are mutual funds?

Then, performance became an important element in mutual fund competition. It soon became clear that funds such as Dreyfus and Fidelity Capital were regularly outpacing the market averages. Fund salesmen, who had once talked retirement goals, began to stress appreciation. New funds were formed which frankly stated that their objective was to achieve maximum capital gains. Gas Industries Fund changed its name to Colonial Growth & Energy Shares. Massachusetts Investors Second Fund was transformed into Massachusetts Investors Growth Stock Fund. Foreign Bond Associates became the Winfield Growth Fund. "Smart" money moved into well-managed aggressive funds. The mutual fund industry was, in fact, revolutionized. In 1949 only two funds used the word "growth" in their name; today, it's commonplace.

As the stock market boomed, top mutual funds delivered impressive performance in the 1950s and 1960s. Then in the slumping stock markets of the late 1960s and early 1970s, profits virtually disappeared and for nearly a decade the mutual fund industry floundered.

The tide has turned. Since 1975 the long-term trend of the market has once again been up. As a result, the mutual fund industry has soared in popularity. It is now the preeminent place for the individual to invest for his retirement and financial needs. Today, mutual funds—now holding over $2 trillion of U.S. equity securities—control nearly 22% of corporate America. Also, you no longer have to be a growth-seeking investor to participate. Money market funds, bond funds, and government securities funds are available for investors who wish to emphasize capital preservation or income, or generally diversify their portfolio among asset classes.

You can't buy and forget

The most striking fact about individual stock funds is that their performance varies tremendously. And it's easy to understand why: Their objectives differ. The over 3,000 equity funds available to the public range in size from less than one hundred thousand dollars to over $60 billion. The number of stocks in their portfolios ranges from a handful to hundreds.

In most years, the performance of individual funds varies from gains of 50% or more—occasionally 100% or more—on the high side to significant losses at the other extreme. Note that "performance" as used in the mutual fund industry and in this book means the fund's performance, not an investor's experience. Your results will vary depending on when you bought a fund, whether it has a load and your personal tax situation.

For various reasons, which we will discuss in detail in the chapters on mutual fund selection, it is highly unlikely that any fund will maintain an outstanding growth record over a long period of time. There are good reasons why funds don't turn in outstanding performances year in, year out. Some are victims of their own success. They become too large and perhaps too complacent. As they get unwieldy, they lose the sharp edge of aggressiveness that originally distinguished their approach. Others become casualties of the market's cyclical ups and downs. It is axiomatic that the aggressive, performance-oriented funds that surpass all others in bull markets are, by nature, the funds that decline most when the inevitable bear market arrives.

The mutual fund industry correctly points out that the greatest rewards usually come to the long-term investor. But that doesn't mean you should marry a particular fund. Holding one fund for your investing lifetime is definitely not the way to maximize your profits.

With the help of *The No-Load Fund Investor* and other resources, you can select funds that should perform better than average for a time—perhaps one to four years. But if you want above-average performance year after year, you must stay flexible. That means you should switch funds or change your allocation among funds from time to time, based on changed in the economic cycle, financial markets, fund performance, and your needs. How to do that in a smart and cost-effective way is the subject of several chapters which follow in this book.

Stay flexible

CHAPTER 2

No-load funds: The modern way to make money grow

Can you imagine an investment that is free of commissions, completely liquid and as safe—or as risky—as you want it to be? That sounds almost too good to be true. What's the catch?

There isn't any, really. No-load mutual funds are as close to the perfect investment vehicle as you can find. You buy them directly from the investment company, so there is never a sales charge. You can cash in—or move your money quickly. And you can invest in almost any type of stocks, bonds or money market instruments. If there weren't such a thing as a no-load fund, someone surely would have to invent it.

Actually no-loads have been around for decades. The first funds to be offered without commissions came out in 1928, only four years after the first mutual fund. Only since the financial explosion beginning in the mid 70s, however, have they reached their ultimate flowering.

Now no-load funds come in wild profusion. Anyone who wants to can invest exclusively in everything from municipal bonds to hi-tech stocks—or in a broader range of securities. You have a wide choice, from funds that buy the stocks of very volatile companies to those investing in the money market. Most firms let you switch your money among different types of funds by telephone. You pay nothing.

Once you have decided how you want to invest your money, no-load funds give you the advantage of professional management. You don't have to worry about picking the best stocks or bonds yourself. A professional makes those decisions for you. For most investors, this is the soundest way to make money.

No-load funds are exactly like their more expensive counterparts, the load funds, in every respect except one. *No-loads are sold without a sales commission* (which in the jargon of the industry is called a "load"). Selling funds without a sales charge is possible if no salespeople are involved in the purchase. No-load fund companies work directly with you, the investor, and you must take the initiative.

The first no-loads were started by investment counseling firms. They needed a depository for accounts too small to warrant individual handling. T. Rowe Price got its start that way, as did Scudder, Stevens & Clark. At first, these counseling firms viewed their mutual funds as a "showcase" for their investment acumen and expertise. Today, it's their main line of business.

The beginnings

Later, some brokerage firms set up their own no-load funds, seeing in them vehicles that would provide a steady flow of new commissions from their portfolio transactions. The Lehman Bros. brokerage house at one time had two such funds. One still survives as the Salomon Brothers Opportunity Fund. The Wayne Hummer Fund is managed by a brokerage house.

In the 70s and 80s, the trend toward no-loads was pronounced. More than 75 old-line load funds "fired" their salespeople and began marketing shares directly to investors. Fund groups that were originally 100% load but are now partially or wholly no-load include the Invesco, Vanguard, American Century, Dreyfus, and Fidelity funds. Later, funds sponsored by insurance companies followed suit. The SAFECO and Selected Funds are now no-load. In the 90s such groups as Skyline, PBHG and Heartland have gone no-load.

The newer money market funds are 100% no-load; early attempts to sell money funds with loads failed completely. No wonder. One dictionary defines a load as "a heavy burden or weight." No investor needs such a burden, but especially not one who is investing in a cash fund.

Including money market funds, no-loads now account for well over half of the industry's total assets.

The difference between loads and no-loads

To understand what distinguishes loads from no-loads, you must understand how funds are sold, managed and valued.

First, you need to understand the NAV, or net asset value per share. The NAV constitutes the real worth of a fund. It is derived by computing each day the total market value of a fund's portfolio, including cash on hand, then dividing this sum by the total number of investors' shares outstanding. You could think of the net asset value as the liquidation value of a fund if it were to sell everything at the end of the day and divide the proceeds among its shareholders. It is what you get when you sell your shares back to the fund. On any given day, you can determine the value of your holdings by multiplying the NAV by the number of shares you own.

The offer price is what you pay to buy shares in a fund. With a load fund, the difference between the offer price and the NAV is the sales charge. Since no-loads carry no sales charge, the NAV and the offer price are the same.

Both load and no-load mutual funds are managed by professional investment advisers who are paid fees for selecting the best stocks, providing judgment in timing the purchase and sale of securities and safeguarding the investor's money. The fee for this service does not come out of the sales commission paid to load funds. It is a common misconception that some—or all—of a sales charge compensates management. Not true. The sales commission is essentially a distribution expense. That commission is shared by the salesperson, his or her brokerage firm and a selling organization usually owned by the mutual fund company itself.

But don't grieve for the investment managers. In both load and no-load families, they are paid separately—typically 0.5% to 1.0% of a fund's net asset value annually. The management of a mutual fund with $100 million of assets will normally be compensated between $500,000 and $1 million per year for providing investment counsel and services to the fund. In the case of load funds, this is in addition to the sales charge.

Load or no-load: a fund marketing decision

It is important for you to know that as far as mutual fund management is concerned, the decision whether to distribute shares through sales people, directly to investors, or through the new fund supermarkets (described in detail in Chapter 22) is strictly marketing. Some fund groups choose the commission route; some companies offer nothing but no-load funds. And some firms have both load and no-load funds. Fidelity markets its funds four different ways: no-load, low-loads marketed directly to investors, front-end load funds sold by brokers, and contractual plans (a kind of super load). Even Vanguard, a virtually pure no-load fund group, has utilized salesmen to launch closed-end funds.

It is not evil to sell products through salesmen—virtually every industry does so. Since funds are compensated on the basis of the amount of assets under management, the greater the assets, the more profitable they are to the sponsoring company. If a fund family can attract more assets by selling directly to investors, without any commission, it will do so. If employing salesmen is more profitable, the company will do that.

The funds' perspective is in sharp contrast to my own point of view. I look at these alternatives solely from the investor's perspective. Since my research proves that no-loads are better for the investor, I am zealous in advocating that you confine your mutual fund investing to funds that carry no commissions.

The marketing of mutual funds is in constant flux. In general, there's been a gradual narrowing of fee schedules throughout the mutual fund industry. Years ago, the vast majority of load funds charged the maximum 8.5%. That's because competition to get the salesmen to sell their funds instead of somebody else's was so fierce. Nowadays the majority of load funds come to market with lower fees because investors are a lot smarter. Fees in the 4%-6% range are common; bond funds may be slightly lower. On the other hand, some funds that have mid-range loads impose an extra annual fee of around one-quarter of 1% a year (called a "trail") to compensate salesmen for servicing their clients' accounts.

Beware! Some funds that look like no-loads aren't

If you buy a fund through a broker, you will most likely pay some sort of commission. Even some funds that are sold directly to investors charge commissions. Not all of these fees are obvious. Here are some of the types of distribution fees that you might encounter along the mutual fund landscape.

12b-1 plans. The name refers to the 1980 Securities and Exchange Commission rule that permits them. Originally, the SEC used Section 12b-1 to enable funds to pass along to investors their marketing and distribution expenses—for example, advertising and the costs of printing and mailing prospectuses and sales literature to prospective investors. These expenses had traditionally been covered by the management fee. Very quickly, though, load fund groups realized that they could use the 12b-1 fee to compensate sales personnel and broker-dealers for their services. Collecting a 12b-1 fee in lieu of a front-end load gave commissionable funds a terrific marketing advantage because the 12b-1 fee is paid to fund management at regular intervals out of the fund's net assets, in just the way that the management fee is collected. Unless a prospective fund purchaser reads the prospectus carefully, the fee is hidden, for all practical purposes. It will come as no surprise to learn that salesmen seldom explain this fee. And until 1988 these funds were listed as N.L. in newspaper price quotations. Consequently, salesmen frequently told their clients they were buying no-loads. What they meant, of course, was that the client didn't pay an up-front sales charge. That's not the same as *no* load. With only occasional exceptions, if a salesman is selling it, assume he is being compensated for his efforts. Ask him what's in it for him and where the money is coming from. You will usually find out you're the one paying the tariff, no matter what it's called.

Contingent deferred sales charges. A few funds have always had redemption fees. Traditionally these fees, typically 1% and never more that 2%, were used to deter trading and were rescinded after an investor had held a fund's shares for from two months to a year. Now, a marketing wrinkle has been introduced to complement the 12b-1 fee: the contingent deferred sales charge (CDSC). At first glance it seems to be a cousin of the redemption fee. But it is really quite different. The deferred sales charge, like the upfront sales charge, is paid to salesmen and their selling organizations. Deferred sales charges can be as much as 5% to 6% for shareholders redeeming in their first year, declining by 1% per year for the next five to six years.

The CDSC makes 12b-1 plans practical. Here's how the system works. The broker or fund salesman is paid 4%-5% to sell the fund's shares—compensation that the salesman receives at the time of the sale. If the fund were using a front-end sales charge, there would be no problem, but under a 12b-1 plan, the shareholder is burdened by an annual charge (no more than 1% a year). At that rate it can easily take four to five years for the fund's sponsor to recoup the money that it paid the salesman. And what if the shareholder redeems in the meantime? Without the CDSC, the sponsors would be out the money. With the CDSC, fund companies are assured of being able to recoup the money that was advanced to the salesman. The shareholder pays one way or the other—via the 12b-1 fee or the CDSC.

An increasing number of load fund groups now market some of their funds three ways: Class (or series) A funds with a front-end load, Class B funds with a 12b-1 plan coupled to a 5%-1% CDSC in lieu of a front-end load, and Class C, the level load—usually 1% per year. The shareholder has a choice. He pays about the same either way the first four or five years, although you wouldn't necessarily know it from the performance. For example, in 1997, the Merrill Basic Value Fund A gained 29.5% while the Merrill Basic Value Fund B gained 28.2%. The fund was the same, the only difference being that in the A version the sales commission was paid up front and didn't affect the reported performance. In the B version, the commission came out of net assets and did affect reported performance. Suffice it to say, in either type of load fund, you're going to fall behind.

No-load investors have no class

Sometimes called *broker* no-loads, these 12b-1 funds have become a salesman's paradise. B shares lack a front-end sales charge. However, they do contain a deferred sales charge (that the salesman tells a prospective investor can be avoided if the investor holds the fund for long enough). And, the D share funds carry 12b-1 charges that are essentially hidden. Does this combination sound like a salesman's paradise? The factors combine to make such funds easier to sell than conventional load funds. Securities regulations prevent salesmen from calling these funds no-load; but unfortunately, what a salesman says in a private conversation can't easily be policed, and brokers frequently call these 12b-1, CDSC funds "no-loads." You ought to avoid broker no-loads just as you would traditional front-end loads. They levy the same high sales fees.

When petitioning the SEC to permit 12b-1 plans, funds argued that they would benefit the investor by enabling the fund to grow larger. This would spread expenses over a larger asset base. As it worked out, these new charges have basically benefitted the fund managers, not the investor.

Historically, there was no time limit on 12b-1 fees. Over the years, they could easily add up to more than the front-end load. Since this was clearly unwarranted, regulators have now put a cap on 12b-1 fees. The NASD (the National Association of Securities Dealers) has capped these asset-based charges at 7.25% of new gross sales if there is no continuing .25% service fee, and at 6.25% of new gross sales if there is a service fee. Annual fees are capped at .75% (plus a .25% service fee). While this new ruling is welcome, for administrative reasons it is applied to the fund, not to the individual accounts. So its benefits to individual investors will vary and, in fact, may be non-existent if the fund's assets grow rapidly.

The *Guide's* companion publications, *The No-Load Fund Investor* and *The Handbook for No-Load Fund Investors*, list a number of 12b-1 funds, but for the most part they are funds with nominal fees of .25% of assets per year or less that are direct-marketed, not sold by brokers. Realize, also, that many 12b-1 funds deduct only the actual marketing expenses incurred, often less than the maximum allowed in the prospectus. Under government regulations which took effect in 1993, funds without a front-end or back-end sales charge and 12b-1 fees of no more than .25% can still call themselves no-loads. I suggest you examine a fund's expense ratio in evaluating this charge. While modest 12b-1 fees are not usually a problem, *I strongly believe that your first preference should always be for pure no-loads.*

Low-loads. A few funds have always carried "low-loads," upfront sales charges typically in the 2-3% range. Historically, the low-load concept was not particularly successful because the low-load did not provide sufficient incentive to salesmen who, for obvious reasons, preferred to put their efforts into selling funds with the standard 8.5% commission. Low-loads were even less attractive to no-load fund investors.

Fidelity has found a way to make low-load funds sold directly to investors work for them in a substantial way. Since 1983, Fidelity has selectively added commission charges to a number of the family's best performing equity funds, and it has found many investors willing to pay the charges in order to obtain superior performance. These low loads don't compensate salesmen, but rather are a marketing charge that Fidelity keeps for itself. Fidelity claims to send out more prospectuses and spend more time on the phone before people buy equity funds than the firm did previously when the easier-to-explain money market funds were the fund group's most sought after product.

However, it seems clear that these low-load fees are being used more to establish advertising dominance than to provide customer service.

Nowadays, Fidelity has introduced a number of exceptions to their low-load marketing policy. Investors can buy most Fidelity low-loads for tax-sheltered accounts such as IRAs and 401(k) plans on a no-load basis.

Besides 12b-1 and redemption fees, a savvy investor needs to be alert to other anomalies, even in the no-load arena. A few no-load funds charge start-up fees and account maintenance fees. For small accounts, these fees can represent a sizable percentage of assets.

When a sales charge isn't

Most sales charges are payable to the adviser or to a sales organization, but a few funds, generally index funds which stay fully invested at all times, collect sales fees that are *payable to the fund*. That means the fee is payable to *you*, since you are one of the owners of the fund. The sums spent come back to you in the fund's return. These fees, generally in the 1/2 to 1 percent range, are levied to ensure that entering and departing shareholders pay their own transaction costs. This is fair since every time a new shareholder signs on, the fund has to buy more stock, and every time a shareholder leaves they must sell stock. If the fund didn't collect this fee, those transaction costs would be mostly borne by existing shareholders. Since many existing investors bought their shares with the intention of holding for the long term, it would be unfair for them to have to shoulder the cost of newcomers. With this charge, the new shareholder pays his own way. In effect this system raises costs for the short-term trader and lowers costs for the long-term investor.

Secondly, this system deters market timers who like index funds because they guarantee participation in a market move. (Market timers are quite annoyed if they buy into a fund just before a big upward move only to find that the fund is not participating in the market advance because the fund's manager has become defensive and sold much of the fund's stocks or, just as bad, has picked the wrong stocks to invest in.)

Some of Vanguard's and DFA's index funds have sales charges payable to the fund. I consider these funds to be *pure* no-loads. Net, net, sales charges paid to the fund are beneficial. In these particular cases, don't avoid funds that have them.

No-loads and loads perform equally well

Performance should always be paramount in your selection of a fund. If no-loads don't perform as well as their cousins that carry commissions, you'd be foolish to invest. Buying an inferior fund simply to save the sales charge is a silly idea. Poor performance can cost you many multiples the commission that you're saving.

However, no-load funds are every bit as good as load funds. Independent research has consistently shown no difference in performance, on average, between the two types when the load is disregarded.

As far back as 1962, a special study prepared by the Wharton School of Finance for the Securities and Exchange Commission found "no evidence that higher sales charges go hand-in-hand with better investment performance." Indeed, the study showed that fund shareholders paying higher sales charges had a less favorable investment experience than those paying less.

One of the best studies was an exhaustive comparison of no-loads versus loads covering income, growth, and stability. It was conducted in 1971 by FundScope, formerly a financial publisher, and concluded: "In the end, because so many no-load and so many load funds perform above average and so many below average, you must reach the conclusion that there just is no relationship, no correlation, between load and results."

In 1979, Computer Directions Advisors, Inc. (now CDA/ Wiesenberger), compared 82 no-load mutual funds with assets of $7.3 billion with 138 load mutual funds with assets of $22.0 billion. They found there was no significant difference in risk, diversification, rate of return or risk-adjusted performance over the one-, three-, and five-year periods ending June 30, 1979.

Consumer Reports looked at the performance of more than 1,000 stock funds over a five-year period 1988 to 1992, and found that no-load funds had an average annual return of 13.5%, compared to 13.3% for load funds.

In 1997, the average no-load equity fund gained 17.2% compared to a 17.5% gain for all equity funds tracked in the comprehensive Lipper Mutual Fund Performance Analysis, which rates all funds regardless of loads. Given that the various categories of equity funds don't match exactly between loads and no-loads, this is a tie.

Look at it this way. The load is a *marketing* expense, and has no bearing on investment management expertise. If a load fund group drops the load, there is no reason for its performance to change. Its management has not changed. In the same vein several groups, for example Dreyfus and Fidelity, manage both load and no-load funds—and in the cases of series funds with both load and no-load series, individual portfolio managers are in effect managing both no-load and load funds. The load makes no difference to the performance of these investment managers?

In sum, a sales charge—or lack of it—is not a factor in achieving performance. The conclusion is inescapable: load or no-load, the basic product is the same. So it's only logical to go no-load and save the commission expense.

By law, the maximum sales charge that load funds are allowed to collect is 8.5%. And for many years the majority of load funds were sold at that level. In recent years, though, competition from no-load funds and increased consumer awareness has forced most load funds to lower their fees somewhat. But even at the lower levels, the costs are far more damaging to your wealth than you may suspect.

First of all, the sales charge that you actually pay is understated because it is expressed as a percentage of the total purchase price (net asset value plus sales charge) rather than as a percentage of the amount you invest in a fund. The 8.5% maximum load is really 9.3%—it's 8.5% of the money you pay out, but 9.3% of what goes to work for you on Day One. That's because if you put $10,000 into a load fund, $850 goes to the sales organization; the balance—$9,150—is actually invested in stocks and bonds. Divide the $850 by $9,150 and you get 9.3%. If you want $10,000 working for you in a load fund, you must put up $10,930. Similarly, a 5.75% load, when calculated correctly, is really 6.1%.

It is amazing that so many investors accept these costs with equanimity. If you bought a stock that plunged by 6% or more the same day you invested in it, wouldn't that make you pretty cranky? But that's exactly the same as the loss you incur by paying the load.

Over the years, mutual fund salesmen have offered many arguments to justify their commissions. One common rationale is the claim that the load amortizes over the years. They argue that over a period of nine years, for instance, an 8 1/2% charge is amortized to only 1% per year. They then conclude that 1% a year doesn't have any real impact, and then imply that after nine years you are home free

The high cost of the load

and clear. This is not only not true, it is in fact the opposite of the truth. If two funds have exactly identical performances, and one carries a commission while the other doesn't, the longer you hold them, the greater the cost of the load. That's because commission money paid to the broker compounds each year. This constant compounding increases the spread between a no-load's and the load fund's returns. Think of it this way: the money you lose in the load continues to grow over the years—*but in the salesman's pocket, not yours!*

Here's the math. Take two funds, one a pure no-load, the other one carrying a 6% front-end load. You invest $10,000 in each. The load fund starts out 6%—or $600—behind. If both funds grow at exactly the same pace, the load fund will always be 6% behind—30 years, 40 years, even 50 years later. Now the salesman will argue "it's 40 years later, your fund is up 2,000%; the no-load is up 2,006%. Big deal."

Well it is a big deal. The $10,000 investment in the load fund may now be worth $2 million. But the no-load will be worth 6% more. That 6% now represents a *$120,000 advantage*, twelve times your original investment! Moral: you spend dollars, not percentages.

Can an average investor grow his nest egg to $2 million dollars? Over, a lifetime it's easy, even if you don't have $10,000 to begin with. Say you start investing in no-load growth stock funds at age 20. For five years you invest $150 a month. At age 25 you are able to increase your savings rate to $500 a month, at 30 to $750 a month, and finally from age 40 to 65, $1,000 a month. At a 12% annual growth rate (the average post-World War II experience with stocks) you will have amassed $2,024,400 (disregarding taxes) by age 65. That is *$121,464 more* than a comparable load fund investment would have achieved. *This is the real difference that the load makes.*

The comparisons obviously envision growth during bull markets. Of course, the bear marauds through the investment markets, too. In that case, a no-load investor doesn't suffer the double-whammy that the load investor faces: starting in the hole because of the commission while his assets are declining in value because of the dropping market.

Furthermore, there are no savings paying with asset-based sales charges (series B or C). A 12b-1 fee of one percent, which results in a high expense ratio, hobbles performance just as the front-end load does. There's a high cost to a load, whether it's paid up-front, at the back-end or on a level all the way along.

No-load mutual funds are investing's greatest bargain. Suppose you wanted to invest $100,000 through a broker. Table 1 shows how much commission you would pay for various investments.

With no-loads there's no commission. And not only that, you don't have to deal with the broker!

Table 1

Commissions on a $100,000 investment

Type of investment	Commission range
No-load mutual fund	zero
Treasury securities	$50
Municipal bond	$500- $2,000
Common stock	$500- $3,000
Unit investment trust	$3,000- $4,900
Load mutual fund	$1,000- $9,300
New stock offering	$3,000-$10,000
Limited partnership	$6,000-$10,000

CHAPTER 3

You can select a top-performing no-load yourself

Choosing the best funds is crucial. You have thousands of different no-load stock and bond funds to choose from, with a wide range of objectives. They vary enormously in performance, and picking the wrong fund can be costly.

The typical investor—and certainly you—can select top-performing funds without any salesperson's help. A comparison of past selections made by no-load and load investors proves this point. As I noted earlier, both load and no-load fund categories feature superior and inferior funds—and money is invested in all of them. In the case of load funds, the investor is assisted in his choice by an adviser or salesperson. With no-loads, the investor is the sole decision maker.

I can prove that no-load fund investors are more sophisticated and do a better job of picking funds than investors working with salesmen. I do that by looking at where the money is going. In other words, are the best funds getting the most money?

Our study found conclusively that no-load fund investors, acting on their own, are more likely to put their money into the best performing funds than are load fund investors, assisted by salesmen or brokers. And here's the proof: fully 52% of no-load assets, I discovered, are in funds whose returns ranked in the top 20% of all equity funds in their categories over a five-year period; only 22% of load fund assets are in these top-performing funds. The categories are based on the Lipper rankings published weekly in the *Wall Street Journal.*

Since many investments remain in the same fund for years, it is possible that some of these funds were better at the time they were purchased than they are now. If this is the case, the load has obviously inhibited these investors from selling when the performance of their funds faltered. How else could so much money remain invested in mediocre load funds?

This study was first done in 1972 and has been repeated periodically since then. The results have been consistent over the years. I

Chart 2
___

Where investors put their money
Percent distribution of

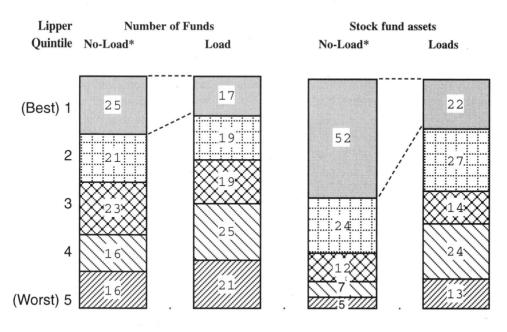

*includes direct sale low-loads
Source: Returns, five years ending June, 1997. Assets June 1997.

think the reason that no-load fund investors continually win is that they have only one interest: the superior performance of *their own money*. Salesmen, alas, have other interests in addition to performance. Some funds pay higher commissions than others; sometimes, the salesman may not be able to sell the best funds. Some studies have concluded that brokerage-house funds are largely inferior in terms of performance.

Here's another caveat: brokerage firms frequently put on educational seminars for potential customers. It's fine to go to learn, but realize that they will inevitably wind up trying to sell you commissionable products.

Shouldn't I buy the best fund regardless of the load?

We're frequently asked that question. The answer is yes, but... Certainly you would be better off if you invested in a load fund that outperforms all no-loads—*but* only if you could count on that fund to continue its superior performance. You can't be certain of such results. Past performance never guarantees future results, as the saying goes, particularly when you are "marrying" the fund, as you are likely to do with a load fund.

Out of the thousands of funds in existence over the years, only two could possibly claim they had a chance of beating *all* no-loads: Templeton Growth, and Fidelity Magellan. Templeton Growth was the number one fund, load and no-load, for the 20 years ending December 1981. Fidelity Magellan was the number one fund for the 20 years ending 1997. Magellan isn't exactly a load or a no-load, but rather a low-load, that is marketed directly to investors. The $12 billion Templeton Growth Fund generally turns in above-average performances in its global category, but was below the average of all equity funds for the three years ending 1997. It has no chance of coming anywhere close to beating all no-loads anymore. Similarly, Magellan, at $63 billion, has seen best days already. It's not even the top fund at Fidelity anymore. These two funds were selected on the basis of very long-term track records, the kind salesmen love to cite. At this point, we see no new Templeton Growth or Fidelity Magellan caliber load funds on the horizon. The top diversified load fund for the three years ending in 1997 is the Kemper-Dreman Hi Return Fund. It ranked eleventh among all diversified funds. Ten no-loads outperformed it.

The differing sales patterns between no-load fund investors and those who purchase funds through an adviser or salesperson confirm the results of my research. Consider this: over the long-term equity funds habitually outperform bond funds. Yet salesmen continually put more emphasis on bond funds than do individuals. The data in Table 3 from the Investment Company Institute compare equity and fixed-income fund sales for funds distributed by sales forces versus those marketed directly. The column labeled Sales Force essentially shows load fund purchases. The next column, labeled Direct Marketed, shows no-load and direct marketed low-load fund sales.

Over the five years ending 1996, 71.5% of no-load sales were in equity mutual funds, and 28.5% were in fixed-income funds. In the case of load funds sold by salesmen, the figures were very different. Only 56.8% of load sales were in equity funds while 43.2% of the money went into bond and income funds. Almost half of all load fund sales went into bond funds during one of the greatest bull markets that stocks have ever experienced.

Considering the brokers' actions, you might say there are four kinds of yields: current yield, yield to call, yield to maturity—and yield to broker!

No-load investors vs. salesmen

Table 3

Mutual Fund Sales by Objective
Five years ending 1996

	Direct Marketed	Sales Force
(Millions of dollars)		
Equity	$634,617	$748,556
Bond & inc	$253,530	$568,891
Percentage		
Equity	71.5%	56.8%
Bond & inc	28.5%	43.2%

Source: ICI, excludes sales due to reinvestments.

Mutual fund salesmen have other tactics to win clients away from the no-loads. One is to scare prospective customers by telling them that no-loads have higher expense ratios than load funds and thus in the long run could prove to be more expensive even taking the load into account. That argument, to put it mildly, is disingenuous. The average no-load doesn't have a higher expense ratio than the average load fund (this is documented in Chapter 14), and in individual cases only a handful of no-loads have higher overall costs. So while it is theoretically possible for commission funds to end up charging lower fees, even including the load, in practice it's quite rare.

As an investor you will find it's easy to avoid a no-load with a high expense ratio. If you'd like to be certain of finding a no-load with an expense ratio lower than whatever fund a salesman is pushing, deal with Vanguard. That no-load company has led the way in reducing overhead costs. The average Vanguard equity fund has an expense ratio of .40; the average Vanguard bond and money market funds have expense ratios of .20% and .23%, respectively.

Another tactic that brokers sometimes use is to complain that "no-loads are not no-load." By this they mean that no-loads also have marketing costs, which ultimately have to be paid by the customer. One load fund advisor asked, "Who pays for all those no-load advertisements in the popular financial press? (The very same press that promotes no-load fund investing.)"

Our response here is that of course no-loads advertise—and of course that costs money. But the expense is picayune compared to the cost of a personal one-on-one sales call. Fidelity is the heaviest advertiser, but the group's ad money comes primarily from the 3% sales commission sales. The second heaviest no-load fund advertiser is T. Rowe Price. This group's long-term funds have a modest average expense ratio of .89%. Vanguard, a sizeable advertiser, breaks out its marketing expenses in its fund prospectuses. Interestingly, the marketing budget amounts to about .03% of assets—that's three one-hundreds of one percent. Advertising is cheap. Even commercials on the Super Bowl, the most expensive ads on TV, cost advertisers only about two cents per each viewing home they reach. A broker can't make a sales call for two cents. Nobody ever claimed no-loads were a free lunch. They have to make themselves known, and advertising is a cheap way to do so. Don't forget, the cost of distributing no-load funds is included in the funds' expense ratios.

Buying no-loads through intermediaries

While I am unalterably opposed to buying funds sold on a commissionable basis, usually through brokers, I recognize that many investors—even after reading this book—will still feel they need the assistance of a professional in selecting funds—even no-loads. If you feel that way, don't despair, you have company. In 1996, 18.3% of no-load purchases were actually made by fee-paid advisors (planners who charge flat rates or a percentage of assets, rather than a commission) or by brokers using wrap accounts (again a non-commissionable arrangement). Add that to the 60% of investors who buy loaded funds, and it's obvious that a lot of investors are insecure.

For those folks, I'd like to recommend several ways to obtain assistance. Least expensive is the popular media: personal finance magazines, newspapers, television and radio programs. The problem with the popular media is that they seldom provide continuing advice. They have their recommendations de jure, but forget from one week or month to the next what they said before. And, they virtually never provide advice you when to sell. However, for some investors, particularly relatively inactive ones, these sources are sufficient.

On the next step up the advice ladder are newsletters. Most of the better ones provide continuing advice by maintaining model portfolios and recommending sales when necessary. Of course, they are more costly than magazines. With some exceptions, mutual fund newsletters sell for $125 to $175 per year. As the publisher of one well-known newsletter, *The No-Load Fund Investor*, I obviously favor this method of obtaining assistance.

Unfortunately, many investors who read newsletters fail to follow the advice promptly. Other investors need additional "hand-holding" or have unusual tax problems. They should consider a personal counselor or an advisor who manages an account on a fee basis. This way is by far the most expensive way to obtain advice, but it offers the advantages of continuous supervision, sometimes market timing, and a big reduction in paper work. The No-Load Fund Investor, Inc. has a sister company, the BJ Group, which manages money on a discretionary basis.

If you are willing to spend some time learning about mutual funds and to do some work evaluating them, you can easily pick top mutual funds on your own. Millions of other no-load investors are doing it right now. So can you. No-load mutual funds can make your money grow and perhaps will do so more conveniently and more consistently than other investment approaches.

It's worth buying no-loads

PART II

Finding the Right Funds For You

Your first steps to profitable investing in no-loads

Buying no-load funds is a challenging do-it-yourself program in which you have to take the initiative. It requires time and know-how. But once you've learned the fundamentals, your periodic review shouldn't take more than one hour a month. And the results will be well worth the effort. When you follow a logical plan, the psychic and monetary rewards of investing in no-loads are great.

Nine steps to success — a summary

Here are the steps you'll need to take to initiate a no-load investment program. I'll discuss each of them in more detail in subsequent chapters.

1. Analyze your specific investment objectives. How much risk are you willing to take? Could you accept great risks for maximum gains? Or would you prefer a more conservative course of investing, with less risk and less potential growth?

2. Learn to recognize which mutual funds are designed to meet your specific investment objectives. This vital step is the one most often neglected by investors. Far too many unknowingly buy funds that are either too speculative or too conservative for them, and their investment programs suffer as a result.

3. Select no-load funds whose objectives coincide with your own. No matter what your investing style, allocate a percentage of your assets to a *core holding* of mutual funds that you can hold long-term

throughout both bull and bear markets. These are generally index funds, conservative funds or, occasionally, more aggressive funds that have a history of selling stocks and sitting with cash when market conditions are uncertain or adverse.

4. Analyze past performance to determine the best two or three funds among those that meet your objective.

5. Learn the criteria for selecting those funds that are most likely to perform well in the future.

6. Write or phone for the prospectuses of two or three top-performing funds.

7. Read the prospectus, in particular the sections detailing the fund's investment philosophy and allowable investments. Look carefully at the fee table and the expense ratio.

8. Then make a decision and invest in one or more funds.

9. Continue to follow the performance of these and other top-ranked funds.

With this plan of action you can design your own financially rewarding investment program. For the details, read on.

Making your peace with risk

Understanding and managing risk is by far the most important skill that you must master in order to be a skilled investor—in mutual funds or any other kind of investment. Here's why. First, *there's no way you can avoid risk*. While everyone understands the risk of losing principal—that is, seeing the value of a security drop—fewer realize that numerous other risks can be just as deadly. For example, the loss of income that occurs when CD rates decline, or the loss of an investment's value in real terms due to inflation.

You need to take equity risks

Generally speaking, stocks are riskier than fixed-income investments and, for that reason, provide greater rewards. Research by Ibbotson Associates indicates that over the long term—72 years—we can expect a total return on common stocks of 11.0% annually. During this period, the Consumer Price Index rose 3.1% a year, on average, which means that the real returns from stocks were about 7% annually. On the other hand, fixed-income investments, as typified by long-term corporate bonds, averaged 5.7% a year—leaving you only a 2.6% edge over inflation.

While the Ibbotson numbers commonly are quoted back to 1926, I have broken out the data for the last 50 years. By doing so, I eliminated the effect of the Great Depression, which I don't see recurring. When the Depression is removed from the numbers, I find that stocks have averaged over 13% a year and inflation has risen to 4.0% a year. But bonds remained about the same, meaning that a conservative fixed-income investor whose investments were entirely in bonds or bills would have seen the purchasing power of his money actually contract after the impact of income taxes was taken into account.

Of course, returns varied greatly during this half-century. Standard deviation is a statistical measure showing variation over a period of time. It is typically used as a proxy for risk. A high standard deviation indicates high volatility: large swings between gains and loses. A lower standard deviation indicates a more conservative security. The standard deviation for stocks over the 50 year period was 16.5, far greater than the deviations for either bonds or Treasury bills, which were respectively 10.2 and 3.1. Look at it this way, if stocks weren't riskier investments than, say, CD's, they wouldn't have better returns than CDs.

Table 4

Long-term historical returns:
Compounded annual returns with income reinvested

	72 years 1/1/26- 12/31/97	50 years 1/1/48 12/31/97	50 years Standard deviations
Common stocks (the S&P 500)	11.00%	13.12%	16.5
20-year Corporate bonds	5.70	6.03	10.2
20-year Government bonds	5.24	5.72	10.6
Treasury bills	3.75	4.99	3.1
Inflation (Consumer Price Index)	3.10	3.94	3.3

While inflation seems dormant for now, even a modest increase in the inflation rate could seriously erode your assets in 15 to 20 years. Today's senior citizens usually live at least that long after retirement. Therefore, investing too conservatively can jeopardize the purchasing power of your assets over a long period of time.

Table 5

Deterioration of $1,000 at various inflation rates
Average annual rate of inflation

Years	3%	4%	5%
5	$859	$815	$774
10	737	665	599
15	633	542	463
20	544	442	358
25	467	360	277

In short, stocks are riskier than fixed-return investments, since they fluctuate more in value. Yet, over long periods of time they are the only investment to decisively outpace inflation. Consequently, it is imperative that every investor keep at least a portion of his assets in equities. As I describe the many varieties of mutual funds in the following chapters, keep this overriding principal in mind.

Risk ordains reward

Usually, over a long period of time the relationship between risk and reward is reasonably fixed. The greater the risk, the greater the reward—and vice versa. Novice investors often make unrealistic demands of financial advisers and money managers: "I'd like an investment that gains 20% annually," is a common refrain from the uninitiated. Another widespread assumption: "If you've earned 15% annually in the past, can I assume you'll make 15% a year for me once I've signed up with your organization?"

Sorry. it doesn't work that way. Reward is ephemeral. It depends on the market conditions, the economy and other factors that are difficult to predict. Risk, on the other hand, is easier to evaluate and predict. Thus in the long run the amount of risk you undertake will determine your investment reward.

Match funds to your investment objectives

As in any carefully planned investment program, the first step in selecting mutual funds is to establish your investment objectives. Next, identify those funds—out of hundreds catering to a wide range of objectives—that meet your goals.

Typically, young investors look for growth. They need to build up their savings for a variety of reasons—emergencies, a new house, their children's college education, eventual retirement. Older investors, who already have an estate, need income to live on in retirement and safety of principal. Since many funds serve each need, you first have to know how to classify mutual funds by their investment objective.

At one end of the spectrum are funds committed to a policy of conservative investing, specifically, to conserve capital and produce income. At the other extreme are funds that invest speculatively for maximum capital gains. In between, funds are spread across every segment of the investment horizon, and it is often difficult to determine minor differences in their investment philosophies.

In Chart 6, I graphically depict the spectrum of objectives as a dial. Conservative funds, appropriate for the investor who wants minimum risk, are at the far left; aggressive funds that offer the possibility of high returns and the accompanying risks, are on the right. The

Chart 6

analogy holds because it is a continuous spectrum. The differences between an income fund and one called growth-income may be slight, just as the difference between traveling 50 versus 55 miles per hour is not great. But at the opposite ends of the dial, the differences are huge.

Chapters 5 though 13 explain the differences between the various types of funds so as to provide you with the proper grounding to make your selections. I start with the most speculative funds, and then chapter by chapter proceed down the risk spectrum.

Chapters 14-21 describe the strategies, techniques and even "tricks" that you can use to obtain the best performance from your no-load funds.

Finally, in Chapters 22 and 23 I guide you through the administrative maze of do-it-yourself no-load investing.

CHAPTER 5

THE NO-LOAD FUND INVESTOR

Aggressive growth funds

Funds that invest for the greatest possible gain are called aggressive growth funds. They also go by several other names: "maximum capital gains," "capital appreciation" and "performance" funds. In the 1960s such funds were called "go-go," a term that fell into disrepute after the 1973-74 stock market debacle. The go-gos went-went.

The principal characteristics of the aggressive growth funds are:

■ They are oriented toward achieving maximum capital gains.

■ To achieve their gains, they take risks, investing in speculative stocks.

■ They are volatile, doing very well in bull markets and very badly in bear markets.

■ They may occasionally use adventurous investing techniques—margined portfolios, options and short selling.

The objective of an aggressive growth fund is to grow faster than all other funds by buying stocks that can outperform the market to the fullest possible extent. Top growth means top returns for management because money pours into the current best performers. Since management fees are essentially determined by the size of the fund, superior growth is a good way for fund management to increase its income. This is especially true for no-load funds. Because they have no sales agents and their advertising budgets are generally limited, an impressive growth record is imperative. With an outstanding record, the fund's advertising stands out and fund management finds it easy to get noticed by the media. That's how no-loads grow.

Greater rewards entail bigger risks

Those who manage aggressive growth funds are not afraid to take risks in order to grow rapidly. Some attempt to call turns in the market. They buy stocks they think have the greatest potential, often highly volatile stocks in vogue industries such as technology. They are quick to sell those that don't measure up.

The profit potential for investors willing to accept the risks these funds take is tremendous. In a bull market, the best aggressive growth funds can give you heady performance. For example, in 1995 and in 1996 more aggressive growth funds appeared in the top 25 best performing diversified funds than any other category.

Mutual fund performance should be calculated in terms of percent changes. However, the psychological impact is greater when you see a spectacular fund's long-term performance expressed in dollars and cents. Fidelity Magellan, for example, went from $3.86 in 1975 to $95.27 a share in 1997, and also distributed $86.90 a share in capital gains.

Now, some investors held individual stocks that performed well in this period but how many had whole portfolios that duplicated the performance of these top-ranked funds? Their growth was achieved over an entire portfolio, including cash reserves held along the way. In contrast to the popular stock averages, this represents net growth after management fees, expenses and transaction costs have been deducted.

On the other hand, I should emphasize that the variations in the performance of aggressive growth funds are particularly wide because the managers are taking great risks. The American Heritage Fund ranked number one among all funds for the three years ending 1993, gaining 230%. Then in the next three years, the fund went to second worst, declining 24.8% *per year!*

In the October 1987 meltdown, the average aggressive growth fund lost 26%. The most volatile funds in the group lost more than 30%. And that included well-managed funds like American Century Vista, which lost 33%. In the milder downturn that began in the third quarter of 1990, the average aggressive growth fund declined 21.9%, while the worst, the Prudent Speculator Leveraged Fund, declined 46.4%. It made the disastrous mistake of being 40% leveraged at the outset.

Because performances vary so dramatically, you have to take great care in selecting aggressive growth funds. And then, keep a sharp eye on them!

The great advantage that aggressive growth funds have is that they are the best way for an investor to buy a portfolio of stocks that's likely to grow dramatically. Because a large fund holds a broad array of stocks, it's less risky for the fund manager to buy secondary stocks than for you to. Even if one company goes bankrupt, it isn't catastrophic if that stock accounts for 2% or 3% or less of a diversified portfolio.

The principal disadvantages of aggressive growth funds are their extreme price fluctuations, lack of defensive strengths in a bear market, and inconsistent performance. However, you can minimize these disadvantages by diversifying your investments. Buy shares in more than one fund, then follow the performances closely.

While the aggressive growth funds' volatility can be a disadvantage in the short run, it has been an advantage in the long run. Since World War II, bull markets have lasted longer and gone further than bear markets.

Pros and cons of aggressive growth funds

To make money in aggressive growth funds you have to be invested during those times when the market is making strong upward moves. Often, bull markets begin with a pop. So, you need to be invested at the end of a bear market. That's when the risks are lowest and the potential rewards the greatest.

On the other hand, investing after strong upward moves in the market diminishes your prospects. Buying stocks in periods of consolidation or, worse yet, near the end of a market advance, changes the risk/reward relationship dramatically.

It's more fun to see your money grow, naturally. The problem is that aggressive growth funds will fluctuate wildly in both directions. Chart 7 shows how the Fremont U.S. Micro Cap Fund performed in 1996 and 1997. Its 48.7% gain in 1996 far exceeded the market, but then failed to perform the following year. Its 7.0% gain in 1997 severely disappointed its shareholders. This a good example of the sort of volatility you should expect from an aggressive growth fund that is usually completely invested in stocks.

A few aggressive growth funds use leverage to increase their volatility. At times when the market is moving dramatically, these funds are frequently among the best—or the worst—performers.

But ... watch out!

Chart 7

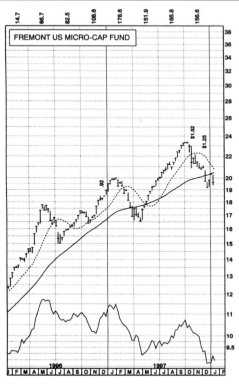

FREMONT US MICRO-CAP FUND

Source: Mutual Fund Trends, January 1998 (Growth Fund Research Bldg., Box 6600, Rapid City, SD 57709).

The bear could get you if you don't get out

The majority of aggressive growth funds stay relatively fully invested at all times, even during bear markets. They reason that their shareholders are paying them to buy stocks, not hold cash. They also know the difficultly of anticipating market tops and bottoms. They take into consideration the cost of selling out and buying back a sizeable portfolio of stocks. It has been estimated that the stock market has to decline about 25% in order to justify a move to cash. Thus, funds are strongly inclined to ride out what may be a minor dip.

Furthermore, fund managers are greatly affected by what their competition does. Savvy investors recognize that aggressive growth funds will perform poorly in a bear market and they will get out themselves when the market declines. These investors are primarily interested in up-market performance. Thus, by staying fully invested during bear markets, a fund is assured of a fast start when the new bull market begins. Too many aggressive fund managers don't care if their fund declines during a bear market; they just don't want it to decline more than their competitors' funds.

So, holding aggressive growth funds in a bear market can be hazardous. If you have a low tolerance for large declines, or a short time horizon, you are best advised to stand clear of aggressive funds. Put another way, you should limit your investment in these funds to an amount you can do without, and invest only those dollars that you can afford to keep invested over a long period, at least three to five years.

And, if you're a sport and can take losses in stride, in Chapter 19 I'll give you some strategies for maximizing profits in aggressive growth stock funds throughout the market cycle.

I use four criteria to determine whether a fund should be classified as aggressive growth. My tests are (1) volatility, (2) analysis of a fund's objectives as stated in its prospectus, (3) dividend yield and (4) the fund's portfolio.

Identifying aggressive growth funds

Volatility can be determined by noting a fund's fluctuations over various periods. You can get an up-to-the-minute guide by checking mutual fund prices in the daily newspaper on the day after a large move in stock prices. Pick a day when the market moves one percent or more. You can use the Dow Jones Industrial Average as a guide, but the S&P 500 and the NASDAQ are better bets. Next, scan the mutual funds section in the financial pages to see which funds outpaced the Dow and by how big a margin. You have to do this quick analysis using percentages; looking at a fund's net asset value in terms of dollars-and-cents changes won't give you a meaningful comparison. *The New York Times* and a some other papers now provide percentage changes. If your newspaper doesn't, you can easily obtain a rough estimate by dividing the fund's dollar change by its NAV.

On active days, some funds will move one-and-one-half times the market indexes or more. These are the aggressive growth funds. Naturally, price movements on any one day can be atypical; but, if you follow the prices over a number of such active days, you can get a pretty good idea which funds are the most volatile.

An easy way to make this comparison without having to flip all over the paper is to compare a fund's daily market action to the Vanguard Index funds. The Small Capitalization Stock Fund is an excellent proxy for small cap funds; the 500 Portfolio, which owns all the stocks that comprise the S&P 500 average, is a representative stand-in for the funds owning large capitalization stocks.

One caution: This is not a method for selecting funds to buy, nor is it a method of predicting future growth. The most volatile funds aren't always the biggest gainers in the long run.

Follow the bouncing betas

A more sophisticated way to measure the volatility of individual stocks, as well as entire portfolios, is called the beta coefficient. The theory behind it is based on two simple ideas: (1) that there is a fairly close correlation between the movement of most stocks and portfolios and the movement of the market as a whole, and (2) that to get higher rewards, you must take greater risks. The beta coefficient measures a fund's sensitivity to, or volatility relative to, the stock market in general. Using the beta is different from the method described in the paragraphs above because it ignores all other factors influencing the price of a stock or a portfolio.

A beta computed for a portfolio of stocks measures the riskiness of that portfolio in relation to the risk of the market. Funds with the same volatility as the market, as measured by a broad based index, have a beta of 1.00. Funds with higher betas are more volatile; those with lower betas are less volatile. The share price of a fund with a beta of 1.20 will typically rise or fall 12% when the broad index rises or falls 10%. On the other hand, the price of a fund with a beta of .80 will rise or fall 8% when the index moves 10%. This makes high beta funds the most desirable in up markets, while low beta funds are preferred in adverse markets.

The average no-load aggressive growth fund had a beta of .87 in 1997; the average growth fund, a .79 beta; and the typical equity fund .74. Among aggressive growth funds, Rydex Nova had the highest beta (1.50).

Table 8

No-load funds
3 yrs ending Dec. 1997

Objective	Avg. Beta
Aggressive growth	.87
Growth	.79
Growth-income	.77
International	.74
Small company growth	.70
Global	.61
Income	.53
Precious metals	.37
Tax-free	.39
Fixed-income	.21
Avg stock	.74
Avg diversified stock	.76

I use the beta as a measure of risk because it allows me to distinguish between two components of total risk—that which is caused by the market's variability and that due uniquely to the securities within an individual fund's portfolio and because it is easily understood and self benchmarked. A beta of .75, for example, is broadly speaking 25% less risky than the market. Betas work best for diversified domestic equity funds. They are far less meaningful for specialized funds such as gold funds, which march to their own drummer, and for bond funds.

Beta has two companions: the alpha and the coefficient of determination. The alpha, which measures non-market-related variability, is considered by some to be an indicator of management ability. The other measure, notated as "r^2," measures the percentage of variability due to the market. Betas are included in the *Handbook* and in *The No-Load Fund Investor* newsletter. Because beta measurements can be relatively volatile over short periods of time, they are generally calculated over a three year period to produce a more stable, useful comparative tool.

Two other measures of risk you should be aware of are the standard deviation and the Sharpe ratio. Standard deviation measures a security's periodic variations from its own average performance, independent of an index. A fund whose NAVs range from $7 to $14 over a period of time will have a greater standard deviation than a fund whose NAVs vary from $9 to $11 over the same period. The disadvantage of standard deviations, in my opinion, is that they are harder for investors to grasp. Standard deviation, while it has a precise statistical meaning, doesn't mean much to laymen unless compared to a benchmark. For example, it's hard to tell in non-technical terms just how risky a fund with a standard deviation of, say, 5.22 really is.

The Sharpe ratio, developed by Nobel prize winning economist William F. Sharpe, measures reward per unit of risk. The latter measure attempts to reduce all portfolio results to the same risk level in order to assess management's ability, that is, a management which produces a mediocre return while taking a large risk with your capital is inferior to one which can produce that same return with much lower risk.

Morningstar, the mutual fund rating service, offers yet another way of measuring risk. Unlike both beta and standard deviation, which take into account both upside and downside risk, *Morningstar* assigns its risk percentile rankings (and stars) based on downside risk only. Downside risk is assumed by *Morningstar* to be any month in which a fund's return is below the Treasury bill return. As a practical matter, most investors *love* upside volatility; it's only downside volatility that we *hate*. So, *Morningstar's* exclusion of upside volatility in computing their star ratings makes a lot of sense.

Note also, the securities industry uses volatility as a proxy for risk because it can be computed precisely. But it's really a very imperfect measure of risk. There are many, many risks that volatility doesn't measure. For example, the likelihood of a company going bankrupt. It's quite possible that a stock's price will be relatively flat (have low volatility) until an announcement is made, and then fall off a cliff. Similarly volatility can fail to capture chronic underperformance. A fund that *consistently* gains 10% a year isn't any more volatile than a fund that *consistently* gains 5% a year.

In a long-term bull market, a decision to take greater risks for higher returns will frequently prove profitable. Yet, only a minority of investors can or should seek maximum risk. Most of us must moderate our risk profile because we can't take a chance of losing substantial portions of our nest eggs.

Analyze a fund's objectives

The second test of an aggressive growth fund is to see what the fund considers its "objectives" to be. Following SEC regulations, every sale of a mutual fund must be made by prospectus, and in every prospectus there is a section labeled "objectives." Aggressive growth funds typically describe their objectives in the following manner:

> Capital appreciation through investment primarily in equity securities of small- and medium-sized companies with sales of less than $500 million which fall outside of the S&P 500 Index. Fund should not be considered as a complete investment program; rather, the fund is designed for those investors who invest for the long term and have the financial ability to undertake greater risk in exchange for the opportunity of realizing greater financial gains in the future— *Kaufmann.*

> Seeks significant capital appreciation by investing in securities, primarily common stocks, that management believes are more aggressive and carry a greater degree of risk than the market as a whole (as measured by the S&P 500 Stock Index)—*Columbia Special Fund.*

Sole investment objective is to realize capital growth. The fund may employ "leverage" by borrowing money and using it for the purchase of additional securities. Borrowing for investment increases both investment opportunity and investment risk—*Value Line Leveraged Growth Investors.*

Seeks long-term growth of capital through investment in common stocks of small, rapidly growing companies—*Price New Horizons.*

Capital growth by investing in a broadly diversified list of special situations. Investing in special situations may increase the risk of possible loss but it may also offer greater appreciation potential—*Value Line Special Situations.*

The statement of objective is not always as explicit as we would like. On the front page of its prospectus, Fidelity Magellan merely says it seeks to increase the value of its shares over the long term by investing in companies with growth potential, but on later pages it goes on to note that it seeks capital appreciation and that no emphasis is placed on dividend income. Thus, Magellan is more aggressive than the impression it conveys in its front-page description. (Magellan's beta is 0.92, above-average for an aggressive growth fund.)

Some other aggressive growth funds are even less explicit. For example the prospectus of the Vanguard Explorer Fund merely says of its objective: ". . . long-term growth in capital." That's why the volatility tests are so important.

The third criteria is dividend income. Funds with the lowest yields are the most aggressive. High percentages of their portfolios are invested in stocks that reinvest their profits for future growth rather than paying their shareholders hefty dividends. The average aggressive growth fund yielded only 0.2% in 1997; many paid no income dividends at all.

Dividends make a difference

Finally, the fourth way to determine the fund's attitude toward growth and risk-taking is to examine the composition of its portfolio. Aggressive growth funds will frequently have heavy weightings in high-tech stocks. So if you see a lot of "ix" and "onic" at the ends of the names of unfamiliar companies in the portfolio, chances are the fund takes an aggressive stance.

Portfolio composition

Small company growth funds

These funds specialize in the stocks of small-sized companies. A strict definition of small cap used by some funds: companies that rank in the smallest 20% of NYSE stocks in terms of market capitalization. (Which means a stock's market price times the number of its shares outstanding. In other words, market capitalization is the total value of all its shares.) Practically speaking, the smallest 20% means companies with market capitalization of $200 million or less.

However, small means different things to different funds. At one extreme is the DFA U.S. Small Company Fund, which strictly adheres to buying stocks in the bottom 20%. At the other extreme are "small company funds" that buy stocks that may rank above the median capitalization of all listed companies. The record for stretching the definition may be held by a fund which was launched in early 1998: the Strong Small Cap Value Fund is permitted to own stocks with capitalizations as large as $2 billion!

Small cap funds don't stay small

In this great bull market it has been tough for larger small-cap funds to find enough companies that are truly small. As stock prices have risen, so, by definition, have market caps. As a result, a common market cap cutoff for small cap funds is now $1 billion. Vanguard now defines small cap as under $1 billion; mid-cap is $1-7.5 billion; and large-cap is over $7.5 billion. On the other hand, the Montgomery funds say micro cap are stocks with a market cap under $600 million; small cap, $600 million to $1 billion; mid-cap, $1-5 billion; and large-cap, over $5 billion. Take your pick. In the end, if the fund's value is rising, what's the difference.

Another reason that the stocks in a typical small cap funds' portfolio are now larger has to do with a practical problem. What do you do with stocks whose price increases have lifted the companies out of the small cap category. It's not necessarily appropriate to sell a good stock simply because its price has risen. The portfolio manager might be selling his biggest winners. Jack Laporte, manager of the T. Rowe Price New Horizons Fund bought Wal-Mart when it was small and sold in the late 80s. He recently figured out that if he still had the stock in his portfolio it would be larger than the entire New Horizons portfolio at the time.

Then there is the matter of relative performance. Some small company funds have been known to vary the size of stocks they hold in their portfolios depending on market conditions. When small stocks are booming, they buy the smallest; when large cap stocks are popular, as they have been throughout much of the last 13 years, these funds edge up to medium cap stocks.

Today, funds that hold the smallest 20% of stocks are frequently termed micro-cap funds. Micro-cap funds ought to be the wave of the future. If they are defined as funds holding stocks with market caps under $300 million, then they can build their portfolios from a universe of almost 7,000 companies, with a total of $495 billion in assets.

To give you some insight into market capitalizations, Table 9 shows the largest companies in each decile group among those stocks listed on the New York Stock Exchange, and how those companies relate to AMEX and NASDAQ stocks.

Table 9

Decile sizes

Market capitalization deciles	Size ($MM)	NYSE Largest company	No. of companies*		
			NYSE	AMEX	NAT'L NASDAQ
1	162,790	General Electric	192	1	18
2	7,096	Federated Dept. Store	192	2	30
3	3,273	Dow Jones & Co.	192	6	55
4	1,938	BJ Services	192	7	83
5	1,175	Federal Signal	192	5	116
6	784	Heilig Meyers	192	12	175
7	524	Zilog	192	20	240
8	352	Marcus Corp.	192	31	430
9	201	Coopers Cos	192	92	787
10	95	Harborside Healthcare	192	391	1,895

Market capitalization = price x shares outstanding as of 12/31/96.
*excludes ADRs, REITs, foreign companies and closed-end funds
Amex and NASDAQ issues are put into NYSE decile groupings

Small cap funds can be categorized in other ways, too. Basically: 1) small company growth funds which invest in high growth stocks; 2) small company value funds investing in undervalued stocks or asset situations; and 3) index funds, which tend to invest across the size spectrum. Small company growth funds outnumber small company value funds by a small margin. An example of a small company value fund is T. Rowe Price Small Company Value. One index fund is the Vanguard Small Cap Stock Fund. In addition, there are also small company global and international funds. You can usually identify these funds by the language in the objectives section of their prospectuses and by inspecting their portfolios.

Since most small company growth funds are in the aggressive growth category, I'm discussing small cap in this chapter. However, many small company value funds belong in the growth category, which I'll discuss in the next chapter.

A distinction can be drawn between small caps and small companies as measured by sales or assets. While the words small cap and small company tend to be used interchangeably, they are not the same. A good-sized company unloved by Wall Street may sell at a low price, and thus have a small market capitalization. Conversely, some very small companies whose stocks are wildly overpriced will have large market caps. The studies that have proven small company stocks are superior are mostly based on market cap, typically listed stocks (which excludes most emerging companies).

Emerging growth stocks can be quite different from small cap stocks. They are typically untried and have high failure rates. Most small company funds do not invest in start-up companies. For example, Twentieth Century Ultra stipulates that the companies it invests in must have at least three years of continuous operation.

Small caps versus large caps

Shares of smaller companies have outperformed the blue chips over the years. A study by Roger Ibbotson and Rex Sinquefield found that a dollar invested in a small cap index in 1926 would have been worth $3,444 at the end of 1997! By comparison, a dollar invested in the stocks of the S&P 500 would have grown to $1,829 over the 72-year period. That equates to average annual rates of 12.0% and 11.0% respectively, a 9% advantage for small cap. (The index I used is the CRSP 9-10, an outstanding long-term measure of small cap prices. It covers the bottom 20% of NYSE, AMEX and OTC stocks, as measured by market capitalization.)

Other studies have found that the returns from small company stocks are sufficient to offset their greater volatility and lack of liquidity. On a risk-adjusted basis, the smallest companies' returns are still significantly higher than the returns from larger company stocks.

Does that mean small cap is always a good buy? Hardly. The long-term averages mask a multitude of variations. In fact, in the fourteen years since 1984, it's been a completely different story; large cap-stocks have surged well ahead of small caps. From 1926 through 1983, small cap stocks averaged 12.3% a year. Since then, they've averaged 10.5% a year—15% less. In contrast, large cap stocks averaged 9.6% a year from 1926 to 1983 and 17.2% since then—79% better. So the small cap stocks' long-term advantage has turned into a 39% disadvantage.

Table 10

| | Avg. ann. return | | |
	S&P 500	CRSP 9-10	% adv.
1926-1997	11.0	12.0	+9.1%
1926-1983	9.6	12.3	+28.1%
1984-1997	17.2	10.5	-39.0%

Probable reasons for the recent superiority of large cap stocks: 1) they have benefitted more from the internationalization of trade (Coca Cola obtains about 80% of its business outside the U.S.); 2) foreigners are more likely to buy blue chip stocks than small company stocks; 3) indexing has become a self-fulfilling prophecy (the better the S&P 500 did, the more money flowed into index funds); and 4) the superior liquidity of large-company shares.

Of course, the overall large cap advantage since 1984 doesn't mean that bigger was better every single year. In four years out of 14 since 1984, small caps excelled—the most recent being 1993. In the following table, the winner is in bold-face. The "point diff" column shows the advantage of large cap over small cap.

Table 11

| Year | Average annual return | | |
	S&P 500	CRSP 9-10	point diff
1984	**6.3**	-11.6	17.9
1985	**32.2**	26.2	6.0
1986	**18.5**	3.5	15.0
1987	**5.2**	-14.2	19.4
1988	16.8	**19.9**	-3.1
1989	**31.5**	8.2	23.3
1990	**-3.2**	-28.0	24.8
1991	30.5	**51.6**	-21.1
1992	7.7	**26.0**	-18.3
1993	10.0	**19.9**	-9.9
1994	**1.3**	-2.3	3.6
1995	**37.4**	33.3	4.1
1996	**23.0**	18.4	4.6
1997	**33.4**	24.0	9.4
Average	17.2	10.5	6.7

Small caps are more volatile

A look at standard deviations shows that small cap investing is more volatile than large cap. Since 1926, the annualized standard deviation for small cap stocks has been 38.8% versus only 20.3% for the S&P. This means the "normal" variation among small caps falls between plus or minus 38.5% of the long-term average. That's a huge range of returns—between 50.5% and -26.5%. In contrast, the returns on large cap funds varied between 31.3% and -9.3%. Confirming this, small caps have had many more losing years than the S&P during this 72-year period—26 versus 20.

Small caps underperform in bear markets

The volatility of small caps is particularly apparent during bear markets. They typically underperform large caps because they are less liquid. Consequently, many professionals are nervous about holding them in down markets. Here's the record for four recent downturns.

Table 12

| | Total return % | |
	CRSP 9-10	S&P 500
October 1987	-28.5	-21.5
Third quarter 1990	-24.5	-13.8
1994	-2.3	1.3
June-July 1996	-14.0	-4.1

One rough gauge of this category's attractiveness is small companies' price/earnings ratios compared to those of large companies. Chart 13, which shows this relationship, is frequently included with quarterly reports distributed by the T. Rowe Price New Horizons Fund. When small company p/e's are only slightly higher than those of large companies (as exemplified by those corporations that comprise Standard & Poor Corp.'s 500-stock index), small company funds generally are a good buy. When their p/e's are twice as high as the S&P 500's, you are better advised to sell them.

I should reiterate one point. If you choose a small fund in order to maximize performance, realize that it is likely to excel primarily because of its maneuverability and its greater propensity to take risks, not because of inherently superior management. The large growth funds own the stocks of multibillion-dollar companies which are unlikely to go bankrupt in any recession. The same cannot be

Chart 13

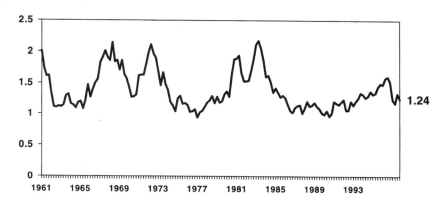

T. Rowe Price New Horizons Fund, Inc.
P/E Ratio of Fund's Portfolio Securities
Relative to the S&P 500 P/E Ratio
(12 Months Forward)
November 14, 1997

Source: T. Rowe Price Associates

said of small companies; and even in booming times there have been bankruptcies in highly competitive fields, especially in the high-tech area.

Yes . . . if you are interested in making your money grow as fast as possible and are able to sustain losses without worrying.

Yes . . . if your income is substantial enough to sustain a "businessman's risk."

Yes . . . if you currently buy volatile stocks, new issues, options and futures, maintain a margin account, sell short, or are a serious student of the market.

Yes . . . if you are willing to take the time necessary to follow the fund and the market.

Yes . . . if you can discipline yourself to sell at the outset of a bear market or when the fund's performance falters.

Performance funds aren't for everyone. But if you found yourself nodding in agreement with these criteria—rather than shuddering in

Are aggressive growth funds for you?

terror—consider putting some of your capital into aggressive no-load growth funds.

Note that older or retired investors should not automatically shrink reflexively from volatile funds. If in retirement your wealth is substantial, and you can sustain losses without jeopardizing your standard of living, then it makes sense to consider the merits of taking above-average risks for above-average gains, at least with a modest portion of your assets. An excessive preoccupation with security can be a mistake. Life is an exercise in uncertainty; often, safety is an illusion that carries its own high price.

CHAPTER 6

Growth funds

Growth funds, often called "long-term growth" funds, focus their attention on capital appreciation over a period of years. They do not attempt to win the yearly performance derby. On the contrary, their aim is to *prudently* grow the money entrusted to them by investors. Some were "go-go" funds in their early years, but have since matured, becoming too big to maintain the percentage increases necessary to keep up the performance pace.

Less hyperactive than their aggressive cousins, growth funds do not employ speculative investing techniques such as leveraging or selling short. And, they are more likely to hold the stocks of large established companies—found in the Dow or the S&P 500.

They are more stable than aggressive growth funds, and as a result, are more consistent performers. In bear markets their losses can be substantial, but they are generally less than the aggressive growth funds'. In bull markets, they grow fast enough to do a superior job of combating inflation, but certainly are not in the vvrroom-vvrroom league of the high-performance aggressive growth funds.

In recent years, popular growth funds have tended to buy blue-chip stocks, the large, well-established companies such as GM, GE, 3M, IBM, Bristol-Myers, Time-Warner, Wal-Mart and so on. Since these stocks have done as well as or better than small companies, growth funds have performed in line with their riskier, aggressive growth counterparts. For example, for the three years ending December 1997, growth funds outperformed aggressive growth funds by a 2.6% margin (24.9% vs. 22.3%). This is something of an anomaly that should not be counted on to continue forever.

In terms of their level of risk, the growth group's betas are on average about 21% *less* volatile than the S&P Index, while the average aggressive growth fund is 13% less volatile than the Index. On the other hand, most other stock mutual fund groups are more stable still. (The only group, besides aggressive growth funds, to have higher betas than growth funds are the highly risky, non-diversified sector funds.)

Chart 14 shows the performance of the Gabelli Growth Fund. It was far less volatile than the Fremont US Micro Cap Fund, as shown on Chart 7.

Chart 14

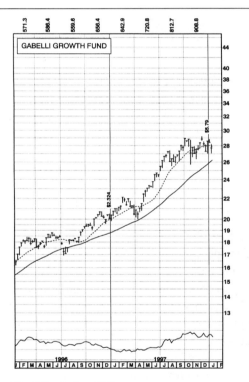

Source: Mutual Fund Trends, Jan. 1998.

How growth funds talk about themselves

A typical growth fund's prospectus will describe its objectives in terms like these:

> Growth of capital through investment in securities of well-known and established companies as well as smaller, less well-known companies—*Fidelity Trend.*

Fund seeks long-term growth of capital. Under normal conditions, will invest in equity securities, primarily common stocks including ADRs and foreign issues, of companies with market capitalizations in excess of $1 billion (with a median market cap of about $2.75 billion) that, in the Advisor's opinion, have an outlook for strong growth in earnings and potential for capital appreciation. May invest in investment-grade convertible securities—*PBHG Large Cap Growth Fund.*

...earn 15% per year compounded, measured over long periods of time (10 years or more)...also seeks to defer shareholder tax liability on the fund's appreciated assets, so that earnings can be generated on money which would otherwise be paid in taxes. Ordinarily invests 90% or more of assets in common stocks, balance will be held in Treasury bills or notes. Central to the investment philosophy is that the value derives from the business, not from the stock—*Torray Fund.*

Sometimes what a growth fund won't do is the key to distinguishing it from an aggressive growth fund. In the "Restrictions" section of the prospectus or the "Statement of Additional Information," many growth funds note that they will not utilize margin, short sales or options, nor will they invest in restricted securities, commodities, nor use other types of investment techniques involving a significant degree of risk.

Growth versus value

Growth can be achieved by buying either "growth" stocks or "value" stocks, or both. This distinction has become increasingly important and more widely understood by investors. Because this issue is so vital to understanding a mutual fund, many publications—newsletters, magazines and analytical periodicals—now specify the sort of companies that funds invest in.

Growth funds buy the stocks of companies whose earnings are increasing, stocks that have relatively high price to book ratios, high price-earnings ratios and low dividend payouts.

Value funds look for undervalued securities. The stocks they buy generally have the following characteristics: their price/earnings ratios and price/book value ratios are low compared to other stocks, and their dividend yields are higher than average. Value fund managers pay lots of attention to the precepts of Graham and Dodd (two professors who wrote the definitive book on stock valuation back in

1934). Such funds can often be identified by the words *value* or *asset* in their name, or by a close reading of the objective section of the prospectus.

Here are the relative characteristics of the Vanguard S&P Growth and Value Index funds:

Table 15

	S&P Growth Index	**S&P Value Index**
Dividend yield	1.0%	1.7%
Price/earnings ratio	31.5x	21.4x
Price/book ratio	9.0x	3.1x
Beta	1.08	.92
3-year earnings growth	23.8%	18.4%
3-year ann performance	32.6%	29.4%

Source: Morningstar, No-Load Fund Investor (As of 12/30/97)

The Growth Index Fund has its largest industry concentrations in consumer staples, health and technology stocks. The Value Index Fund has its largest concentrations in financials and service industry stocks.

In terms of performance, growth funds and value funds tend to alternate in cycles, much like the small and large capitalization stocks. Notwithstanding the cycles, though, other studies have shown that over the long-term, value has outperformed growth. Perhaps that's because growth stocks, with their higher price/earnings multiples, are simply poorer bargains. An interesting study developing this point of view was published in 1987 using both "excellent" and "unexcellent" companies described in the Tom Peters book, *In Search of Excellence.* The excellent companies were far superior based on all the standards that accountants use to measure success. Yet, as shown in Table 17 (page 60), the unexcellent companies' stocks posted far greater returns.

Finally, just to confuse the issue, some portfolio managers feel that growth and value are two sides of the same coin. These managers search for undervalued companies that have good growth potential.

Here's how William Miller III, the portfolio manager of Legg Mason Value Trust put it in an interview printed in the February 1997 issue of Rukeyser's Wall Street newsletter:

"Our approach...we look for quality companies with excellent managements at bargain prices. Some people believe that companies that are growing can't represent good value. We think this is a false

Table 16

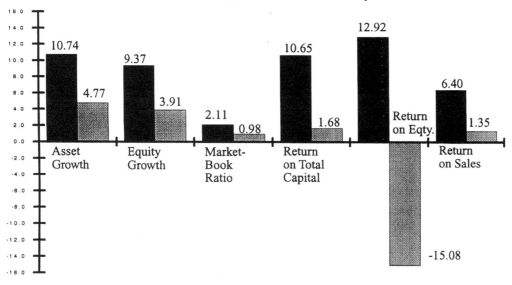

Excellent vs. unexcellent company ratio
1981-1985

Source: Clayman, M., "In Search of Excellence: The Investor's Viewpoint"
Financial Analysts Journal, May-June 1987

dichotomy...We look at present value, liquidation value, private market value, and historical and prospective valuations—things like price/earnings and price-to-book and price-to-cash-flow. Then do a careful analysis of business fundamentals: company prospects, what the products are like, what management's like—how they allocate capital—and what their competitive position is."

Style boxes

Style boxes are a useful innovation for maximizing diversification. As popularized by the *Morningstar* rating service, the construction is a nine box grid, based on two variables. For equity funds, the variables are growth versus value on one axis, and capitalization size on the other. Thus, funds are categorized as large cap value, small cap growth, etc.

Table 17

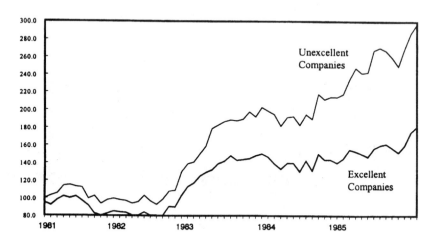

**Excellent vs. unexcellent company portfolio returns
1981-1985**

Source: Clayman, M., "In Search of Excellence: The Investor's Viewpoint"
Financial Analysts Journal, May-June 1987

Morningstar determines categories by an inspection of the fund's portfolio. The growth/value placement is determined by relating the funds' average price/earnings ratio to that of the S&P 500. Consequently, the categories can and do change from time to time. Also keep in mind that the style boxes represent the *average* stock in a portfolio. Therefore, the characterization may be a simplification of the fund's actual policies. A fund designated medium cap might actually hold mostly large and small cap stocks. Usually this isn't a problem, but if you are combining a number of funds, you probably won't get exactly the diversification you are aiming for.

Similarly, the *Fidelity Mutual Fund Guide*, a paid publication covering all Fidelity funds, provides style boxes for its equity funds showing not only the historical style, but also the current one.

Are growth funds for you?

Yes . . . if you don't want the risks of an aggressive growth fund.

Yes . . . if you do want your money to grow, keeping you ahead of inflation.

Yes . . . if current income is not a pressing need.

Chart 18

Equity style box

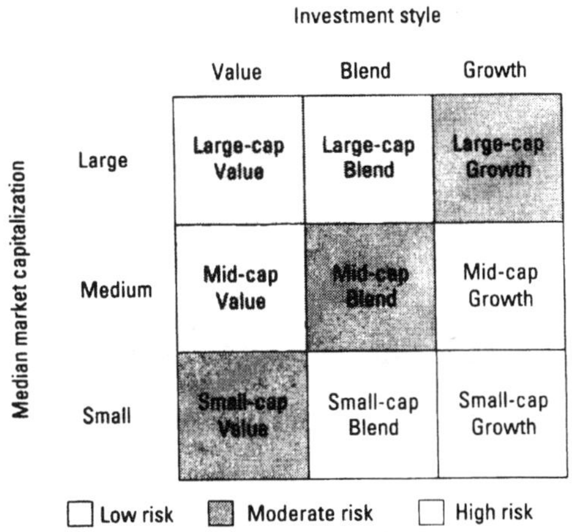

Investment style

Median market capitalization

	Value	Blend	Growth
Large	**Large-cap Value**	**Large-cap Blend**	**Large-cap Growth**
Medium	**Mid-cap Value**	**Mid-cap Blend**	Mid-cap Growth
Small	**Small-cap Value**	Small-cap Blend	Small-cap Growth

☐ Low risk   ▦ Moderate risk   ☐ High risk

Within the equity style-box grid, nine possible combinations exist, ranging from large-cap value for the safest funds to small-cap growth for the riskiest.

Source: Morningstar

Growth funds are suitable for almost all investors. Nearly every-one should consider putting some investment dollars into them.

CHAPTER 7

Growth-income funds

Growth-income funds aim to give their investors a combination of price appreciation and current income. That's called *total return* in the industry. The result with this sort of fund is a return that's usually reasonable, though usually not stupendous. Here's an easy way to distinguish between the three different categories of common stock funds. In 1997, the average no-load growth-income fund had a dividend yield of 1.8%. The dividend yield of growth funds, by contrast, averaged 0.6% and was just 0.2% for aggressive growth funds.

Because dividends help cushion market volatility, growth-income funds provide relative stability for an equity investment. They are ideal for conservative investors and, in uncertain times, aggressive investors who want to reduce their risk.

An above-average growth-income fund over the past few years is Mutual Shares (Z class). As Chart 19 shows, it had a very stable performance in 1996 and 1997. Compare its performance with those of more speculative funds shown in Charts 7 and 14.

The case for conservative equity funds

Growth-income and income funds have done very well in recent years. Here are some of the reasons:

Characteristically, they hold stocks with higher yields than do growth funds. Generally, high-income stocks are more conservative because the yields provide downside protection. But somewhat surprisingly, it doesn't necessarily mean that they lack upside potential. It's possible for them to be conservative on the downside, yet not necessarily conservative on the upside.

Chart 19

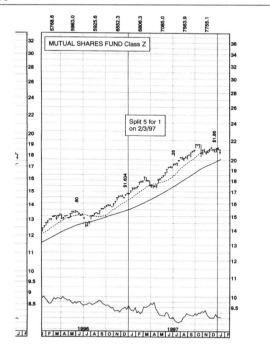

Source: Mutual Fund Trends, January 1998.

Growth-income funds can perform well compared to growth funds because their dividend yield gives them a headstart. A growth fund has to beat its growth-income cousins by the amount of the yield differential during any particular year just to tie. That's not as easy as it may seem.

Advocates of growth-income stocks point out the two ways you can make money on this type of stock. One is that the company's prospects may improve relative to analysts' expectations, and the stock may thus appreciate in value. The other is that, even if it doesn't, the stock market may have already oversold it and discounted its problems (or apparent problems). Thus these funds are, in any event, left holding cheap stocks.

Furthermore, the income portion of the return always gets underestimated. People do not adequately take into account the compounding effect of income, which is an enormous part of the total return. Here's an example: The Standard & Poor's 500 Stock Index, from September 1987 to September 1997, a 10-year period, went from 321.83 to 947.28—626 points, not counting dividends. But when you include reinvested dividends, the index shoots up not just from 321 to 947, but in effect to 1,594! The Index has a 395 percent increase in value by reinvesting the dividends, but only a 194 percent increase if you don't include the reinvested dividends. You get a doubling in performance simply from the compounding effect of income. Because income is such an important component of total return, as an investor you ignore it at your peril.

Finally, in years when the market favors large established companies, that's an additional plus for growth-income funds, since these stocks are among their favorite holdings.

Growth-income objectives

In their prospectuses, growth-income funds state their objectives as follows:

> Long-term growth of principal and income; reasonable current income secondary—*Dodge & Cox Stock.*
>
> Long-term capital growth. However, in order to provide a reasonable current return to shareholders, the fund to some extent limits the emphasis on the growth objective by investing a portion of its portfolio in securities selected for their current income characteristics—*Fidelity Fund.*
>
> Seeks long-term growth of capital, a reasonable level of current income and an increase in future income through investment in income-producing equity securities which have prospects for both growth of capital and dividend income—*T. Rowe Price Growth & Income.*

A word of warning

Sometimes, it is difficult to place funds in their proper categories. If you are still wondering after you have applied the four tests of stated objective, portfolio, dividend yield, and volatility, rely most heavily on volatility. Reason: some funds change their tactics with market conditions and at times can be out of phase with or have outgrown their stated objective, while others deliberately push the outer limits of their category in order to be the best performers within the particular category.

On occasion, a fund's category needs to be revaluated. For example, my newsletter used to place the Neuberger-Berman Guardian

Fund in the growth-income category, but because of its then 1.00 beta I moved it to the growth category. (Some other rating services still call it growth-income; I disagree.) If an aggressive-growth fund has grown larger and is buying the stocks of bigger companies, I may recategorize the fund to growth or growth-income. For example: the Dreyfus Fund, once the epitome of aggressive growth, is now a growth-income fund. Conversely, some funds with "income" in their name may be managed quite aggressively. I may move these funds from our income category to growth-income, or perhaps even growth.

Occasionally, the impetus comes from a renaming. Back in the 70s, American Century had a fund named Twentieth Century Income Investors. I categorized it as a growth-income fund because of its name, even though the fund's fine growth record, dividend payout, and prospectus language were more characteristic of a growth fund. Twentieth Century eventually recognized the incongruity and changed the name to Twentieth Century Select Investors. With the name change, the *Investor* moved the fund to the growth category, where it remains. So you need to look behind a name before you invest.

Are growth-income funds for you?

Yes . . . if financially or psychologically you cannot accept the greater risks of the growth or aggressive growth funds.

Yes . . . if the market is favoring the blue-chip, dividend-paying stocks held by growth-income funds.

Yes . . . if you have been investing yourself—and not too successfully—in blue-chip stocks.

CHAPTER 8

Income funds

Income funds are the most conservative category of mutual funds that invest in common stocks. Also known as equity-income funds, they usually invest half of their assets or more in income-producing stocks, though at times they take defensive measures.

The balance of their portfolios contain convertibles and bonds. At year-end 1996, the portfolio of the average no-load income fund, excluding the cash portion, was 70% invested in equities, 30% in bonds. By comparison, no-load growth-income funds had 93% in equities, 7% in bonds; growth funds were 98% in equities, and aggressive-growth funds were 99% in equities. Simply put, if a fund holds almost entirely stocks, it's probably not an income fund, even though it may be labeled as such. If it is an income fund, its risk, growth potential and dividend yield put will place it somewhere between growth-income and bond funds.

Accenting income even more than the growth-income funds do, the income funds' average yield was 3.3% in 1997. While exceeding the yield of other diversified equity funds, it was still substantially less than the 6.3% that the typical long-term corporate bond fund achieved. In the last decade or so, income funds have done almost as well as the other, more speculative, categories—and with far less risk. This unusual performance resulted from an unprecedented situation. In the current era, both stocks and bonds have posted high returns due, in part, to the nearly uninterrupted and at times very steep decline in interest rates.

While typically their objectives focus on income, it is not uncommon for these funds to have growth as a secondary objective. Note these prospectus extracts:

> High income consistent with the preservation and potential growth of capital—*Fidelity Puritan.*
> As much current income as in management's judgment is consistent with reasonable risk—*Wellesley Income.*
> Income, as high and dependable as is consistent with reasonable risk. The secondary objective is capital growth—*Value Line Income.*
> Regular income, conservation of principal and an opportunity for long-term growth of principal and income—*Dodge & Cox Balanced.*

Categorizing mutual funds is a judgemental process. Authorities may and do differ in their classifications. I use the income category as a catch-all for a number of different types of mutual funds that have the common attributes of relatively low volatility and reasonable dividend income. These include the balanced funds, asset allocation funds and convertible securities funds.

Balanced funds

Among the earliest mutual funds organized in the United States, balanced funds offer a "complete investment program," as a matter of policy, keeping percentages of their assets in a combination of common stocks, preferred stocks and bonds. Their prospectuses usually require that 20%-50% of their assets be in interest-bearing securities. This differentiates them from common stock funds, which are not required to hold any bonds.

In the inflationary and high interest rate environment of the 70s, balanced funds tended to underperform both growth-income and equity income funds. That was primarily attributable to the losses suffered by the bonds in their portfolios. Thus, for many years the industry shied away from balanced funds. The oldest no-load fund, the Scudder Stevens & Clark Balanced Fund, changed its name to Scudder Income and dropped its policy of balance in 1977. At the time, Scudder said the change was a "progressive step that would enhance current income." In 1984 the Stein Roe Farnham Balanced Fund became the SteinRoe Total Return Fund.

Still, there is life in the genre. With inflation low, interest rates dropping and bond prices rising for many years, the balanced funds have staged a strong recovery.

Roughly speaking, balanced funds can fall into one of three types: 1) Regular, which typically have a ratio of about 60% stocks to 40% bonds. Vanguard Wellington is an example; 2) Income oriented, where the ratio is weighted in favor of bonds. Vanguard Wellesley is an example. Typically, only about a third of its portfolio is in stocks; and 3) Domestic asset allocation funds, where the ratio between stocks, bonds and cash is more variable. These are also known as Flexible Portfolio Funds. Asset allocation funds typically carry larger cash positions than balanced funds.

Many, but not all, balanced funds have "Balanced" in their names. The asset allocation funds typically have Asset Allocation or Asset Manager (or some variant) in their names.

Since balance is a policy, not an objective per se, balanced funds can have income, growth-income and, occasionally, even growth as their objective, depending on their volatility.

The advantage of a balanced fund is that it provides diversification, a low minimum investment and a professional manager to do the required reweighting or make the asset allocation decisions. Thus, you need not take such an active role in the apportionment of your portfolio. If you have only a small sum to invest, it's by far the best approach.

Who should not buy them

Opponents of balanced funds, including myself in some instances, think of them as mutual funds with training wheels. So, for several reasons, I recommend that most sophisticated investors who have enough assets to invest in three or more funds—perhaps $50,000 or more—can do better handling their own asset allocation.

First of all, there is *no need* to buy a balanced or asset allocation fund to get proper diversification. When balanced funds were first offered in the 20s there were virtually no bond funds available. Even when the Wellesley Income Fund was launched in 1970 there were only ten bond funds in existence. Today, every large group has a wide selection of stock, bond, and money funds. Thus you can easily "balance" your own holdings, simply by apportioning your investments among two or more stock and bond funds to suit your objectives.

If you do it yourself, you'll know exactly what you have. There are great differences among asset allocation funds in the percentage of the portfolio invested in various classes. Here's how some bal-

anced and asset allocation funds allocated their portfolios at the end
of 1996.

Table 20

Percentage of Portfolio
Ranked by % in bonds

	Stocks	Bonds	Cash
Balanced funds			
Vangd Wellesley Inc	38	60	2
Htchks & Wly Balanced	40	60	0
Vangd Tax Mngd:Bal	46	54	0
IAI Balanced	54	45	1
AARP Bal Stk & Bd	57	41	2
Price Balanced	59	39	2
Janus Balanced	57	39	4
Dodge & Cox Balanced	54	37	9
Price Pers Str-Bal	60	36	4
Dreyfus Balanced	63	35	2
Vangd Wellington	62	35	3
Invesco Balanced	58	34	8
Fidelity Balanced	65	33	2
Founders Balanced	66	27	7
Warbg Pincus Balanced	59	27	14
CGM Mutual	74	4	22
Asset allocation funds			
Vangd Lifestrat:Income	30	70	0
Vangd Lifestrat:Cons Gro	50	50	0
Montgmry Asst Alloc	51	49	0
Strong Asst Alloc	57	41	2
Crabbe Hsn Asst Alloc	58	39	3
Fidelity Asst Mgr Inc	20	32	48
Fidelity Asset Mgr	48	32	20
Invesco Total Ret	67	31	2
Vangd Lifestrat:Mod Gro	70	30	0
Value Line Asst Alloc	48	29	23
Vangd Asset Alloc	47	28	25
Dreyfus Asst Alloc	77	26	-3
Fidelity Asst Mgr Gro	70	17	13
Invesco Multi-Asst	50	15	35
Vangd Lifestrat:Growth	90	10	0

This means that you must research funds carefully to select the
asset allocation mix you seek. My guess is many investors don't.

By doing your own asset allocation you can *control the risk level*
to suit your exact needs. Bonds and cash are less risky than equities.

So by varying your asset allocations, you can control overall risk level.

Some funds are keyed to investors of certain ages, but other funds' allocations are based more on market judgments. In any case, one size does *not* fit all. When you do it yourself, you can take into account these factors as well as others such as your income and wealth levels.

Regarding market judgments, most (but not all) balanced funds maintain relatively fixed portions in asset classes. Asset allocation funds, particularly those that do tactical asset allocation, vary their mixes depending on the relative desirability of different asset classes.

I reviewed the trends of some of these funds' allocations over a four-year span and found that the results were mixed. Some made astute allocation judgments, while others made mistakes. The majority (including the balanced funds) didn't vary their holdings sufficiently to make a significant difference. Varying asset mixes won't achieve huge differences in performance when stocks and bonds move in the same direction, as they have tended to do in recent years.

If you do your own asset allocation, you will have *greater flexibility* in both your equity and fixed income selections. On the equity side, the funds probably emphasize blue chips and other mid-to large-cap stocks. That's generally fine, but perhaps you would prefer a heavier weighting in small caps.

On the fixed-income side, almost all hold corporate and government securities, generally intermediate-term. However, some, including Vanguard Wellington, Star and IAI Balanced, hold long-term bonds. Short- to intermediate-term maturities generally have better risk/reward ratios. Even more pertinent, with only a few exceptions, all these funds hold taxable bonds, while muni bonds may be preferable for your bracket. Two exceptions: USAA Growth & Tax Strategy Fund, which owns both long- and short-term muni bonds, and the T. Rowe Price Tax-Efficient Balanced Fund which invests at least 50% in long-term muni bonds with the balance in mid- to large-cap stocks.

There is also one other *tax advantage* that can be very important. If you own stocks and bonds in separate funds, you can take a loss in one without having to sell the other for a profit. You could take a tax loss in, perhaps, a bond fund to offset another gain (including mutual fund capital gains distributions). Or you could deduct up to $3,000 of a net loss from your ordinary income.

It can be comforting to own low volatility balanced and asset allocation funds, but you'll usually get better investment results on your own. Buying the funds individually, you can target equity funds currently in favor, adjust the asset mix to your own risk level and income needs, and buy bonds or bond funds that are right for you. In sum, asset allocation funds are most suitable for small or uninvolved investors, or investors who find standard allocation funds appropriate to their needs.

Global asset allocation funds

Also called global flexible portfolio funds, they provide broad diversification across five or six different markets (or asset classes). They are similar to domestic asset allocation funds, but add overseas exposure and frequently add a holding in precious metals. Global asset allocation funds do not necessarily move in tandem with the U.S. stock market. As a result, losses in one or two markets may be offset by gains in others.

These funds started in the mid-80s and performed very well for a time, particularly in 1987, when their international sectors buoyed performance and offset sharp declines in the U.S. stock market that year. From 1988 to 1992, they were underachievers because their gold and international sectors underperformed, and because they have quite high expense ratios due to their wide diversification. Since then these funds have changed their prospectuses to allow them to deemphasize gold, but have still lagged the domestic asset allocation funds in recent years. At this time most global asset allocation funds have loads. Two no-load standouts are the USAA Cornerstone Fund and the Vanguard Horizon Global Asset Allocation Fund.

Convertible securities funds

Until 1985, no no-loads invested exclusively in convertibles. Since then, funds with this specialty have been launched by Vanguard, Fidelity, Value Line and others. In addition, several closed-end funds invest in convertibles.

Convertible securities are bonds or preferred stock that can be converted to a fixed number of shares of another security—usually common stock—issued by the underlying company whenever the investor wants. Essentially, convertible funds are substitutes for stocks. Companies usually sell convertible securities when conditions (for instance, low stock prices) make it difficult to issue common stock and/or the credit markets demand such unacceptably high interest rates that issuing bonds is unappealing.

The conversion feature of a convertible is a "sweetener" to persuade investors to accept a lower interest rate in the hope that eventually the company's stock, into which the issue can be converted, will appreciate in value, thus increasing the worth of the convertible. When the company's common stock is valued below the conversion price, the value of its convertible bonds are based on their yield, without regard to the conversion feature. But when the common rises above the conversion price, the convertible's value moves up with the stock price.

Proponents of convertibles believe that they offer the best of both worlds. They believe that convertibles will rise more when stock prices are advancing than they will fall when prices are declining. That's because when stocks rise, convertibles rise, too. They usually don't go up as fast as the common stock, though. When stocks fall, convertibles generally fall less. At some point the convertible becomes attractive for its yield.

Detractors argue the opposite. They think convertibles get the worst of both worlds. Investors, they feel, don't get the maximum gain during rising stock markets. Just as bad, the yield an investor receives is less than straight bonds issued by the company would produce.

I think the detractors have the best case. While they have delivered good gains in the fast-rising stock and bond markets of the 90s, they just haven't provided much protection in down markets. Here's the record in five downturns going back to October 1987.

Table 21

Convertibles' performance in down periods		
Total return %		
	Avg convertible bond fund	Avg dvsfd. fund
October 1987	-19.1	-21.0
Third quarter 1990	-11.7	-16.6
1994	-3.8	-1.4
June-July 1996	-4.7	-6.9
March 11-April 11, 1997	-3.1	-7.4

You see this pattern because convertible bonds, notwithstanding their high yields, are much more of an equity substitute than they are a quasi bond.

Yes . . . if you are a conservative investor who needs income and is willing to accept moderate risk to achieve some growth.

Yes . . . if you have fixed-income investments that are not providing the total return you desire.

Yes . . . if you have been investing yourself—and not too successfully—in income-producing stocks.

Are income funds for you?

CHAPTER 9
THE
NO-LOAD
FUND INVESTOR

Bond funds

Here's an interesting notion that you've probably never considered. If you're typical, you'll receive over your lifetime four times as much interest income as you'll spend in interest payments. You'll lend money to banks, corporations and governments. And in this enterprise, no-load bond funds can be an important ally, providing you with maximum returns at reasonable risk.

From 1981, when inflation began to ebb and interest rates started their long plunge from historic highs, bond funds have delivered an enviable combination of interest and capital gains with very low price volatility.

This great performance is something of an historic anomaly, though. For many years before, and in 1994 when the Federal Reserve Bank raised interest rates repeatedly, bond funds were very poor investments. Their returns were eroded by inflation, their prices fluctuated wildly with swings in interest rates, and the purchasing power of their interest payments steadily declined. If inflation stays low, bond funds will continue to be outstanding investments in the 90s. On the other hand a resurgence of inflation will give bond funds the negative total returns that they often had in the 70s.

Bond funds have two advantages over individual bonds: liquidity and diversification. A no-load bond fund can always be sold at net asset value, with no commission cost. (A sizeable commission can well be the cost of disposing of individual bonds. And obviously, if you paid a load for your bond fund, if you sell your shares you may have to eat that commission.) In terms of diversification, a fund lets you buy little stakes in a great many bonds; that's beneficial because bond issuers occasionally default on their obligations. Along those lines, a mutual fund allows you to hold a portfolio of bonds of a lower grade than would make sense if you were buying just a few individual bonds yourself.

On the other hand, it is important to understand that owning a bond fund is not the same as owning individual bonds. The latter have specific maturities; you can get your principal back in full, at least in nominal terms. This is not true of bond funds, and that's a disadvantage in times of rising interest rates. For all practical purposes, a bond fund has no maturity. For example, a fund portfolio that currently has an average life of five years, will usually have an average life of five years at any time in the future. That's because when one bond matures it is replaced by another with a similar maturity. This means you always sell a bond fund at its current market value, not its face value.

> # *Price impacts yield*
>
> The price volatility of fixed-income investments can significantly increase or reduce their yield. For example, if a bond fund yielding 6% and selling for $10.00 per share has a change in price of a single penny, that's the equivalent of gaining or losing six days' interest.

A few years ago I received a letter from the widow of a close friend. She wrote in part:

Riding the teeter-totter

> Well Sheldon, it is almost six years since Frank died. As a result of his death I had to become a real adult and take charge of my life. It has been a long journey, but I am proud of myself, and more self-confident. In the process of growing up, I discovered that I had to take full responsibility for my estate, so I began to read the business sections of the newspapers and to study the language. My son Andrew was my coach. After a lot of patiently explaining the concepts to me, I finally understand why bonds go down in price when interest rates go up, or ... is it the other way around??

No, she had it right the first time. Interest rates—that is, yields—and bond prices move in opposite directions, much like a child's teeter-totter.

Chart 22

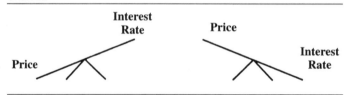

It's easy to remember the relationship when you understand the underlying rationale.

Let's say you bought a bond at par (100) that was paying a 6% interest rate. Now let's say that a year later interest rates in general had risen, perhaps because of a rise in inflation. Obviously, a bond issuer would now need to offer whatever the current rate was. Let's say it's 7%.

Here's where most people trip up in trying to puzzle this out. The key is that newly-issued bonds are sold right alongside of existing bonds that have yet to mature.

Therefore, when you think about it, how could anyone with an old 6% bond sell it if new bonds of the same quality and maturity were yielding 7%?

Obviously, something has to happen, since bonds of all types are constantly being bought and sold. What happens is that the bond market has a self-correcting mechanism. If interest rates currently are higher than the rate on any particular bond, its price is dropped accordingly. This is called a "discount." And vice-versa. When rates are lower than an older bond carries, it sells at a "premium."

That explains why the bond market is said to be "rallying" when interest rates are dropping. Because the volume of existing bonds is so vastly more than the trickle of new bonds being issued, most of those being sold at any given time are not new issues.

Just remember the key: where your bond (or fund) is in relationship to the current interest rate environment, and the current trend—rising or falling—in interest rates.

Or, you can just remember this: when yields go up, bond prices go down.

From here to maturities

How much the price of a bond rises or falls with a change in interest rates depends largely on the bond's maturity—the date when you can redeem your bond for full value. The longer the maturity, the greater the volatility. The following table illustrates the approximate changes in value that can be expected from a $10,000 investment in various government securities when interest rates change 1%.

Table 23

$10,000 investment

U.S. gov. security	Change in value if interest rates move:	
	Up 1%	Down 1%
3-mo. Treasury bill	$ -24	$ 24
1-year Treasury bill	-93	94
5-year Treasury note	-383	401
10-year Treasury note	-617	672
30-year Treasury bond	-940	1,123
30-year zero coupon bond	-1,989	2,665

Source: American Century—Benham

What beta is to stocks, average maturity and/or duration is to the bond fund investor. It's a measure of risk. The longer the maturity of the holdings in the fund's portfolio, the greater the price gains or losses you should expect for a given change in interest rates. Funds with bonds maturing in the near future typically are less volatile—and usually yield less—than funds holding long-term bonds.

Longer maturity means greater risk

Illustrating this principle, Table 24 shows the maturities and yields of the bond funds offered by three major fund groups: Vanguard, American Century-Benham, and T. Rowe Price.

Vanguard offers a number of separate U.S. Treasury portfolios ranging from a short-maturity money market fund to a long-term bond fund. The Money Fund's investments had an average maturity of only 66 days at year-end 1996. Its price, like those of virtually all money funds, is fixed at $1.00. Next, the Vanguard Short-Term Treasury Portfolio had an average maturity of 2.3 years; its price varied by 3.7% from high to low in 1996. Vanguard's Intermediate and Long-Term Treasury Portfolios had longer maturities and consequently and greater volatility—8.7% and 15.2% respectively. The yields also rose as maturities lengthened. This is the normal pattern. However, occasionally when the Federal Reserve is tightening short-term rates the reverse is true: bonds with short maturities have higher yields than bonds with longer maturities. This abnormal situation is called an "inverted yield curve."

I've shown similar data for T. Rowe Price tax-free funds and Benham zero coupon bonds. The yields for the zeros are imputed. Their volatilities and yields also varied with maturities, the zeros having the greatest variations because they don't actually pay interest.

Table 24

Bond funds
How average maturity affects yield and volatility

	Average maturity 12/31/96	1996 Yield	1996 Net asset value High	Low	Volatility
Vanguard					
Treas. Money Mkt	66 days	5.0%	$1.00	$1.00	0.0%
Treasury Short	2.3 yrs	5.8	10.39	10.02	3.7
Treasury Intermediate	7.5 yrs	6.2	10.93	10.06	8.7
Treasury Long	20.9 yrs	6.6	10.79	9.37	15.2
Rowe Price					
Tx Expt Money Mkt	57 days	3.4	1.00	1.00	0.0
TF Short-Inter	3.5 yrs	4.3	5.41	5.27	2.7
TF Ins. Inter.	8.1 yrs	4.4	11.01	10.47	5.2
Tax-Free Inc	17.8 yrs	5.3	9.88	9.23	7.0
American Cent./Benham					
Cash Res. MM	58 days	5.0	1.00	1.00	0.0
Target 2000	3.9 yrs	5.6	82.83	77.28	10.7
Target 2010	13.7 yrs	6.3	46.93	39.79	17.9
Target 2020	23.7 yrs	6.6	26.29	20.18	30.3

Choose your risk

While the real risk of holding bonds or bond funds is the risk that inflation will erode their value, there is also the default risk. Bond funds offer various degrees of protection from that risk. Some invest in government bonds that are totally safe from default, others in bonds that are insured. Some funds buy high quality, investment-grade bonds issued by corporations. Their risk of default is infinitesimal. Others invest in low-grade speculative issues, termed "junk" bonds, which may have a significant likelihood of default. I'll detail their risk later in this chapter.

Risk is usually evaluated by the two national rating agencies, Standard & Poor's and Moody's. The prospectuses of many bond funds list their quality standards using these ratings. Annual reports sometimes summarize the portfolio bonds using these ratings. The lower the rating of a portfolio, the more speculative it is, and the higher its return should be. Bonds rated in the first four grades (AAA to BBB in S&P) are called investment grade; those with ratings below the first four grades (BB and below) are called high-yield or "junk" bonds.

And here's one other risk you need to be aware of: With long-maturity bonds, the risk of losing principal is high, while the risk of losing income, at least over a period of years, is low. With short-term bonds, the reverse is true: the risk of losing principal is low while the risk of losing income is high. That's because long-term bonds, whose maturities are possibly years away, don't have to rolled over very often. So the yield obtainable at the time they are rolled over is not a matter of great concern. On the other hand, by their very nature, short-term bonds need to be rolled over far more frequently. If interest rates are lower when the time comes to roll over the bond, you will find your income is severely diminished. Many savers found this out to their sorrow when they rolled over CDs in the early part of the 90s.

Careful about the name

A fund's name should tell you a lot about its average maturity. Short, intermediate and long in a name have fairly consistent meanings. Short generally means maturity of from 1 to 5 years; intermediate, 5-10 years; and long, over 10 years. However, the name limited can mean either short or intermediate. Some examples:

Fund	Avg. maturity (Dec. 1997)
Neuberger-Berman Limited Maturity	2.0
Vanguard Muni Limited Term	3.3
Fidelity Spartan Ltd Maturity Gov.	4.6
Fidelity Limited Term Muni	8.0

I recommend that the long-term fixed-income investor should generally buy intermediate term maturities, typically in the five-to-ten year range. Intermediate bonds capture most of the yield of the long-term bond funds, but with substantially less volatility.

What's the best maturity

Short-term bond funds are a great substitute for money funds when interest rates are falling. But when interest rates are rising, you are better off scuttling back to the money funds, even if their yield is substantially less. You will come out ahead on total return. And make no mistake, when interest rates rise significantly, you can definitely lose principal in a short-term bond fund, as investors began realizing to their discomfort in the fall of 1993. By 1994, rising interest rates caused the worst bond market selloff in decades.

Another way to beat money fund rates when prices are falling is to buy one- or two-year Treasuries. They're less liquid, but you can hold them to maturity and be assured that your principal is safe.

Duration

While average maturity is useful, there is a better measure—called duration. It differs from average maturity in that it takes into account a bond's cash flows from current interest payments. Average maturity doesn't take cash flows into account. Here's an example that shows the difference. The AARP High Quality Bond Fund and the Benham Target 2005 Fund both had similar average maturities, about 11 years, at year-end 1994. (I've used 1994 as an example because it was a down year for bonds.) But the AARP Fund had a far shorter duration, 5.2 years vs. 10.8 years for the Benham Target Fund.

The reason for the difference is that the AARP Fund makes regular interest payments, which shorten the time needed to receive the sum total of interest and principal due you over the life of the bond. The Benham Fund is a zero coupon bond fund that doesn't make any distributions until its zero coupon bonds mature. With lower duration, the AARP Fund lost less in the rising interest rate environment of 1994. Its total return declined 4.5%, while the Benham 2005 Fund declined 8.9%, twice as much.

Table 25

Duration vs. average maturity

Fund	Avg. maturity	Duration	1994 total return
AARP High Quality	11.0	5.2	-4.5
Benham Target 2005	10.8	10.8	-8.9
AARP diff.		-51.9%	-49.4%

Duration is a far more accurate measure of volatility due to interest rate changes. You can multiply a fund's duration by a change in interest rates and get its price movement. A fund with a duration of five will lose 5% of its value with a 1% increase in interest rates. A fund with a duration of 10 would lose 10% of its value. Conversely, a 1% decline in interest rates would result in 5% and 10% gains in total value, respectively. If interest rates change by 2%, then double the figures. You can't use average maturity to make these determinations. Duration data are not quite as universally available as average maturity data, but if you can get it, by all means use it. Otherwise, rely on average maturities when you analyze bond funds.

■ Generally speaking longer-term bonds have higher yields and thus have higher durations. However, if two bonds both mature at the same time—say, 20 years—the bond with the higher yield will have a shorter duration, and thus be less volatile. That's because more interest is paid along the way. By the same token, changes in interest rates and yields will shorten or lengthen durations.

■ Like maturity, duration can be calculated more than one way. In addition to figuring duration to the maturities of the bonds in the portfolio, it can also be calculated to the dates that the bonds may be called—that is, redeemed early by the issuer.

■ Several factors can reduce the accuracy of duration figures. If a fund holds convertible bonds, they may be excluded from the calculations. Similarly, foreign bonds, which may not track domestic interest rates, can throw the figures off. Derivatives are another problem. They may have different volatilities and a lack of liquidity can affect their prices, regardless of their theoretical value. Sometimes nobody will buy them at a fair price, or even at any price.

■ Duration is less meaningful for junk bonds. Interest rate changes are only a small part of the risk of holding them.

The subtleties of duration

Don't make the mistake of thinking that bond funds with high yields are always better buys than funds with lower yields. Compare total return— the sum of yield and changes in NAV. For the twelve months ending December 1997, Lexington GNMA had a yield of 6.2%, and a total return of 10.2%. By contrast, the Dreyfus 100% U.S. Treasury Intermediate-Term Fund had a higher yield, 7.2%, but a far lower total return, 7.6%. In 1990 during the S&L crisis, junk bonds boasted high double-digit yields, yet had negative total returns.

When the yield is higher than the total return, you are losing principal. The truest measure of your return is total return. Some retired investors who live on their investments may say that they don't care what happens to the price of their bonds as long as they continue to receive their interest income. I think this point of view is incorrect, par-

Emphasize a fund's total return

ticularly if virulent inflation were to return. Back in the 1950s, 30 year corporate bonds provided 2-3% yields. If you bought one of those bonds for $1,000 and held it until the 1980s, you lost your shirt from a total return, after-inflation standpoint, even though you received your $1,000 back at maturity.

Similarly, during periods of high inflation, it's a mistake to spend all your interest distributions. The reason: high interest rates primarily reflect high inflation and thus provide a return of capital.

Economists believe that during times of no inflation, bonds should return about 3% per year. During inflationary periods, interest rates above 3% compensate a lender for the loss of purchasing power on his principal when it is paid back. Let's say that inflation is running at a 3% rate and bonds are yielding 6%. Three percentage points is pure interest; the remaining three percentage points is demanded by lenders to preserve what they believe to be the real value of the principal.

How does this affect you? If you are holding $10,000 worth of bonds for the long-term, and they pay $600 per year, don't spend the entire $600 unless you want to eat into your principal. Spend only $300 and reinvest the balance. If you don't, you will suffer when non-inflationary times return. That's because when your bonds mature, they will have to be rolled over into new bonds yielding far less. I've used the example of individual bonds to make the point clearly, but the same holds true for bond funds. The fund's portfolio holdings mature or are called, and the managers must replace them with lower yielding bonds. Similarly, if the fund sells more shares it must dilute its high-coupon bonds with newer ones that have lower coupons.

While total return is the best measure to use when looking at past performance, it's a poor gauge of future performance. Under SEC regulations, when the funds quote yields, they must also show total return performance figures for the latest one-, five-, and ten-year periods (or the life of the fund, if less). In some respects this policy is ill-advised.

If you examine only total returns when you purchase a long-term bond fund, there are occasions when you may be riding for a fall. Here's why. Total return figures look best after a long decline in interest rates. Yet, if the trend reverses and interest rates start rising, that will be the worst time to buy. The best time to buy long-term bond funds is when interest rates are high—and starting to decline. Unfortunately, that is the time when total returns look the worst. In sum, total return tells you how you have done, but is of little help in predicting how you will do in the future. It is best ignored when timing purchases. Yield is a better fore-caster of the future.

Two other variables in determining performance are a fund's will-ingness to protect against price declines either by going to cash equiva-lents or by shortening the maturities of its portfolio during periods of falling bond prices. The funds most likely to vary their maturities this way are those with the word "flexible" in their names.

There is a tendency to ignore expense ratios, in part because the total return and yield figures used to analyze performance are net of all expens-es. Too often we excuse high expenses if a fund is doing well or if it fills a niche in the investment spectrum. It's very important to keep investment expenses as low as possible, particularly in the case of bond funds.

To illustrate, I've compiled a comprehensive list of all domestic, investment-grade bond funds, load and no-load, that meet two criteria: a five-year performance history and a 1997 expense ratio of 1.5% or more. (The median no-load bond fund has an expense ratio of .72%.) Out of a universe of 992 bond funds, 103 funds met the criteria, about 10% of all funds. I next compared the performances of these 103 high-expense bond funds to all bond funds and found that over the five-year period, high-expense bond funds were far more likely to be underperformers. Using my standard quintile analysis, only 8% of them were above average (1st and 2nd quintiles) while a full 74% ranked in the bottom two quintiles.

Watch expense ratios

Table 26

Bond funds with expense ratios of 1.5% or more		
Percent distributions **by five-year quintile performances**		
Quintiles	**# funds**	**% Distribution**
1 (best)	4	4%
2	4	4%
3	19	18%
4	14	14%
5 (worst)	62	60%
Total	41	100%

Source: Morningstar, 5 yrs ending June 1997

You can find a fund's expense ratio in the prospectus in the chart usually titled "Per Share Income and Capital Changes." Table 44 in

Chapter 14 provides averages you can use as benchmarks. Make a point of checking this important figure before buying any fund.

Other selection criteria

Don't waste your time looking for "star" fixed-income managers. There is expertise out there, but fixed-income managers (with the possible exception of PIMCO's widely-respected guru William Gross) just don't get the publicity treatment accorded hot equity fund managers. It's best to make your investment decisions based on a group's fixed-income expertise and a particular fund's long-term performance record—a minimum of a year, preferably three to five years.

It's not necessary to select insured bond funds. In most cases the loss from defaults is less than the cost of the insurance. (Single state munis, described in the next chapter, may be an exception.)

Most bond funds pay interest monthly; however, a few pay quarterly or even annually. However, if you need the income to live on, you may prefer to receive your dividends monthly.

Next, let's look at some of the major bond categories that you may wish to invest in.

Corporate bond funds

These are short, intermediate, or long-term bond funds in which corporate bonds predominate in the portfolio. Many of the funds also own government bonds. (The SEC requires that 65% of a fund's portfolio be in assets that are implied by its name.) The prospectuses of most corporate bond funds simply call for the purchase of investment grade bonds, which are the four highest grades: AAA, AA, A, and BBB. However, some funds in this category restrict themselves to a higher standard, usually A-rated or better. Funds in the latter category include Dreyfus A Bonds Plus, D. L. Babson Bond Trust L, which mandates that 80% of its portfolio be in the top three grades and/or government bonds, and the AARP High Quality Bond Fund, which keeps 80% of its portfolio in the top two highest quality grades, or in government-issued securities.

Warning! Some investment grade bond funds may quietly take on extra risk. Some buy junk bonds. In the first quarter of 1997, Scudder Income Fund boosted its junk bond allocation to 18%, close to the 20% limit allowed by prospectus. Dreyfus Short-Term Income Fund increased junk from 8% to 26% over a 2.5 year period. Some also buy the higher-risk emerging market bonds.

Government bonds are the ultimate in credit safety. They are backed by the "full faith and credit" pledge of the U.S. government, and include instruments such as Treasury bills, notes, and bonds as well as government agency securities that are fully backed by the government such as GNMAs and FNMAs. Nevertheless, government bonds, like all bonds, fluctuate with interest rates. Since 1980, annual total returns on long-Treasury bonds have been as high as 40.4% (in 1982) and as low as -7.8% (in 1994).

For years, government bond funds have been popular among investors. Interestingly, most of the action centers on load funds, which are heavily pushed by salesmen. They have accounted for over two-thirds of sales in past years. While their total returns have been relatively high through much of the past decade, equities usually offer more potential over the long-term. This may be another case of salesmen making the easy sale instead of doing what is best for the investor.

In many large states, avoiding state and local taxes can be almost as important as avoiding federal taxation. Thus, you may reap substantial benefits from some bond funds that invest only in Treasury bonds, which are not taxed at the state level. However, for many years the IRS refused to allow treasury bond funds the same exemption. However, since a 1984 Supreme Court decision on a related matter, the fund industry has won a slew of court battles prohibiting states from taxing Federal interest distributions made by mutual funds. But it's a slow battle. As recently as 1997, the funds won a court fight with New Jersey. Your fund can tell you the tax status in your own state.

While I almost always prefer using professionally managed mutual funds to holding individual securities, whether they be stocks or

Government bond funds

All fixed-income funds are not created equal

Fixed-income investing may seem simple, but don't be fooled. More than 30 categories of funds could nestle in your fixed-income portfolio. And they have wide variations in performance.

Fixed-income funds
Ranked by 10-year cumulative total returns
through 9/30/97

Target maturity (zero coupon bonds)	246.4
Convertible securities	185.0
High current yield (junk bonds)	168.7
Flexible income	151.2
General bond	149.0
General US trsy	148.0
Corporate debt BBB-rated	147.8
Corporate debt A-rated	143.3
Multi-sector income	131.6
GNMA	131.1
Intermediate investment grade	129.0
General municipal debt	124.6
High-yield municipal debt	124.2
US mortgage	123.0
Insured municipal debt	122.2
Intermediate US trsy	120.7
Intermediate US gov't	120.1
General US gov't	118.1
Short-intermediate US gov't	110.2
Adjustable rate mortgage	104.8
Intermediate municipal debt	102.9
Short US trsy	102.9
Short-intermediate investment grade	101.9
Short investment grade	99.9
Short US gov't	91.3
Short world multi market	89.0
Short-intermediate municipal debt	79.8
General money market	69.8
Short municipal debt	68.7
US gov't money market	67.8
US trsy money market	67.1
Tax-exempt money market	43.7

Source: Lipper Fixed-Income Performance Summary

bonds, Treasury bond funds may be an exception for the long-term holder. Since there is no credit or call risk, nor any need for diversification, you are better off holding individual Treasury bonds, particularly if you want the money back at some pre-determined time in the future. This way you save the management fees which add up over the years.

GNMA funds

These government funds invest in mortgage-backed GNMA (or "Ginnie Mae") certificates endorsed by the Government National Mortgage Association. The principal and interest are guaranteed by the United States government. GNMA certificates are created by an "issuer," which is an FHA-approved mortgage banker who assembles a pool of FHA, FmHA, or VA-insured mortgages that have similar interest rates, maturities and dwelling types. The certificates are most commonly marketed to investors as "passthroughs," in denominations of $25,000. There are also $5,000 participation certificates, but they pay interest semi-annually, not monthly, as the passthroughs do.

These Ginnie Mae certificates have a stated life of 25 to 30 years, but because some mortgages are prepaid or are foreclosed, the typical certificate has about a 12-year life. In periods of declining interest rates this is a disadvantage since this limits their potential price gain and reduces the ability to lock in good yields for long periods of time, because maturities will shorten as home owners pay off their old mortgages. That was a dramatic drawback in 1993 as rates plunged and refinancings soared. The average GNMA gained only 6.8% that year, well below the returns for other intermediate and long-term funds. However, by actively managing the underlying GNMA certificates, funds can control maturities better than individuals generally are able to.

Holders of GNMA certificates receive both interest and return of principal. If you own the certificates themselves you have to be careful not to spend your monthly returns, because doing so wouldn't just be spending your interest, you'd actually be eating into your capital as well. When you buy a GNMA fund, your capital distributions are automatically reinvested, thus maintaining your equity.

Many large fund groups now have GNMA funds. In addition, other fixed income funds like Strong Government Securities Fund, invest in GNMAs, as well as in other mortgage-backed securities, such as Fannie Maes and Freddie Macs.

GNMA bond funds are not all the same. They can hold GNMA certificates at par, or at a discount or premium. Discount GNMA certificates represent mortgages with interest rates significantly below current market rates. As refinancing in these circumstances gives homeowners few advantages, such GNMAs have a low repayment risk and their maturities are longer than average. They have a high sensitivity to interest rate changes.

Premium GNMAs, which have coupon rates above current market rates, have greater repayment risk and shorter-than-average maturities. They are less interest-rate-sensitive and their prices are more stable. Current-coupon GNMAs, at around the current market rate, are the most sensitive of all to interest rate changes.

When interest rates are rising, premium GNMAs can offer the most stable returns. When rates are falling, discount GNMAs generally have the greatest potential for price appreciation. (GNMA fund managers can move from one to another, or may even have some of both. You rely on the manager's expertise to pick the best ones.)

Junk bond funds

When you see the words "high yield" in a fund's name, that's usually a dead giveaway. Such funds invest in bonds rated below the top four grades—in other words, BB or lower. There are two types of junk bonds, "fallen angels" and "original issue." Fallen angels are bonds that once were investment grade; original issue bonds, pioneered by Michael Milken, enable young companies with poor credit ratings to tap public markets. Junk bond funds hold both types of securities. They also differ from each other in the grades they hold. Some junk bond funds stick to the BB issues—almost investment grade. Others dip down to the far more speculative CC and C grades.

Junk bonds are not as interest rate sensitive as higher quality bonds, which perhaps give them an aura of safety, but the risk of default is many times higher. That rate has varied tremendously over the years. It peaked at 9.33% in 1991 during the S&L crisis. However, since the default rates are tied to the economy—which has been outstanding in recent years, it was .6% for the first nine months of 1997. Of course, when the next recession comes their default rates will rise. By way of comparison, the 1997 default rate for investment grade bonds was .07%.

Chart 27

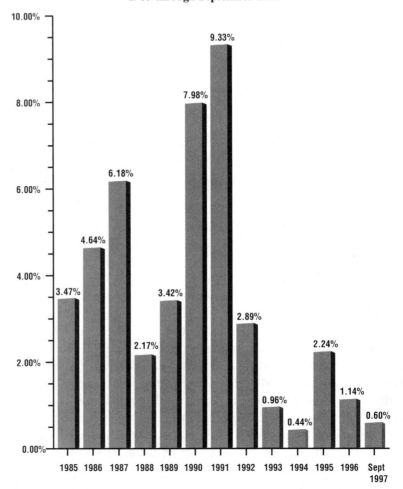

High Yield Market Default Rate*
1985 through September 1997

Default rates are at historic lows.

*based on par value

Source: T. Rowe Price, CS First Boston

A prudent investor should think of high-yield bonds not as safe debt, but as an equity substitute—a way to achieve appreciation along with generous income. Well-known mutual fund manager Mario Gabelli calls them "SIDs," stocks in drag. The following table compares the total return of junk bond funds with diversified equity funds and intermediate term investment grade bond funds over a ten-year period. I used the intermediate term category since most junk bond funds are not of long maturity. As you can see, the performance of junk bond funds falls between equities and investment grade fixed-income funds.

Table 28

Junk bond funds vs equities and investment grade bond funds **10 years ending 1997**	
	Total return percent
Diversified equity	15.8
Hi-yield	11.6
Fixed-income investment grade	
Corporate intermediate	8.5
Gov. Intermediate	8.0

Junk bonds turned in terrible performances in 1989 and 1990 primarily as a result of the S&L crisis. This resulted in their being oversold. Junk bonds then bounced back with a vengeance in 1991, advancing 30.4% on average. They have continued to make strong gains since then. In bear markets they generally held up far better than equities but not as well as investment grade bond funds. The exception was in 1994 when they performed better when the Federal Reserve raised rates because they are not as interest-rate sensitive as other types of bonds. As a general rule junk bonds will do well when the economy is strong, because that reduces the chances of default by the bond issuers. Conversely, when the economy is weak, the number of defaults will increase, often sharply, and junk bond funds will be poor investments.

Table 29

Bear market performance **Total return %**			
Down period	**Avg high-yield bond fund**	**Avg investmnt grade Inter-term bond fund**	**Avg dvsfd. equity fund**
October 1987	-4.0	3.2	-21.0
Third quarter 1990	-6.3	0.6	-16.6
1994	-2.2	-3.4	-1.4
June-July 1996	-0.8	1.4	-6.9
March 11-April 11, 1997	-2.6	-1.3	-7.4

In summary, junk bond funds are most appropriate for equity investors. When buying, look for the best managed funds. You need a manager who knows credit analysis, because avoiding defaults is the name of the game. Diversification is a must. Do not buy individual junk bonds. Choose funds with a large number of different issues and no disproportionately large individual holding. A very high-yield fund probably indicates that the manager is buying the riskiest junk; lower yields, a somewhat better grade. Ironically, when these funds are doing well, the riskier variety can do best. But don't look just at yield; the real bottom line is total return.

I previously noted that you should not spend that part of the interest distribution that reflects an inflation premium. Similarly, in the case of junk bond fund investments, don't spend that part of your distribution that compensates you for loss through defaults. If you spend all the interest you receive you are, in a very real sense, eating into your capital. In 1996, the average no-load junk bond fund we follow yielded 8.6%, while the average long-term corporate bond fund holding investment grade bonds had a yield of just 6.0%. That extra yield is not a free lunch.

Flexible bond funds

As the name indicates, these funds can move between various types of fixed-income bonds and vary their maturities. They can invest in corporate, government, mortgage-backed, international and junk bonds, convertibles and income producing common stocks. Maturities can vary from very short to very long.

Flexible bond funds have the advantage of being able to move into the fixed-income sectors that are currently the best performers, saving you the chore of switching.

Their disadvantages: 1) their selections and timing can be off, and 2) you never know exactly how the fund is invested.

Some examples of the class: Dreyfus Strategic Income, Janus Flexible Income, Merriman Flexible Bond, Price Spectrum Income, and USAA Income.

International bond funds

A new genre was started in 1986 when the T. Rowe Price International Bond Fund was launched. For the first time, it provided no-load fund investors with the possibility of higher returns by investing in foreign bonds. Other groups such as Scudder, Fidelity and Warburg, Pincus followed with international and global fixed-income funds.

International bond funds are attractive because they benefit from weaknesses in the dollar, and because often the yields being paid on bonds in other countries are higher than in the U.S. Of course, a rising dollar can shrink and even offset foreign bond returns, so the returns on these funds are erratic. In 1987, the Price International Bond Fund gained 28.1%, to rank 14th among all no-load funds. The next year it lost 1.3% and was one of the worst performing of all funds.

International bond funds tend to invest in high-quality, intermediate-term securities, frequently issued by foreign governments. They may enter into currency hedges in countries where a fund's manager feels that the currency is weak against the dollar.

The newest innovation in international fixed-income investing is the emerging markets bond fund. Fidelity, T. Rowe Price and Scudder all now have them. When first introduced in 1993, emerging markets bond funds offered high yields and good total returns. But the following year was another story. These funds were hard hit by currency devaluations and fears of default. Fidelity New Markets Income, which had gained 38.8% from its inception in May 1993 through December 1993, lost 16.1% in 1994. It then bounced back, gaining 41.4% in 1996 and 17.2% in 1997. These funds will probably deliver good returns in the long-run, but with extreme volatility.

Zero coupon bond funds

Two fund groups—Benham and Scudder—offer no-load mutual funds investing in zero coupon bonds. Typically, the funds hold U.S. Treasury securities that have been stripped of their interest coupons. You buy the corpus at a deep discount from the face value, which is paid when the bond matures. The primary advantage of zeros is that they eliminate the reinvestment risk. You don't have to reinvest interest payments periodically at varying, and possibly lower rates. One major disadvantage: you pay taxes each year on the interest as if you had received it. This is true for both individual bonds and funds. (In fact the Benham fund declares an annual dividend solely for tax purposes, followed by a reverse stock split to maintain the fund's NAV, since the zeros pay no dividend.) This tax disadvantage is eliminated by purchasing zeros in tax-sheltered accounts, such as IRAs, Keoghs, and IRA rollovers.

The Benham Target Maturities Trust has six portfolios maturing at five-year intervals through 2025. The Scudder Zero Target Fund now has a single portfolio maturing in 2000. When a Benham Target fund reaches maturity, it is liquidated. Shareholders have the option of moving to another fund or taking cash. At Scudder, a target fund is converted into a permanent fund, usually short- to intermediate-term.

Investors interested in holding zero coupon bonds should carefully consider the relative merits of buying a fund versus buying individual securities. The fund's advantages: (1) no-load; (2) low minimum and subsequent investment amounts—typically $1,000 to begin, and then $100 to add to your investment; (3) greater liquidity: if you want to sell before maturity you are not at the mercy of the secondary market; (4) the ability to switch effortlessly—and cost-free—between series; (5) call protection (some municipal zeros can be called, and it's very hard to know if that's happened, since there are no regular interest payments; if there were, you might notice one missing); and (6) ease of investing within an IRA or other tax-qualified plan.

The major negative: fund expenses, which range from .58% to .67% per year excluding brokerage fees, taxes, and interest. Benham's management fee is approximately .35% per year. If you are buying a fund with the intention of holding it to maturity, you're paying these expenses unnecessarily. For all practical purposes, you then have an *unmanaged* investment. By buying the bonds individually you avoid the fees—a considerable savings in the long run. Here's a rule of thumb for cost effectiveness: if you plan to hold less than four years, buy no-load funds; more than four years, buy the individual bonds.

If you are a long-term holder, the best way to profit from zeros is to buy the individual U.S. Treasury bonds from a broker when interest rates are high and peaking—then hold them until a particular maturity, which you have selected in order to return your capital at a time when you need it. (I recommend you avoid corporate zeros and municipal zeros unless they are general obligation bonds. You don't want to assume any default or possible premature call risks.) For example, if interest rates are at 6%, a zero coupon bond maturing in 12 years could be bought for approximately half its face value, then held until maturity for a guaranteed 100% profit. The only way an investor can lose is if inflation averaged 6% or more over the entire period. Why take the risk of having to always be correct on your interest rate forecast if such a desirable alternative is readily available?

Zero coupon bonds, whether in a fund or outside, are extremely volatile, rising and falling in response to interest rate fluctuations. At various times zero coupon bond funds have been at both the top and the bottom of the fund rankings. In 1995, the Benham Target Maturities Fund 2020 portfolio was third ranked among all no-load stock or bond funds, up 61.3%. But just a year earlier—1994—the fund lost 17.7% when interest rates spike up after the Fed tightened. As a rule of thumb, you can figure that the zeros' profit or loss potential is about three times that of ordinary bond funds.

Of course, this presents a great opportunity for capital appreciation if you have strong feelings that interest rates have peaked—at least for the time being—and are poised to decline. An investor who bought a long-term Benham or Scudder zero-coupon fund in April 1997, for example, could have made a large gain. At the time, the 30-year Treasury bond was at 7.15%; by early 1998, the yield had dropped to 5.7%. Anyone who bought in April and sold the following January would have reaped something like a 40% capital gain, extra sweet if it was in a retirement account and thus exempt from taxation.

On January 29, 1997, the U. S. Treasury, for the first time, auctioned off the ultimate worry-free investment—inflation-adjusted 10-year notes. These Treasury inflation-adjusted notes differ from regular Treasury securities in one important respect. Twice a year, the face value of the bonds is adjusted for inflation. For example, if the Consumer Price Index rises 3% annually, the note's $1,000 original face value will rise to $1,030, a 3% increase over the year. The following year, the bond will pay interest on the larger principal amount. Thus, investors are protected from inflation eroding the bonds' purchasing power. But even if we have deflation, investors will get back no less than the $1,000 face value at maturity.

If Congress changes the computation of the CPI, as has been discussed, the Treasury will base the adjustment on an appropriate alternate index. In periods of high inflation these bonds should deliver a higher total return than regular bonds. In periods of falling inflation, deflation, or even a constant inflation rate, the reverse will be true. In

Inflation-adjusted Treasury notes

that event, you will have to justify the lower return as an insurance premium, the insurance being protection against higher inflation.

In designing these notes, the U.S. Treasury unfortunately slipped in two ways. You don't get the inflation adjustment in cash. It's added to the face value, which you won't get until sale or maturity. And, as in zero coupon bond funds, you will pay taxes on the annual adjustment as if you had actually received it in cash. This makes holding the bonds in non-tax-sheltered accounts somewhat less attractive than in tax-sheltered accounts. Even more important, realize that all you are getting when you buy these bonds is inflation protection. There is no protection from market forces. For example, if foreigners stop buying our Treasury bonds, values on the indexed Treasuries could fall just the same as those for other bonds.

Because of the inflation protection, the basic yields on these notes are lower than comparable non-inflation notes. And given their lower yields, these notes will not generate much current income for many years. So why buy them? Three reasons: They provide the ultimate in safety. Unlike regular bonds or bank savings accounts, you are guaranteed the return of your principal in real terms. They may be less volatile than regular bonds, because inflation fears create much of the volatility in today's bond market. And, they offer great diversification, providing either low positive correlation or negative correlation with regular bonds.

You can buy these notes directly from the Treasury, or you can buy a mutual fund that holds a portfolio of them. Owning them through a fund has the advantage of greater liquidity, monthly distributions that can be reinvested, the ability to manage maturities, and the ease of dealing through a fund group.

The American Century/Benham Inflation-Adjusted Treasury Fund was launched on February 10, 1997 for individual investors. Its monthly distributions represent both interest and an inflation adjustment. Thus, fund investors taking cash distributions will avoid the possible mismatch between distributions and imputed taxes. (If you reinvest, the tax mismatch is academic since, as with all reinvestments, the taxes come 100% out of your pocket.)

At this time, inflation-adjusted notes or funds seem best suited for conservative investors who are overweighted with traditional fixed-income investments without inflation protection. These investors can benefit from additional diversification of bond or bond fund holdings, particularly in tax-sheltered plans. The notes may also be appropriate for wealthy older investors who can live comfortably off the smaller interest.

Because inflation has been such a minimal issue in the '90s—it was just 1.7% in 1997—the Benham Inflation-Adjusted Treasury Fund has fared poorly in its initial year. To benchmark the fund's performance, I have compared it to the Vanguard Short-Term and Intermediate-Term Treasury Bond Funds. As you can see in the following table, the new Benham fund has seriously underperformed both bogies.

Table 30

Total return percent gain March 1 - Dec. 30, 1997	
American Cent. Benham Inflation Adjusted Sec	1.6
Vanguard Inter Trsy	8.8
Vanguard Short-Term Trsy	5.8

While the Inflation Adjusted Security Fund has been an underperformer so far, at some point the market will adjust prices to a level where it will be worth owning. At that time, even a whiff of inflation could make it a winner.

Derivatives

Derivatives are such exotic financial instruments that they are virtually unfathomable to the public, and confusing even to some pros. So it's probably not surprising that these mysterious creatures got a number of bond funds in trouble in 1994. The investment climate was very hostile. Rising interest rates turned supposedly prudent risk-taking into unmitigated disasters. Most adversely affected was the Piper Jaffray Institutional Government Income Fund, a supposedly safe short-term fund. It declined in value a shocking 28%.

The universe of derivatives ranges from some that are intended to reduce risks to others that are highly speculative. The most common include options, futures, etc. The fact that some derivatives went awry hasn't persuaded all mutual fund managers to discontinue their use. Derivatives are a weapon that's simply too important in fund managers' arsenals. So by and large, the funds are sticking with the conservative instruments and avoiding risky, exotic derivatives. Vanguard, one of the more conservative fund groups, continues to use futures, options, planned amortization class CMOs (or PACs), and synthetic short-term notes (or floaters). But the fund family is *not* employing interest-only strips (IOs), principal-only strips (POs), inverse floaters, interest-rate swaps, caps, floors, collars, and swaptions.

Can you avoid funds with derivatives? That is difficult to impossible. In late 1994, *Money* magazine sent a questionnaire to 592 retail bond and money market funds. A staggering 292 or 49% refused to answer their questions regarding the funds' derivative holdings. Although derivative holdings should be included in the funds' quarterly reports, they are hard to decipher.

The best advice: beware of a free lunch. If a fund's yield is suspiciously high compared to its peers, and it is not waiving expenses nor is there any other obvious explanation, the answer may well be that the fund is using derivatives to enhance its performance. There are no giveaways in investing. Higher yields mean higher risks. If that makes you uncomfortable, stay away.

I can offer one note of reassurance. The worst excesses occur among the load funds. They are goaded to use derivatives in order to offset high 12b-1 fees that make their reported performances uncompetitive.

Yield quotations

At one time, the yields compiled and quoted in mutual fund advertising, which many investors used as a prime determinant for making their selections, were frequently misleading. Instead of the more illuminating total return, yields were quoted without reference to gains or losses in principal. As a result, a fund might be tempted to use any means at its disposal to show higher yields. One ploy: ignoring the eventual capital loss of portfolio bonds bought at a premium. For example, if a bond due to mature in 12 years had a 10% coupon, it might be selling for 110. Taking that premium into account, the real yield would be about 9%. And the most accurate comparative measure, called the yield to maturity, would be around 8%. That's because the bond holder gets only 100 at maturity, not the current 110 value. Similarly, some U.S. government securities funds with Government Plus in their names claimed that they were enhancing yield by writing covered options on bonds held in their portfolios. Options are no magic potion. The premiums received from the sale of the options are, in effect, a return of capital. They're not interest.

In 1988, the SEC handed down new rules to curtail the ingenuity with which funds misrepresented their performance. These rules, still in effect, mandate a standardized, government-prescribed way to compute yields that has sharply restricted the potential for abuse.

■ Today, yields must be shown for the last 30 days, except for money funds, which show 7-day yields. Tax-exempt funds can advertise a tax-equivalent yield.

■ Premium income from option writing is excluded.

■ For bonds selling at discounts or premiums, yield-to-average-maturity must be computed, or yield-to-call if there is a likelihood of the bond being called.

■ GNMA funds must reduce their advertised yields by any reductions realized from homeowners repaying their mortgages early.

What this boils down to is that the SEC yield is essentially a yield-to-maturity, amortizing bond discounts and premiums.

Two yield figures are available, the SEC yield, discussed above, and the distribution yield, which is based on actual payouts. The funds will generally give you the SEC yield. In fact, information dispensed by automated telephone answering systems comes under the SEC guidelines. But what a fund representative tells you may not. So it doesn't hurt to ask what you're getting. A few funds give both yields.

The SEC figures are not a perfect representation of the yield, but they make comparisons between funds much more reliable. Funds holding discount bonds now report higher yields; other funds holding premium bonds may report lower yields. In practice, these new procedures apply to fixed-income funds, but can apply to equity income funds if yields are quoted for them.

It is important to understand that these reporting procedures in no way affect dividend payouts. Think of the 30-day advertised yields as essentially measuring a fund's earning power. The actual dividend payouts, on the other hand, are different. They do not take into account accruals, and may include short-term capital gains realized by a fund either on the sale of its portfolio securities or by selling options on its portfolio securities (a strategy used by some funds to enhance income). Depending on the length of the month, the dividend distribution could be for 28 to 31 days. The advertised yields are always 30 days. If the distribution yield is well above the SEC rate, say two or three percentage points, you should be very wary.

Outside rating services (including ours) provide a 12-month "distribution" yield by taking the dividends actually received for the latest year and dividing by the NAV. It is not possible for outsiders to compute yields according to the SEC's methods because they would need to know every security in the portfolio, information that a fund need not disclose. And for that matter, even the funds need expensive software programs to derive their figures.

Are fixed-income funds for you?

Yes . . . if you are a conservative investor who needs stable income with a lower risk of capital loss.

Yes . . . if you lack the capital to properly diversify individual bond purchases.

Yes . . . if you want to diversify against the risks of equity ownership.

Yes . . . if you wish representation in specialized fixed-income areas such as mortgage-backed securities, international bonds, ARMs or zeros.

Yes . . . if you think declining interest rates will generate capital gains.

CHAPTER 10

Municipal bond funds

Before municipal bond funds debuted in 1976, individuals had no way to invest small amounts of money in managed portfolios of tax-free bonds. Today, municipal bond funds give that opportunity to anyone with as little as $1,000 to invest. Even investors who have the means to spend $5,000 or more for individual bonds can benefit from muni funds. Here's why:

In addition to offering tax-free income, muni funds provide professional management, diversification, liquidity, convenience, and reduced commissions in acquiring bonds.

Professional management is especially important. Fund managers closely scrutinize their bonds' credit standing. This is a boon to individual investors, who otherwise are at a decided disadvantage because less information is available on municipal bonds than, say, for publicly held corporations. Tax-exempt issues are relieved of many disclosure requirements by the Securities Act of 1933. Surveillance by the rating agencies is spotty and often occurs only when an issue is sold.

The funds have the ability to buy and sell large amounts, thus avoiding odd-lot fees and commissions that most individual investors would pay. Dividends are almost always paid monthly and can be reinvested without charge. Individual bond owners generally receive their interest twice yearly; and there's no simple means of reinvesting the proceeds in other tax-free securities.

While stocks trade in an auction market, with quotes freely available in daily newspapers, bonds trade in a negotiated market, mostly by telephone. The prices of individual municipal bonds—and even the unmanaged municipal trusts—do not appear in daily papers. As a result, in the 1970s millions of bond holders were unaware of the extent to which the value of their holdings had declined because of inflation. And investors could be blindsided again. Not so with muni bond funds. Their prices are available daily, and can generally be found in your daily paper's mutual fund tables. Thus muni bond owners know exactly what their investments are worth on any given day.

Should you own taxable or tax-free bonds?

Deciding whether to invest in municipal bonds rather than taxables, issued by corporations or the federal government, is simple. It depends solely on their respective after-tax yields. Check Table 31 to determine whether you can benefit from tax-free income. Find the line with your taxable income (be careful not to confuse taxable with gross income) and read across. If you're in the 28% bracket, tax-free income of 6% is equivalent to an 8.3% taxable yield. In other words, if the going rate for taxable bonds of the same quality is less than 8.3%, then 6% munis will provide you with greater after-tax income. The higher your bracket, the greater the benefit munis will provide. Otherwise, there'd be little incentive to purchase them, since a U.S. government bond, for example, has no risk of default.

When you're doing these computations, make sure you are comparing like bonds; you need to look at short maturities versus short, investment grade versus investment grade.

Relative yields change. Tax brackets change. So it's a good idea to review your choices of taxable versus tax-free funds at regular intervals.

Table 31

Tax exempt/taxable yield equivalents for 1998					
Single return	$0 $25,350	$25,350- $61,400	$61,400- $128,100	$128,100- $278,450	over $278,450
joint return	$0 $42,350	$42,350- $102,300	$102,300- $155,950	$155,950- $278,450	over $278,450
Tax bracket	15%	28%	31%	36%	39.6%
Tax-exempt yields (%)		Federal Taxable yield equivalents (%)			
2.0	2.4	2.8	2.9	3.1	3.3
3.0	3.5	4.2	4.3	4.7	5.0
4.0	4.7	5.6	5.8	6.3	6.6
5.0	5.9	6.9	7.2	7.8	8.3
6.0	7.1	8.3	8.7	9.4	9.9
7.0	8.2	9.7	10.1	10.9	11.6
8.0	9.4	11.1	11.6	12.5	13.2

When municipal bond funds started out, they spread their investments over many states. But soon it became apparent that investors could get even greater tax advantages by buying bond funds that invested only in bonds issued within their own states. That's because only muni bonds issued by your own state (or its communities and agencies) are totally tax-free to you. The interest you get from out-of-state munis generally is fully taxable at the state level if your state or municipality has an income, dividends or interest tax. This holds true for both municipal bonds and municipal bond funds. If the fund purchases bonds issued by municipalities outside your state, you will have to pay state and local taxes on the interest you get from them (though not federal income tax, of course). Only that portion of a national fund's assets that is invested in your state's bonds can be exempted from your state tax.

Almost every rule has an exception. Four states—Illinois, Iowa, Oklahoma, and Wisconsin—tax even the income from some or all of their own bonds. On the other hand, the District of Columbia, Indiana and Utah give tax-free status to muni bond interest, no matter where the bonds are issued.

Single-state municipal bond funds did not exist prior to 1983. Now, they are far more numerous than national bond funds; there are about 1,400 versus 300 national. The first no-load municipal bond fund investing in the securities of a single-state was the Fundamental New York Muni Fund. Its popularity has now led to the formation of additional single-state no-loads benefiting investors in Arizona, California, Connecticut, Florida, Georgia, Hawaii, Kansas, Kentucky, Louisiana, Maryland, Massachusetts, Michigan, Minnesota, Missouri, New Jersey, New York, North Carolina, Ohio, Oregon, Pennsylvania, South Carolina, Tennessee, Texas, Virginia, Washington, and Wisconsin.

These single-state bond funds are available from Benham, Dreyfus, Fidelity, Rowe Price, SAFECO, Scudder, USAA, Vanguard and others.

By sidestepping state and/or local income taxes you can dramati-

Single-state bond funds

WARNING!

It's a big mistake to buy a municipal bond fund or bond (or any other tax-favored investment, such as an annuity) for tax-advantaged investment vehicles such as IRAs and Keoghs. You can't shelter something twice. By placing muni bonds into a tax-deferred retirement account you effectively convert a tax-free investment into a low-earning taxable one. In the case of the new Roth IRAs, which aren't taxed on withdrawal, you reduce your return by substituting a lower yielding bond for a higher-yielding taxable one.

cally increase your after-tax returns. A New York City resident who is in the new 39.6% federal income tax bracket can zoom to a combined federal, state and city income tax bracket of 46.6%. That means that a 6% yield from a fund invested in a New York bond fund is worth an after-tax equivalent of 11.2% to a top-bracket New York City resident. A California resident in the 39.6% federal tax bracket and a 46.2% combined state and federal bracket would similarly benefit.

To calculate the equivalent taxable yield, divide the tax-free yield by 1 minus your tax bracket denoted as a decimal. For example, here are the calculations for someone in a combined federal and Massachusetts state bracket of 39.28%: 6% tax-free yield / 1.00 - .3928 or .6072 = 9.9% equivalent taxable yield.

Single-state muni bond funds are more likely than national funds to be insured. Which is a good thing, since they aren't as well diversified. The debacle surrounding Orange County, California's default in late 1994, hit the California single-state funds the hardest. However, there's always a downside. Insured bond funds may be a bit more volatile than their uninsured counterparts. That's because the cost of the insurance lowers their coupons, making durations higher.

Performance of single-state bond funds

In deciding whether to purchase a single-state or a national fund, don't automatically assume that a single-state fund for your state is preferable. You have to calculate after-tax equivalent rates of return. A surprisingly wide variation in returns exists, due to the states' differing tax rates and investor demand relative to the supply of municipal bonds in any particular state.

Table 32

What tax free yields are worth

Tax-free Yield	Tax-equivalent yield Federal taxes only	CA	CT	Tax-equivalent yield if free from state taxes					
				MA	MI	NJ	NY	OH	PA
4%	5.80	6.51	6.07	6.59	6.06	6.19	6.56	6.23	5.96
5%	7.25	8.14	7.59	8.23	7.58	7.74	8.20	7.78	7.45
6%	8.70	9.77	9.11	9.88	9.10	9.29	9.83	9.34	8.95
7%	10.14	11.40	10.62	11.53	10.61	10.84	11.47	10.90	10.44
8%	11.59	13.03	12.14	13.18	12.13	12.38	13.11	12.45	11.93

Tax-equivalent yields are based on a 31% federal tax rate New York rates include New York City rates

As background on the matter of choosing between national or single-state funds, it is interesting to learn the rationale a fund group goes through in deciding whether to offer a single-state fund in various states. At Vanguard, managers first want to make sure the state issues an adequate *supply* of high quality bonds to obtain sufficient diversification. They want to make sure the *insurance costs*, which decrease yield by about 0.2%, don't make the after-tax yield lower than that of a general muni. And finally, *state taxes* must be high enough to give you an after-tax advantage.

As the table of the next page shows, almost half of single-state muni bond funds underperformed the average general municipal fund in the five years ending September 1997. In some cases the differences between individual state funds and a general municipal bond fund are small; in other cases they are significant enough so that there may not be a tax advantage. If you live in a state whose own bonds are poorly performing, be sure to check general bond funds before buying single-state funds. My annual *Handbook* lists the combined federal and state marginal tax rates for all states. Using it you can then calculate the after-tax yield of a single-state fund and compare that with the equivalent return for a national fund. The easiest way to do this is to convert both to a taxable yield basis.

Pricing bond funds

Tens of thousands of municipal bond issues exist. But only a small fraction of them actually trade on any given day. Thus, no accurate current prices exist for the vast majority. Since the funds need to price their shares each day that the bond market is open, they use the services of an outside pricing firm, which estimates the prices of the bonds that have not traded. Such companies price bonds by using a matrix. Essentially that involves applying a mathematical formula that takes into account the bond's coupon rate, maturity, discount or premium and call features. When interest rates are stable, these estimates are reasonably accurate. But in times of flux, it may be another story. None of this matters very much unless a fund suffers massive redemptions that force its managers to sell bonds that may be mispriced (usually overpriced). It's unlikely you will be able to anticipate such situations. But if you think you may need to bail out at an inopportune time, redeem sooner rather than later.

Table 33

Long-term single state bond funds

Fund (#)	Avg % gain 1992-1997
Colorado (24)	41.2
Washington (8)	41.0
Texas (20)	40.2
Georgia (34)	38.9
California (114)	38.9
Pennsylvania (66)	38.8
Florida (67)	38.5
Alabama (11)	38.4
Kentucky (10)	38.0
Massachusetts (57)	37.9
Louisiana (16)	37.9
General munis (252)	37.9
Arizona (39)	37.8
Ohio (56)	37.5
Missouri (24)	37.5
Virginia (34)	37.4
South Carolina (19)	37.1
Connecticut (25)	37.1
All other states (73)	37.0
Maryland (36)	36.9
Hawaii (10)	36.8
Michigan (53)	36.8
Tennessee (23)	36.7
New York (100)	36.7
North Carolina (40)	36.7
New Jersey (60)	36.6
Minnesota (47)	35.8
Kansas (12)	35.7
Oregon (23)	35.6

The number of funds in each average is in parentheses.
Source: Lipper Analytical Services, 5 years ending Sept. 30, 1997

Funds vs. trusts

Unit investment trusts (UITs) are an alternative to no-load municipal bond funds. (At year-end 1996, there was $43 billion in assets invested in 11,400 tax-exempt UITs.) The trusts have fixed portfolios and for that reason can lock in high yields for many years. Their portfolios are not managed; consequently there is no management fee, only a minuscule trustee fee of about .15% annually. On the other hand, the trusts are sold with a 4%-5% sales charge. For the long-term investor, trusts can provide higher yields than funds. They are liquid and can usually be sold back either to the sponsor or in a secondary market. But the sales charge penalizes short-term investors. Thus, the trusts lack practical liquidity during the early years. If you plan to hold for six years or more, consider the unit investment trusts. Otherwise, no-load bond funds are more economical. (One exception: bond index funds, which have expenses almost as low as the UITs.)

When the municipal bond funds were first organized, their sponsors claimed that their management ability would enable them to outperform the unmanaged trusts. The managed funds can go to cash in adverse markets and have the ability to dump bonds whose credit standing has declined.

How has the performance of funds compared with that of trusts? No comprehensive analysis has been done in many years. But early studies showed that in down years (i.e., when interest rates are rising), the funds, with their ability to sell bonds and move to cash, out-performed the trusts. In rising markets, when interest rates were dropping, the reverse was true. The fully invested trusts outpaced the funds.

Most UITs are acceptable alternatives under certain circumstances. Be sure that you are not buying a problem investment. Check the trust's portfolio before you buy. You're going to be living with it for the duration of the investment. Because these trusts are sold mainly on the basis of yield, there is a great temptation to stretch by buying lower quality bonds. About 25% of the WPPSS (Washington Public Power Supply) bonds that went into default a number of years back were owned by trusts. On occasion, the brokerage firms that underwrite bonds put them into retail trusts when they can't drum up institutional interest.

It is hard to follow UITs. No newspaper coverage of their bid and asked prices exists, and no advisory services track them. I suggest that if you own UITs, you leave them in a brokerage account. That way you'll get a monthly or quarterly review of prices, saving you the trouble of having to call the Trust for a quote. Two other tips before you buy. Find out the yield-to-call, as well as the yield-to-maturity, and see how many of the bonds can be called. Unlike mutual funds which reinvest the proceeds from called securities, the trusts return the principal to you. Thus, after a few years, the outstanding value of your investment can be significantly lower. In the early 1990s, most muni UITs made huge return of principal distributions as interest rates dropped. Next, see if the portfolio contains any long-term zero coupon bonds. If their maturities extend beyond that of other bonds, you will not receive face value when the trust is liquidated.

Are municipal bond funds for you?

Yes . . . if you are a high-bracket investor needing tax-free income.

Yes . . . if you want fixed-income investments with immediate liquidity.

Yes . . . if you lack the capital to properly diversify individual bond purchases.

In sum, when you buy municipal bond funds, keep in mind their quality and maturities. If you live in a state where single-state bond funds are available, consider them first for additional tax savings.

CHAPTER 11

THE NO-LOAD FUND INVESTOR

Money market funds

The money market fund was invented in 1972 as a way to allow individuals to benefit from the high interest rates prevailing at the time. Prior to the invention of the money fund, the only place an ordinary person could invest cash was in the bank. And the banks' ability to pay market interest rates was restricted by Regulation Q, a Depression era law that had been passed to prevent banks from overpaying for their deposits and running the risk of going bankrupt. By the 1970s, the situation had reversed. Regulation Q was limiting the interest on bank savings accounts to 4 1/2%, an amount far less than they could afford.

The first money fund was launched by Harry Brown and Bruce Bent of the Reserve Fund; the second came a few weeks later, founded by James Benham. The money fund took advantage of a loophole in Regulation Q, the lack of an interest rate cap on jumbo CDs of $100,000 or more. Using the mutual fund structure, the money funds could buy these jumbo CDs and pass along high market rates of interest—over 8% at the time—to shareholders who had invested as little as $1,000 in the funds. Furthermore, the Reserve Fund had a new innovation that made it unlike any other mutual fund—a fixed share price of $1, thus fostering the impression money funds were like bank accounts. This was accomplished by varying the yield, computed daily, instead of the price.

One further wrinkle was needed to turn money funds into a preferred way to manage cash. This came about in 1974 when Ned Johnson of Fidelity brought out Fidelity Daily Income Trust, the first money fund that offered check-writing redemptions. Prior to FDIT, the fund industry had made it hard to redeem shares; now it became easy.

Since then, money funds have become the gateway to the mutual fund industry. Millions of individuals who were once afraid to make equity investments were exposed to mutual funds, where they learned of the benefits of stock and bond fund investing. They turned the industry into a financial supermarket that has become the preferred investment vehicle for all Americans with savings.

Money market funds have three objectives: preservation of capital, liquidity and the highest possible current income consistent with these objectives. While the fixed NAV is not guaranteed, money funds have done an outstanding job of preserving capital. They have virtually instant liquidity, but their yields are extremely variable—far more than for long-term bond funds. A money fund's yield and total return are identical.

You can use money funds in three basic ways. Probably the most important for the no-load investor is as a convenient "parking lot." Until profitable new stock market opportunities arrive, you leave your assets in a money fund. For this reason, almost every mutual fund group now has such a fund. Money market funds can also be used as a free checking account. There is, typically, a $250 or $500 per check minimum, although a few money funds have no minimum. The great advantage with a money market fund check is that you benefit from the "float," earning interest until your check is cashed and returned to your money fund's custodial bank. Finally, you can obtain money market interest rates that are generally higher than those paid by banks, not only with liquidity but also safety. For all these reasons, some of your cash should stay permanently in a money market fund.

The main types of money funds available for your use:

General money funds

The most common type is the general taxable money fund. It holds a wide array of investments but typically has a preponderance of assets in commercial paper. Most general money funds are "first tier" but a few are "second tier." First tier funds must have all their commercial paper holdings invested in companies of the highest rank; second tier funds can have up to 5% of their commercial paper holdings with lower ranked companies. Money funds' portfolios are not insured, but they have compiled a remarkable record for safety.

There are *risk differences* between general money funds. But in the main they are relatively small, particularly compared with stock and bond funds. The possibility of a portfolio security defaulting on interest or principal is known, technically, as the credit risk. Since money funds are not insured, this has been of modest concern to investors.

Keep the risk in perspective, though. First, money funds are diversified like other mutual funds. They don't generally invest more than a limited percentage of their net assets with any individual issuer. The average fund owns securities of more than 30 individual issuers, so that the default of a single one should not be catastrophic.

The only time individual investors in a money fund actually lost principal was in the early days of the money funds. In 1978 a small fund, First Multifund For Income, extended its average maturity out over 600 days, betting on a decline in interest rates. When rates rose instead, redemptions shot up. Investors switched to money funds with shorter maturities that had been able to reinvest matured securities more quickly at the higher yields. Further aggravating the situation, the fund did not mark its portfolio to market (that is, price it to current value rather than the value at maturity). The fund finally bit the bullet, selling its securities at a 6% loss. There was no credit problem. First Multifund's principal investment was Citibank paper, which had the highest corporate credit rating. As a result of this loss, the SEC restricted average maturities to 120 days or less. By today's standards, we would not call the First Multifund For Income a money fund.

In the subsequent years several other close calls occurred, due to actual or potential credit losses. This raised the possibility of a loss that would chop NAVs below $1 a share. To avoid that—and the shareholder exodus that would likely follow—advisers reached into their own pockets to make the funds whole.

Because of these close calls, in 1991 the SEC placed new restrictions on the kinds of securities that money funds can hold. Under current guidelines, no money fund can invest more than 5% of the fund's assets in less-than-top-grade commercial paper. In addition, no single issue can make up more than 5% of the fund's holdings if the issuer is top rate; below that, 1%. The previous limit had been 25%. (Because there's no credit risk, investments in U.S. government securities are not restricted.) Another step taken by the SEC was to reduce the maximum average maturity of the portfolio securities to 90 days.

Unfortunately, these steps didn't prevent a number of money funds from losing money investing in derivatives in 1993 and 1994. In fact, the trade newsletter, *Fund Action*, tallied 16 such close calls in 1993 and the first half of 1994. In every case but one, the fund's managers assumed the loss because they didn't want to be the first fund to "break the buck," as they term it, which means causing a money fund shareholder to lose money.

Then, in September 1994, it finally happened. A small institutional money fund in Colorado, overloaded with derivatives, was liquidated with a 6% loss to its shareholders. The culprit was the Community Bankers U.S. Government Money Market Fund, all of whose owners and shareholders were community banks. The shareholders could have been bailed out for a mere $2 million, but there was no point since the owners of the fund were the shareholders. It would simply have been a transfer of money from one pocket to another. No individual investors were involved. The loss, dutifully reported by the press, did not have any effect on mainstream money funds.

I think it's inevitable that a retail money fund, probably a small one, will someday pass on a loss to its shareholders. When that happens, there will be even more adverse publicity, but the chances are the loss will be moderate—a couple percentage points or less.

Several insured money market funds used to exist, but no longer do. Until early 1989, the Vanguard Money Market Trust had both an insured and an uninsured portfolio. The Insured Portfolio, yielded 7.3% for the five years ending 1988, while its uninsured counterpart, the Vanguard Money Market Trust, Prime Portfolio, yielded 7.96% in the same period. The insured fund's yield ranked in the bottom 20% of money funds, the uninsured fund's yield, in the top 20%. That's a steep price to pay for insurance against a minimal risk. In 1989, Vanguard announced that the Insured Money Market Trust was being converted into a U.S. Treasury money fund, a sensible move. Its portfolio securities are, of course, fully insured, and its yield is greater.

Government money funds

The greatest distinction between money market funds is whether or not they hold government or government-guaranteed securities. If you are a very conservative investor, you can choose a fund that buys only government securities. Most major no-load fund groups now have one. Investors in these groups can easily switch from a general money fund to a government-only fund if they feel economic or political storm clouds are gathering. The yield penalty varies, but in recent years, government money funds have generally lagged the regular funds by 0.4% or less. In some individual instances, government money funds equalled or bettered the return of general money funds, particularly if they were waiving expenses. Treasury-only money funds, tax-free at the state level, easily exceeded it on an after-tax basis.

Government funds invest in Treasury bills, obligations issued by government agencies such as the Federal Home Loan Mortgage Corp (Freddie Mac) or Student Loan Marketing Association (Sallie Mae), and repos. Funds that invest in Treasury bills are the safest. They're backed by the full faith and credit of the U.S. government. They're even safer than insured bank accounts. Agency securities (like the FDIC) have only the moral backing of the government, yet they're considered quite safe. To compensate for the slight addition of risk, agency paper pays about 10 basis points (one-tenth of one percent) more.

Many government funds buy repurchase agreements or "repos." A few funds hold only repos. These are short-term loans collateralized by government or agency securities in which the borrower agrees to buy back the securities at a fixed price including the interest and at a fixed time. A number of years ago, repo holders had some scary moments when a few firms that dealt in them went bankrupt and the holders didn't have possession of the collateral. That's changed. The SEC now requires money funds to take possession of the collateral, insuring the safety of the investment even if there are problems with the dealer. Repos also pay slightly higher yields.

Like the bond funds that invest only in Treasury securities, U.S. Treasury money funds can pass the state tax exemption along to their shareholders. That can add significantly to your return, in many cases giving them a better after-tax return than the regular money funds—and with greater safety. In addition, short-term securities issued by the Farm Credit Program, Home Loan Bank, Student Loan Program, and the Resolution Trust Corp. can be tax free at the state level. The Benham Government & Agency Fund, which holds such securities, has tax-free pass-through status.

Tax-exempt money funds

These funds invest in short-term municipal securities. Historically, their average maturities have been longer than those of regular money funds. When they have longer maturities, the tax-free funds' yields increase more slowly as interest rates rise and decline more slowly as rates fall.

Tax-exempt money funds are appropriate for high-tax-bracket investors who need to keep a portion of their money both liquid and tax-free. When you are considering a money market fund, you need to compare the relative yields of the regular versus tax-exempt funds at your particular tax bracket, just as you would when investing in longer term bond funds.

Single-state tax-exempt money funds

For the same reasons that people in high-tax states are often better served by investing in single-state municipal bond funds, it also makes sense for them to invest in single-state, tax-exempt money market funds. Not surprisingly, fund managers have launched a number of these funds. The first were born in 1984 for New Yorkers. Advisers then followed with single-state money funds for residents of 18 large states. Single-state funds are available from Benham, Dreyfus, Fidelity, Rowe Price, Schwab, Scudder, the Reserve Fund, USAA, Vanguard, Warburg Pincus and others.

You can't always assume that single-state funds are better for you than national, or even than taxable, funds. Vanguard has sponsored New Jersey and Pennsylvania tax-free money market funds since 1988, but didn't launch a New York T/F money market fund until September 1997. That's because the fund group found that yields on New York money market instruments had been uncompetitive because too many investors were chasing a limited supply of paper. As a result, their national tax-free money fund had frequently delivered higher yields—on an after-tax basis—than the average New York T/F money fund. Investors in single-state money funds should check their current tax-equivalent yields and switch to other funds, taxable or tax-free, when that proves advantageous. However, unless you keep very large six or seven-figure amounts in these cash accounts—and then for significant lengths of time—don't drive yourself crazy by worrying about minuscule differences in after-tax yield.

Some other short-term bond funds, which may appear similar to money market funds, are not classified as money funds. They have variable NAVs, and consequently are listed with bond funds. They typically maintain dollar-weighted portfolios with average maturities not much longer than one year. So their price fluctuations are minimal. But as long as the NAV fluctuates, they can do better or worse than a money fund.

In the taxable category, the Strong Advantage Fund can provide investors seeking a higher total return than conventional money market funds provide, minimal risk to principal, and liquidity. It aims to enhance yield by lengthening the average maturity of its diversified portfolio of money market instruments up to 360 days. How much riskier is it? In 1997 the NAV varied from $10.12 to $10.05, a difference of 0.7%. At year-end it had an average maturity of 0.5 years. In 1996 the differnce was only 0.4%, but in some other years the difference has been as much as 2%. This fund—and other similar funds such as IAI Reserve, and Harbor Short Duration—is listed with other stock and bond funds in the papers.

These funds are superior on a total return basis when interest rates are declining, but inferior when rates are rising. When you are evaluating these funds, call the adviser for latest maturities. One caveat: I recommend you don't write checks on these quasi-money funds. Since their NAVs vary, every time you write a check, you are selling fund shares. That's a capital transaction, with potential capital gain (or loss) tax consequences.

Fluctuating NAV liquidity funds

I believe that yield is only one consideration when you are choosing a money fund, and perhaps a minor one at that. Yield differences among money funds are small.

Some funds have higher than average yields, which they obtain by temporarily waiving their management fees and absorbing some expenses. When that happens, shareholders get a windfall. That's great, but be wary. These free rides are often temporary. In the case of new funds, the sponsor may gradually phase in management fees. If you buy shares in a money fund that is waiving expenses, keep a close eye on yields; don't expect the fund to tell you when it stops waiving expenses. According to the *IBC Money Fund Report*, 58% of all retail money funds waived at least a portion of their expenses in 1996.

Selecting your money market fund

Since expenses are a major determinant of yields, funds that have historically been top performers are likely to remain so.

Bear in mind that the yields quoted in the papers and by the funds are annualized rates. You get them only if you hold the money fund for a full year—and rates stay at that level throughout the period. But don't bank on either eventuality. Money fund yields fluctuate from week to week. It's far more realistic to think of a 4% annualized yield as a rate that yields 0.33% per month, or even 0.08% per week.

Convenience is important. If your investments are concentrated in a no-load fund group that has a money fund, I strongly recommend you use that group's money fund to facilitate switching between funds.

Here's a checklist of services you should consider in picking a money market fund:

■ A reasonable minimum amount for check redemption. Most funds require you to write checks for at least $250-$500. However, some have lower minimums. American Century Benham's Capital Preservation Fund, for instance, allow checks for $100. Money funds that are part of central asset accounts usually have no minimums. Some funds will let you write small checks for a service fee.

■ Expedited redemptions. If you redeem today, how soon do you get the money? Almost all money funds will redeem via fed wire, which provides you with same- or next day service. In addition some funds provide other types of bank wires. They take two to three days, but usually are free.

■ Speed. How fast your money goes to work for you can differ from fund to fund, and check to check. How soon you can withdraw money invested by check also varies. You can wait up to two weeks after you make a purchase before you have "good" funds. The deadline for same-day investments made by wire or in person can vary from 11 A.M. to 4 P.M.

■ Minimum investments. They usually range from $1,000 to $2,500, but a few funds have lower or higher minimums. The Fidelity Spartan money funds and Vanguard Admiral funds deliver above-average yields for individuals who can meet high minimums.

In selecting a money fund, *size* has its advantages. Other things being equal, the larger funds should pay higher rates because their expenses are spread over a bigger base. They are also more diversified.

Try to *avoid funds that carry 12b-1 charges* and those with *high expense ratios.* They benefit the fund group, while cutting your yield. Zurich Money Market and Cash Equivalent Fund, both managed by Zurich Kemper, are similar funds. They have similar portfolios and maturities. Yet Zurich Money Market yielded 5.37% in 1997 as compared to 4.89% for Cash Equivalent Fund. The basic difference is that Cash Equivalent has a 12b-1 charge of .38%, which is used to pay outside organizations for bringing assets into the fund, a higher management fee and other expenses. The total expense ratio for Zurich is .45%, for Cash Equivalent, .89%. Since gross yields vary only slightly, the differences in expense ratios account for almost all the yield differences.

Watch out for *additional charges.* Some funds charge for check-writing, exchanges and even withdrawals.

Pay attention to average maturity. The shorter the maturity, the safer a fund is, and the quicker the yield will respond to changes in interest rates. In periods of rising interest rates, funds with the shortest maturities will increase their yields the fastest. On the other hand, if interest rates are declining, funds with longer maturities are in a better position because their high yields are locked in longer.

In the case of government funds, check to *see if state and local taxes are deductible.*

Here's a tip for maximizing your money fund returns: Don't take your monthly distributions in cash. If you do, the fund will collect the float. It's better to have the distributions reinvested and then write a check when you need money. That way you get the float.

Money funds versus the banks

Many investors find it convenient to keep some liquid funds in bank money market accounts. How much to have there depends on the type of services you need and the extent to which small differences in yield are important to you.

If you're using liquid asset accounts primarily for yield, it pays to compare funds and banks closely. It is important to understand that banks and money funds have totally different ways of determining yield payouts. Money fund shareholders participate in the earnings of a pool of money invested in money market instruments. You get a share of whatever that pool of money earns, minus the fund's expenses.

Not so with the banks. Their payout bears no necessary relationship to what their deposits actually earn (although, of course, they must cover their expenses, which generally are higher than a fund's). They establish their yields based on the supply/demand relationships for the deposits. The yield depends on how high a rate they have to offer to keep the money in the bank.

The banks have discovered that money market account customers are not particularly sensitive to interest rates. Those who are generally buy CDs. So the banks now compete with the money funds for this business. Consequently, in recent years, bank money market accounts have tended to yield significantly less than the money funds.

The banks' major advantage is FDIC insurance. If this is important to you, compare bank yields to the government money funds, particularly those that own Treasuries. They're just as secure.

Note, however, that there is another reason to rest easy when you invest in a money fund: shareholders own the assets of the portfolios on which they have claims. Even if every shareholder wanted to redeem his dollars at the same moment, everyone eventually would get paid. Banks, on the other hand, create money by lending out more than their deposits. They cannot pay every depositor at once; that's why a run on a bank can be devastating.

Check newspapers for current yields

You can find money fund statistics in *The Wall Street Journal*, *Barron's* and many other large daily papers on a once-a-week basis. If your fund isn't listed in the papers, don't hesitate to call. Most funds have 800 numbers with recorded announcements that provide you with the fund's current yield.

CHAPTER 12

THE NO-LOAD FUND INVESTOR

A fund to meet your every need

Without half trying, you can find a mutual fund that's as general or as specialized as you might want. As you browse through the landscape, you will encounter investment opportunities that seem alluring, as well as those that are baffling—or downright scary. When you start thinking seriously about funds that you might invest in, be introspective. Don't let a fund's glossy brochures and glowing verbiage entice you into making an investment that is out of keeping with your goals and risk tolerance.

In this chapter, so that you will have the information you need to make your investment decisions, I will run down the different varieties of specialized mutual funds. For your convenience, so you can refer back to various sections, I list them in alphabetical order.

All-weather funds. The basic definition is funds that long-term investors can safely hold throughout a complete market cycle. Specifically, I divide funds that you can use for all-weather investing into three distinct categories.

The soundest way to achieve the goal of all-weather investing is to select low volatility funds that don't track the market too closely. Some funds have an admirable record of reasonable profits in rising markets and below average losses during downturns. Of these funds some, such as Third Avenue Value and Lindner Dividend, have eclectic portfolios. Others are value funds, or funds that tend to raise cash if they don't see values in the market, such as Greenspring or Price Capital Appreciation.

A second approach to all-weather is to use asset allocation and balanced funds described at length in Chapter 8.

Finally, a few funds attempt to time the market or to allocate assets among stocks, bonds and cash depending on market conditions. Ideally such a fund stays fully invested during rising markets, then minimizes losses during bear markets by keeping a high percentage of its assets in cash. In practice these funds have performed poorly. But since they frequently hold large amounts of cash, they do have the advantage of low volatility. All-weather investing is a desirable strategy for conservative investors and for long-term investors, particularly in uncertain times.

Balanced funds. They keep a relatively fixed percentage of their assets in a combination of common stocks, preferred stocks and bonds as a matter of policy. Balanced funds have a variety of risk levels.

Bear market funds. Over the years, mutual fund groups have marketed portfolios designed to prosper in bear markets. Most have failed to attract assets for the simple reason that the market has been in a long-term upward trend. Nevertheless, the industry hasn't stopped trying. Now, finally, the mutual fund business has developed some funds that actually make sense in a bear market.

One that's designed solely for bear markets is the Rydex Ursa Fund, launched in January 1994. This fund engages in short sales, options and futures that will profit when the S&P 500 declines. As its name implies, Ursa is a pure bear market fund. *It will lose money in any up market.* Even more so than with cash, your timing needs to be nearly perfect to make money with this fund. The fund has a $25,000 minimum investment and is marketed mainly to professionals. But it is available to everyone. Another fund in this category is the Prudent Bear Fund which has been about 60% short, 30% in cash, and 10% long in stocks.

Common stock funds. If a fund invests primarily in common stocks, as some 3,000 do, it is a common stock fund. This broad classification encompasses many degrees of risk.

Contrarian funds. Trendy managers brought out several funds in 1994 that promised good performance in down markets. The two that attracted the most attention: the Robertson Stephens Contrarian Fund and the Lindner Bulwark Fund, which bill themselves as all-weather or inflation hedge funds as well as bear market funds. Both stock their portfolios with gold and base metals, natural resource stocks, and T-bills. They also engaged in short selling, an investing technique used by those who want to profit from market declines. Another fund in this category because it can go short is the Heartland Small Cap Contrarian Fund.

Robertson Stephens Contrarian lost 5.5% in 1994, gained 30.9% in 1995 and was up 21.7% in 1996, primarily because of good gains in gold. In 1997, it lost 29.5%, primarily because of losses in gold. Lindner Bulwark lost 11.2% in 1995, gained 28.8% in 1996, then lost 22.3% in 1997. The Heartland Fund gained 18.9% in 1996 and 13.7% in 1997 when small caps soared. So whether these funds go in the same direction as the market or in an opposite direction, either way it's a mixed blessing. Worse, how well they will do in a real bear market is open to serious question; they have yet to be tested. Here's their limited performance history in down periods:

Table 34

| | Total return % | | |
	Lindner Bulwark	**Rob Steph Contrarian**	**Avg dvsfd. fund**
1994	7.2	-5.5	-1.4
June-July 1996	-6.6	-1.1	-6.9
March 11-April 11, 1997	0.4	-6.2	-7.4
October 1997	-5.5	-5.9	-3.6

Diversified and non-diversified funds. This is a legal distinction that does not relate to whether a fund's investments are concentrated in particular industries, but rather to the magnitude of the investments concentrated in particular stocks. Most mutual funds are diversified. The Investment Company Act requires funds to keep 75 percent of their assets well diversified. That means that they can't put more than 5% of their assets into one stock or hold more than 10% of the outstanding voting shares of a particular company. (However, if a holding grows to more than 5%, they don't have to sell off the excess.) A fund that's classified as non-diversified theoretically could concentrate its entire portfolio in one stock. But to qualify for the specialized tax treatment available to investment companies under Subchapter M of the Internal Revenue Code—a powerful incentive—a fund must keep no more than 25 percent of its assets in the securities of one issuer and at least half the assets (instead of 75 percent) must be well diversified. Non-diversified funds are riskier than diversified funds.

Focus funds. Also called Selected funds, these are funds that concentrate their portfolios. I've never seen a precise definition of such funds, but a working definition might be: "Either 1) a fund holding 25 or fewer stocks; or 2) a fund in which the top ten holdings account for 50% or more of its total assets." In the case of funds with multiple managers, the test would be stocks per manager.

The concept behind focus funds is that many individual money managers have a limited number of great investment ideas. When managers are too widely diversified, the impact of their best selections will be diluted. A concentrated portfolio therefore allows managers to get the greatest mileage out of their best ideas. It's a way to stand out from the pack. It's also a resurrection of an old idea—with "fewer eggs in the basket," the manager can watch each one more closely.

The concept seems to be gaining popularity. We now have Montgomery Select 50, PBHG Select Equity, Oakmark Select, Masters Select Equity, and Vanguard Selected Value, as well as the Neuberger-Berman, CGM, Marsico and Yacktman Focus funds. (Such older funds as American Century Select, Selected American and Special Shares, and Fidelity Stock Selector are not particularly concentrated, despite their names. The 38 Fidelity Select sector funds are concentrated, but by industry.)

Industry funds. While some think industry funds are the latest fad; in truth, they are not new. Century Shares Trust, which holds insurance stocks, began in 1928. The Energy Fund (now Neuberger-Berman Focus Fund) was founded in 1952. But as the number of funds has continued to grow, so have the industry funds. And no wonder. With their concentrated portfolios, they can stand out from the crowd. Depending on which segment of the stock market is in favor, some non-diversified fund is almost always at the top of the rankings, which makes it easier for fund managers to achieve one of their primary goals: selling their shares to investors. In fact, some industry funds have been launched basically as marketing gimmicks. At one time, eleven environmental funds coexisted; now, only three remain, because they never performed particularly well. I'll discuss industry fund investing in more detail in the section on Sector funds.

Warning: Some supposedly diversified aggressive growth funds are little more than sector funds in drag. In 1995 many aggressive growth funds had 50% or more of their portfolios in technology.

Make sure you don't have unwanted sector exposure through these funds.

International funds. In the 1970s, the U.S. economy was so large that investors could adequately diversify their assets within the domestic market. The U.S. accounted for two-thirds of global GDP and two-thirds of the capitalized value of the world's liquid markets. Over the last two decades, though, these numbers have been whittled down as other countries' economies have achieved growth rates two to three times that of the U.S. In 1995 the U.S. accounted for only one-third of world stock market capitalization. (It's somewhat larger today because our market has boomed while Japan's has declined.)

Today, it makes sense for American investors to look offshore. Disregarding international investments would mean ignoring many of the world's best investment opportunities. America invented color TV, but now manufactures only a small share of TV sets. If you're seeking world-class steel producers, ship builders, consumer electronics manufacturers and car makers, you need to look beyond our shores. If your investment adviser is familiar only with domestic corporations, he would compare the advantages of Ford, GM and Chrysler. An internationally minded investor would also look at Toyota, Daimler-Benz, BMW, Japanese tire manufacturers and even rubber producers in Malaysia.

Overseas you will find:
- 10 of the 10 largest steel companies
- 9 of the 10 largest banks
- 8 of the 10 largest electronic companies
- 7 of the 10 largest auto companies
- 6 of the 10 largest chemical companies

Over the past several years, countries that have led or embraced change and development have also provided investors with some of the most attractive returns. The U.S. stock market has been a top performer in just one of the ten years ending 1996.

Diversification in international investments can lower the overall risk in your portfolio. The world's stock markets often have their own rhythms; over the long-run, their cycles don't move in lock-step with our markets. Investing internationally is also a way to protect yourself against weaknesses in the U.S. dollar. When the dollar weakens, foreign funds enjoy the benefit of favorable currency fluctuations in addition to the inherent growth potential of their foreign stocks. (By

Table 35

		Top-performing markets			
Rank	**1996**	**1995**	**1994**	**1993**	**1992**
1.	Venezuela	Switzerland	Brazil	Poland	Columbia
2.	Hungary	**U.S.**	Finland	Turkey	Thailand
3.	Zimbabwe	Sweden	Peru	Philippines	Hong Kong
4.	Poland	Spain	Chile	Indonesia	Malaysia
5.	Turkey	Belgium	S. Africa	Hong Kong	Philippines
	1991	1990	1989	1988	1987
1.	Argentina	Greece	Argentina	Brazil	Turkey
2.	Brazil	Chile	Mexico	Korea	Portugal
3.	Mexico	Mexico	Thailand	Mexico	Greece
4.	Chile	U.K.	Greece	Taiwan	Taiwan
5.	Philippines	Hong Kong	Austria	Belgium	Zimbabwe

Source: Morgan Stanley Capital Int'l, annual returns of indexes in U.S. dollars.

the same token, a rising dollar hampers the performance of international funds.)

But don't consider international funds bear market havens. In the short run, which has characterized bear markets since 1982, they have almost always moved in lock step with U.S. stocks. This is particularly true on a daily basis.

Buying foreign stocks on your own is tough. It's difficult to get meaningful investment information on foreign companies. Accounting, auditing and financial reporting practices vary enormously and are frequently spotty. Many foreign countries lack powerful regulatory bodies such as the SEC, which provides protection for American investors.

Think of it another way. When you buy U.S. stocks, you could make one basic mistake. You could pick the wrong company to invest in. Investing internationally, you have three ways to go wrong. You could pick the wrong country or the wrong stock. Or, you could end up on the wrong side of currency fluctuations.

Thus, the ideal way for the American investor to exploit today's overseas investment potential is to buy a fund that specializes in foreign securities. The fund's managers have the expertise to make profitable, rather than perilous, international investments.

Global or *international?* These two buzz words refer to a significant distinction among investments. An international or foreign portfolio is invested exclusively overseas; a global portfolio invests both in the U.S. and abroad. The advantage of an international fund is that it gives you the opportunity to allocate your investments precisely between domestic and international markets. You can then easily change the allocations to fit your own preferences. The advantage of a global fund is that the professional money mangers who run these funds are equipped to examine worldwide currency and stock market trends and make domestic/international asset allocation decisions for you. My general feeling about global funds is the same as for asset allocation funds: if you are sophisticated, do your own allocating. It will be far more precise.

More and more often, you get international diversification without even asking for it. About three-fourths of all equity funds that are considered domestic have, in fact, some foreign exposure. And 12% invest 10% or more of their equity portfolios overseas. You should take this into account when you allocate your money between the U.S. and foreign funds.

If you want to diversify internationally, you confront a wealth of choices. You can choose among both large and small cap international and global equity funds, either in the open-end or closed-end structure. You also have choices of objectives. Most international funds are growth oriented, but a few have proclaimed growth-income objectives. Small company international funds should probably be considered as aggressive-growth funds. In addition, international and global fixed-income funds are becoming commonplace.

Some funds can invest in geographic regions such as Europe, Latin America and Asia. A new category that has become important in the last few years is the emerging markets fund. While definitions may vary somewhat, the following countries are generally considered developed or mature markets:

In Asia—Japan, Australia, and New Zealand; in North America— the U.S. and Canada; and in Western Europe—all the countries as far east as Germany and Scandinavia. All other countries are considered emerging markets.

Emerging markets funds invest in developing countries that have high economic growth rates, pro-business governments and good long-term potential. Funds with Emerging Markets in their names, Latin American funds, and those investing in the Pacific Basin region (except Japan) are all in this category.

In contrast, many of the general or European funds make most of their investments in the developed countries. They tend to select large-cap stocks in countries that are heavily weighted in the EAFE international index. This is the Morgan Stanley Europe, Australia, Far East Index, which is generally used as a benchmark for international performance.

More than 30 no-load funds invest in 13 specific foreign countries, with Japan, China/Hong Kong and the United Kingdom the most popular places. Another 50 single-flag funds are marketed as closed-ends because small stock markets in developing countries lack easy liquidity. While these single-flag funds provide easy access to specific countries, I think you should avoid them unless you have specific fundamental knowledge of the markets and the investment potential in these countries.

While the funds are mostly affiliated with major U.S. fund groups, they are run by managers expert at foreign investing. In many cases, American fund managers have teamed up with established foreign investment counselors. T. Rowe Price International, for example, has joined with British-based investment counselors. The Invesco funds are owned by a British investment concern, Invesco Mim PLC, which provides expertise for their international funds.

International funds should be a permanent component of every investor's equity holdings. A 15% to 30% allocation is suitable for most investors. But don't get carried away and invest in a number of these funds. If yours is a small portfolio, figure on selecting a general international fund that can invest in any foreign country. If you have a larger portfolio, you may benefit from holding several international funds that have regional concentrations in Europe, the Pacific (with or without Japan) and in the emerging markets.

Life-cycle funds. These funds are targeted at specific age groups. If their portfolios never change, they are indistinguishable from asset allocation funds. The Vanguard Life Strategy and Rowe Price Personal Strategy funds are examples.

However, some life-cycle funds adjust their asset mix over the years so the fund gradually gets more conservative as its shareholders age. These funds can usually be identified by a year in their name. Example: Fidelity Freedom Funds, which have portfolios targeted for the years 2000, 2010, 2020, and 2030. These portfolios do not terminate when they reach their target dates. Rather, they continue on with a very low level of risk.

Multifunds. In theory, a fund that invests in the shares of other funds ought to offer expertise in both selection and market timing. In practice, the funds have not had notable success. Several such funds appeared in the late 60s and early 70s—First Multifund, Pooled Funds, Inc., Fundpack, Hyperion, No-load Selected. They tended to buy into a dozen or more growth funds, spreading their investments. Many of the best performing funds were small, and couldn't stand to take in too much money from one source, especially one that might suddenly redeem its shares. The result was unwanted diversification, which diluted performance.

Worse, the funds' ability to time the market was none too good. Furthermore, their practice of layering investment fees (their own plus the management fee of the funds in which they invested) significantly increased their expense ratios. All the original no-load multifunds were liquidated by 1979, although not necessarily because of these shortcomings.

Other multifunds have been launched since then. In 1984 FundTrust came into existence with four different portfolios. Each one has a different investment goal—Aggressive Growth, Growth, Growth & Income, and Income—and each invests in about ten different mutual funds, both no-load and load. More recently, Markman Capital Management, a Minneapolis advisory, and Eric Kobren's Insight Management, have launched similar fund groups. Surprisingly, more than 70 multifunds are now available.

Taking another approach, Vanguard some years ago formed Star fund, a multifund whose portfolio consists solely of ten other Vanguard Funds—seven common stock funds, two fixed-income funds, and a money market fund. Vanguard now offers an international version of Star, as well as four Life Strategy funds.

In 1990, T. Rowe Price followed with its Spectrum Fund, which has both Growth and Income portfolios. As with Star, Spectrum invests in other Price funds. The Income Portfolio invests mostly in fixed-income funds. Unlike the other multi-funds, there is no layering of fees with Star or Spectrum. Neither Vanguard nor Price charges a management fee.

Multifunds were originally prohibited from owning more than 3% of another fund's assets. The SEC has granted exceptions over the years, but mainly to firms looking to create portfolios consisting of funds within their own fund families. Now, the National Securities Market Improvement Act of 1996 makes it easier for firms to open in-house funds of funds. It permits mutual funds that want to invest in other funds within their own family to do so without applying to the SEC for a regulatory exemption. The SEC is also now more likely to let regular multifunds exceed the 3% limitation.

How have the multifunds performed? On occasion, Spectrum and Star have done fairly well. But in general, because of their wide diversification and layering of fees, most of these funds-of-funds have produced sub-par performance compared with individual funds.

Here's another way to think about these funds. You might make a case that they are more akin to managed mutual fund portfolios than to individual funds. If the multifund owns other mutual funds in various risk categories, then it might make sense to compare it to a similarly diversified portfolio of funds. On the other hand, if the portfolio funds of a multi-fund all have similar risk levels—say, all growth funds—then the best comparison would be with an individual growth fund. But you can't just compare raw performance; you need to take risk into account. The average performance of several funds might likely be less than a single fund but the volatility should also be significantly less.

Multifunds are best suited for the small investor because they provide diversification with a low minimum investment. This is especially appropriate in an IRA account. Another category of individuals well suited to multifunds: those who don't want to follow their investments.

Multi-national funds. If you want to benefit from growth overseas without buying an international fund, you can. Multi-national funds buy globally diversified U.S. companies who receive a significant portion of their profits from overseas operations. Coca Cola is a good example of such a company; approximately 80% of its income is foreign. Other multinational stocks are Gillette and Intel. Leading mutual funds specializing in multinational stocks are Papp America Abroad, Fidelity Export & Multinational, U.S. Global Leaders and Buffalo USA Global.

Market timing multifunds

The Rightime Fund, a multifund organized in 1985, is different. Manager David Rights is a market timer who basically substitutes funds for stocks as his equity vehicles. His fund's performance, which depends primarily on the accuracy of his market timing, has been quite erratic, varying from the top to the bottom 20 percent. Overall, his performance has been poor. Others in the market timing multifund category are the Merriman Asset Allocation Fund, Merriman Capital Appreciation Funds, and the Flex Muirfield Fund. As with Rightime, they have generally done poorly. Yet, any of them can look good temporarily if they correctly time a bear market.

Open-end and **closed-end funds.** Open-end funds, also called mutual funds, create new shares when they receive money from investors. They redeem shares when an investor wants to take money out. Thus the number of shares outstanding in an open-end investment company varies. By contrast, closed-end funds raise a set amount of money initially, and thus have a fixed number of shares. Once formed, a closed-end trades on a stock exchange or over-the-counter. The fund does not sell shares directly to investors, nor will it buy them back. I'll take a closer look at closed-end funds in the next chapter. Open-end and closed-end funds both come in many forms, with all degrees of risk.

Option income funds. Fund managers, moving to take advantage of a provision in the Tax Reform Act of 1976, brought out a new type of mutual fund early in 1977. Certainly here is an area where expertise is needed. If you have dealt with stock options, you know how complex the investment decisions can be: which stock to buy or sell options on; what specific option to write; if and when to repurchase the option.

Option income funds are conservative, writing covered-call options on stocks they already own to generate additional income beyond that derived from dividends and capital appreciation. But they aren't magic. When the market is rising, the call options, in which the writer bets that the market will go down, limit upside potential. Managers of conventional equity funds depend solely on dividends and capital appreciation. By contrast to the option-writing funds, however, their potential is unlimited.

Option income funds have been poor performers in this long-running bull market, Consequently, their numbers have dwindled. At the peak, 21 option income funds existed, most of them load funds. Today only two are left. Analytic Option Equity Fund, the only no-load, typically ranks in the bottom 20% of all funds in its category. Except during market corrections. Then it shines.

Precious metals funds. No industry group has achieved more popularity than the precious metals funds. Forty-eight gold oriented funds exist, 14 of them no-load. You can buy gold funds that invest heavily in South African gold stocks, funds that totally avoid South Africa by concentrating investments in North America and other parts of the world, funds that offer a mixture, and even funds that keep a portion of their holdings in gold bullion, which is typically less volatile than the stocks of the gold mining companies.

Although there are exceptions, a rule of thumb is that the shares tend to have a beta of 1.5 to bullion, meaning that their price fluctuations are one and one-half times as volatile as the price of bullion. Not to mention that bullion is more liquid, and provides greater diversification in a portfolio.

Most gold funds tend to hold the shares of the larger, established gold mining companies. Some, though, buy new ventures—the prospectors. The people doing that call it growth gold investing. They contend they can make money no matter what the price of gold. Still, the greatest differentiation among the funds is their asset allocation by country.

The performance of the gold funds is erratic, to say the least. In some years they are the best performing fund group, in others the worst. Their salad days came in 1986, 1987, 1989, and 1993. Yet, in spite of their go-go years, gold funds have not shone over the long term. Far from it! In the 10-year period ending in December 1997, gold funds were the worst performing category *losing* 26.5%. The average equity fund gained 238% in this period. Keep in mind that if you are buying shares of stock, they are subject to the same influences all stocks are subject to—future earnings, which depend not only on the price of gold but the costs of mining it, new gold strikes, existing mines playing out, etc. A statistical study found that only half the movement of the typical gold fund is explained by the price of bullion.

Because of many structural changes in the world (including the decline of inflation), gold seems well on its way to becoming a commodity that will eventually move to an industrially based price. Its price has stayed low in part because central banks have sold into price rises, preferring cash to the sterile, non-interest-paying yellow metal.

Popular mythology holds that gold is a great bear market investment. Don't be so sure. Gold is much more of an inflation or disaster hedge than a bear market hedge. Gold had double digit declines in five of the last six stock market downturns. As a disaster hedge, it did well only in the third quarter of 1990, the Gulf War bear market.

As with other industry funds, gold funds make sense only if you believe that they have immediate appreciation potential. Although some advisors suggest holding gold funds as a kind of "portfolio insurance," I do not advocate that approach. Here's why: Let's assume that you have $100,000 to put into stocks. Say you invest

Table 36

	Total return %	
	Average gold fund	**avg dvsfd. fund**
October 1987	-31.4	-21.0
Third quarter 1990	0.9	-16.6
1994	-13.0	-1.4
June-July 1996	-16.4	-6.9
March 11-April 11, 1997	-13.3	-7.4
October 1997	-17.0	-3.6

$90,000 in diversified funds and put the other $10,000 into gold funds as "insurance" against financial calamity. Suppose the worst happens: the economy, the markets, in fact the world, all get into trouble. Your diversified funds decline 30%, and your gold funds double. That means you lose $27,000 on one side of the ledger, but gain $10,000 on the other. You're still down $17,000. I don't think the Prudential or GEICO would call that insurance. I'll show you better strategies.

Real estate funds. Traditionally, real estate has been the investment of choice for those who want steady, long-term returns. That objective is especially popular in times of inflation. Most real estate investing is direct—owning your own home or personally managing income producing property. Another common investment vehicle is the limited partnership, which invests in a number of different properties. However, participation commonly requires that you have a substantial net worth, and that you tie up your money for a number of years. Yet another way is investing in individual real estate companies, frequently in the form of real estate investment trusts (REITs) or master limited partnerships (MLPs). Complementing these vehicles, the real estate mutual fund has emerged as an investment with good liquidity and the advantage of active management.

Because real estate has done extremely well since the S&L crisis, the funds that invest in this sector have exploded; 75 now exist, twelve of which are no-load. Most invest in REITs including one that's a REIT index fund. But a few invest in operating companies in the real estate field. They couple an investment goal of current income with the potential for capital appreciation. Their portfolios contain many REITs, which give investors access to investments in shopping malls, medical facilities, office buildings and apartments. They also provide the opportunity for direct investments in companies within the real estate industry. Advantages of the funds: professional management, diversification, low minimum investments and liquidity. Disadvantages: an investor is several times removed from a pure real estate investment, having to contend with the movements of the stock markets as well as the underlying real estate.

The average real estate fund has gained 15.2% annually for the five years ending December 1997. Their yields can be as much as 4%, which is great for an equity investment.

Regional funds. Some funds specialize in a particular area of the United States. The IAI Regional Fund in Minneapolis, for instance, must keep 80% of its portfolio in the stocks of companies headquartered in Minnesota, Wisconsin, Iowa, Nebraska, Montana and the Dakotas.

The managers of regional funds feel that they gain an edge by investing close to home. Of course, it all depends on where home is. The IAI Fund has had some very good years. But not every regional fund has fared as well. For many years, San Antonio's USAA Investment Management Corp. ran the Sunbelt Era Fund, which invested in the common stocks of smaller, emerging growth companies in the Sunbelt region. The fund was a loser. In 1989, Sunbelt Era changed its name to the USAA Aggressive Growth Fund and dropped all geographic restrictions. Similarly, in 1995 the Northwest Growth Fund, specializing mainly in companies situated in Washington and Oregon, dropped its regional orientation and became the Sextant Growth Fund. Another Pacific Northwest fund, the SAFECO Northwest Fund, has been a lackluster to poor performer.

Sector funds. In the early and mid-80s, smart marketers discovered a way to jazz up industry funds. The new wrinkle was to put several different industry portfolios under the umbrella of one fund, add switching capability between portfolios and a related money fund, and call them sector funds.

Sector funds can offer you the opportunity to own diversified portfolios in various segments of the stock market. If you think energy stocks, technology stocks, bank or financial service stocks or health stocks are ready for gains, here is a convenient way to buy the sector. You get a working portfolio of stocks that will benefit if that sector moves. The potential rewards are great because, unlike well-diversified funds that embrace many different industries, you can use sector funds to zero in on those areas of the stock market that you think are primed to really move.

This concept was pioneered by the Fidelity Select Fund in 1981. Select began by offering specialized portfolios in six stock market sectors, and has since expanded the total to 38, including Select's own money fund.

In 1984, two other groups followed Fidelity's innovation. The Invesco funds came out with Invesco Strategic Portfolios and Vanguard offered the Vanguard Specialized Portfolios. Invesco has one significant advantage over the other two—it's truly no-load. Fidelity Select charges entrance and exit loads, as well as fees for switching between portfolios. Vanguard, the least hospitable to switchers, levies a 1% redemption fee on five of its funds when money is moved to other funds in less than a year.

Sector funds are frequently hot topics in the press. Newsletters have been organized to cover them exclusively. The reasons are not hard to fathom. Since they are non-diversified, they have a better chance of producing superior performance than do diversified funds. Hardly a period goes by without one or more sector (or industry) funds posting first-rate performance. And, of course, top-ranked funds generate a lot of publicity, interest—and money.

By the same token, though, sector funds have a better chance of doing poorly. The range of performance among these specialized investments is very wide, much more so than among diversified growth funds. Fidelity's multitude of sector funds are typically among the best—and the worst. In some years, they encompass practically the entire spectrum of mutual fund performance. In 1997, their performances ranged from +62.3% for Select Brokerage & Investment Management to -8.0% for Natural Gas.

How sector-fund investors go wrong

Notwithstanding their often excellent performances, surprisingly few sector fund investors actually pocket large gains. The problem is they fail to appreciate how different sector funds are from diversified growth funds. The latter almost always move with the market. Individual stocks, on the other hand, frequently move in the opposite direction. In this respect, industry and sector funds perform much more like individual stocks than do their conventional cousins, diversified mutual funds. Consequently, it is dangerous to use the usual criteria—prior track record and management ability—when you are evaluating sector funds.

To illustrate: consider the fate of the majority of investors who bought Fidelity Select Biotechnology Fund in 1991.

Launched in mid-December 1985, Fidelity Biotech had a lackluster performance until 1989 when the health and biotech stocks took off. Fidelity Biotech, a major beneficiary, gained 43.9% in 1989, 44.3% in 1990, and 99.0% in 1991. The fund was #1 in 1990 and #3 in 1991. Biotech's total assets grew from $40 million at the beginning of 1989, to $1.1 billion in 1991, with $663 million in new money pouring in during the final six months. It ended the year with 118,000 shareholders.

However, 1991 proved to be the top. Biotech stocks began a major multi-year correction. The fund lost 26.2% in the next three years. It ranked 3,574th among all funds in 1994. Yet, its shareholder list never fell below 83,000—a decline of only 25,000. Its assets were still at almost $400 million, which indicates that large investors were quicker to bail out than small investors. One indication: the average account size was cut in half from the peak. Those who bought near the top—an unhealthy majority of Biotech's shareholders—suffered losses. Most investors *bought* too late and either *sold* too late, or more likely, didn't sell at all.

Table 37

Fidelity Select Biotechnology

Year	Annual performance %	Total net assets at year-end $ Mill.
1986	3.5	39.6
1987	-3.3	57.4
1988	4.1	39.9
1989	43.9	69.7
1990	44.3	223.9
1991	99.0	1,146.5
1992	-10.5	799.3
1993	0.7	551.8
1994	-18.2	396.7

Once a sector fund's stocks fall out of favor, the manager has few weapons to stem the fund's losses. Unlike diversified funds, he can't buy stocks in other sectors. He could sell his stocks and raise cash, but historically that's been a little used option, for one thing because investors expect that they are buying stocks—not cash—when they purchase shares in a stock fund. When you buy a diversified fund you are really buying the manager's expertise. But when you buy a sector fund, you are doing so because you want to own the stocks in that sector.

Because sector funds perform differently from diversified funds, you should develop your own assessment of an industry's potential for appreciation before you buy a sector fund representing that industry. If you don't have first-hand knowledge of the industry, stay away from sector funds! You are best off if you think of them as proxies for individual stocks. If you like an industry, but are either not sure which will be the best performing stocks, or want to buy several stocks in the industry, then buy a sector fund. In some cases the commissions will be lower than buying stocks individually.

Sector funds are not for buy-and-hold investors, and they're certainly not for novices. If sector investing were easy, you would think that Fidelity or Invesco would organize multifunds where their professional money managers would assume the task of switching into the top-performing sectors for you. The fact that they have not done so suggests that these sophisticated professionals appreciate how difficult is the task of divining which sector will be the next winner in the stock market's relentless rotation. Thus, long-term investors are better off sticking to diversified stock funds.

If you are attracted to a given sector, limit your holdings to 5% to 10% of your equity portfolio. And don't hesitate to switch to another sector or a money fund when your sector's move is over. Most of the time you will be better off buying on weakness rather than strength. It can be brutally injurious to your portfolio's welfare to buy near the conclusion of an upward move. Still another word of caution: don't hold sector funds in bear markets; they are apt to get hammered worse than broadly diversified funds.

Finally, don't get too caught up with the excitement of sector funds. Despite all the hoopla in the press, the year-end assets for the Fidelity, Invesco and Vanguard sector funds combined were only $27.4 billion. That's only 1.1% of the total $2.4 *trillion* invested in all equity mutual funds.

Social conscience funds, sometimes termed socially responsible funds. Several no-load equity funds aim at purity in their investments. The Pax World Fund's prospectus states that the fund tries through its investment objectives to make a contribution to world peace. It buys shares in companies that produce life-supporting goods and services in such fields as health care, education, food and leisure. The fund avoids liquor, tobacco and gambling stocks as well as companies doing business with the Pentagon. Like most other socially conscious funds, it used to avoid South Africa, but that is no longer the case. Other social conscience funds: the Dreyfus Third Century Fund, which invests in companies that enhance the value of life in America; two Ariel funds; the Domini Social Index Trust, a social conscience index fund. In addition, there are social conscience money funds, such as the Calvert Social Investment Money Market Portfolio and Working Assets Money Fund.

If you believe, as I do, that defending America *is* socially responsible, then perhaps these funds are better named "politically correct" funds.

Another fund that you might think of in this category is the Amana Growth Fund, which is designed to provide investment alternatives that are consistent with Islamic principles. The fund does not invest in such businesses as liquor, wine, casinos, pornography, gambling and banks and associations that are not based on Islamic principals. Muslims do not believe in receiving interest, which rules out domestic banks.

Similarly, the American Trust Allegiance Fund avoids investments in tobacco, pharmaceuticals, biotechnology, medical diagnostic services and products, gambling and liquor industries. As such it is invested in accordance with the principles of the Christian Scientist church.

Social conscience funds are for people who feel strongly about how their money is invested, to the point that they are willing to accept somewhat lower returns for their principles. Studies have shown that restricting a portfolio manager's options hurts performance. A thorough study of ten no-load and load funds for the five years ending with 1988 was conducted by Samuel A. Mueller, a sociologist at the University of Akron. He found that, risk-adjusted, the average social conscience fund produced returns about one percentage point less than the returns that could have been made in comparable funds

---

Women's social conscience, too

The Women's Equity Mutual Fund is designed to invest in companies that have growth potential and meet the fund's ten criteria on women's issues. These include companies that promote women to senior executive positions or to their board of directors, offer employee benefits that address work/family concerns, choose women-owned vendors, contribute to women's organizations, and present positive images of women. The fund has identified a universe of 300 "pro-women" companies. Naturally, Women's Equity is managed by women.

not subject to the restrictions that the ethical funds have imposed on themselves.

Another bit of evidence: your intrepid author is one of five investment advisors participating in a fund selection contest sponsored by *The New York Times*. With the contest four and one-half years old as of January 1, 1998 (latest figures at press time), I was leading with a 113% cumulative gain. In next to last place was an investment advisor with a portfolio of eight socially responsive funds. His portfolio had gained only 83%.

Financial author Timothy Middleton explains the extent of the problem: He interviewed the representatives of eight social conscience funds and found that one or more ignored the ten largest companies in America. All ten are engaged in business activities that some consider antithetical to social goals. General Electric, AT&T, and IBM all have military contracts. Merck, Procter & Gamble, and Johnson & Johnson engage in animal testing. Coca Cola opposes bottle bills. Wal-Mart imports from child labor law violator Bangladesh, and, rounding out the top 10, there's Exxon and Philip Morris!

As a result, I was not surprised when in April 1996, Co-op America, a Washington DC group that promotes social conscience investing, released a list of environmentally unfriendly mutual funds. Topping the list was the Vanguard Index 500 Fund, with 81 energy, tobacco, chemical and other "toxic" companies. Essentially, Co-op America is indicting our entire society.

If you are able to separate your wallet from your "social conscience," as most of us do, here is a suggestion. Why not find a good-performing diversified fund, and then give your "excess profits" to your favorite charity. If you do that, you'll be following the example of Alfred Nobel. He made millions selling explosives, but then used the profits to create a charitable foundation that has fostered enormous world-wide good.

Special-interest funds. Some funds are differentiated not by what they buy, but to whom they sell. The General Electric S&S Program is a no-load offered only to employees of that company. State Farm Growth Fund is offered only to agents and employees of State Farm Insurance Companies and members of their families. Another example: institutional funds, which have high minimum investments so only large institutions can afford them.

Five no-loads are designed specifically for children. They either make good presents, offer some tax-sheltering possibilities, or get children started on good life-long investing habits. They are: American Century-Twentieth Century Giftrust, Royce Giftshares, Stein Roe Young Investor, USAA First Start Growth and Strong Step 1 Money Fund. The first two set up irrevocable trusts that run for ten years.

Tax-efficient funds. With the capital gains rate lowered to 20% it once again pays to look at funds that try to maximize your *after-tax* return. Some funds fitting the bill are the Vanguard Tax-Managed Fund with its Balanced, Capital Appreciation and Growth & Income Portfolios, the J.P. Morgan Tax-Aware Disciplined Equity and Tax-Aware U.S. Equity funds, and the T. Rowe Price Tax-Efficient Balanced Fund. Furthermore many index and low-turnover funds are tax-efficient.

Utility funds. Some fund groups include utility funds with their sector funds; others hold them out as separate industry funds. Fidelity, with its enormous selection of funds, does both.

Historically, utility stocks have tracked along with bond prices. The higher bond prices go (and the lower bond yields fall), the better utilities generally have done. When interest rates surged in 1994, the average utility fund returned a negative 8.5%. When interest rates fell in 1995, the average utility fund returned a positive 30.5%. However, utilities have underperformed the overall stock market in recent years through periods of both rising and falling interest rates because the outlook for both electric utilities and the telephone companies has been clouded by deregulation issues.

Now, the deregulation horizon has cleared for the telcos and will soon begin to clear a bit for the electrics. So utilities are responding positively once again to falling interest rates. As long as the outlook is for little or no inflation and for stable to lower interest rates, utility funds should continue to do well.

At the same time, deregulation is about to change the very nature of the utility industry for the better. Besides being loved by investors as defensive plays, the best-performing utilities could also become attractive for their growth potential. No longer is the typical utility a government-regulated bureaucratic enterprise, lulled into lethargy by the certainty of earning a decent return come hell or high water. Deregulation—a negative in the short run—ultimately will turn the best utilities into lean, mean, competitive players. It will give them incentive to cut expenses, diversify into other industries and seek opportunities outside their traditional market areas. Utilities traditionally have been heavy borrowers of cash.

Traditionally, utilities were favored for their defensive characteristics. But they never were no-risk investments. They were low-risk investments—government-regulated entities whose earnings were essentially protected against bad times and severe fluctuation. The beta of the average utility mutual fund is .56—about half as volatile as the S&P 500, but this could increase in the coming years.

There are marked differences among utility funds. Some emphasize either electric utilities or telecommunications companies, while others put a significant portion of their portfolios in energy-related companies. Performance can vary considerably between various utility funds with their areas of concentration accounting for much of the difference.

Most utility funds try to deliver something in the way of income dividends; yields tend to cluster around 2%. A few utility funds aim for growth and sacrifice dividends—Fidelity Select Utilities Growth, with a 1% yield, being a prime example. Because the utility industry is in flux, it makes sense to stick with utility *funds* rather than trying to pick the individual winners. Leave stock selection to experienced portfolio managers.

Value funds. *See Chapter 6.*

In summary

No-load stock, bond and money-market funds come in an endless and ever-changing profusion. From funds that buy the entire stock market to those that invest only in stocks of socially conscious corporations, from funds that ramble the world looking for bargains to ones that stay within the Pacific Northwest region, no-loads can provide you with just about any investment specialty you could want. In the right time and place, all can help you earn profits. Be cautious, though. Not every fad and fancy proves profitable.

CHAPTER 13

THE NO-LOAD FUND INVESTOR

Closed-end funds

No-loads are bought and sold at their net asset value. How would you like to be able to buy funds at a discount? Such bargain-basement funds exist. They are the closed-end or "publicly traded" funds.

Mutual funds, no-load and load, are called open-end funds. They do not maintain a fixed number of shares. They issue additional shares whenever anyone wants to invest in the fund, and they redeem shares when investors want to sell out. In sharp contrast, closed-end funds issue a fixed number of shares at the time of their initial offering. Thereafter, they infrequently change the number of outstanding shares.

Some closed-end funds have been in existence since the 1920s. However, in the 1980s and early 1990s new closed-ends were launched at a heady pace. Some fund advisors prefer to bring out closed-end rather than open-ended funds because they incur a one-time marketing expense. After that, shareholders who wish to buy or sell do so on a stock exchange. Because the fund will not take back shares, closed-ends are a *virtual annuity* for their managers. All fund managers are paid a percentage of the assets under management. Closed-end managers can lose assets only if the value of their portfolio declines. In sharp contrast, open-end managers can lose assets if they suffer redemptions—though of course they can also gain by taking in additional money, either from existing or new shareholders.

More than 450 closed-end funds now exist, with total assets over

$140 billion (a tiny fraction of the open-ends' $4 plus trillion. Closed-end funds come in many varieties. Fixed-income funds are now the most numerous type, accounting for more than two-thirds of the total.

Equity funds are divided among into four categories. The largest: globals and internationals, accounting for over half of all equity funds. Specialized and diversified funds account for most of the rest. There are also nine convertible securities funds. The Adams Express Fund and Tri-Continental Corp. are examples of closed-end general common stock funds. Many of these were started in the 20s. Newer equity funds are more likely to fall in the specialized equity and convertible funds category, which includes gold funds, single country, and regional international funds.

Unlike mutual funds, some closed-ends have more than one class of shares. Example: Source Capital has both common and preferred stock. The existence of senior securities gives some leverage to the common shares, which increases both risk and volatility.

Closed-end funds offer several advantages:

■ As with their open-end cousins, closed-ends provide professional management and diversification among securities.

■ When they sell at a discount, the funds provide investors with real bargains. This is particularly true with closed-end bond funds, which will then generally have higher yields than comparable open-end fixed-income funds, an advantage even if you ultimately sell at the same discount.

■ The closed-end funds do not have to worry about redemptions. (The next chapter discusses how net redemptions can hurt fund performance.) Consequently, they can hold less-liquid securities than the open-end funds. That's why almost all single country funds choose the closed-end structure. The Nautilus Fund, one of the top performers of the 1980s, held 360,000 unregistered shares of Apple computer (32.6% of the fund's assets) before the stock went public. (In 1985, Nautilus became an open-ended fund.)

■ The yields of closed-end bond funds are not diluted by new money. In periods of declining interest rates, open-end funds may see the high yields of older bonds diluted by new money pouring in. That causes fund managers, flush with this fresh capital, to buy new, lower yielding bonds. This can't happen with closed-ends.

Closed-ends don't sell at NAV

Because closed-ends don't redeem fund shares—they are traded like any stock on a regular exchange or over-the-counter—there is no fixed relationship between their NAV and the current market price. Closed-ends commonly sell at a discount to their net asset value, but at times their price exceeds NAV and the funds sell at a premium. In 1989, single country international funds were very hot and many of these closed-end funds sold at substantial premiums to their NAVs. In 1990, they cooled off considerably; their premiums disappeared, and newer funds went to discounts. When you buy or sell a closed-end, you pay a stockbroker's commission.

You can find the closed-ends' NAVs and discounts from NAV in *The Wall Street Journal* on Mondays and in some other papers on Saturdays. NAVs and discounts are also available weekly in *Barron's*.

Don't buy closed-ends on the initial offering

You should almost always avoid purchasing a closed-end when it first comes to market. At the initial underwriting, a closed-end is like a load fund, with the price reflecting the NAV plus the salesman's commission. The SEC's Office of Economic Analysis did a study of 64 closed-end funds that came to market between 1985 and 1987. The study revealed that on average, closed-end funds lose significant value during the first 120 trading days following their IPOs (initial public offerings). In this period U.S. closed-end stock funds lost 23.2%, foreign stock funds lost 17.7% and bond funds lost 6.2%. After the first 24 weeks, U.S. stock funds traded at an average discount of 10.0%, foreign stock funds at an average discount of 11.4%, while bond funds traded at approximately NAV.

Of course, in all cases, the funds began at a sizeable premium due to the salesmen's commissions, but then trended downward. Finally, the study found that these IPOs were far more likely to be sold to individual investors than to institutions.

Closed-ends' prices tend to move from premiums to discounts for several reasons. Since the funds are traded like stocks, their market prices are subject to the same laws of supply and demand that influence stocks, which may sell for more or less than their book value. In exactly the same manner, closed-end funds sell at discounts or at premiums from their net asset value. Brokers make a great effort to sell closed-ends at the time they are launched because the underwriting commissions are fat. They usually sell enough shares to satisfy the demand from all interested investors. Afterwards, the brokers tend to ignore these funds, thus lowering demand. That's because once the funds are exchange traded, the commissions are the same as for any stock. But since investors are likely to hold them for longer periods than regular stocks, the brokers' second commission is delayed. At that point brokers favor other underwritings, open-end load funds or unit investment trusts, all of which generate higher commissions.

A second reason is that closed-end funds generally lack aggressive advertising or public relations. There's no incentive for the management company to spend its own money for promotion, since that won't bring in new assets. Nor can they levy 12b-1 fees. Thus, most of them soldier forth in obscurity.

Some other reasons that may explain discounts:

■ Poor performance may increase the discount.

■ The market cycle may affect discounts.

■ In some cases there may be a discount because the portfolios contain illiquid stocks. Or as an offset against potential capital gains liability.

A good rule of thumb is to buy a closed-end fund only when its current discount is 5% wider than its average annual discount, provided that the discount is not less than the average discount of similar funds. It is difficult to conceive of a reason to buy a closed-end bond fund at a premium, and generally you should also avoid stock funds that are selling at premiums. The major exceptions are those funds that own a franchise. For example, for many years there was only one fund that owned Korean stocks. It sold at a healthy premium during those years. If you own a fund selling at an above normal premium, you should consider selling it.

Rights offerings

Closed-end funds can raise additional money through the medium of a rights offering. That happens when shareholders are given rights in a fixed ratio to the number of shares they own. Then, with an additional investment, these rights can be converted to additional shares.

If you don't exercise the rights, your stake in the fund will be diluted, and the value of your shares may have declined. Your value can be preserved by exercising the rights but at the cost of an additional outlay.

In some cases, the rights can be sold in the open market. If that's the case, you may profit by selling your holding immediately, then buying back after the offering is completed.

Eliminating the discount

It would be profitable to goose up a closed-end fund's worth by eliminating the discount, and investors have sought ways to do so. The simplest is to open up the fund. As a regular mutual fund, it must sell at its true net asset value. Stratton Monthly Dividend REIT Shares, the Japan Fund and T. Rowe Price Media & Telecommunications Fund are all examples of closed-ends that transformed themselves into open-ends. In many cases the management of a closed-end is enlightened enough to decide that it's in everyone's best interest to go open-end. But, when a reorganization proposal is initiated by outside stockholders the odds are strongly against the fund's becoming open-ended. In such cases management usually resists because its fees are based on the fund's size, which surely will shrink if redemptions are permitted.

Still, in 1997, dissident shareholders were startlingly successful in open-ending closed-end funds. There were nine open-endings in '97 versus five in '96. Closed-end fund analyst Thomas Herzfeld found that one of every five proxy statements he looked at in 1997 included either a dissident shareholder proposal or something related to a promise in the prospectus to cure persistent discounts.

Among the funds open-ended in 1997 were Alliance Global Environment, GT Global Developing Markets, Inefficient Market, New Age Media, Pilgrim America Bank & Thrift, Worldwide Value and the capital shares of Convertible Holdings, Gemini II, and Quest for Value Dual Purpose Fund.

In an effort to close the discount, some funds are authorized to purchase shares in the open market or make tender offers. Other funds guarantee a minimum dividend payout. One of the first to try this was the Zweig Fund, which pays a 10% annual distribution. Such payouts are made whether they are earned or not. If the dividend and realized short-term capital gains aren't sufficient, the balance is made up as a return of capital (that is, you get your own money back). Perhaps it could be argued that this is unimportant because over the long run the fund should appreciate by 10% a year or more. On the other hand, it is likely that many shareholders will believe the fund is yielding more than it really is (just as many holders of individual GNMA passthrough securities fail to recognize that part of their dividend is a return of their capital). Such a practice is not desirable. Consider also that the investors in these funds paid a commission to buy the fund. As an investor, you don't get a rebate of part of your commission when you receive some of your own money back. Other funds that guarantee a minimum payout: Baker Fentress, The Europe Fund, Gabelli Equity Trust and Liberty All-Star.

Open- or closed-end? Which is better? Which should you prefer? While every fund has to be evaluated individually, here are some very general guidelines.

Open-end vs. closed-end funds

■ Among diversified equity funds, as a general rule, you should prefer open- over closed-ends, since usually the open-end funds have more aggressive management. That's because they can be penalized for poor performance. The managers of closed-end funds know that shares of their funds can't be redeemed, only sold to a third party the way stock is, on an exchange or over-the-counter.

■ Buy specialized closed-ends when no comparable open-ends are available. Prime example: single country funds.

■ If the same group manages both open- and closed-end funds, prefer the closed-ends when they are selling at exceptional discounts that may well narrow. For example, compare Gabelli Asset to Gabelli Equity Trust, which have the same manager.

■ Buy comparable fixed-income closed-ends when the discounts more than make up the transaction costs.

Traditionally, only open-end funds had dividend reinvestment plans. That's changed. The majority of closed-ends now offer the privilege. The closed-end funds obtain the necessary shares either by buying them in the open market or, less commonly, issuing new shares. Reinvestment price is generally the market price if the funds trade at a discount. If the funds trade at a premium, the reinvestment price would be the higher of net asset value or 95% of the market price.

PART III

Mutual Fund Selection and Strategies

CHAPTER 14

How to select the best equity funds

By this point, you are familiar with the various types of funds. So the next step is to learn how to pick the best funds in each category. In order to do so you need to look at the factors that determine performance. By far the most important is past performance. In this chapter, I'll discuss past performance and other factors pertinent to various situations, including the portfolio manager, the fund group, fund expenses, size, cash positions, cash inflow and portfolio composition.

Let me say at the outset that using past performance as the criteria for picking mutual funds is a very imperfect method. It's a matter beyond dispute that past performance is no guarantee of future performance. Nevertheless, past performance is almost universally used as the major predictor of a fund's future. The reason is simple: all other ways of forecasting future performance are even more imperfect. In fact, you might argue that there really is no other way. So, like it or not, you will inevitably wind up making past performance a major criteria in your fund selection. With that understanding, you'll find that you can maximize your chances of picking a top-performing fund by judiciously choosing which past periods to examine.

Note that the discussion in this chapter primarily concerns diversified funds, where the performance of the manager is paramount. As I pointed out in Chapter 12, you ought to invest in sector and industry funds only after you have done a fundamental analysis of their indus-

Past performance as crystal ball

tries. The methodology is also different for passively managed funds such as index funds. They are discussed in the next chapter.

The long and the short of it

Which time period or periods to consider is a matter of great controversy. About the only thing experts seem to agree on is that you shouldn't buy a fund simply because it made the top rankings over some short period of time. (But even here, I have found exceptions.)

Historically, when load funds predominated, "experts" (usually salesmen) argued that a very long record—at least ten years—was the best predictor of future performance. In recent years analysts have leaned toward shorter periods—usually one to five years. Here's my take on the subject.

First of all, there is a very practical reason for selecting shorter time frames. If you limit yourself to funds of great age, you eliminate hundreds of promising candidates. About half of all funds are less than five years old, and 69% are less than ten years old. Thus a universe of relatively new funds exists, many of which have already demonstrated top performance.

Furthermore, not only are most funds new, their managers are even newer. A compilation by *Morningstar* found that the average manager tenure is 3.1 years. An old fund run by a new manager is no different than a new fund.

If old funds were better performers than new funds, it might make sense to restrict your selection to this smaller universe. But that isn't the case. Examining the performance of funds over several periods—those organized since 1988 with their older cousins—you see that either the same or a higher percentage of the youngsters placed in the top 20% of all funds than was the case with their elders. For example,

Table 38

% of equity funds in first quintile

by age over various periods

Period	Organized 1988 or later	Organized before 1988
Latest 12 months	20%	20%
Latest 3 years	24%	16%
Latest 5 years	20%	20%

* All periods end Oct. 1997

24% of all funds organized since 1988 ranked in the upper fifth of all funds for the three years ending October 1997, but only 16% of funds organized before 1988 did.

The conclusion: age is not a significant factor when selecting a fund. It is foolish to ignore a fund merely because it doesn't have an extensive performance record. Disregard the advice you so often hear to "concentrate on the ten-year (or some other extended) track record."

What time period makes most sense, then? That depends on how you expect the markets to perform in the immediate future. Ideally you want to examine the most recent previous time period during which similar market conditions prevailed. That's the best benchmark for determining how funds will perform in the future.

For example, if you think small capitalization stocks (and hence small company growth funds) will excel in the immediate future, hunt for prior periods when there was a bull market in that type of stock. See which funds did best, then note whether the fund has the same manager as it did in the previous period. Similarly, if you think the direction of the market is south, then look for funds that have done well in adverse markets.

You need to make a market prediction in order for all this information to be usable. And since predicting is difficult, especially if it involves the future (a bon mot that has been attributed to a wide range of celebrities, ranging from Lord Keynes to Samuel Goldwyn to Casey Stengel), that explains why we aren't all millionaires.

It also explains why opinions on the matter are sharply divided. If all you rely on is a gross five- or ten-year period, the results you get will depend heavily on the on the types of markets that were prevailing during the period. And bear in mind: if you alter your starting and ending dates even slightly, you may get a different crop of winning funds. Therefore, it's important that you take a more multi-dimensional view.

Furthermore, don't just look at the performance of a single fund over even a ten-year time frame. Even adding or dropping a single month can sometimes make a big difference. For example, $1,000 invested in American Century/20th Century Ultra Fund over the ten years ending September 1997 grew to $5,488. One month later, for the ten years ending October 1997, $1,000 invested in the fund grew to $7,623.

Why the big jump? Simple. If you had invested—in that fund or most any other U.S. stock fund—in September 1987, your money would quickly have lost significant value when the stock market took its big hit the next month. But if you had waited a month, until after the big crash on Black Monday in October 1987, you would have fared substantially better.

That illustration only dramatizes the concept that adjusting the time period slightly can influence the returns of a fund as well as your own results. Depending on the type of fund and how aggressive its strategy is, a slight time adjustment can be of minor or major importance in the reported performance. Many fund managers, in fact, looked forward to substituting October 1997 for October 1987. Although October 1997 was a lousy month that contained "Grey" Monday, when the Dow declined 554 points, it was nothing like October 1987. The Ultra fund, for instance, benefited from the substitution of months. While it declined 6.2% in October 1997, the drop in October 1987 was a gut-wrenching 32.5%. The smaller decline, even spread over ten years, made a large difference.

What to do

Since few people consistently make accurate predictions of the future, here are some practical guidelines you can rely on.

Begin your quest by examining the current winners. Then see which of them have also done well over longer periods of time. You will generally see two types of long-term performance data: presented annually and/or in bull and bear market spans. Either one can be useful.

But here's a warning: If you're investing in aggressive growth funds, you should focus your attention first on bull-market periods. If you investigate down periods, keep in mind that the aggressive funds that fared *worst* in bear markets are the ones most likely to do *best* during bull markets. Volatility can work in your favor.

Keep in mind that you have to compare your potential selection with other similar funds. This way you can quickly see which performed best, given their level of risk. You want to compare aggressive growth funds to other aggressive growth funds, income funds to other income funds. Put another way, an aggressive growth fund that outperforms a growth-income fund in a sharply rising market may not be desirable when you take risk into account.

In a long-running bull market, such as the one we've experienced in recent years, the quintile ranks, as presented in our companion publications, have provided reasonable predictive power. In the

Table 39

Stock and bond fund performance comparison

No-Load Fund	NAV 1/30/98	Total return percent with quintile ranks by objective						Beta/ Sharpe	% Cash 1/98	Total Assets		Yield %
		Jan 1998	Latest 3 mo	Latest 6 mo	Latest 12 mo	3 yr ann cmpnd	5 yr ann cmpnd			$ Mil 12/31/97	$ Mil 9/30/97	
		AGGRESSIVE GROWTH FUNDS										
AARP Capital GroØ	52.67	1.1²	4.3¹	0.3³	26.9¹	28.6¹	17.0²	1.09-A	3.6	1,217.9	1,228.4	0.5
Amer Cent-20th GiftrustØSC	22.41	-3.8⁵	-9.0⁵	-10.0⁵	-5.7⁵	13.5⁵	15.1³	1.26-F	11.8	986.0	1,130.3	0.0
Amer Cent-20th GrowthØ	24.59	2.4¹	4.0¹	0.6³	21.7²	23.1³	13.2⁴	1.21-D	1.1	5,165.8	5,368.6	0.0
Amer Cent-20th UltraØ	27.78	1.8¹	5.2¹	-3.0⁴	15.1³	26.5²	17.5⁵	1.34-C	1.3	22,420.3	23,012.6	0.0
Amer Cent-20th VistaØ	12.37	-0.4³	-9.2⁵	-10.3⁵	-12.1⁵	15.2⁵	9.6⁵	1.09-F	9.6	1,605.9	2,070.2	0.0
American Heritage SC X	0.85	-13.3⁵	-14.1⁵	-20.6⁵	16.4²	0.4⁵	-1.8⁵	0.41-F	0.0	20.6	23.1	0.0
ahson Enterprise IIØSC	23.80	4.8⁵	-2.2³	2.0²	26.0¹	25.2²	15.0³	0.56-A	5.3	87.7	81.9	0.2

newsletter, quintile ranks (a quintile of one means it's in the top 20% of funds in its objective category; a quintile of five, the bottom 20%) are shown for six or seven different time periods ranging from one month to five years. (The quintile is the small superscript number to the right of the total return figure.)

Short-run performance can measure portfolio momentum. Funds that develop superior momentum have put together a portfolio of stocks that will, in the short-run anyway, most likely continue to outperform other portfolios.

The longer-term record, when available, reassures you that the fund's performance is due to skill, not luck. If an older fund has been mediocre in the past, and its management has not changed, high-ranked current performance may be due to a few lucky stock picks or market-sector selections. But even here, going back five years is usually sufficient.

If a fund achieves quintiles of one or two—meaning that it is in the top 20% to 40%—in most time periods, it generally has enough momentum to continue to be an above-average performer. But don't forget to consider a fund's performance in light of your expectations for the market. If small cap stocks are not in vogue, then the aggressive growth funds investing in them can hardly do well.

The "Mountain"

The "mountain" is a fund's performance chart shown on an annual basis. Funds are not required to provide such a chart. But if they've performed well, they may elect to use it as a gloating device, in prospectuses as well as promotional literature. To avoid misrepresentation, the SEC requires that performance data cover the life of the fund, or periods of ten years or longer (over ten years in multiples of five). The longer the period used, the more impressive the "mountain," since money has been growing longer. However, since the periods shown vary from prospectus to prospectus, it is extremely difficult to use mountain charts to compare different funds directly or even to tell how the particular fund in question has done in recent years.

To illustrate just how misleading these charts can be, I have shown the mountain for Dean Witter Diversified Growth Securities. The chart appeared in an ad placed in *Kiplinger's Personal Finance* magazine. The mountain is impressive because the fund turned in an outstanding performance in its latest year, and also because the growth (the vertical axis) is drawn with an arithmetic scale instead of the more proper ratio scale.

In the box, the fund shows its performance, numerically, two different ways—with or without the impact of the load. While a casual reader may think the second line (labeled SEC standardized avg. annual total return) is a benchmark surpassed by the fund, the fine print at the bottom reveals that it is simply the fund's total return deducting sales charges.

A clue that things may not be as good as the chart makes them appear is the choice of benchmark used at the bottom of the graph. There, a comparison to the CPI reveals that the fund handily outperformed the inflation rate. When a fund compares itself to the CPI, it almost always means it underperformed its relevant stock market index. In this case the Dean Witter fund gained 333% during the most recent ten years; the S&P 500, with dividends reinvested, gained 437%.

Thus, you are best advised to make molehills out of mutual funds' "mountains." And certainly, don't make investment decisions based on them. Your guideline should be numerical performance data for more recent periods.

Finally, you will find annual performance data in the prospectus or other fund literature. If the numbers differ significantly from published data, check to see the period covered. Funds frequently show these annual figures for their fiscal year, not the calendar year that most investment publications use to put all funds on an equal footing.

Chart 40

Don't you wish you had seen this ad in 1981?

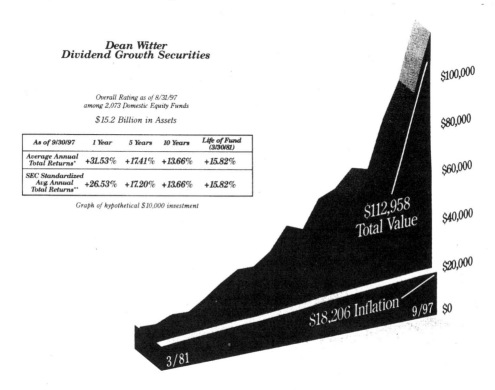

Dean Witter
Dividend Growth Securities

*Overall Rating as of 8/31/97
among 2,073 Domestic Equity Funds*

$15.2 Billion in Assets

As of 9/30/97	1 Year	5 Years	10 Years	Life of Fund (3/30/81)
Average Annual Total Returns*	+31.53%	+17.41%	+13.66%	+15.82%
SEC Standardized Avg Annual Total Returns**	+26.53%	+17.20%	+13.66%	+15.82%

Graph of hypothetical $10,000 investment

$100,000

$80,000

$60,000

$112,958
Total Value

$40,000

$20,000

$18,206 Inflation   9/97 $0

3/81

Of course you do. Over the past 16 years, the Dean Witter Dividend Growth Securities fund, in up markets and down, has provided consistent growth and income for 800,000 investors.

But the impressive numbers don't end there. Dean Witter has a network of over 9,400 Account Executives, each with the experience to give you the investment advice that's right for your individual goals.

Remember, past performance cannot guarantee future results, and you may have a loss or gain when you sell your shares.

Call Dean Witter today for more information on these and other impressive numbers. And for the office nearest you.

How adept is the manager?

The ability of a fund's management is a most significant factor in evaluating a diversified mutual fund. Although the word "professional" carries the connotation of excellence, alas, this is not universally the case. While many professional fund managers do an outstanding job for their shareholders, some are mediocre. And more than a few are so poor that their shareholders would be better off selecting stocks by throwing darts at the financial pages. With the total number of funds surpassing 6,800 and the number of equity funds over 3,000, the chances of mediocre management is increasing.

Invariably, investors are exhorted to select well-managed funds. But how to evaluate management's ability? Here are some guidelines:

The prospectus may be of some help in evaluating the management of a fund. Since July 1993, the SEC has required that the name or names of the portfolio manager(s) be listed in the prospectus along with the length of service and experience for the last five years. The prospectus is "stickered" for new investors and for current shareholders acquiring additional shares when there is a change in portfolio managers. Other shareholders receive the news in the fund's next regular mailing. Money funds, index funds, and funds run by committees or teams are excluded from this requirement.

New managers

Many investors select a fund because the manager has received favorable publicity. But write-ups in the financial press don't always indicate true expertise or predict outstanding performance. Nor does a lack of publicity imply poor management. The facts are that financial columns on occasion profile the managers of funds that perform well over short spans and neglect other managers who have been equally outstanding over long periods.

Similarly, television interviews are, at best, an imperfect way to select a fund manager. The most eloquent portfolio managers are not necessarily the best stock pickers! Conversely, some of the best managers are not particularly outgoing, so their firms do not promote them to the media.

The fact that some fund managers are profiled and others aren't is due primarily to their attitude regarding publicity. Some managers love the limelight and eagerly seek it; others shun it. Be skeptical of publicity. Don't select a fund on that basis.

Magazine and newspaper profiles, while they generally make interesting reading, often fail to provide actionable information for prospective fund investors. They should include a measure of the fund's objective and risk, the type of investor who would find the fund suitable, the fund's performance, properly benchmarked, and even the phone number and minimum investment accepted, if it's unusually high. Instead, they all too often emphasize a portfolio manager's winning stock selections. That's not what fund investing is about. If a portfolio has enough stocks, some of them are bound to be winners. In one profile, former New York Times business columnist, Robert Metz, noted in exasperation: "Mr. _____ would rather discuss his successes." The fund manager's strategy is to identify companies with the best growth!!!

Funds run by committees

Sometimes it's hard to tell what you are getting when you buy a fund run by a team or committee. In some cases the committee may be composed of members all having equal voices; or, more commonly, there will be a team leader who makes the major decisions with the rest of the team being essentially assistants or analysts. Only fund management knows the roles played by specific individuals in the everyday business of the fund and the extent to which they contribute to its success or failure. So while you're flying blind to a certain extent, if the fund group has a record of excellence, you aren't taking much of a risk.

There has been a marked increase in the number of funds that claim team or committee management since the SEC began requiring funds to name their portfolio managers in the prospectus. Some mutual fund companies don't want to spotlight their managers, fearing that if they become "stars," they might be wooed to another fund company or leave to start their own fund groups. So they take advantage of an exception to the rules: funds run by committees don't have to name names. A 1994 study by *Morningstar* found that while only 15% of all funds were piloted by more than one person in 1989, the figure is now 35%. Funds that recently made the switch to team management are suspect. It's quite likely that one particular individual among the fund's management is still controls the decision making.

Yet another incentive exists for a group to promote its "team." Star owners, such as Michael Price of the Mutual Series funds, sometimes sell out to larger organizations. In this case the terms of the sale require Price to stay on for a five-year transition period (although he need work full-time for only the first two years). Nobody ever heard of the team of assistants at Mutual Series backing up Price before the sale. Now that group is being trumpeted to reassure shareholders that it wasn't a one-man show.

Teams versus individual managers

Who would you think performs better at managing your money, one person or a team? Conventional wisdom says individuals. Committees have a reputation for being staid and unadventurous. Not true, says a study that appeared in the personal finance magazine *Bloomberg Personal.* The study made a comprehensive comparison of funds managed by individuals versus those run by teams. Funds co-managed by two people were included in the team count.

Bloomberg found that the teams outperformed individual managers over various periods ranging from three to fifteen years—without taking more risk. The superior performance by teams was believed due to their greater discipline. In other words, the managers may adhere more strictly to the fund's investing philosophy. The team may well make fewer hasty decisions, and therefore fewer mistakes. They may take a longer-term approach. And, if a manager leaves, there is less disruption.

While the study didn't get into it, I suspect that teams also are better at managing today's mammoth funds. It's one thing for an individual to manage a few hundred million. Managing several—or many—billions is undoubtedly much harder. This may well be one of the problems besetting gargantuan Fidelity, which still relies on individuals.

The Bloomberg study named the following no-load funds as the best team-led: Twentieth Century Giftrust, Kaufmann, SteinRoe Capital Opportunities, Warburg Pincus Emerging Growth, First Eagle of America, and Brandywine.

Table 41

Teams vs. individual portfolio managers		
	teams	**individuals**
annualized returns		
10-year	12.5%	11.7%
5-year	15.7%	15.2%
3-year	16.1%	15.2%
Portfolio turnover	54.0%	80.0%
Expense ratio	1.4%	1.4%
Beta	0.92	0.91
# domestic equity funds	264	1,836

Source data: Morningstar

If the fund has a new manager, that may be a reason for caution. At the very least, you'll need to ignore the fund's prior performance record, which was compiled by someone else.

However, one study found that when a poorly performing fund had a change of managers, frequently that worked out for the better. On the other hand, the replacement managers for top performing funds often did not live up to their predecessor's record. I think that's logical.

And then there is the situation where a manager eases out of day-to-day control. In January 1986, Sir John Templeton, one of the most successful fund managers of our time, announced the sale of shares of his privately owned management company to the public. The master cashed in. While the octogenarian Templeton continues as the "public face" of the company, he is no longer president. Mutual fund salesmen still sell the Templeton name, but current shareholders are getting the services of a large, diversified organization which manages more than 70 different funds worldwide (and is now a component of the Franklin Funds). You may see a Templeton advertisement with Sir John's picture prominently displayed, but in the fine print there will be a disclaimer saying he "is not involved in investment management decisions, which are made by the fund's investment manager."

New managers

Here's a situation you may be able to relate to. You own a fund, and you're happy with it. But suddenly you see the fund's manager on TV, and you realize—egad!—he's only 28. Should you worry yourself sick? Usually not. But in any case there may not be a lot you can do about it. Portfolio management tends to be a young man's game. A *Morningstar* study found that 38% of portfolio managers are in their 30s and another 32% are in their 40s.

Old fossil "experts" are frequently quoted as saying the youngsters will get killed in the next bear market, because they aren't old enough to remember the last one. I don't believe there's much truth to the assertion. When the next bear market arrives, the type of fund you've invested in will be a greater determinant of your success or failure than the fund manager's age. Aggressive growth funds and many fully invested funds will decline the most, regardless of the portfolio managers' age.

This question came to a panel discussion I was part of. I answered the question as above. The next panelist, portfolio manager Garrett Van Wagoner, thought the younger managers might actually do better

The manager is just a kid!

because the old ones, having been through a bear market, might be too cautious. A third panelist, fund manager Art Bonnel, no spring chicken, noted that his aggressive fund would decline substantially in any bear market.

Does the manager invest his own money in the fund?

Some managers personally invest large sums of money in the funds they manage. Many others do not. The ones who do will frequently publicize this fact. When a manager puts his own money into his fund it's a definite plus. However, where the advantage shows up is less in published returns, which are pre-tax, than in the unpublished after-tax returns. Managers with their own money in a fund, are simply going to take more care that their realized gains are long-term, subject to the 20% or 28% long-term capital gains tax, than managers without their own money in their fund.

On the other hand, in most cases the absence of personal money has no particular significance. The lack could be due to any number of valid reasons. The fund's objective may be different from the manager's personal objective. The manager may be part of a large group, with the expectation of short tenure at his present fund.

For most managers, high salaries and substantial bonuses are sufficient motivation. The personal investments are just icing on the cake.

Transferring performance records

Who owns a fund's performance record? While you'd obviously think it was the fund, lately that hasn't always been the case. In 1994, Elizabeth Bramwell, then the manager of the Gabelli Growth Fund, left Gabelli to start her own Bramwell Growth Fund. Since she intended to manage her new fund in the way that she did her old Gabelli fund, why not, she thought, cite the Gabelli fund's performance record. She figured it would be a valid indication of how her new Bramwell Fund would perform. To the surprise of some, the SEC agreed with her, giving her permission to use the old performance record in promoting the new fund in the prospectus and in advertising.

While everybody agreed this was a responsible decision, the SEC soon found out it had stumbled into a mine field. Quickly other investment advisors asked the SEC for permission to use the performance of unregistered incubator funds (see Glossary), institutional funds that had converted to retail funds, and even new funds whose managers' previous funds had had somewhat dissimilar objectives. The pre-launch records of many of these funds were far less relevant than Elizabeth Bramwell's. Many in the fund industry saw this as a way for competitors to take undue advantage. They complained, and the SEC began backpedaling. That's where things stand at the moment.

While the practice of hitchhiking on someone else's record may be legitimate on occasion, be alert to the practice. Be critical of performance records compiled before the birth of the fund that you are evaluating. Let management prove to you that the pre-launch record is meaningful.

There is, of course, expertise in the mutual fund field. But it's difficult to identify. So recognize that the best way to measure a manager's ability is to concentrate on fund results. Continual gains in the value of a fund's shares are the most eloquent testimony a manager's ability.

In summary

With today's exaggerated media hype, it's all to easy to overestimate the importance of the portfolio manager. The fact is that in most cases the manager is not indispensable. I estimate that in about 90% of the cases, a change in portfolio managers will not materially affect a fund's performance. Here's the general guideline:

The larger the advisory organization, the less likely it is that a departure will cause significant problems. The portfolio manager is not as crucial in a larger organization as in a smaller one, since it is far easier for a larger organization to replace a departing manager with someone equally skilled.

Fidelity is the obvious example, here. It has achieved strong performances with young managers who seem to move around frequently. This means that the people managing the various funds are for the most part fairly new to their particular portfolio. *The No-Load Fund Investor* did a special study and found that the median fund manager at Fidelity (as of September 1997) had been running his or her current fund for only 17 months. Here's the breakdown. I've separated sector funds from other equity funds because Fidelity seems to use them as a train-

The importance of the fund family

ing ground before giving a manager responsibility for a diversified fund. I found that only 18% of all the Fidelity fund managers were in place before 1995, and in the case of sector funds, only 6%.

Table 42

Tenure of Fidelity portfolio managers*
Percent distribution
As of September 1997

Year began	Sector	Other equity	Fixed-income	All
1992 & earlier	3%	13%	9%	8%
1993-94	3%	20%	7%	10%
1995-96	38%	45%	51%	45%
1997	56%	22%	33%	37%
Total	100%	100%	100%	100%
Median start	Jan '97	Mar '96	Jan '96	May '96
Median tenure	9 months	19 months	21 months	17 months
# managers/funds	36	60	43	139

Source: Fidelity Mutual Fund Guide. Money funds excluded.

Bear in mind that I am measuring tenure on the *current* fund. Many Fidelity managers managed other Fidelity funds before assuming the helm of their present post.

A number of Fidelity funds had mediocre performances in 1995 and 1996, so the manager turnover is partly a response to that. It was also in response to a desire to get the Fidelity managers to hew to their stated objectives, which hadn't always been the case previously. Nevertheless, I had done a similar study in early 1995 and found similar results. Another independent study found high turnover in 1992 and 1993. Fidelity funds were turning in outstanding performances those years.

Fidelity has more than its share of top-performing funds. You have to conclude that the group's high turnover of managers has *not* affected performance to any significant degree.

How do they do it? The key to Fidelity's success is the strong organization that backs up its portfolio managers, including an army of skilled research analysts and traders.

And while I've used Fidelity as an example, I think the same truth applies at other major fund groups. Vanguard, T. Rowe Price, Scudder, Stein Roe, Strong, just to name a few, also have solid organizations. As a result, good managers leave all the time—without necessarily causing any deterioration of performance.

Because of this tendency, I believe that if you are considering two funds that appear similar, the odds favor buying the fund that is part of the larger group.

Still other advantages: Your account will likely receive better service and administration in the larger group. And if the fund should falter, it's a lot simpler to switch to another excellent fund. If you're in a stand-alone fund, you face a time-consuming redemption and reinvestment process.

Does that mean that we oppose the all-American dream in which the little guy triumphs? Not at all. And sometimes a Monetta, a FAM Value, a Meridian or a Kaufmann does. But the sardonic cliche is true: The biggest don't always win, but that's the way you bet it.

It's just as important to pay attention to expense ratios when you are buying stock funds as when you are buying bond or money funds. It's a mistake to excuse high expenses if the fund is doing well. Now, with the 12b-1 distribution fees, expense ratios are increasing, particularly for 12b-1 funds with fees of 1% or more.

In the case of stock funds, there's no doubt that superior management can overcome the drag of a high expense ratio in a given month, or even over a one- or two-year period. But it's much more difficult for fund managers to offset this drag over long periods of time. So if you want to be a successful investor over the long haul, it is essential to keep investment expenses as low as possible.

The performance of index funds confirms this axiom. The Vanguard 500 Portfolio is an index fund that buys the stocks that comprise the S&P 500. The fund has no manager or management fee, and it has one of the lowest expense ratios of any fund in the business. In the five years ending in 1997, the average expense ratio has been 0.19%, one-eighth that of the average equity fund. Given that its portfolio is an exact duplicate of the S&P index, you would think that its performance would also be on a par. But it isn't. In the five years ending 1997, the Vanguard Index 500 Fund fell 1.5% behind the index,

Watch expense ratios

which of course, has no expenses. The S&P 500 index, with distributions reinvested, grew 151.6% in this period vs. the fund's 150.1%. Over this period of time, 31 other S&P 500 Index funds were in existence, all of them considerably smaller than Vanguard's. Even more telling, their average performance was only 148.2%, 3.4% behind the Index. The worst performer in the group, Stagecoach Corporate Stock Fund, was up only 138.6%. If the Index funds, with their ultra low expense ratios, can vary so much in their performance, imagine how serious the impact of a high expense ratio would be.

To illustrate, I've compiled a comprehensive list of all funds, load and no-load, that meet two criteria: a 1997 expense ratio of 2% or more, and a five-year performance history. About a tenth of all stock funds with five-year records (126 out of a total of 1,360) met the criteria. Overall, these high-expense funds had decidedly inferior performances. Only 24% ranked in the first or second quintile of all funds (the top 40%). Seventy-six, or 61%, ranked in the two bottom quintiles. In other words a high expense ratio fund is more than twice as likely to be below average as above average in terms of performance!

Table 43

Stock funds with expense ratios of 2% or more

Percent distributions
by five-year quintile performances

Quintile	# funds	%
1 (Best)	14	11%
2	17	13%
3	19	15%
4	31	25%
5 (Worst)	95	36%
Total	126	100%

Source: Morningstar, five years ending June 1997

What's a good expense ratio?

To give you benchmarks for evaluating expense ratios, I've calculated medians. As in all my analyses, I try to compare similar funds. So I first grouped funds by size. As a rule, the smaller the fund the greater its expense ratio. I used medians (the middle number in a group) rather than the mean (the average) because a few funds have extremely high expense ratios, which would seriously distort the picture. I've shown equity and fixed-income funds separately. The expense ratios for equities include international funds which typically have higher expense ratios than domestic funds. Fixed-income funds have lower costs—and keeping them low is more important, since the funds' expenses are deducted from dividend income.

I've also compared the median expense ratio for no-loads to the expense ratios of load funds. In 1997, the median no-load equity fund had an expense ratio of 1.16%, 36% below the median expense ratio for load equity funds. No-load international funds had a median expense ratio of 1.50%; the ratio for international load funds was 2.21%. Among fixed-income funds, no-loads had a 38% overall advantage.

Table 44

Median expense ratios

Stock funds

Assets in millions	No-loads	Loads	No-load Advantage
$1,000 +	0.87%	1.10%	0.23%
$500-1,000	1.00	1.44	0.44
$250-500	1.01	1.54	0.53
$100-250	1.15	1.57	0.42
$50-100	1.21	1.81	0.60
$25-50	1.40	1.80	0.40
$10-25	1.37	2.00	0.63
$10 and less	1.51	2.05	0.54
Total	1.16	1.80	0.64
Fixed-income funds			
$1,000 +	0.57	0.92	0.35
$500-1,000	0.61	1.16	0.55
$250-500	0.65	0.96	0.31
$100-250	0.69	1.07	0.38
$50-100	0.73	1.04	0.31
$25-50	0.79	1.13	0.34
$10-25	0.80	1.24	0.44
$10 and less	0.80	1.32	0.52
Total	0.72	1.17	0.45

Base counts: Equity funds - no-load: 1452, load: 2562;
Bond funds - no-load: 862, load: 2422"
Data: 1997

The essential difference between load and no-load funds, the major reason for the no-load advantage, is the higher 12b-1 fees that many load funds charge. Unlike front- or back-end sales charges, these are continuing expenses and as such are included in the expense ratio. By the way, I excluded institutional funds from the no-load averages; if they'd been included, the no-load advantage would have been still greater. The data clearly refute salesmen's claims that load funds are managed more economically.

All fund expenses affect performance results. But, generally, minor differences in expenses among funds are insignificant compared to the wide variations in performance. Still, you need to screen out the high ratios. Make a point of checking the expense ratio before buying any fund.

Who's got the lowest expenses

In this contest, Vanguard wins hands down. Here's a list of no-load fund groups which offer 12 or more equity funds. The group average expense ratio is obtained by weighting each fund by its asset size. (Second ranked Dimensional Fund Advisors is an institutional group.)

Table 45

Avg. expense ratio	
Vanguard	0.29%
Dimensional	0.63
SEI	0.84
T. Rowe Price	0.85
Fidelity	0.87
USAA	0.95
Dreyfus	0.95
Janus	0.96
American Century	1.01
United Asset Mngt	1.02
Stagecoach	1.04
Invesco	1.06
Scudder	1.15
Strong	1.29
Wright	1.31
Warburg Pincus	1.34
Lexington	1.36
Gabelli	1.39
Montgomery	1.54
Robertson Stephens	1.94

Source: Mutual Funds Magazine, November 1997

Fund size—the total net assets a fund has under management—is another factor affecting performance. All else being equal, well-managed small funds frequently have an edge over large funds. This advantage is most pronounced in the case of small cap funds.

Size

An examination of fund rankings generally shows small funds doing better than—and also worse than—larger funds. Some small funds land at the bottom of the rankings because of poor management. They can't afford the management expertise provided by larger funds and groups. But if a fund, often a younger fund, has good management it frequently excels. In 1996, 36 of the top 50 best performing load and no-load equity funds had $50 million or less in assets at the start of the year, and 41 funds had assets of less than $100 million. I have tracked these statistics for many years and I've found that these results are always similar.

Table 46 shows the 1996 gains of the 25 top-performing diversified no-load stock funds. The largest of the 25 has assets of $1.3 billion; the second largest had $382 million. Only one other fund was over $100 million. They are contrasted with the lesser performance for the 25 largest diversified no-loads, which have assets of $4.2 to $53 billion. I've determined asset category according to a fund's size at the beginning of the year. In 1996, as you can see, there was no duplication between the two lists. This has generally been true in previous years. Size militates against aggressive growth. The best performers in 1996 had gains of from 56.2% to 31.9%. The best performing large fund had a 26.4% gain. The average gain for the 25 funds was 17.8%. This is remarkable considering the fact that the markets in 1996 favored the large cap stocks usually held by these big funds.

One reason small funds can outperform large ones is they can make meaningful investments in small capitalization companies. Big funds can't take meaningful positions in minuscule companies. Only a small amount of stock is available, and legal as well as practical considerations limit the amount of voting stock of any one company that a fund can own.

Consider the case of a promising industrial corporation with only $10 million worth of outstanding stock. No single fund can buy more than $1 million. Suppose a fund with $1 billion in assets has $1 million worth of this particular corporation's stock. If the stock doubles, its value is increased to $2 million, but the large fund's total assets are increased to $1,001,000,000, up only one-tenth of 1%.

Table 46

Performance of diversified no-load equity funds

	Best performers	Assets Mill. $ 12/95	1996 % gain		Largest funds	Assets Mill. $ 12/95	1996 % gain
1	Warbg Pincus Small Co Val...........0.1		56.2		Vangd Windsor.........................13,646.2		26.4
2	Fremont US MicroCap.................10.0		48.7		Brandywine...............................4,210.5		24.9
3	Rydex OTC... ....30.4		43.5		Vangd Windsor II....................11,012.9		24.2
4	Robrtsn Stph Partners... ....7.5		43.3		Vangd Idx 500..........................17,371.0		22.9
5	Lindner/Ryback Small Cap............6.4		41.2		Fidelity Contrafund.................14,831.7		21.9
6	Oakmark Small Cap.....................25.8		39.8		Fidelity Eqty Inc... ....10,492.1		21.0
7	CRM Small Cap Value.................39.0		38.9		Mutual Shares... ....5,224.9		20.8
8	Dreyfus Agg Val...........................4.6		38.9		Price Eqty Inc... ....5,214.8		20.4
9	Fidelity Export & Multi... ....382.0		38.6		Fidelity Gro & Inc... ....14,818.6		20.0
10	Legg Mason Value...................1,340.4		38.4		Janus Fund... ....12,466.2		19.6
11	Dreyfus Emg Ldrs.........................17.4		37.4		Fidelity Eqty Inc II... ....11,977.0		18.7
12	Dreyfus MidCap Val... ....0.1		37.3		Nbrgr-Ber Guardian...................4,389.4		17.9
13	Montgmry Sm Cap Opp.................0.1		37.3		Fidelity Value............................5,745.8		16.9
14	Weitz Ser Hickory... ....5.0		35.4		Fidelity Growth Co... ....6,278.8		16.8
15	SteinRoe Young Invest... ....41.9		35.1		Invesco Indust Inc......................4,256.1		16.7
16	Dreyfus Sm Co Val... ....0.1		34.2		Vangd Star:Star... ....4,841.0		16.2
17	Heartland Val Plus.........................19.0		33.8		Vangd Wellington....................12,656.0		16.2
18	Salomon Capital............................104.3		33.3		Fidelity Blue Chip... ....7,801.9		15.4
19	Sound Shore... ....67.6		33.3		Fidelity Puritan... ....15,628.3		15.2
20	Thompson Plumb Growth.............13.0		33.0		Amer Cent-20th Cent Growth... .4,849.0		15.0
21	PBHG Core Growth... ....0.0		32.8		Amer Cent-20th Cent Ultra... ....14,551.2		13.8
22	Montag & Cldwl Growth... ....48.9		32.7		Fidelity Asset Mgr... ....11,165.4		12.7
23	White Oak Gro...............................10.9		32.3		Fidelity Magellan.....................53,702.3		11.7
24	Bridgeway Agg Gro... ....0.7		32.2		Vangd Wellesley Inc... ....7,180.7		9.4
25	Strong Gr & Inc... ....0.1		31.9		Fidelity Balanced.......................4,880.1		9.3

On the other hand, a $20 million fund has $1 million of the same stock. When the stock doubles, the small fund's total assets increase to $21 million, and its net asset value goes up a very substantial 5%.

If the $1 billion fund specializing in these small growth companies puts no more than $1 million in each, it would need to buy 1,000 different stocks. To properly analyze and manage so many stocks is a difficult undertaking, to say the least. As a result, the larger growth funds prefer substantial holdings in major corporations. Just as important, large funds can't quickly dispose of their huge holdings without depressing a stock's price. Diminutive funds are more nimble. They can sell their holdings almost as readily as individual investors can, without disrupting the market.

As a practical matter, fund size is most significant in the performance of small company funds and then only when small company funds are outperforming large funds. While small company funds have outperformed larger funds over broad periods of time, their ascendancy tends to run in cycles. When large cap stocks are the best performers, large funds—which of necessity own mostly large cap stocks—can do as well as small funds.

In the case of bond and money market funds, size is an advantage. You should prefer larger funds because of their lower expense ratios.

I should reiterate one point. If you choose a small fund in order to maximize performance, realize that it is likely to excel primarily because of its maneuverability and its greater propensity to take risks, not because of inherently superior management. The large growth funds own the stocks of multibillion-dollar companies, which are unlikely to go bankrupt in any recession. On the other hand, some emerging growth companies favored by the small performance funds do go under during a recession. And even in boom times, bankruptcies in highly competitive fields are scarcely unheard of, especially among high-tech firms.

Many large funds grew to their present size because they performed well in their early years, when they were still small. The Dreyfus Fund is a classic example. Its greatest gains came in the 50s and early 60s, when the fund was quite small and was aggressively managed. Back then, it regularly outpaced the NYSE Index by two to one or more. The Dreyfus Fund is no longer a superior performer, and it's now classified as a growth-income fund.

The Fidelity Magellan Fund has occasionally appeared to be an exception to the smaller-is-better rule. Defying gravity, the fund maintained respectable performances between 1993 and 1995 despite incredible size ($36 billion at the start of 1995). I think a major reason for Magellan's continual good fortune is the strength of Fidelity's management team. However, if the fund were not so large it might be doing even better.

In 1989, Peter Lynch authored a book on investing called *One Up*

When size doesn't matter

The Windsor Fund's big bets

In 1996, the $15 billion Windsor Fund held $994 million of Chrysler, $727 million of Citicorp, $704 million of Seagate Technology, $662 million of Ford Motor, $631 million of Burlington Resources, and $621 million of Georgia Pacific Corp. The fund held only 93 common stocks. The average holding was $151 million.

on Wall Street, in which he noted: "My biggest disadvantage is size. The bigger the equity fund, the harder it gets to outperform the competition. Expecting a $9 billion fund to compete successfully against an $800 million fund is the same as expecting Larry Bird to star in basketball games with a twenty-five-pound weight strapped to his waist. Big mutual funds have the same built-in handicaps as big anythings—the bigger it is, the more energy it takes to move it."

Fund closings

Because of the disadvantages of being too large, about 75 no-load funds have stopped selling shares at one time or another when they reached a certain size. Most—but not all—are small company funds.

The fact that these funds have closed their doors tells you how important their managers feel modest size is. They are voluntarily depriving themselves of one of the only two ways they have to increase income. (The other way is internal growth through increases in NAV.)

What's the optimum size that a fund should be before its managers consider closing it? It's hard to pinpoint a number, so let's consider the size of some of the funds that since 1991 have locked out new investors. Oberweiss Micro-Cap closed at $56 million. Babson Enterprise closed at $125 million. Skyline Special Equities shut out new investors when it grew to $150 million. Nicholas Limited Edition figured that $170 million was sufficient. Montgomery Small Cap was about $165 million when it closed. And Quantitative Numeric was $100 million. These funds clearly closed before their assets grew too large to be manageable.

On the other hand, Janus Venture announced in September 1991 that its then portfolio manager, Jim Craig, felt that $750 million was about all he could handle. Unfortunately, Janus permitted the fund to grow by an additional $350 million in the period between the announcement and the final cutoff of sales. Similarly, Monetta closed at $500 million in 1993. These two funds were too large when they closed.

And, of course, the worst example of a fund closing after it had grown far too big was Fidelity Magellan's 1997 closing with assets of $63.8 million. Magellan's closing, like most, was for new investors only. Existing investors can still make further investments. In the case of Magellan, the fund will continue to grow because it is still open to its 4.3 million current shareholders as well as all new participants in its hundreds of 401(k) and other retirement plans. The closing had nothing to do with maintaining performance; it was meant to reassure existing shareholders.

Some funds announce closings as a marketing ploy. If a fund with, say, $300 million in assets, announces they plan to close when assets reach $500 million, or when a fund sets a closing date 1-2 months off, don't get excited. That fund is really saying, "Hey sucker, help me grow larger, fast." (Some funds announce a closing date at the time they are launched, usually at a very low level. For example, the PBHG Limited Fund closed at $100 million in assets the very first day it was offered for sale! That's a completely different situation.)

Raw size isn't the only criterion. FAM Value closed at $212 million and that proved to be more than the managers could handle. On the other hand, Fidelity Low-Priced Stock Fund closed and reopened in 1992, and then closed and reopened again in 1993. It since has increased its assets to $10 billion. It has managed its growth by increasing the price limit on the stocks it can hold. The fund originally would not buy any stocks selling for more than $15. The limit was then increased to $25. Now it's up to $35. Not exactly "low-priced," but at least the higher price greatly broadens the universe of stocks available to the fund. The major difference: FAM is a pint-sized shop, while Fidelity has enormous resources to back up its portfolio managers.

Buy funds that close when assets are still manageable; pass on the rest. All else being equal, choose funds with the smallest assets.

Cloning

Cloning existing funds is another method of relieving pressure on further growth. In 1983, when the Twentieth Century Growth and Ultra funds had grown bulky, the adviser introduced the Twentieth Century Vista Fund. Similarly in 1987, Twentieth Century introduced the Heritage Fund. While there are some differences among these funds in style; all have essentially the same growth objective. Other examples of cloning: the Mutual Series Funds, Windsor II, Babson Enterprise II, and Skyline Special Equities II. Unfortunately, in many cases, when a small cap fund is cloned, the new fund frequently invests in mid-cap stocks.

Is small size a detriment?

Can a fund be too small? Unequivocally, the answer is yes. Small funds often lack the wherewithal to afford good managers and purchase top quality investment research. I suggest that you avoid, or at the very least be skeptical of, established funds (say, those five years or older) whose assets are still below $25 million. And if a fund can't attract enough investors in five years to reach at least $10 million, then it clearly should be avoided. (An exception might be made for a rare, limited-sale fund, such as a small fund run in-house for a number of years before being marketed.) Similarly, be wary of a new fund that remains quite small even though it has attracted reams of publicity, usually because of some unique marketing gimmick. One example of this is the Women's Equity Mutual Fund. More than four years after its founding, it still has only $5.8 million in assets.

Sector neutral portfolios

This term refers to how the fund's portfolio is weighted. If the fund allocates its industry positions roughly the same as the broad market, the fund is termed sector neutral. The opposite strategy is for a fund to "heavy up" in certain industry categories. The latter strategy works if the manager correctly forecasts the market environment. It becomes a losing strategy if the forecast is incorrect. In 1995, a number of ostensibly diversified funds had half or more of their portfolios in technology stocks. For example, the Wasatch Mid-Cap Fund, the number one diversified no-load that year, had a technology weighting of 48%. It was, in reality, a closet industry fund. Since technology was red hot that year, overweighting in technology enabled Wasatch and other overweighted funds to make the top ranks.

That was great while the party lasted. Unfortunately, it didn't last through 1996. Many of 1995's top funds turned in dismal performances the next year.

You don't get such stomach-churning swings if you buy broadly diversified growth-stock funds that are "sector neutral." I think that's a better bet for most investors.

The following table details the sector weighting of two Vanguard Index funds: S&P 500 and Total Market Stock Index. The latter attempts to replicate the Wilshire 5000 Index, a summary of all traded U.S. stocks. If your fund's industry weightings are in line with this allocation, then the fund is sector neutral. Note that in the broad universe of U.S. stocks, technology has a 13%-14% weighting.

Table 47

Industry weightings	S&P 500	Wilshire 5000
Financial	15.8%	18.4%
Industrial cyclicals	15.6	15.0
Technology	14.3	13.4
Services	11.9	13.8
Consumer staples	10.6	9.1
Health	10.4	10.8
Energy	9.3	7.0
Retail	5.3	5.4
Consumer durables	4.0	3.7
Utilities	2.7	3.4

Based on distributions in Vanguard Index funds

Some funds whose philosophy is to stay sector neutral are: the Babson and Turner funds, Hotchkis & Wiley Small Cap Fund, as well as most enhanced index funds.

How much cash is in the till?

A fund's cash position is the portion of its assets that are not invested for the long-term. This includes cash and cash equivalents such as short-term government securities, bank CDs and other money market instruments plus receivables, minus current liabilities. The amount of cash that a manager holds should be appropriate for the market conditions.

Here are the rules for an appropriate cash position:

In a bull market, a fund should be fully invested or even leveraged, in order to take maximum advantage of rising prices. Conversely, in a bear market, a high portion of assets should be in cash or cash equivalents in order to minimize losses as stock prices tumble.

In essence this is market timing. As I noted earlier, a majority of equity funds do not time the market to any appreciable extent. However, a sizeable minority (perhaps one-third) of funds do. In a bear market, these defense-oriented managers may place 20% to 100% of their assets in cash.

In practice you will find three somewhat distinct types of funds that run high cash positions on occasion: market timers, asset allocators, and value funds. Market timing funds vary their cash positions by typically using technical analysis (an explanation of that term appears in the Glossary). Asset allocators move their assets among stocks, bonds, cash and other asset classes by using models to determine which class is expected to have the most potential. The value funds use fundamental analysis to determine whether a stock is over- or underpriced. They sell stocks they feel are overpriced, and remain in cash if they cannot find undervalued replacements. Because stocks tend to be overpriced at market peaks and underpriced at market bottoms, their actions amount to market timing. Technicians sometimes call these people "bottom up" market timers, while they themselves are "top down" market timers.

Not surprisingly, fund managers are not infallible when it comes to correctly timing the market. Those who go to cash at the onset of a bear market frequently fail to reinvest in stocks at the bottom. The evidence: a number of funds had high cash positions at the beginning of 1991, and consequently missed the beginning of the new bull market that began when U.S. troops attacked Iraq during "Desert Storm." Funds like Flex-Muirfield (67% cash), Fontaine Capital Appreciation (49% cash), Mathers (92% cash), Strong Opportunity (39% cash) and Valley Forge (80% cash) lagged badly because of their inappropriate cash positions.

> # *Where to find cash position data*
>
> Our newsletter, *The No-Load Fund Investor,* is one of the few comprehensive sources of cash positions. It provides current data for virtually all popular no-load equity funds. You can also find cash position data in the funds' quarterly reports, but that information is usually out of date by the time you get it.

A few funds have managed to stay largely in cash during this great bull market. The Mathers Fund, ostensibly an equity fund, has placed two-thirds or more of its assets in cash or Treasury securities throughout much of this great bull market. The fund, which had been in the top ten in the seventies and early eighties, became bearish under the direction of its current manager, Henry Van der Eb. In the ten years since January 1, 1988 it has averaged only a 5.2% gain per year. (And in the last five years, that declined to a 1.2% annual gain.) The fund's founder, Thomas Mathers, who is no longer involved with the fund, reportedly became so perturbed at this turn of events, he attempted to force the fund to change its name.

Value funds seldom carry cash positions over 30%. The funds with higher cash positions are usually congenital bears, like Van der Eb, or market timers. While there may be some exceptions, in general, you should avoid funds with cash positions that exceed 30%.

Funds that do not attempt to time the market feel that they lack the ability to forecast the market's direction consistently.

If you do your own market timing, choose a fund that is always fully invested, and then move back and forth yourself between the stock fund and its companion money market fund. If you're a buy-and-hold investor, and want a fund to time the market for you, select one fund that has demonstrated its adroitness.

In sum, a fund's cash position gives you an important indication of how its management views the future. It is also a measure of risk and reward. In a bull market, funds that are fully invested offer the greatest potential for gain. If you are willing to take the risk, by all means buy funds that are completely invested or even leveraged at key market junctures. But, if the outlook is uncertain, funds with greater cash reserves provide you with some defense.

An investor can obtain leverage in either of two ways. First, invest in a fund that is internally leveraged. Unfortunately, only a few funds use that strategy, and they are seldom the most desirable funds. One that fits the bill is the Rydex Nova Fund, which uses futures and options to achieve returns 50% greater (or less) than the S&P 500 index.

Second, you can get more leverage on your favorite funds than they themselves employ by buying their shares through a discount broker which trades in mutual funds. Charles Schwab, Fidelity or Jack White are well-established brokerage firms that permit you to borrow to the current 50% margin limit. Using that ability to the fullest would enable you to obtain two-for-one leverage, providing for greater gains in bull markets—as well as much bigger losses during market declines. The procedures are similar to buying stocks on margin. Chapter 22 and the *Handbook* provide more information on discount brokers.

Leverage will maximize profits

New money coming into a fund, termed cash inflow, can aid performance, particularly if it arrives at a measured pace. Here's why:

■ With new money coming in, a fund's management can buy securities on market dips or simply raise its cash position without selling securities.

Cash inflow and outflow

■ A positive cash flow means that a fund does not need to sell good or promising equities in order to meet redemptions, or to raise cash for defensive purposes.

■ With fresh money coming in, a fund need not sell existing holdings to take advantage of new or special market situations. Thus, decision-making is simpler; a manager has to decide only what to buy, rather than what to buy and what to sell.

■ With more money to spend, a fund can attract the advice of the best analysts.

■ With ample cash, fund managers try harder to find promising new investment opportunities.

■ A fund can "bootstrap," directing new money into additional shares of stocks already in its portfolio. If the stock's "float" is not too large such investments can raise its price—and the value of the fund's shares.

But if the fund is particularly hot, that's another matter. When the new money arrives in torrents, that can cause problems. The manager may then have difficulty finding attractive new investments. This usually results in excessive cash positions, a drag on performance, or unwise investments made in haste.

Beware of net redemptions

While excessive cash inflow can present problems, net cash outflow clearly hinders performance. A fund experiencing net redemptions must either keep abnormally large cash positions, thus diluting its performance in up markets, or sell stocks to meet redemptions. The fund tries first to sell the stocks that are the weakest. But eventually it may be forced to sell promising holdings prematurely. A fund in net redemptions is forced to forgo valuable investment opportunities. As its size diminishes, its expense ratio will likely increase. Net redemptions virtually always work to the detriment of the fund's shareholders.

Everyone's got recommendations

Maybe it just seems that way because it is my business and I read all the investment literature, but everywhere I turn I encounter investment recommendations. You can't get through an edition of Wall $treet Week without Lou asking his guest for some stock picks. Recommendations are an important feature in all the personal finance publications and investment newsletters (including my own). Brokers live by their recommendations.

All that advice is fine—if properly used. But I worry that many investors don't know how to use it effectively. Beware of some recommendations: The *fund of the month* or *novelty syndrome.* The obsession of many publications to tout "hot" funds or stocks in every issue generates a flood of recommendations, some outlandish. Some examples:

World's Best Fund?

The 6 Best Investments For '97

Superstar Funds

Best Mutual Funds to Buy Now

The 7 Best New Mutual Funds

Rookie funds with great prospects.

25 Best Funds to Buy Today

The Greatest Funds of All Time

How to Find POWER FUNDS

The excerpts above are from headlines found on the covers of our best-known personal finance magazines. They were all written simply to sell magazines, particularly on the newsstands. And these headlines work, too, or else the magazines wouldn't stick with this format.

The reason these "grabber" headlines work is that most investors still focus on the "recommendation." I get this all the time—when I'm interviewed for print or broadcast media and by individuals. "Sheldon, what's your favorite fund? Which small-cap fund will be top-rated next year?" etc. I think this tradition goes back to the old days when most investors held stock portfolios bought on the advice of brokers. Push a stock; make a commission. That's how brokers paid the rent. Perhaps it's also human nature to converse along these lines—"What's the best movie you've seen lately?...The best book you've read?"

Rest assured, not every recommendation will be top-notch. Moreover, the timeliness factor in these sorts of recommendations is usually vastly overstated, since most funds are meant to be held long-term. While my *No-Load Fund Investor* newsletter has continuing model portfolios, a form of recommendation, major write-ups are not a regular feature. It only recommends funds that it thinks are special or especially timely.

The *"one best" fallacy.* This type of recommendation generally comes about from a reporter's desire for simplicity, although occasionally unsophisticated individuals ask for it. It goes like this. A reporter will say: "I want your one, single best recommendation." In the real world, of course, no such thing exists. Advice has to be conditioned on a fund's appropriateness within a specific portfolio. And while it seems obvious that no single fund could be best for everybody and at all times, this common sense fact tends to get ignored in the quest to be catchy or concise.

It's certainly possible to own just one fund (an asset allocation fund would be suitable). But for a variety of reasons, you are much better off investing in several.

The David Letterman delusion. We're referring to Letterman's well-known top ten lists. In investing, securities that have performed well in the past get memorialized, often in Top Ten lists, or starred (****), honor rolled, given "A's," written up, or singled out in some other manner. Nobody actually says they are recommendations, but most readers assume that they are. Why else is a fund in the limelight? But we all know that good past performance never guarantees future performance. Thus, there is a difference between an acknowledgment of the past and a recommendation for the future. The top fund lists are not forecasts of future performance. The Best Buy recommendations in my *Investor* newsletter are forecasts. They aren't always right, but that is the goal of the recommendation.

Past performance is, of course, the basic starting point for any recommendation. But constructing a sound portfolio involves a lot more. If past performance were the only criterion, then many securities would be recommended at their peak. In addition to past performance, you need to look at the future potential in terms of the types of markets you might reasonably anticipate. You also need to take into account such factors as continuity of management and fund expenses.

In this regard, you should also be wary of "recommendations" that appear in contests sponsored by publications. Such games have little meaning because they typically focus on just a few selections, mandate artificial holding periods, up to a year, and ignore risk. Once the holding period is selected, the ability to make changes is sharply restricted. These rules are devised for the publications' convenience and bear no relationship to real-world investing. Consequently, the experts in the competition will pick securities differently than when they are selecting for a client. There may be a tendency to pick risky stocks or funds because there is great publicity value in winning, and virtually no penalty for coming in second, or even last. Don't use these contest selections as a basis for your own decisions, unless the objectives and risks correspond to your own.

Unsuitable recommendations. Most recommendations have merit. But that doesn't necessarily mean they are appropriate for you. The most common error is, of course, buying securities—either funds or individual stocks—that are too risky. Many printed recommendations fail to disclose all the risks. In 1994, the United Services funds launched the United Services China Region Opportunity Fund, a fund that clearly has great long-term potential, but also carries great risk. The fund was initially sub-advised in Boston by Batterymarch, an institutional money manager with $11 billion in assets including $2 billion in emerging market stocks. I attended a supper in Boston hosted by Batterymarch to promote the fund. The firm's president commented to me that this would be a great fund for dollar-cost averaging, because "you won't believe how many chances you will get to buy low." She was right. The fund has had great swings over the years. I dutifully repeated her admonition in my newsletter writeup. Not many other publications did.

Undeserving candidates. Not all funds or stocks are deserving of a favorable nod. They may be recommended as a result of an effort by a public relations agent, or they may result when a publication looks for something different. Be leery of articles with titles like: "Five undiscovered funds," or "Rookie funds with great prospects." (This last title, in a major magazine, generated a considerable response for a fund that hadn't even been launched yet.)

Sifting through recommendations to find the ones that work for you. The single most important criterion is, "Does this recommended security fit into my portfolio?" If it doesn't, you don't need it, no matter how glowing its prospects may seem. Avoid owning a randomly selected list of securities that don't blend into a coherent whole that will meet your own objectives. This chapter is all about determining the proper fit.

The *bottom line:* to be in control of your portfolio you need to proceed carefully in evaluating recommendations. I have long felt that the best way to deal with your broker's recommendations is to tell him or her, "Don't call me, I'll call you." The same concept holds true with other recommendations. When you perceive a need to make a specific change or addition to your portfolio, then look at the relevant recommendations and pick the best. That way, you'll always be on top of your investments. Here's a bit of wisdom. Don't be a dilettante. Picking the trendy fund of the day that some advisor or publication is touting, is foolish at best and disastrous at worst.

Track funds on your own

Once you own no-load funds, it's a good idea to follow them periodically. You should review your conservative fund holdings at least quarterly, although monthly is better. And definitely check on more speculative funds at least once a month. If the market has been turbulent, don't hesitate to keep an eye on your holdings weekly. Many newspapers and magazines provide good monthly or quarterly data. But the easiest way to track funds weekly is to follow the total return figures in *The Wall Street Journal, Barron's* and major papers such as *The New York Times*.

If your local newspaper doesn't show total return data, see if it has a weekly summary of mutual fund performance in its Sunday edition. You can compute fund performance from this information by simply dividing the gain or loss for the week by the NAV from the preceding week. Be sure to add to the ending NAV any distributions that the fund made during the week. They are noted in the paper with an "x." If you buy aggressive growth funds that are not listed in the papers, call them each week for their NAVs when the market is in the midst of a major move.

Newspapers list funds alphabetically, either individually or under their group names. (Incidentally, information on some small funds is often not published because the fund has either fewer than 1,000 shareholders or less than $25 million in assets, the threshold levels required by the N.A.S.D. for listing.)

Summary: effective stock fund selection

Our discussion has analyzed a number of factors that you ought to consider when you are selecting a mutual fund. The most important one influencing future performance is the fund's performance over various periods in the past. But the other criteria can also be significant. All else being equal—which it never is—I favor the in-depth management at the larger fund groups. In upcoming chapters I will give you strategies to meld the individual funds that you have selected into a coherent portfolio. We will also discuss ideal holding periods for your funds. This is the really the key to investing success.

CHAPTER 15

Index fund investing

Most investors prefer to buy actively managed funds. They select funds that have expert portfolio managers who buy and sell securities in an attempt to maximize profits. In previous chapters I described the procedures for choosing such funds.

Yet another investing strategy has much to recommend it: passive investing through index funds.

Invented in 1971, such funds are a logical outgrowth of the Random Walk theory. That's the notion that the stock market fairly values stocks. Thus an investor cannot consistently find bargains. Theoretically, that means that your results would be just as good if you picked stocks at random.

Another way to accomplish the same thing is to purchase all the stocks in a given market or index, or at least a large statistical sampling of them. Then, you wouldn't have to worry whether you did or did not select top-performing stocks. If this sounds like a coward's way out, investing so broadly has much to recommend it. For example, it ensures that you will always match the performance of the market—or whatever share of it you've invested in.

Indexing is an especially useful strategy for pension funds. When hundreds of millions or even billions of dollars are invested, as is the case with major corporate and government pension funds, it becomes difficult, if not impossible, to beat the market. Some pension funds are so large they virtually *are* the market. Accepting this fact of life, large institutions have adopted the old adage, "if you can't beat 'em, join 'em." They find that they can save substantial sums of money on research, management fees and trading commissions by simply duplicating a broad cross-section of the market, such as the S&P 500. That way, they automatically achieve the same returns as the overall market.

Wells Fargo Investment Advisors, the leader in index fund management, claims that active management must outperform the market by 2% to make up for the transaction costs and higher management fees. Since the market is in a long-term uptrend, and institutions have far longer time horizons than individuals, they find that indexing can be a profitable strategy. With the institutions in the forefront, about one-fourth of all equity assets are now indexed.

Index funds also have a place in individual investors' portfolios. Already, about 6% of all stock mutual fund assets are indexed. Jack Bogle, Senior Chairman of Vanguard, predicts that one-fourth of the equity assets in mutual funds will eventually be invested in index funds. Here are some reasons why you should include index funds in your own portfolio:

■ Since the market is in a long-term uptrend, index funds—which by definition are always fully invested—maximize your potential for long-run gains. You won't lose out at the beginning of a strong uptrend, which can happen if an active manager has a high cash position.

■ Index funds have the lowest costs of any investment. That's very important! In the last chapter I showed that high expenses are a major reason for underperformance.

■ Index funds are tax efficient. Most have low turnovers, thereby minimizing transaction costs and taxes. The following table shows how two Schwab index funds deliver better after-tax returns than comparable actively-managed funds.

Table 48

	Before tax returns	**After tax returns**	**% lost to taxes**
Schwab 1000 Fund	18.86%	18.10%	0.76%
Avg large-cap fund	16.74	14.31	2.53
Schwab Small-Cap Index Fund	20.00	19.74	0.26
Avg small-cap fund	20.93	18.40	2.53

Source: Charles Schwab, returns 3 years ending June 1997, annualized.

Many index funds also keep expenses and turnover low by discouraging market timers, which they do either directly, or indirectly by levying a small sales charge payable to the fund, refusing to accept telephone exchanges and charging redemption fees.

■ You avoid the need to sort out the many contradictory market forecasts. Index funds are as close to a "no-brainer" as you can find in investing.

■ While expertise is needed to keep the fund tracking the index, and to keep expenses down, index funds aren't managed in the same sense as actively managed funds. That means you don't have the problem of a star fund manager quitting. You also won't have the problem of the manager's strategy going out of style.

I think index funds will become even better investments in the future because the market is becoming increasingly efficient as a result of increased competition, better communications, disclosure regulations, and powerful computers.

A variety of investors can benefit from index funds:

1) long-term, buy-hold investors, including dollar-cost-averagers (who are most affected by the drag of high expenses) can profit from the minimal expenses of index funds;

2) buy-and-hold investors who are comfortable with the return and degree of risk provided by the various index funds (betas are 1.00 plus);

3) market timers who are looking for guaranteed (as opposed to potentially superior) performance in their equity vehicles and who want a pure stock fund, rather than one in which a manager may take defensive cash positions in uncertain markets, can get predictability from index funds;

4) index funds are also ideal for people who don't want to pay a great deal of attention to their investments. This makes them suitable gifts for a young grandchild. The money isn't typically needed until college. The child's parents, with all the expenses and distractions of a new family, may not follow the financial markets closely. If you can afford only one fund, the best one to buy is the Vanguard Total Market Index Fund—it invests in everything.

While I believe strongly in this investment category, several factors can make it unsuitable for some investors. If you don't have a five-to-

Who can benefit from index funds?

ten year time horizon, or if you can't stand the volatility of a fund that is always fully invested, you are better off selecting a managed fund that has a record of building cash in unsettled markets. (Funds that remain fully invested throughout the market cycle will not do better than index funds. The Vanguard Index 500 Fund declined 21.7% in October, 1987, only slightly more than the average diversified fund, which was off 21.0%.) Furthermore, if your goal is top performance, you obviously won't find it in an index fund.

Another potential problem is that in long-running bull markets, index funds have large unrealized capital gains which will be realized if redemptions exceed purchases, as they might during bear markets. Unrealized capital gains amount to 34% of the assets of the Vanguard 500 Fund (as of June '97). However, Vanguard plans to minimize the potential tax-bite in that event by selling off the more recent, highest-cost purchases first (HIFO), and by funding redemptions from dividends when possible.

Index funds for individual investors have proliferated, so it's now easy to benefit from their relative performance certainty. They tend to fall into distinct categories: (1) pure no-load index funds designed for the long-term investor, which emphasize low costs; (2) somewhat higher-cost index funds or quasi-index funds designed for market timers; and (3) loaded index funds. I recommend funds in the first category, infrequently in the second, and never in the third. Index funds that carry commissions are a contradiction in terms. The point of an index fund for the long-term investor is low cost. You cannot get that with funds that carry commissions.

Low turnover index funds

Index funds keep expenses low by minimizing trading. But there's always an exception. In this case, the ASM Index 30 fund which has catered to market timers.

Fund	Index	Avg ann % turnover*
Vangd Spec-REIT Idx	real estate	0
Price Eqty Idx	S&P 500	1
Schwab 1000	largest US companies	2
Fidelity Spart Market Idx	S&P 500	2
Vangd Idx Total Stk Mkt	Wilshire 5000	2
Vangd Idx Europe	MSCI large cap	4
Vangd Idx Pacific	MSCI large cap	5
Vangd Idx 500	S&P 500	5
Dreyfus MidCap Idx	S&P Mid-Cap 400	18
Vangd Idx Extend Mkt	Wilshire 4500	18
Vangd Idx Balanced	Wilshire 5000/ Lehman Bd	26
Vangd Idx Growth	S&P 500	27
Vangd Idx Sm Cap	Russell 2000	27
Vangd Idx Value	S&P 500	29
ASM Index 30	DJIA	641

* Three-year average where available

S&P 500 Index funds

Index investors began by investing in the S&P 500. It's a broad group of large blue-chip stocks, yet a more manageable universe than, say, all the stocks traded on a particular exchange (for example, the New

York Stock Exchange). The S&P 500 is the most widely tracked index. Over thirty fund groups offer S&P 500 Index funds to individual investors.

Surprisingly, the variation in the funds' performances is significant. Since all have the same portfolios, the only difference is in their expense ratios. For the five years ending December 1997, their performances varied from 138.6% to 151.7%.

The leader in the field is Vanguard, whose 500 Index Portfolio, at $49 billion, is now the second largest mutual fund. It has achieved explosive growth, not so much because millions of investors have been converted to the merits of indexing, but because of its outstanding performance. For the three years ending with December 1997, the Vanguard 500 Portfolio ranked in the top 9% of all no-load equity funds. That's amazing for an investment whose goal is to be "average." But of course, during that period, large cap stocks outperformed small caps dramatically. (See Appendix A for our discussion of the index.)

Everybody agrees that the market for large capitalization stocks is very efficient; they trade at their true value because they are closely followed by many analysts who uncover their secrets.

Small cap index funds

By contrast, it is thought the market for small cap stocks is considerably less efficient because many of the smaller companies either are followed by only one or two analysts or are not followed at all. Thus, an active manager doing good research can find undiscovered gems among small cap stocks and achieve superior performance.

Probably there is a good deal of truth to this idea, but there's an offsetting disadvantage. The cost of trading small stocks can be significant. While the commission costs that mutual funds pay to buy and sell stocks are very low—particularly in contrast to what most individuals pay—that's not the whole story by any means. The real cost of trading is the spread between the bid and ask prices, which can be many times the commission cost. The ask price is what you pay to buy shares "at the market." The bid price is what you get for selling them "at the market." So, the spread is what you lose if you buy and immediately sell back the same shares.

Bid-ask spreads are not reported anywhere, but the Dimensional Fund Advisors group (an institutional fund group) has done an extensive analysis of their impact. DFA says spreads vary considerably based on market cap size. Among the largest and most actively traded blue chip stocks, the bid/ask spread is nominal; among micro cap stocks, however, it is frighteningly large. As shown in the table below, the DFA study ranked stocks by the decile size of their market caps. For the first decile (the 10% of stocks with the largest market caps), the spread was 0.5%. For the last decile of very small stocks, it was 6.2%—eleven times as large. The table also includes the average daily trading volume (per stock) by decile. The daily trading volume of an average decile-one stock is $47 million, roughly 400 times that of an average decline-ten stock.

Table 49

			Trading costs by capitalization size	
			Daily trading volume per issue	
Size Decile	Average price	Percent spread	Shares	Dollars
1	$58.10	0.43%	1,025,300	$60,395,991
2	43.11	0.54	532,300	20,527,366
3	38.62	0.63	333,913	10,632,328
4	32.84	0.82	251,164	6,054,271
5	28.57	1.02	164,599	3,627,266
6	26.20	1.31	109,518	2,474,907
7	22.54	1.52	88,308	1,613,991
8	20.40	1.95	57,545	807,078
9	15.66	2.71	33,014	385,640
10	8.99	5.81	18,637	165,649

Source: Bridge, 3/6/97

The proof is in the performance. My *Investor* newsletter follows 51 small-cap, no-load funds where five-year performance data is available. Included in my data base are two small-cap index funds. The best one, the DFA U.S. 9-10 Fund, ranked fifth. The Vanguard Small Cap Index Fund, was also nicely above average, ranking 20th.

Choose your index—and fund

A number of index funds now target other indexes. And some even invest passively in set lists of stocks of their own devising. In my opinion this is a welcome addition because the S&P 500 is dominated by large capitalization stocks. Thus index funds that follow the S&P 500 are investing in just that portion of the market, and as a practical matter, are really driven by the 50 largest stocks because of the way the index is weighted.

There is a place for funds that track indexes of small and medium cap stocks, international stocks, and bonds. First, let's examine some of the other index funds you may wish to employ. Then, at the end of this chapter, we will construct a full portfolio of index funds.

The Vanguard Extended Market Portfolio and the Fidelity Spartan Extended Market Index Fund seek to provide investment results that correspond to the performance of the universe of publicly-traded stocks that are outside the S&P 500. Its strategy is to buy a stratified sample of the small and medium sized companies in the Wilshire 4,500 stock index.

The Vanguard and Fidelity Total Stock Market Funds aim to match the Wilshire 5,000, the broadest stock index in the U.S. Because they are weighted by capitalization, these funds still emphasize big companies. For example, S&P 500 stocks account for 70% of the Total Market Funds. Mid-cap stocks are just 20% and small caps only 10%.

Vanguard also offers a Small Capitalization Stock Fund, which invests in 500-700 small companies from the Russell 2000 index. Owning the Extended and Small Cap portfolios would be particularly advantageous should the S&P 500 stocks lag. Charles Schwab also has a small cap index fund.

Both Vanguard and Wilshire now have index funds that are even more targeted. The Vanguard Index Growth and Index Value Funds split the 500 into those respective stocks. Wilshire splits the Wilshire 5000 four different ways: large company growth, large company value, small company growth, and small company value. I believe these narrowly based index funds are fine for sophisticated investors; however, they do require judgments as to which sector is best. Investors who want a "no-brainer" are better off buying everything: the Total Market Index for equities.

There is an index fund that holds the 30 Dow Jones stocks. But since Dow Jones & Co. only recently gave marketers permission to use their magic name, the fund is known as the ASM Index 30.

Souped-up index funds

Not to be confused with index funds are enhanced-index funds. They aim for a high degree of predictability relative to the S&P 500 Index. The Vanguard Growth & Income Fund (formerly called Vanguard Quantitative) matches the characteristics of the index. But the fund tries to outperform it by weighting its portfolio toward stocks that its computer models identify as the most attractive.

The Vanguard Index funds have expense ratios as low as 0.19% partly because they do not have portfolio managers. Unlike these funds, Growth & Income does have a portfolio manager. As a result, its expense ratio is about 0.38%. Of course, that compares with an expense ratio of over 1.5% for the average managed equity fund.

Other enhanced index funds are: Smith Breedon Equity Plus, Gateway Index Plus, and Pimco StocksPlus.

Vanguard also has four fixed-income index funds. The firm began with a Total Bond Market fund. Then in 1994 the fund group added three more: with short-, intermediate-, and long-term durations.

And just to put everything together in one fund, Vanguard next brought out a Balanced Index Fund, which combines the Total Market and Total Bond Index Funds in a 60/40 ratio.

International index funds

You can also invest passively overseas. Various index funds concentrate on Europe, the Pacific, emerging markets, and the EAFE Index.

I find the case for international index funds less persuasive than that for domestic stocks. The problem is not that the basic concept of indexing is less valid overseas. It's that the international index funds currently available don't, in my opinion, provide the proper allocations for minimizing risk.

The heart of most international index funds is the country allocation, which in most cases is based on the capitalization of the country's stock market—the larger the market, the greater the weight. This has not been a problem for index funds investing in the developed countries of Europe. However, it has been an actual or potential problem for index funds investing elsewhere.

In June 1997, the Vanguard Index Emerging Markets Fund allocated 13% of its assets to Malaysian stocks and 6% to Indonesian stocks. When these countries suffered currency devaluations and plunging stock markets two months later, the index fund was hard hit, declining 15%. That was a sounder drubbing than any actively-managed diversified emerging market fund took that month. It's one thing to have a few U.S. companies go down the tubes, perhaps representing 1-2% of a domestic index fund's assets. It's quite another problem when a whole country takes a hit.

Worse yet, there is the potential for further disappointments in the future. As of August 30, 1997, the fund's largest positions were in Brazil, 17%; Hong Kong, 15%; South Africa, 13%; Mexico, 12%; and Malaysia, 10%. Consider the 13% weighting in South Africa. What happens to the country after Nelson Mandela? The fund's weighting mirrors the Morgan Stanley Capital International Select Emerging Markets Index. Actively managed funds can and generally do avoid the special political and economic risks of South Africa. (Only two other no-load emerging markets funds have more than a

2% weighting in South Africa.) An index fund is stuck. It can't easily drop a country where problems are arising.

There's one other potential downside. For liquidity reasons, the Vanguard fund invests in only 14 of the 26 emerging markets in the Morgan Stanley Index. They may be missing good growth prospects down the road.

Similarly the Vanguard Pacific Index Fund has 77% of its assets in Japan. The Fidelity Spartan International Index Fund, which is based on the Morgan Stanley EAFE Index, has its largest holding in Japan—29%. Since 1982, bear markets in America have been short-lived. Japan has been through a long multi-year bear market.

Passively invested specialty funds

A number of funds follow indexes of their own creation or simply invest passively. The Schwab 1000 fund invests in an index of the 1,000 largest stocks. American Century Global Gold Fund invests in a universe of North American gold stocks. The American Century Global Natural Resources Index Fund holds energy and basic materials securities of companies that are in the Dow Jones World Stock Index. Rushmore's American Gas Index buys stocks of companies that are members of the American Gas Association. The adviser to the Domini Social Index Trust has developed her own index of 400 companies that meet certain social criteria.

Essentially these funds are investing passively. The major difference between them and standard index funds is that they don't have to track a well-known index. This can be an advantage because they reduce their costs by not having to replace stocks simply because Dow Jones or Standard & Poor's does. Any low-cost, passively managed fund can achieve the same objectives.

While Vanguard dominates the retail sale of index funds, you should be aware of Dimensional Fund Advisors (DFA), a large institutional group based in Santa Monica. The group has 22 domestic and international funds, which are classic examples of funds that achieve good results by investing passively. The DFA Japanese Small Company Fund has twice been the number one fund—in 1987 and 1994. DFA funds are available to individuals through investment advisors participating in Charles Schwab's FAS program. My *Handbook* has a comprehensive list of index funds.

How to use index funds

Given the low cost and low tax liabilities, long-term investors are well advised to build index fund positions into the core portion of their portfolios. That's the part of your portfolio that you keep through all kinds of markets.

Table 50 shows one way to set up a long-term buy-and-hold core portfolio using equity index funds. Up to half your fund assets can go into this core portfolio; the balance then can be actively managed.

I suggest that you put the biggest slice into the Vanguard Total Market Index Fund. However, since it is capitalization weighted, it mirrors large cap stocks more than the small cap stocks. But small companies sometimes are the best performers. Therefore, I've added medium and small cap index funds. Moreover, a properly diversified portfolio should contain some international exposure. But in view of the problems that I have cited above, I only recommend including an international index fund for Europe.

In order to make the figures easy to understand without using fractions, the percentages total 100%. If index funds comprise half of your portfolio, divide each percentage by two.

Table 50

Indexing a core portfolio with equities

Vanguard index fund	% Allocation
Total Market Portfolio	50%
Extended Market Portfolio	15%
Small Cap Fund	25%
Index Europe	10%
Total equity index funds	100%

In Table 51 it is the same core portfolio, but with a bond fund added.

Index funds belong in almost every portfolio. But they are not a total solution to successful investing. Most investors should have top-performing actively managed funds to balance their risk/reward goals.

The first index fund?

Simply matching the indexes is a relatively new concept. So I find it interesting that in 1938, long before anybody dreamed of index funds, a fund was organized that possessed most of the characteristics of today's modern versions. Founders Mutual, the oldest fund in the Founders group, was limited by its original charter to holding 40 stocks that were considered suitable for long-term investments—37 industrials, one insurance company, one railroad and one utility (AT&T). All were selected at the fund's inception. IBM was its largest investment. Other major stock holdings were Eastman Kodak, Sears, du Pont, Union Pacific, and Proctor & Gamble. Whenever new money became available, equal dollar purchases were made in every issue, in effect applying the principle of dollar-cost-averaging. No stock was ever sold. But by the end of 1983, 45 years later, the portfolio was down to 36 stocks—four had merged or gone bankrupt. Over the years the fund's performance was, as you might expect, roughly average. In 1983, Founders received permission from its shareholders to shed the original charter and provide the fund with active management. It is now called the Founders Blue Chip Fund.

Table 51

Indexing a core portfolio with equities and bonds

Vanguard index funds	% Allocation	
Equities	75%	
Total Market Portfolio		37%
Extended Market Portfolio		11%
Small Cap Fund		19%
Index Europe		8%
Bonds	25%	
Bond Market Intermediate		25%
Total	100%	

If you are a conservative investor, the actively-managed portion of your portfolio should be invested in growth-income, equity-income, and speciality fixed-income funds, such as GNMAs, that are less risky than index funds. The latter, of course, provide no downside protection whatsoever.

If you are an aggressive investor, then the actively managed portion of your portfolio can be placed in technology funds, other speculative sector funds, or even risky stocks or derivatives. Both types of investors should add actively-managed emerging market international funds, and possibly a Japan fund.

You will note that, for the first time, I made specific fund recommendations in this chapter. With index funds, I can do that. But it just isn't responsible to recommend the more erratically performing, actively-managed funds in a book. Such recommendations I reserve for my monthly newsletter.

One final item: if you implement an index fund strategy at Vanguard, as most investors do, you should be aware that their index funds also have a $10 annual account maintenance fee for investments under $10,000. With the minimum $3,000 investment this amounts to an additional charge of 0.33% charge, which more than doubles the expense ratio.

If you're still not convinced of the merits of indexing, listen to what the best active manager in the country—Warren Buffett—said about index funds in his 1997 Berkshire Hathaway annual report: "Most investors, both institutional and individual, will find that the best way to own common stocks is through an index fund that charges minimal fees. Those following this path are sure to beat the net results (after fees and expenses) delivered by the great majority of investment professionals."

CHAPTER 16

THE NO-LOAD FUND INVESTOR

Investing in new funds

Every year hundreds of new funds are launched. Since 1990, these launchings have averaged 472 a year, or more than one a day. And it will probably take a severe bear market to end this trend. Not that investors need more funds. But they keep sprouting up, for several reasons. More funds means more income to a fund group, and as experienced fund managers leave established groups they start funds of their own.

On the load fund side, salesmen push brand new funds or new series of old funds, perhaps thinking their customers will equate them with new issues of stocks. On the no-load side, the salesmen are within the marketing departments of the mutual fund groups. They attempt to attract investors to new funds by blitzing them with heavy publicity.

In fact, investing in brand-new funds is at best a mixed bag. There are some instances when you should jump in, other cases where you should wait until a fund has demonstrated its ability to perform.

In this chapter, I'll define a new fund as an initial offering, the same as a new issue of stock. A fund with even a short performance record is not considered a new fund.

When you buy an established fund, evaluating its performance is comparatively easy because it has a record. And it's relatively simple to get a fix on its investment objective by analyzing its portfolio and volatility. On the other hand, the initial offering of a mutual fund is a relatively untested commodity. You are essentially relying on the reputation of the portfolio manager and the fund group, since the prospectus provides little information on potential performance. With hundreds—or even thousands—of funds that have a known track record, there is certainly no need to take the blind risk of buying an unknown commodity.

As you might suspect, the performance of new funds varies greatly. I began analyzing new fund performance as far back as 1972 and generally found that about half outperformed their asset class benchmarks, and the other half underperformed. Thus, new funds performed about as well as established funds, on average. The odds of turning in above-average performance was generally a coin flip. That alone is sufficient reason to avoid new funds. While many are immediate winners, without performance records to analyze, identifying which ones will be is a more difficult task than selecting established funds by their track records.

Performance of new funds

But in recent years, this pattern may have changed. The funds that were launched in 1995 significantly outperformed their established counterparts the following year. The advantages were the greatest for the small company, aggressive growth, and technology—three categories with significant overlap. In 1996 new funds in those three categories again outperformed established funds, but lagged somewhat in the more conservative categories. The data for the income category is shown, but as noted in Chapter 8 this is a catchall. So the results are less meaningful.

Why are new funds now outperforming their established cousins? The answer, I think, is evidence of the tremendous growth of the industry. Small funds outperform large funds, and new funds almost always start small. As long as the bull market continues, the best-performing established funds are going to grow beyond their optimum size well within the three-year period some advisors prefer to see before they buy.

If the fund in question buys small cap stocks, there's also a good chance it might close to new investors before it establishes a three-year performance record. Artisan Small Cap and Montgomery Micro Cap closed in less than a year; ni Growth and ni Micro Cap funds closed in fourteen months; Oakmark Small Cap, Heartland Small Cap

Table 52

Performance of funds begun in 1995 and 1996

	1996 returns		1997 returns*	
	Avg. new fund	Avg. fund	Avg. new fund	Avg. fund
All stock funds	20.2	18.3	17.8	15.8
Diversified stock	21.3	18.6	21.5	21.0
Aggressive growth	25.2	19.1	22.4	16.5
Growth	22.9	19.0	22.9	23.8
Growth-income	20.3	20.7	22.2	24.5
Income	14.6	13.7	15.8	18.5
Small company	28.1	19.7	26.2	19.5
Technology	28.1	21.4	25.0	16.1
Global equity	19.1	16.8	9.7	11.2
International	13.0	14.9	-0.3	-1.6

Based on 134 new no-load funds launched in 1995
Based on 137 new no-load funds launched in 1996

*First 11 months

Contrarian and Wasatch Micro Cap all closed in less than three years after they were launched.

In addition to superior performance in many cases, new funds have two other advantages over existing funds:

■ *The new fund may offer a tax advantage.* If you buy existing successful funds with substantial appreciation, which is often the case during a long bull market, you are buying somebody else's tax liability (as I discuss in Chapter 22). This can't happen with a new fund.

■ *A new fund may be favored* by a large fund group. Although the fund group will vehemently deny it, I believe that some new funds get first crack at hot new stock issues and other favored stocks.

The first month study

With the avalanche of new funds in recent years, we are seeing more funds doing quite well right from the opening bell.

With my suspicions aroused that some large fund groups might be favoring their new offspring in some way, I decided to do some rigorous analysis in my newsletter. I wanted to see whether there was any truth to my suspicions. My methodology was to take each new fund's performance during its first calendar month and compare that with the average fund in its objective category. To simplify the study,

I restricted my appraisal to actively-managed, diversified, domestic equity funds. From 1989 through October 1994, 105 funds met my criteria.

I found that the new funds did slightly better than average in their initial month. They posted an average 1.1% gain for the month, as compared to a 0.3% gain for the benchmarks. However, this 0.8% differential drops to 0.3% if I compute the median fund, perhaps a fairer measure, since two new funds had extreme success in their first month. For example, Monetta Mid-Cap Equity gained a phenomenal 16.7% during its first full month, 13.1% better than the average growth fund that month!

Table 53

Best first-month's performance

	New fund	Adv. over benchmark
Monetta Mid-Cap Eqty	16.7	13.2
Janus Enterprise	13.9	12.1
Fidelity Emerging Gr	14.8	6.6
Robrtsn Steph Contrarian	6.9	6.4
Janus Balanced	6.4	6.0
PBHG Emerg Gro	10.9	5.8

My next step was to see if there was any pattern by fund family. Do some large fund families favor new funds by loading them up with IPO's? Are other funds in the group buying the new fund's stocks to drive up the price? And can you profit from this knowledge?

I took an average of each fund family's new funds to see if there was any pattern. Families with only one new fund are excluded from the following table.

I want to emphasize that my evidence is *statistical*. My results may be due to chance or nothing more than fortuitous timing. (That was certainly the case when the Robertson Stephens Contrarian Fund was launched during a month when the market was taking a pounding.) Nevertheless, if you like the concept of a new fund or a particular manager's record and want to take a flyer on it, I think you would have a better chance with a new fund from Janus, Fidelity, Strong, Price or Lindner. The odds seem especially good at Fidelity; nine of the family's eleven new funds surpassed their benchmarks.

Table 54

Average difference in total return New funds versus their benchmarks		
Family	**# funds**	**Avg diff**
Janus	4	5.5
Robertson Stephens	2	4.4
Lindner	3	2.6
Strong	3	2.0
Fidelity	10	1.9
Price, Rowe	4	1.6
Evergreen	3	1.4
Crabbe Huson	2	1.3
Mean	—	*0.8*
IAI	4	0.6
Royce	3	0.3
Median	—	*0.3*
Benham	3	0.2
Columbia	2	0.1
Dreyfus	5	0.0
Merriman	4	-0.2
Invesco	4	-0.3
USAA	2	-0.4
Montgomery	3	-0.5
Loomis Sayles	3	-0.8
Portico	3	-1.0
Scudder	3	-1.1
Capiello Rushmore	3	-2.1

When to buy new funds

Best reason to buy a new fund: you find one focused on a *new investing concept or niche*, or an established approach first becomes available without a load.

A good example occurred in 1990, when *The No-Load Fund Investor* newsletter recommended the newly formed T. Rowe Price New Asia Fund. It was the first no-load to specialize in buying stocks in the fast-growing Pacific Rim countries (excluding Japan). Managed by Price Fleming International, Inc., the fund has exemplary lineage. That firm has had outstanding results with four other Price international funds. My recommendation proved sound. The fund ranked second among all international and global funds from 1991 to 1993. (The number one fund was a single country fund buying only stocks in Hong Kong.) Similarly, in April 1996 the *Investor* recommended the Vontobel Eastern European Fund, the first no-load to invest in this emerging area. Launched in February, the fund was up 76% for its first 12 months.

Another type of new fund that's perfectly all right to buy: an index fund. For obvious reasons, age makes no difference.

Flying solo ain't easy

When a popular, experienced fund manager moves to a new fund, either in his group, or with another established family, that may be a reason to buy his new fund. However, when he goes off to start his own fund group, prudence suggests a wait-and-see attitude before buying. Usually the manager is leaving a well-oiled investment management machine, with in-depth support of all sorts, for the dubious advantage of building his own organization from the ground up. That takes courage, but it also takes time. Some cases in point.

Gerry Tsai left Fidelity to start the Manhattan Fund in 1967. A legend at Fidelity, Tsai did not do nearly as well on his own. Manhattan fund performed poorly until Neuberger-Berman took it over years later.

Richard Fontaine put together an outstanding record at T. Rowe Price. Since 1989, though, he has been the principal in the Fountaine funds, a small group of three funds. None of them could remotely be considered a star.

Donald Yacktman compiled a superior record running the Selected Funds. His Yacktman Fund was the fourth worst equity fund in 1993, its first full year. (There was a dramatic turnaround in 1994—which was the time to buy the fund.)

In late 1995 Garret Van Wagoner left the top-performing Govett Small Companies Fund to launch his own group of three funds. They opened to new Investors on January 1, 1996. For the first four months, all the funds turned in exceptional performances and attracted a billion dollars in assets. But then, when technology stocks corrected in June, 1996, Van Wagoner's funds declined far more than other aggressive funds. As I write, he has yet to recover. The average Van Wagoner fund was *down* 16.5% in 1997, while the typical aggressive-growth fund gained 17.0%.

Of course, not every new operation strikes out. Elizabeth Bramwell, formerly with Gabelli funds, went out on her own in 1994. In its first year, her Bramwell Growth Fund performed well above average. Similarly, in late 1994, Carlene Murphy Ziegler, the co-manager of the Strong Common Stock Fund, and her husband Andrew Ziegler, the president of the Strong funds, left to start their own group. Their new fund, the Artisan Small Cap Fund, gained 39.9% its first year, an above average performance.

If you run across a situation where you believe it makes sense to follow a star manager when he or she sets up their own group, ask what kind of support they'll have within their new organization. Do they have several analysts working for them? Or are they essentially on their own? Who is going to do the back office work? Will they have the time to spend running the fund? Or must they devote hours and days being a media star in order to gather assets quickly? It makes a difference?

Clones

Some new funds are "clones" of older funds. In 1985, for example, Vanguard closed Explorer and Windsor, then offered in their place Explorer II and Windsor II. The new funds had new managements. (Don't bother hunting for Explorer II; in 1990 Vanguard folded it back into Explorer.) Other funds have launched clones using the same management—Mutual Beacon and Nicholas II are well-known examples.

In recent years, a number of small cap funds have spun off other funds that appear to be clones, but really aren't. Some examples: Babson Enterprise II, Skyline Special Equities II and Quantitative Numeric II. All of them buy larger company stocks than their originals. In most cases they were cloned because the original small cap fund had closed to new investors, or was about to.

It's best to evaluate these clones as if they are totally different funds. In some cases they have different policies or managers. Others perform differently, even with the same policies, because they were initially smaller.

Sales people love to sell new funds

New funds are easy to sell. That's why every fad brings new funds. When options burst onto the investing scene back in the late 1970s, fund groups rushed to bring out option funds. Sales were brisk, even though it was an untried concept with no record of success. At the peak, 21 option funds existed, 19 of them load funds. None has ever done particularly well. They were just a jazzy sounding product—a natural for salespeople.

An artificial marketing period pressures investors

One reason why salespeople find new load funds easy to sell is that the funds' sponsors often set a limited period of time for the original underwriting. There is often no commission during this period—only an underwriting fee.

After the period ends, the fund often closes for sales for a short time. In June 1992, Dean Witter Reynolds launched the North

American Government Income Trust, a fund that owns U.S., Canadian and Mexican bonds. The initial prospectus noted that the initial offering period was from June 24th to July 24th. A continuous offering period was to commence two weeks later. (In addition, load fund marketers sometimes reduce the minimum investment during the initial offering period, although in the case of the Dean Witter Fund there was no difference.) These sales tactics, although they frequently are successful, are nothing more than psychological gimmicks to make the offering seem more desirable. The underwriting fee is the same as the load. Closing the fund for a short period is done only to force investors to make a decision before the underwriting period ends. You don't save anything, and money can always be invested elsewhere during the closed period.

With the huge popularity of mutual funds in recent years, an unbelievable amount of money has poured into the initial offerings of funds. Sales of fixed-income funds were especially popular until 1994, when rising interest rates drove bond prices down and investors away. Previously, though, investors had poured billions into government bond funds, mostly those with loads. The new funds weren't superior to existing funds. They didn't have greater yields than existing income funds with comparable objectives and policies.

New bond funds

What difference does it make whether you buy an existing fund that already owns certain bonds, or a new fund that goes out and buys the same bonds? In either case, you receive the same dividend. The same is true for equity funds investing in dividend-paying stocks. A fund may be new, but it's buying old stocks.

Three no-load short-term global income funds were launched in 1991. They attracted a lot of money, but the new concept's initial results disappointed shareholders. They generally underperformed similar domestic funds in 1992.

In sum, while no absolute rules exist in the selection of mutual funds, and while some new funds will become instant successes, you'll fare better in the long run if you buy funds that have at least a few months' experience. For growth or aggressive growth funds, which are often more erratic, wait at least a half-year, and preferably a year. Let somebody else go through the growing pains with new offerings. Don't buy until you see proof of a fund's success.

Watch out for gimmick funds

Be particularly careful before you buy new funds that are being launched purely for marketing reasons. The HomeState Year 2000 Fund is an example. It was first offered in October 1997 in the hopes of cashing in on companies trying to provide solutions to the year 2000 problem. (You have read about this nightmare: allegedly, many of the world's computers will go berserk on December 31, 1999 because years are programmed in just two digits—00. Thus, computer programs ostensibly will mistake 2000 for 1900. Everybody has been aware of the problem for several years.) Here's the rub. The fund is essentially a technology sector fund. But since the market anticipates, many of the stocks of companies working on the 2000 problem have already had their runup. Naturally, this fund carries a load. Who would voluntarily buy it?

Some other examples: In August 1996, the Sportsfund was launched to capitalize on the Summer Olympic games and the interest in professional sports. The fund never performed and was liquidated some eight months later. At the same time the WWW Internet Fund was launched to capitalize on the interest in cyberspace. As I write this, the fund, now with $2.3 million in assets, is bumping along at the end of the pack; it's one of the worst funds in the technology sector.

In 1990, Lord Abbott, a load fund group, launched a new fund called Lord Abbott Equities. It featured an unusual selling point. If 10 years later, in the year 2000, your assets in the fund were worth less than your purchase price, the fund would make up the difference. Of course, you had to have reinvested all distributions over the decade. Some deal! The guarantee is backed by insurance which will cost you a stiff 0.5% per year. The guarantee is in nominal dollars—not inflation-adjusted—and in no decade since 1929-38 have stocks declined. For the five years ending September 1997, the fund lagged the average large value fund by 1.3% per year (more than one-third of that difference due to the insurance premium). While the fund's marketing gimmick reassured a few investors (assets are a low $63 million), it proved costly for them.

Some of the new closed-ends launched in recent years could also be considered gimmick funds. Some were single country international funds, launched without great regard for the prospects of equities in the country. Others offered guaranteed yields, which are in part a return of capital.

Don't be gulled by such gimmicks. Insist that a fund specializing in the latest investment fad demonstrate that its concept makes sense before you buy.

Another somewhat unsettling trend: writers of financial newsletters starting their own funds. A number of the best known authors of market timing and stock advisory newsletters have launched funds. One might think that newsletter advisory skills are transferable, but the evidence seems to indicate otherwise. Actually managing money is different from merely recommending action in a publication.

In 1987, Al Frank, publisher of the highly successful Prudent Speculator newsletter, became the sub-advisor to the Prudent Speculator Leveraged Fund. The new fund gained 12.7% in 1988, its first full year of operation. The newsletter's recommendations had a 49.2% gain that same year. Again, wait until these funds are performing before you buy. In 1989, the Prudent Speculator Leveraged Fund was the second worst no-load equity fund; in 1990, it was the third worst. As a result Frank was replaced by another advisor.

Similarly, Stephen Leeb, the editor of the Personal Finance and Big Picture newsletters, launched the Leeb Personal Finance Fund in 1991, Now renamed the U.S. Global Megatrends Fund. it's been a mediocre performer the latest five years.

Finally, don't get excited because a firm with proven funds trots out a new one. That's no guarantee of success either. Every fund family now wants a complete product line. The fact that a group has done well with domestic funds, for example, is no guarantee that it will be able to manage a superior international fund.

New funds are different from new stocks

There are times to buy new funds, but don't buy them just because they are new. Don't confuse a new fund with an IPO—initial public offering—for new stocks.

New stocks often are profitable because a fixed number of shares is available. If demand is great, the price increases, sometimes sharply. We've all read about the difficulties of obtaining shares of these new issues in joyful anticipation of windfall profits. On August 10, 1995, Netscape Communications, a company many thought could achieve a dominant position in software for the Internet, offered 5.75 million shares in a public underwriting at $28 a share. (The underwriters had originally priced the new issue at $14 per share, but seeing the demand, had doubled the price a few days earlier.) The stock opened far higher, at $71, as eager investors, mostly institutions, who were unable to place orders at the original offering price, fought for the limited number of shares available. The stock surged to as high as $74.75 by noon before finishing the day at $58.25.

Open-end mutual funds are entirely different, and in fact almost opposite. They can create an unlimited number of new shares as public demand increases. Since all shares are sold at the fund's net asset value, buying early provides no advantage whatsoever.

Some quick arithmetic illustrates this point. Assume a fund has $100,000 of assets and 100,000 shares outstanding. Each share is, therefore, worth $1. Now, suppose a new investor wants to purchase 10,000 shares. In the case of an open-end no-load mutual fund, the new investor would also pay $1 per share—the net asset value. Ten thousand new shares would be created. The total asset value of the fund would increase to $110,000. The number of shares would increase by the same percentage. And the per-share value for both old and new investors would remain the same.

Table 55

	Sales don't change NAV		
	Total assets	**Number of shares**	**Price per share**
Originally	$100,000	100,000	$1
New sale	10,000	10,000	1
After sale	110,000	110,000	1

Unlike stocks, there is no advantage to buying early. You always pay net asset value for mutual fund shares—no more, no less.

CHAPTER 17

THE NO-LOAD FUND INVESTOR

Creating a profitable portfolio of mutual funds

It's a New Age dilemma—where to put how much of your assets. The answer, of course, depends on your personal circumstances and your prospects. As either one changes, you want to transfer part of your wealth from one type of investment to another, searching for a portfolio mix that's both right for you and right for the time.

In previous chapters, I explained how various types of funds—aggressive growth, growth, income—were suitable for some investors, but not for others. Here, I put it all together, showing you how to lay out your investments so that your investment portfolio can achieve your objectives. It's wrong to buy a fund, or any security, in a vacuum. You should always consider its place in your overall strategy.

Understanding the securities you own is half the battle. Begin by grouping them according to their objectives. Put the riskiest funds (or stocks) in the aggressive equities section, growth and growth-income funds in the conservative equities section, bond funds (corporate or municipal) in the fixed-income category and any money market funds in a separate section. Group sector funds with diversified funds of like risk levels. Do *not* make gross, undifferentiated categories. Stock mutual funds, for example, is too general a category. Another guideline: don't make distinctions without a difference. Bonds and bond mutual funds should be in the same category.

Know what you own

The categories are not hard and fast. For instance, if you are primarily interested in income, you may want to put growth-income and income funds, which contain high-dividend stocks, in your income category. Growth funds could be lumped in with the aggressive growth category.

Table 56 gives you a model that you can adapt to your own situation. If you own a personal computer, you can set up a sophisticated tracking system. However, you can easily keep your portfolio up-to-date with only an inexpensive pocket calculator.

Here's how to lay out your portfolio: In the first column to the right of each fund's name, write the number of shares you own. Second, put the market price of each. Third, the current market value (price x number of shares = value). In the fourth column, calculate the percentage of your total portfolio that each fund (and each category) makes up. This is essential because it helps you to make certain that your portfolio is in roughly the proportion you have decided on, and allows you to keep it that way.

At least quarterly, update your figures by noting the number of shares and the current price of each fund or security and then determining the worth of your portfolio. That way you can easily keep track of your overall allocations, as well as spotting funds that are performing poorly.

You will also want to take note of the yield you are receiving from your funds. First get your dividend per share for the latest twelve months. If you have owned your fund for more than one year, you will find that data complete in the statements your funds send you. If the information's not there, you can call the fund directly and ask. Also *Barron's* lists annual per share dividends each week.

Next calculate your total dividend by multiplying the dividend per share by the total number of shares you own. Finally, figure your yield by dividing your dividend by the market value of your shares.

The yield is an interesting yardstick for comparing various investments. But it is much more important in evaluating bonds than stocks. If you are primarily interested in receiving income from your funds, keep track of current yields (but don't forget total return). Growth stock investors will be much more concerned with the current market value and total return of their holdings.

The simple form you have now created provides you with a wealth of information. It tells you your exact asset allocation. If you are heavily invested in speculative stock funds, you know you will be selling when the market goes down. If inflation surges, you know to what extent you will need to lighten up on bonds. You know how much cash you have on hand. By subtracting the amount you need to keep aside for emergencies or for needs in the near future, you will then know how much is available for investment.

Note that in the model portfolio in Table 56 I included only those assets, primarily financial, that are "investments," which I define as:

■ Assets you can control; assets that you would be willing to sell for spending money, or that generate income. The cash value of a life insurance policy is an investment that can be included in the fixed-income category. If you own rental property, that can be listed. I would include a 401(k), which you can control. But I do not suggest including your potential Social Security entitlement or a defined benefit retirement plan.

■ Assets that can be valued. I would exclude furniture, antiques, jewelry, most stamp collections if they are hard to value and hard to sell. Stock options on your company's stock are certainly assets, but if they have no present value, they're best left out.

■ To be included, an asset must have substantial value. Otherwise it's not a meaningful addition. One test: If the asset were not included in the portfolio would you structure the portfolio differently?

■ Consumption assets should be excluded. A consumption asset is a depreciating asset. A car is a consumption asset even though it may have considerable liquidation value. That's because if you dispose of a car, you generally need another. It's basically an expense.

If you want to know your total assets, for example for estate planning, you can easily compose an overall financial statement. Simply add your home, cars, valuable household belongings, pensions and Social Security entitlement. You then deduct mortgages, loans, bills, and other liabilities to get your net worth.

How wealthy should you be?

Whatever your age, whatever your income, how much should you be worth right now. Thomas Stanley and William Danko, the authors of *The Millionaire Next Door* have developed a simple rule of thumb to compute your expected net worth. Simply multiply your age times your realized pretax annual household income from all sources except inheritances. Divide by ten. This, less any inherited wealth, is what your net worth should be.

For example if you are 40 years old, make $90,000 a year, and have

Table 56

Personal financial assets

Model portfolio

Security	No Shares par value	Market price $	Market value $	% of total	Dividend per share	Dividend total $	Yield %
Aggressive Equities							
Vontobel Eastern European	941.512	15.25	14,358	3.3	0.00	0	0.0
Neuberger-Ber Manhattan	1,575.375	11.01	17,345	4.0	0.01	16	0.1
Hotchkis & Wiley Small Cap	642.431	24.92	16,009	3.7	0.05	32	0.2
Vanguard Total Stk Market Index	798.671	22.74	18,162	4.2	0.32	256	1.4
Total aggressive equities	—	—	65,874	15.2	—	303	0.5
Conservative equities							
Dodge & Cox Balanced	587.256	66.78	39,217	9.0	2.22	1,304	3.3
Fidelity Convertible Securities	1,526.677	17.51	26,732	6.2	0.70	1,069	4.0
Neuberger-Ber Partners	1,437.444	26.30	37,805	8.7	0.19	273	0.7
Pacific Telesis	200	25.75	5,150	1.2	2.13	426	8.3
Lngleaf Partners Reality	1,354.231	17.35	23,496	5.4	0.13	176	0.7
Vanguard Wellington	1,238.562	29.45	36,476	8.4	1.12	1,387	3.8
Windsor II - IRA acc't	1,455.871	28.62	41,667	9.6	0.66	961	2.3
Total conservative equities	—	—	210,542	48.5	—	5,596	2.7
Fixed income							
Janus Flexible Income	851.204	9.87	8,401	1.9	0.68	579	6.9
Fidelity Global Bond	645.547	9.09	5,868	1.4	0.50	323	5.5
Fidelity Ltd Term Muni	861.345	9.94	8,562	2.0	0.49	422	4.9
Monthly Payment Series # 276	10	548.00	5,480	1.3	40.05	401	7.3
My company savings plan	800	16.80	13,440	3.1	0.95	760	5.7
Rowe Price Spectrum Income	1,540.431	11.66	17,961	4.1	0.71	1,094	6.1
Cats 0% 8—15—99 - IRA	15,000	0.83	12,450	2.9	0.07	1,050	8.4
USLIFE Income Fund	1,300	10.13	13,163	3.0	0.76	988	7.5
Vanguard U.S. Treasury Int.	3,273.057	10.67	34,924	8.0	0.65	2,127	6.1
Total fixed inc.	—	—	120,249	27.7	—	7,743	6.4
Cash							
Vanguard Prime MM	31,250	1.00	31,250	7.2	0.05	1,563	5.0
Bank money market account	6,125	1.00	6,125	1.4	0.04	245	4.0
Bank checking account	350	1.00	350	0.1	0.00	0	0.0
Total cash	—	—	37,725	8.7	—	1,808	4.8
Total Financial	—	—	434,390	100.0	—	15,450	3.6
Recap							
Total aggressive equities	—	—	65,874	15.2	—	303	0.5
Total conservative equities	—	—	210,542	48.5	—	5,596	2.7
Total fixed income	—	—	120,249	27.7	—	7,743	6.4
Total cash	—	—	37,725	8.7	—	1,808	4.8
Total Financial	—	—	434,390	100.0	—	15,450	3.6

investments that return another $10,000, multiply $100,000 by 40—that equals $4 million—and divide by ten. Your net worth should be $400,000. If it's not, you probably should be saving more and spending less.

"Absence makes the heart grow fonder."
"Out of sight, out of mind."

"He who hesitates is lost."
"Look before you leap."

"It's not whether you win or lose, but how you play the game."
"The end justifies the means."

In investing, there are two theories about diversification:

1) *"Don't put all your eggs in one basket."*
2) *"Put all your eggs in one basket—and watch that basket!"*

The first advice, a way of saying "diversify," is the easy winner. The contrary advice ("put all your eggs in one basket—and watch that basket") is simply unworkable. Look what happened within a few months back in 1995:

First there was the Mexican Peso crisis which was unanticipated by virtually every layman and professional. It's part of the reason why a number of the Fidelity funds were underperformers that year. With the investment expertise available at Fidelity, literally hundreds of investment professionals and their extensive information sources, you'd think that the company wouldn't have any trouble "watching that basket," and reacting in time. But they did.

Next was the Orange County California derivative fiasco—also a surprise to Wall Street. In this case, the significant fact is that not a single no-load tax-free fund was significantly impacted. That's because even the funds investing exclusively in California munis all were properly diversified.

Another reason why "watching the basket" doesn't work is the possibility of fraud. The non-diversified American Heritage Fund was top-rated from 1991 to 1993. Then in early 1994, the fund took a big hit as a result of sharp declines in Spectrum Technology, one of its largest hold-

Reaffirming the importance of diversification

ings. After the stock had declined from about 11 to 3, Heritage's port-folio manager, Heiko Thieme, bought another large block virtually doubling his bet.

Since I had strongly backed the fund when it was top-rated, Thieme called me to explain his strategy. He believed the fundamentals were still there. He talked about using his block of stock to make changes in the Board of Directors and management. There was no doubt he was watching that basket closely. My immediate reaction was that he had become dangerously undiversified. In the *Investor's* next issue, I said, "Sell American Heritage." It was the only time in the history of the newsletter that I ever put sell advice in the headline. As a result of my warning, long-term subscribers who heeded my message escaped with the bulk of their profits intact. The fund ended the year down 35.4%, one of worst performances of 1994.

On January 26, 1995, Spectrum Technology filed for bankruptcy. On March 23, 1995, the company's former president and nine of his business associates were indicted for fraud. While fraud is not unknown, luckily it is uncommon. But the sad reality is that when it happens, there is really no protection—other than diversification.

Allocating your assets

Once you know just what you own, you can evaluate your portfolio, and make changes as necessary to ensure that your assets conform to your personal objectives.

In earlier chapters, I characterized the main types of mutual funds and their appropriateness for various sorts of investors. But obviously, just because you are looking for aggressive growth you wouldn't put all your assets into aggressive growth funds. A major part of your wealth should be in more conservative investments for proper diversification. Similarly, even if your objective is current income, don't bet the ranch on fixed-income funds. Some of your money should be in income-producing stock funds to provide you with protection against inflation.

In constructing your own portfolio, apply the principle of the financial pyramid. In this paradigm, safe investments go at the base of the triangle. Every investor should have some foundation investments (money market funds, bank deposits, short-term bond funds, conservative equity income funds). The next level of investment is securities that provide for long-term growth of capital. These should be comparatively conservative, such as dividend-paying growth funds, balanced funds or intermediate-term bond funds.

Depending on your situation, a greater or lesser portion of your portfolio should be in growth investments. Then, a smaller amount of your investments go into more speculative vehicles, which are higher up the pyramid. These are primarily aggressive growth stock funds. And finally, at the top of the pyramid are the highly speculative investments that most investors will omit. At most, a very small amount of your money will be allocated to such high-risk investments that promise a very substantial return if they are successful, but may also result in a major loss if they're not. Here, we're talking about initial public offerings, speculative over-the-counter stocks, and the like.

Chart 57
_____

The most important decision you will ever make

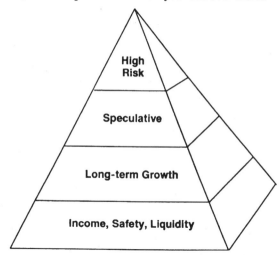

In Table 58, I show three different investment programs, each with differing risk levels. I then show sample fund portfolios for each program. This table is taken from the February, 1998 issue of my *No-Load Fund Investor* newsletter. An up-to-date version with current fund and cash position recommendations appears every month in the newsletter.

While model portfolios are sometimes categorized solely by risk orientation—for example, a portfolio with nothing but aggressive growth funds, etc.—I don't buy that approach. A portfolio of funds that all have the same risk level is not a complete investment program. Moreover, investors often don't understand which risk category is most appropriate. So I offer various model portfolios oriented by life-style goals. Each portfolio represents a complete investment program—using the concept of the financial pyramid—for all your financial assets. I have not shown the amount of cash you may need for emergencies or for everyday expenses. That depends on your personal circumstances.

The *Wealth Builder Portfolio* is designed for working investors whose goal is capital accumulation. It takes above-average risks to achieve its goals. Current income is not a factor in this portfolio, so bond funds are generally excluded.

The *Pre-Retirement Portfolio* has a more conservative outlook than the Wealth Builder. Designed for investors who are within ten years of retirement, it generally avoids the aggressive growth funds that can suffer the most severe short-term losses. This portfolio normally invests in equity income, growth-income and lower volatility growth funds, as well as fixed-income or money market funds.

The *Retirement Portfolio* emphasizes income and capital preservation and growth since a major portion of the portfolio is generally invested in equity income and growth-income funds. It is usually best suited for couples in their sixties and early seventies who anticipate spending many years in retirement. Bond or money funds provide current income and minimize price fluctuations.

I emphasize that these are models and should be adjusted to your own risk preferences and lifestyle. For example, if you are retired yet are still reinvesting your dividends, the Retirement Portfolio may be too conservative for you. Consider staying with the Pre-Retirement Portfolio. Furthermore, low tax bracket investors should use taxable bond funds; high bracket taxpayers will generally benefit from municipal bond funds. Note that bond fund recommendations are for stability and income; if money funds are recommended, they are for stability when equity market conditions are unsettled.

Average betas are computed to show the risk differences between portfolios.

What percent of your portfolio should be in stocks?

The answer really depends on the amount of *risk* that you are willing to take, and your *time horizon*. An all-stock fund portfolio will, over the long-run, achieve higher returns, but at the expense of taking greater risk. Portfolios balanced between stocks and bonds will typically provide lower returns than an all-stock portfolio, but will not be subject to as much downside risk. That is why my newsletter's Wealth

Table 58

Model investment portfolios

Fund	Obj	Beta	February returns	Latest 12-month returns	Rec. portfolio % Dist.
Wealth Builder Portfolio					
Hotchkis & Wiley Sm Cap	growth	0.60	6.7	37.4	10%
Neuberger Berman Partners	growth	0.87	7.9	30.8	20%
Babson Growth	growth	0.97	7.7	33.1	10%
Montgomery Emerging Mkts	int'l	1.00	6.8	-17.8	5%
Price European	int'l	0.47	7.3	29.6	10%
Amer Century Inc & Growth	gr-inc	0.94	8.9	38.2	15%
CGM Realty	sector	0.25	-3.7	18.0	10%
Price Equity Income	income	0.63	4.8	27.5	20%

Avg beta: 0.72

Int'l 15%

Long-Term Equities 85%

Fund	Obj	Beta	February returns	Latest 12-month returns	Rec. portfolio % Dist.
Pre-Retirement Portfolio					
Gabelli Growth- **N**	growth	1.05	8.6	47.2	10%
Third Ave. Value- **W**↓	growth	0.60	6.2	24.4	10%
Montgomery Emerging Mkts	int'l	1.00	6.8	-17.8	5%
Vanguard Index Europe	int'l	0.52	7.8	37.5	10%
Baron Growth & Income	gr-inc	0.80	4.3	31.0	15%
Price Equity Income	income	0.63	4.8	27.5	15%
Fidelity Real Estate	sector	0.25	-1.8	15.3	15%
Price, Rowe Spectrum-Inc	bond	0.24	1.0	13.0	20%

Avg beta: 0.57

Bonds 20%   Int'l 15%

Long-Term Equities 65%

Fund	Obj	Beta	February returns	Latest 12-month returns	Rec. portfolio % Dist.
Retirement Portfolio					
Vanguard Windsor II	gr-inc	0.83	7.3	32.5	10%
Amer Century Inc & Gro- **W**↑	gr-inc	0.94	8.9	38.2	15%
Heartland Value Plus	gr-inc	0.24	2.6	27.1	10%
Janus Overseas	int'l	0.59	7.7	23.0	5%
Price European	int'l	0.47	7.3	29.6	5%
Dodge & Cox Balanced	income	0.60	3.3	21.8	10%
Cohen & Steers Realty	sector	0.16	-1.3	16.2	10%
Vanguard Short-Term Corp	bond	0.09	0.0	7.3	15%
Price, Rowe Spectrum-Inc	bond	0.24	1.0	13.0	20%

Avg beta: 0.44

Bonds 35%   Int'l 10%

Long-Term Equities 55%

N = New selection this month   **W** = Change in portfolio weighting ↑↓

Source: The No-Load Fund Investor, March, 1998.

Builder portfolio, which I've just described, seldom includes bond funds. The two more conservative portfolios usually do. Wealth Builder is for younger investors with longer time horizons. The other two are for investors who typically have less time.

I've described my three model portfolios in terms of age, a method that assumes that the amount of risk you can take declines with age. It's a common way to identify the suitability of a portfolio.

Unfortunately, age is a poor proxy for time horizon, the real criteria. Funds that provide these age-based models fall back upon simplistic formulas because they can't possibly know the personal needs of each shareholder. So, they reduce the allocation design process to three or four convenient baskets—take your pick. Investment publications simplify the concept for much the same reason, and also because they have space limitations.

But there is far more to finding the suitable risk level than checking your age. Nor are there any other "cookie cutter" solutions that really work. Everyone's needs are unique. You should give much time and thought to the design of your personal asset allocation portfolio to achieve the proper risk level. This is more important than stock or fund selection. Here are the important investment considerations you should take into account:

Your time horizon. That is, how much time do you expect to have before you need to begin using the money for either income (e.g. retirement) or a lump-sum payment (e.g. a house, your kids' college educations)? This consideration outweighs your age in importance, because financial objectives vary for people of the same age. A twenty-year-old could be saving for a retirement decades from now, or to buy a house in just a few years. The investment guidelines for reaching these objectives differ because the cost of a bad investment varies according to your time horizon. In the first case, the investor can afford to take a substantial risk because even if the investment were made at the worst possible moment, the mistake can be overcome by holding on. The second investor, who needs his money in a few years, should invest more conservatively because it's difficult to overcome bad timing in such a brief period.

Don't assume that you must be conservative because you are older, or aggressive because you are younger. It's truly your time horizon that counts most. For purposes of establishing your investment time horizon, focus on when you expect to need access to all your income or assets, assuming all goes well. Bear in mind that a person retiring at age 65 doesn't need all his retirement funds at once. Assuming a 20-year life expectancy, the average retirement dollar is needed ten years later, or at age 75.

Your wealth. Another premise of asset allocation is that risk can be increased with wealth. For example, if you are retired and living on investment income and the return on your assets is just sufficient to make ends meet, then you can't afford much risk. On the other hand, if your assets are great enough that a major loss won't affect your lifestyle, then you can afford greater risks.

A simple yet effective way of determining how much risk you can afford, based on your accumulated assets, is to multiply your equity assets by 8%. Consider this a conservative estimate of what assets might earn, *after inflation*, over a long period of time. For example, if you have $1 million in equity-based assets, that should provide a total return of $80,000 a year. Add, say, $20,000 in Social Security payments or a pension, and you might generate an annual retirement income of $100,000. Now, suppose you lose one-fourth of it. The $1 million shrinks to $750,000, and your 8% return declines to $60,000 per year, or a total of $80,000 with the pension. For many people that would still be sufficient.

On the other hand, if you have $400,000 of financial assets all invested in equities, your total return would be $32,000 plus $20,000 or $52,000. In this case, a 25% loss slices away $100,000. Your return is now $24,000 plus $20,000 for a total of $44,000. That might not be enough to maintain your standard of living.

For money invested in bonds, a comparable test is to multiply assets by 4%, which represents a rough estimate of what fixed income assets can return after inflation. It would be unusual for short- to intermediate-term bonds to decline more than 6%. This loss would reduce a $1 million portfolio to $940,000. Assuming a 4% after-inflation return, the income would drop from $40,000 to $37,600; adding in the $20,000 from Social Security, the drop would be from $60,000 to $57,600. For most people, such a reduction would be tolerable.

Your propensity for risk. No matter how great your need for income, you shouldn't take risks you can't tolerate. This principle might be called "investing up to your sleeping point." In September, 1996 I received a letter from a middle-aged subscriber to my newsletter asking that I cancel his subscription. The letter said he had first invested in stock mutual funds in May 1996, just before the 10% correction. Then "after losing thousands of dollars," he sold out two months later. Unfortunately in this case, if he had just stayed with his investments a few weeks longer, he could have recouped his loss and gone on to greater profits.

It was obvious to me that this subscriber had invested beyond his sleeping point. He remarked that he was comfortable in fixed-income investments but could not handle the volatility of equities.

Your investing goals. Do you want to live off your capital or build an estate that can be distributed to heirs or charities? If your goal is to die broke (and you'd be surprised how many people have that goal), then you should probably take fewer investing risks because you will be making large withdrawals. A table of financial life expectancy on page 345 tells how many years your money will last at various withdrawal rates. If you match the withdrawal rate to your life expectancy (and live just that long), you will enjoy your money for all it's worth, and leave nothing behind.

However, if you want to leave an estate behind, then you have a longer time frame and perhaps more flexibility in assuming risk. For example, a few years ago a doctor went to a financial advisor I know and asked that the $500,000 in his pension plan be invested as aggressively as possible. The advisor demurred since it was pension money that is normally invested conservatively. The doctor explained that he didn't need the money; he had other sources of wealth to support his retirement lifestyle. "If I can make a killing with the money, I can endow a wing in my hospital and be remembered a long time. And if I lose, let someone else be remembered," explained the doctor.

How much money do you want to amass? ike the doctor above, if your goals are lofty, you'll want to concentrate more heavily in risky equities (aggressive growth, small-cap and international funds, or individual stocks), the best bet for the highest returns over the long run.

Amount of diversification needed. This goes hand-in-hand with the amount of risk you want to take. Less diversification among asset classes will enhance the possibility of greater returns. Less diversification within an asset class (i.e., owning one fund or stock instead of many) gives you a greater chance to outperform the equity averages. Unfortunately, the reverse is also true; less diversified portfolios can also lose more.

Relative valuations in the market. While the primary reason for selecting various asset classes is to implement your personal strategy, asset classes should on occasion be adjusted to maximize returns under varying market conditions. From time to time, *The Wall Street Journal* publishes the asset allocation weightings recommended by the major brokerage firms and investment banks. These allocations vary based on the firms' perception of the relative value of stocks versus bonds. They can be used as a starting point for your own tactical allocations.

Investment experience. In asset allocation, there is something to be said for having been through the ups and downs of investment markets. The first time an investor experiences a sudden dip in net worth, it is a little like that first plunge on a roller coaster. In general, wouldn't you prefer to get this experience with a smaller rather than a larger portion of your assets?

Now here's an iconoclastic thought: what if you just bought stocks?

A provocative research study conducted by Peter L. Bernstein, noted economist and securities analyst, arrived at that advice. Bernstein's research lead him to make a case against the common asset allocation strategy in which the normal portfolio composition is 60% equities and 40% bonds. Many balanced funds use that sort of allocation. Bernstein argued that a portfolio allocation consisting of 75% equities and 25% cash is at least as good, and in many market climates, probably better.

Bernstein first undertook his study in 1988 using the S&P 500 as a proxy for equities, the 30-year Treasury as the bond component, and 90-day Treasury bills as cash. The original research found that from 1954 until the middle of 1988, a portfolio 60/40 stocks to bonds had an annual compound total return of 9.17% with a standard deviation (a measure of risk) of 5.78. Over the same period, a portfolio that was 75% in stocks and 25% in cash generated a 10.24% total return— 12% greater! Yet, the standard deviation rose only 4%, to 5.99%. Thus the stocks/cash portfolio delivered a substantially larger gain with only slightly more risk.

However, most stock market research is maddeningly sensitive to particular time periods. A strategy that's magical in one period, may not work at all in another. The 1954-1988 period covered many bad years for bonds, and that biased the results toward the stocks/cash strategy.

To take that bias out, the study was redone in 1994 for the two decades from 1974 to mid-1994. That period included the great bull

The no-bond study

market in bonds, from 1982 when interest rates began to decline, until 1994, when rates climbed dramatically.

Not surprisingly, the advantage of the stocks/cash plan almost disappeared. Over the last 20 years, the stock/bond portfolio averaged 11.40% per year, while the stock/cash portfolio averaged 11.18%. The standard deviations were 6.51% versus 6.29%. Thus, the stock/bond portfolio had a 2% advantage in performance at the cost of a 3.5% higher standard deviation.

Bernstein also replicated his study using other asset classes. Instead of using the S&P 500 to represent equities, he substituted a mix of 70% S&P stocks with the remaining 30% in small company stocks. Secondly, he substituted an intermediate-term bond for the long bond. The addition of small company stocks raises both the risk level and returns of the portfolio. Shortening bond fund maturities has the opposite effect. Making these changes improves the risk/reward relationship of both portfolios. The new mixed-stock portfolio plus cash outperformed the new stock/bond portfolio but at a greater risk—though it is not as statistically significant as it appears in the accompanying chart.

Since these latest readings don't show one strategy clearly dominating the other, why should you consider such a radical departure from conventional asset allocation?

Here are three reasons for eliminating bonds and substituting cash in your portfolio:

■ Bonds can suffer negative returns, cash cannot.

■ The original reason for balancing a stock portfolio with bonds is that, historically, the two asset classes did not move in tandem. This has been less true in recent years. Stocks and bonds now decline simultaneously much of the time. From 1974 through June 1997, there have been 25 quarters (out of 94) when the S&P 500 declined. Long bonds declined in 19 of these 25 quarters.

■ I believe the great, decade-long bull market in bonds is over. After all, interest rates are at low ebb as I'm writing this. Therefore, the original study may be more relevant than the update.

When bonds are in a bear market, the stocks/cash plan is clearly superior. When bonds are in a bull market, the two strategies are roughly comparable. This tilts us toward the stocks/cash plan. However, in making your own decisions, your feelings about the direction of interest rates—and of the stock market, for that matter—

Chart 59

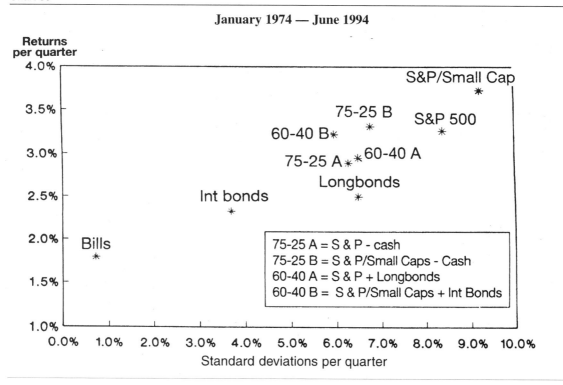

January 1974 — June 1994

Returns per quarter (y-axis)

Standard deviations per quarter (x-axis)

S&P/Small Cap
S&P 500
75-25 B
60-40 B
75-25 A   60-40 A
Longbonds
Int bonds
Bills

75-25 A = S & P - cash
75-25 B = S & P/Small Caps - Cash
60-40 A = S & P + Longbonds
60-40 B = S & P/Small Caps + Int Bonds

could change the equation. A substantial decline in interest rates in the remaining years of this century would enhance the appeal of the stocks/bonds strategy. On the other hand, a resurgence of inflation would poison bonds, cash would be king in your portfolio.

If you believe that the long-term bull market in bonds is essentially over, I suggest one way to gradually switch over to a stock/cash allocation is to stop reinvesting bond fund distributions. Either have the fund send you a check each month, or, if you're at one of the larger fund groups, direct your distributions to a good stock fund or money fund.

Note that following the stocks/cash strategy doesn't necessarily mean you never hold bonds. It means that stocks and cash are your permanent investments. Cash becomes your diversifier and risk-reducer. You buy bonds opportunistically, if you believe interest rates are about to decline. Then a play in bonds can produce attractive returns. (With a traditional stock/bond allocation, the reverse is true. Cash becomes your opportunistic purchase.)

How many funds should you own?

A common question put to mutual fund experts is, "How many funds should I own?" While it may seem that this is a simple issue, in fact it's not. Of course, this doesn't stop "experts" from responding. But I get the feeling that their answers display no science and little art, typically being made off the top of the head or intuitively. The most common answer I see is, "Not too many funds. Otherwise, you will be diluting your performance." Or: "Enough for proper diversification." Or: "Not so many that you can't easily manage them."

I'd like to provide some solid information in an area where analytical answers seem hard to come by.

As a preface to this discussion, I should remind you that we are talking about no-load funds. So, an investor never has to increase a purchase within any one fund family in order to hit what are called break points—the level in load funds where the commission begins to decline. You don't need to limit the number of funds you own for that reason. On the other hand, the paperwork consideration can be all too real. The more funds, the more paperwork—a bother both in keeping track of your investments and in filing your tax return. If you have a limited tolerance for paperwork, this may be reason enough to prefer a smaller number of funds.

Years ago, I used to take the position that smaller was better when it came to the number of funds in your portfolio. Over the years, I've modified my thinking. I now believe proper diversification is paramount and a million-dollar-plus portfolio could easily include twenty funds (fewer if a major portion of the portfolio is indexed).

It's the size of your portfolio that should be the major consideration in deciding how many funds to own. If you have only a small amount of money to invest, the minimum investment restrictions that some funds impose can be a problem. People with only small sums to invest need to locate fund groups—such as Montgomery and Invesco—that have low minimums. Alternatively, they should consider funds that provide internal diversification, such as balanced funds, asset allocation funds or multi-funds like Vanguard Star and T. Rowe Price Spectrum. If your assets are greater, then this problem is eliminated. You can diversify on your own to greater advantage.

I think that owning more funds can provide greater diversification, which is advantageous. When you analyze the model investment portfolios in Table 58, you see that they follow the principle of the financial pyramid. This strategy can entail owning quite a few funds. For example, I allocate most of our money to fairly conservative funds, keeping relatively small portions in the speculative funds categories. However, unless the market is quite high, I think it's preferable to own more than one aggressive growth fund. One diversification I advocate is holding a small cap fund plus an aggressive fund that does not take size into consideration when picking top growth stocks.

In the growth and growth-income categories, it makes sense to diversify between an earnings-driven (growth) fund and a value fund. Completing the financial pyramid, virtually all portfolios should have an equity income fund. And, diversifying into international funds is a must for today's investor. That can be accomplished by investing in one fund; but large portfolios might do better buying one or two regional funds plus an emerging markets fund. I don't think specialized funds are necessary, though sometimes they can enhance the total return of a portfolio.

Many different types of bond funds exist, providing all sorts of diversification possibilities. Most fixed-income money should be invested in funds with intermediate-term maturities. If you use only one fund, it should probably be one that invests in government securities or investment grade munis. Investors who buy two or more can add a high-grade corporate bond fund and, possibly, global, international or junk bond funds. But don't diversify willy-nilly. Three or more fixed-income funds in the same category, say long-term corporate bond funds, won't provide you with meaningful diversification.

Here are some rules of thumb for relating the number of funds you should own to the size of your portfolio.

Table 60

Portfolio size	Number of funds you should own
$2,000-5,000	1-2 funds
$5,000-20,000	2-4 funds
$20,000-50,000	4-7 funds
$50,000-200,000	7-10 funds
$200,000-600,000	10-15 funds
$600,000-1 million	15-20 funds

While I don't see any absolute limit to the number of funds in a portfolio, trivial holdings are pointless. I have seen portfolios containing mutual fund positions amounting to less than $1,000. Think of it this way: if you have so little in a particular fund that it's less than

1% of your total nestegg, is that really worth the paperwork? Except for an occasional very offbeat or high-risk investment, every position should be at least 4%-5% of your portfolio.

Will holding a great many funds dilute performance? In theory, a portfolio composed of just three or four of the best funds should have greater potential, but it's exceedingly difficult to pick the three or four funds that will turn out to be the best. And even if you do, the portfolio could be dangerously undiversified, since the best—and worst—performing funds at any moment are likely to be similar. On the other hand, more diversified mutual fund portfolios can produce greater rewards for the same amount of risk, or the same rewards with less risk, provided you are diligent in selling off your losers (a practice that's essential no matter how many funds you own).

I did some research to document this point. For example, I compared the performance and variability of two portfolios of aggressive growth funds over a three-year period. The first portfolio consisted of five aggressive growth funds. The second had 20 aggressive growth funds (including the five in the first portfolio). I selected funds to give both portfolios about the same total return (40.5% vs. 40.9%). The larger portfolio had a standard deviation of 5.08, while the smaller portfolio's standard deviation was 5.80.

Similarly, I assembled a portfolio of eight funds similar to my Wealth Builder Portfolio. I then compared it to a similar portfolio with 20 funds. Again the results were similar. The larger portfolio had less variability and a slightly higher total return.

Table 61

Portfolio	Total return	Std Dev.
8 funds	53.5%	4.44
20 funds	54.1%	4.21

Can you achieve the same results with low-cost index funds? Yes, but they can't do the whole job. They have relatively high betas due to their policy of always staying fully invested. So conservative portfolios need additional funds that would bring down the overall level of risk. Nor do index funds allow you to concentrate on hot sectors of the market in order to maximize your return. I think index funds belong in the core portion of almost every portfolio. But I don't think they are a total solution to minimizing the number of funds you need.

Because of its inherent inflation protection, real estate undoubtedly should play a role in most investors' financial plans. However, its exact participation depends heavily not only on your circumstances, but also on your inclination toward the management of property.

Generally, individually chosen and managed real estate is your best investment. (If the equity in your home represents 20% or more of your assets, that may well be sufficient.) If sole ownership is impractical, though, you should consider a no-load real estate fund, such as we described in Chapter 12. Bear in mind that a large mortgage can offset the deflation protection afforded by long-term bonds. If that applies, you might consider replacing a regular bond fund with an American Century Benham Target Fund that holds zero coupon bonds. This will give about triple the protection for the money.

While allocating your portfolio is of utmost importance, no set formula can be applied to everyone. You need to tailor your investments to your own situation. Happily, you can construct portfolios for all seasons by using no-load funds. And you can easily adjust the proportions as your needs change.

Real estate

Rebalancing is a strategy designed to maintain a portfolio's desired weightings. For example, you have a portfolio set up with a 5% weighting in gold funds. If, by some chance, gold should double, its weighting in the portfolio will approximate 10%. You would rebalance by selling half your gold holdings, and putting the profits in sectors that did less well.

No question that the theory is sound. The practice, though, is less so. Some authorities suggest regular rebalancing. My feeling is that unless the weightings in your portfolio change significantly—by more than 10%—you probably don't need to bother. You will increase your tax exposure (in a non-qualified account) to gain a marginal advantage.

The book *Bogle on Mutual Funds* by Vanguard head John Bogle contains a study comparing two $10,000 investments. Both start with a 50/50 distribution between stocks and bonds. One portfolio is rebalanced annually (enough of the best performing category is sold and reinvested in the other to bring it back to the 50/50 weighting). The other portfolio is not rebalanced. After 25 years, the portfolio that is rebalanced is worth $100,590; the other portfolio is worth $97,910. Annualized the difference

Rebalancing

is 9.7% versus 9.6% per year. And this is before tax consequences are taken into account! Not to mention the sheer administrative nuisance that rebalancing your portfolio every year would cause you.

On the other hand, while it's problematic that rebalancing will significantly improve performance, it does have some ability to reduce a portfolio's risk level. That's because rebalancing reduces the size of your positions in the funds that have had the greatest runups. These are the funds that will typically decline the most in a downturn.

If your holdings are concentrated within a major fund family, one easy way to rebalance comes cheaply. Just direct the fund group to send the dividends distributed by your overweighted funds to your underweighted funds. This should work well in the long run. If that's not enough, add additional investments to your underweighted holdings.

How to compute the exact return on your investments

You can probably cite the yield on your bond or money fund. You may know your stock fund's precise return. But *your* return may be different from the *fund's* return. That can happen when you've made additional investments or withdrawn money during the measured period. Sometimes it happens because you did not own your investment for exactly the period that you're comparing with (one calendar year, for instance).

Calculating your total return is a bit of work. But wouldn't it be nice to know how well *you* did—as opposed to how well your mutual fund manager(s) did?

Professional investors can figure the precise rate of return by performing a complex calculation that takes into account the exact timing of cash inflows and outflows. Mutual funds do it every day. But you don't need such precision. Fortunately, it is possible to arrive at a reasonably accurate figure for your return by using a simple formula. Nearly all the information is in the records you need to save anyway. The formula assumes that additions and withdrawals are made in the middle of the measured period. Here are the steps:

1. Compute the beginning value of your initial investment including sales charges, if any. For example, on Jan. 1, your investments are worth $10,000. Then calculate the value of your investments at the end of the period—say, $12,350 on March 31. Calculate net additions or withdrawals—say $2,000—during the course of the quarter.

2. Subsequent purchases are considered to be additions. Dividend,

interest or capital gains distributions taken as income are counted as withdrawals. Reinvested dividends are ignored as they are a wash. If you want your computations to be after-tax, count taxes on distributions as additions. When you pay tax on gains for a security that has appreciated over several years, your calculation will understate the return for the year in which you paid the taxes, and overstate the returns for previous years. You can correct the distortion by allocating a pro-rated share of the tax payment to prior periods and then recalculate your annual returns.

3. Multiply net additions or withdrawals by 0.5 (note that a net withdrawal will be a negative number). Example: 0.5 x $2,000 = $1,000.

4. Subtract the result of step 3 from the ending value. Example: $12,350 - $1,000 = $11,350.

5. Add the result of step 3 to the beginning value. Example: $10,000 + $1,000 = $11,000.

6. Divide the result of step 4 by the result of step 5. Example: $11,350 / $11,000 = 1.032.

7. Convert to a percentage by subtracting one and multiplying the remainder by 100. Example: 1.032 - 1 x 100 = 3.2%. This is your quarterly return.

8. To annualize the figure, multiply the decimal value in step 6 by itself three times and convert the result to a percentage. Example: 1.032 x 1.032 x 1.032 x 1.032 = 1.134 = 13.4%.

9. To get your actual returns for a year, multiply the decimal value (as in step 6) of your quarterly returns together and convert back to a percentage. Example: 1.032 x 1.042 x 0.98 x 1.048 = 1.1044 = 10.4%.

If you want still greater accuracy, compute your returns monthly.

CHAPTER 18

THE NO-LOAD FUND INVESTOR

Choosing a fund family

Just as with your own family, the company you keep in your investments has a major bearing on the quality of your life. We'll try not to strain the analogy too much, since your portfolio, admittedly, is not the centrally important theme of your life. And then, too, you can *choose* the investment company you keep.

Increasingly, that choice is a pleasant one. As mutual funds have expanded the range of their services, the importance of the family you select has grown increasingly important. And, in an odd way, also less important.

As we will discuss in detail in Chapter 22, you can avail yourself of an investment supermarket by opening a brokerage account with a discount broker like Fidelity, Charles Schwab or Jack White. That lets you move among mutual funds in different families.

For many if not most investors, though, remaining within the bounds of a single mutual fund family makes sense. For instance, if yours is not a huge portfolio, if you are not trading oriented, if you don't need to diversify among a large number of good funds, you can certainly select and stay with one fund group.

In the no-load universe, more than 150 firms are now prepared to serve investors' needs with one or more stock, bond and/or money market funds. About 85% of all no-load stock and bond funds belong to these groups. As a result the question that you are most apt to be asking yourself is *which* family of funds is best for you, not so much which particular fund.

This is especially true if you want to use a fund group for your IRA or Keogh, since you can move money around in a tax-qualified plan at will, without worrying about tax consequences every time you switch from one fund to another. (When you are investing outside of a tax-qualified plan, every time you move from one fund to another—unless it's a money market fund—you have either a taxable gain or loss.)

No single fund family is right for everyone, of course. As we will discuss presently, different groups have different strengths. Your choice depends upon your individual needs. Here are some considerations to help you choose.

The first and most important is the type and quality of the group's stock funds. The greatest differences between families exist here, particularly in performance. Most groups have growth or growth-income funds that perform respectably. But relatively few have outstanding aggressive growth funds. So if that's where you plan to make significant investments, it's an easy basis on which to select a group.

These days, international investments have a place in every portfolio. Since they're very popular among knowledgeable investors, every major group now offers them, making it easy for you to allocate a portion of your investments overseas. But be careful. There are wide differences in the quality and types of these various international funds. American Century, Fidelity, Invesco, Janus, Montgomery, Rowe Price, Scudder, Vanguard and Vontobel have particular no-load expertise in this area.

After you've found one or more groups that satisfy your stock fund requirements, look next at the group's bond funds. The important differences here are in the variety of fixed income funds available, and their operating cost.

First, does your tax bracket incline you toward taxable or tax-free bond funds? Some groups have one kind but not the other.

Next, look for a group whose bond funds have low expense ratios. Vanguard is usually the best among large groups in this regard.

Finally, consider whether the group that you are investigating offers funds with different maturities. Most fund groups have long-term bond funds. Short- and intermediate-term bond funds are less common. Since these are the better performers in adverse markets, their availability makes a group more desirable.

After you are satisfied with a group's stock and bond funds, examine its money market funds. Variety, rather than performance, is the major criterion. A fund group that includes all three types of money funds—general purpose, government-only and tax-free—has the edge.

Another consideration is the existence of specialty funds. Various groups offer gold funds, energy funds, financial funds, real estate funds, etc.

Is the fund group completely or only partially no-load? Totally no-load is better, of course. Needless to say, when you are selecting a fund, I recommend ignoring any in a group that carry loads.

In addition to applying the above techniques, some special considerations apply with a tax-deferred account.

■ Obviously, you ignore a group's tax-free bond or money market funds in your evaluation. Their dividends are already tax-free.

■ Make sure that all the group's funds you are considering accept IRA or Keogh accounts. A few groups exclude certain funds from tax-sheltered programs.

You should put your money into a tax-sheltered account early in the year so the income will be tax-sheltered for the entire year. If you haven't decided on a specific fund, start your IRA in the mutual fund group's money market account. Later you can always switch to a stock or bond fund.

Tax-sheltered investing

Whether investing for growth or income, mutual funds offer the best investment vehicles for tax-deferred retirement savings plans such as Individual Retirement Accounts, Keoghs and many 401(k) plans.

Good no-load families offer a broad range of investment choices—a vital feature as you get older. Not only are you likely to have more money later in life, you may also want to consider moving your retirement nest egg from riskier to more conservative investments in order to preserve principal.

An IRA account within a mutual fund family provides you with the opportunity to maximize your profits by buying and selling equity funds or switching to bond or money funds without having to pay any taxes until you cash in the account, usually years later. And all the paperwork covering years of contributions comes from a single company. So, for a tax-deferred retirement account, your first choice should be a family of no-load funds.

Finally, it is quite possible to move your IRA from one management group to another as often as you wish. The necessary paperwork is less than it used to be. However, all else being equal, it's preferable to stay within one no-load fund group, but don't feel that your money is imprisoned there.

Because your income and capital gains are not taxed until you begin withdrawals, the investment strategy for IRAs and Keoghs may be different from the ones you'd use in an account that is not tax-sheltered. However, basic investing fundamentals still apply.

The quick answer is: the same amount of risk you would take in a regular taxable account. Here's how to allocate investments between taxable and tax-deferred accounts: First establish the overall asset allocation that will provide your desired risk level. Then select a number of funds to implement this allocation. Next, divide these funds between your tax-sheltered and taxable accounts, not by risk level, but by *tax-efficiency*.

The reason you don't allocate by risk is that, taxable or tax-deferred, it's all your money. Don't fall into the trap of saying the retirement money has to be conservative while it's O.K. to take risks with the taxable money. To allocate investments this way is akin to thinking it makes a difference whether you put money in your right pocket or your left pocket.

How much risk should I take in an IRA?

Your aim is to allocate your assets to achieve the greatest after-tax return over your entire portfolio. Some considerations: Your allocation will vary depending on the capital appreciation that you anticipate, whether your investment provides you with ordinary taxable income, capital gains, or tax-free muni income, how long you hold a security before you sell and how long your money remains in your tax-sheltered account. Importantly, it also depends on your tax bracket now and when you retire.

The advice I am about to give you is quite different from the recommendations I offered in my first edition of the *Guide* because of the changes made in the tax code as a result of the Tax-Reform Act of 1997. Under the old rules there was not a lot of difference between ordinary income and capital gains taxes. Most people were in the 28% bracket for capital gains and the 28% or 31% for ordinary income. Now the Federal

Allocating assets by returns and tax efficiency

capital gains rate is as low as 20%, and the ordinary income rate is as high as 39.6%. It makes a much greater difference.

Buy and hold investors may obtain the greatest after-tax income by putting income producing funds in a tax-deferred account such as an IRA and growth funds, which distribute little or nothing in the way of dividends, in regular taxable accounts. That's because the income is taxed at ordinary tax rates if its held outside a tax-shelter, and all distributions are taxed at ordinary rates when withdrawn from a tax-sheltered account upon retirement. On the other hand long-term capital gains, particularly when taxed at 20%, are already partially sheltered. This strategy has the greatest potential if you think you will stay in a high tax-bracket after retirement. If your tax-bracket at retirement is 15%, then you might do better by putting high growth funds into the tax-sheltered account for greater gains since they would be taxed at a low rate when withdrawn after retirement.

If you are a trader, the picture changes considerably. If you hold funds for less than a year, your capital gains will be taxed at the ordinary income rate. If you hold less than 18 months, they will be taxed at the 28% rate. If that's the case, it's better to trade these investments in the tax-sheltered account, particularly if you think your tax bracket will be lower in the year that you begin withdrawing money.

How long the money is tax-deferred makes a great difference. A study by Fidelity compared $2,000 investments in tax-deferred accounts for an investor in a 28% tax-bracket, now and at the time of distribution, to investments in a taxable account which were turned over every two years thus qualifying for long-term capital gains rates. With a 6% return, the taxable account wins over both five-year and 25-

Table 62

	Value of a $2,000 investment after taxes **6% return**	
Years invested	**Taxable account**	**Tax-deferred account**
5	$2,531	$1,927
25	6,498	6,180
	12% return	
5	$3,175	$2,578
25	20,243	24,480

Source: Fidelity

year periods. However, if the investments generate a 12% annualized return, the taxable account still wins over the short period, but not the longer one. Here's an investment maxim you should remember: The value of the tax-deferred account grows with time and with the rate of return on your investments.

Fund group profiles: It's all in the family

Whether you are investing for retirement, or putting money into no-load mutual funds for some other purpose, you should select one or more fund families that best suit your needs. But how do you know which group to select?

In the following sketches, I'll give you an overview of the 33 major fund groups you are most likely to consider. Some of these are household names, others more obscure. Some appeal to all investors, others are specialty shops. Some you've heard of. Others you'll no doubt be introduced to for the first time.

Regarding the rankings: I've ranked the groups according to the amount of assets they manage. Our universe is those families that primarily market no-loads to individual investors. In keeping with the spirit of this book, I've naturally excluded groups that market primarily to institutions and broker/dealers.

American Century

American Century Investments was formed in February 1995, when the Kansas City based Twentieth Century mutual funds company acquired the Benham Group of Mountain View, California. The resulting merger created the sixth largest no-load fund group.

In early 1998, 45% of the company was sold to J.P. Morgan & Co. for approximately $900 million. Morgan has the right to purchase another 5% of American Century in the year 2000. James Stowers Jr, the founder of American Century and his family, retains control.

In January, 1997, as the 20th century was winding to a close, the fund company changed its name from Twentieth Century/Benham to American Century. At the time, its approximately 70 funds were realigned into three fund groups: The Benham Group, with bond and money market funds; the American Century Group, with asset allocation, balanced, speciality and moderate-risk equity funds; and the Twentieth Century Group with domestic and international growth stock funds.

Twentieth Century began life in 1958 with two funds, Twentieth

Century Growth and Twentieth Century Select. Both of them are among the top five performing funds for the 23-year extended bull market period that began in 1975. Though it began life as a load fund group, Twentieth Century in 1974 became an early convert to no-load investing.

Its investment motto: money follows earnings. In other words, stocks with consistently improving earnings tend to continue upwards in price. In essence, the group invests only in companies with at least a three-year history of *accelerating* earnings. James Stowers, Jr., Twentieth Century's founder, describes stocks as "chicken eggs" or "tennis balls." Chicken eggs, he explains, "don't bounce back after a bear market; tennis balls do." The latter are the stocks of companies with accelerating earnings that he buys.

Unlike other mutual fund groups that rely on individual managers, Twentieth Century runs its portfolios with two and three-manager teams who make the investment decisions for the equity funds. These individual managers have the authority to make buy and sell decisions as the need arises. A computerized database of over 18,000 companies helps to screen investment choices.

Over the long run, the Twentieth Century growth funds have been top performers. But they are well known for their volatility. Twentieth Century funds remain fully invested at all times, which makes them naturals for market timers. To discourage timing, the company limits switches to six per year. The funds' volatility as well as their minuscule initial and subsequent investment minimums make Twentieth Century funds a natural for dollar-cost averagers—especially young people and/or those who are planning for their children's or grandchildren's college bills some years down the road.

Twentieth Century has an innovative college investment program, utilizing the group's Select and Cash Reserve funds. The program initially puts investments intended for college in Select, a growth stock fund. This serves to achieve a build up of the portfolio during the early years. Then, four to six years before a child is going to need the money for college tuition, Twentieth Century gradually moves the investment into Cash Reserves, where it is sheltered from market volatility. If you choose to rebalance from Select to Cash Reserves during a four-year period, Twentieth Century will automatically move 25% to cash each year; if you choose the five or six year rebalancing plans, 20% or 17% is shifted over per year.

By contrast to Twentieth Century, a leader in growth stock investing, the Benham funds have been a pioneer in first money-market and
then bond fund investing. Founder James Benham, introduced the
first Treasury-only money fund, Capital Preservation, in 1972, and
went on to become one of the largest organizers of fixed-income and
money-market funds. However, it wasn't until 1993, 21 years after
launching Capital Preservation, that Benham brought out its first general money fund.

Not all of the Benham funds are meant for conservative investors.
In 1986, the family came out with the first portfolio of zero-coupon
bond funds. Given today's constantly changing interest rate environment, these funds can easily be as volatile as aggressive growth funds.

In what seems to be an increasing trend as both the industry and
its leading lions age, James Stowers, Jr. has, by and large, turned over
the management of the company to his son, James Stowers, III.
Meanwhile, Jim Benham has retired.

Babson

Jones & Babson, which manages the Babson funds, was founded in
Kansas City in 1960 with one mutual fund, the Babson Growth Fund.
Now Babson is the 28th largest no-load family with 29 mutual fund
portfolios. Included are the five Buffalo funds which are sub-advised
by the Kansas City money manager, Kornitzer Capital Mngt. and
responsibility for ten United Missouri Bank (UMB) Scout funds
(about 38% of Babson's assets under management), and the four Five
Star Funds for the Armed Forces Benefit Association. All told, Babson
has $4.1 billion in assets under its wing.

Babson has always contracted out its portfolio management to the
David L. Babson Co. of Cambridge, Mass. for all funds except two of
the UMB Scout funds, which the bank itself manages. David L.
Babson is an independent investment counseling firm and a principal
owner of Jones & Babson.

The group's Shadow Stock Fund is derived from the concept in the
AAII Journal (a publication of the American Association of Individual
Investors). The notion is that small company stocks *neglected* by the
institutions may produce superior returns.

Babson takes a value-oriented approach to both equity and fixed
income investing. In stock funds, Babson tries to emphasize quality
stocks, whether large cap, small cap or international. Its portfolios are

kept fully invested, consistent with the belief that attempting to forecast short-term market trends is futile.

Berger

Bill Berger is a true western pioneer. His great great grandfather started the first bank in Denver in 1862.

Almost a century later, in 1959, he started Colorado's first mutual fund, the Centennial Fund—the country's first exchange or swap fund. (That was a fund where you could turn over appreciated securities, rather than cash, for shares in the fund without paying capital gains taxes. Because of changes in the tax laws, they are no longer available.) In 1962 Berger launched an aggressive growth fund—the Gryphon Fund. Four years later he decided to merge with the Founders group. Gryphon became the Founders Growth Fund. But the merger didn't take and by 1969 Berger was back on his own.

Then in the 1970s, Berger was asked to take over the managment of two troubled funds, the 100 and 101, which he promptly renamed the Berger 100 and Berger 101. They became the foundation for the present company, though no more funds were launched until 1993, when a Small Company Fund was added.

In 1994, Berger sold his stake in Berger Associates to Kansas City Southern, the railroad conglomerate that also owns the Janus fund family. This has provided for further growth. The Berger group now manages nine funds. They are primarily stock funds; seven of them, including an international fund, hold equities. Another fund is balanced. Telephone switching is available with Kemper Money Market Funds. Assets now total $3.2 billion.

Berger's promotional material notes that the fund's prescription for success is founded on the belief that "Patient, courageous investors who stay the course through the market's ups and downs are the most successful investors over time." To implement that goal, the Berger funds emphasize capital appreciation, but achieve it in a wide variety of ways. The firm offers both small and mid-cap growth and value funds. In its advertising Bill Berger, who's now 72, is the group's visible symbol. In reality, the funds are now run by a group of young turks.

Columbia

The name, which Easterners would undoubtedly misunderstand, comes from the great Columbia River. That's because the mutual fund family is based in Portland, Oregon.

Although the Columbia group is only the 23rd largest no-load family of funds, with 12 funds and $6.6 billion in assets, it is a showpiece for the management company behind it. That company, Columbia Advisors, has more than $22 billion in its investment advisory business.

Columbia uses a team investment approach to portfolio management, though each fund designates one person who is ultimately responsible for the fund's performance. These managers are top-down investors who do sector rotation.

The group's forte is aggressive growth investing; it now offers both large and small-cap funds. Flagship Columbia Growth has an above-average long-term record. Over the years, Columbia has added other equity funds including a real estate fund, as well as a full complement of fixed income funds. The group is pure no-load, but does have a fee-based managed account service that provides assistance to large shareholders by guiding them among Columbia's funds.

Dodge & Cox

Dodge & Cox originally managed funds just for individuals. But today the firm finds that tax-exempt institutional clients are a substantial portion of its business.

Established in San Francisco in 1930, the group has only one office, and its 24 shareholders are all employees of the firm. Overall, Dodge & Cox has $34 billion under management, of which $10 billion is in its three funds. That's sufficient to rank 18th among no-load fund families.

The firm's oldest fund, Dodge & Cox Balanced, was launched in 1931, hardly a propitious time to launch a new investment vehicle. The Stock Fund was added in 1965 and the Income Fund in 1989.

Conservatism is Dodge & Cox's hallmark; yet that hasn't prevented the group's funds from turning in fine performances. The Stock Fund has been in the top 20% of funds in its growth-income category for the five years ending 1997.

Dodge & Cox uses fundamental analysis to select solid, well-established companies for the long-term. On the fixed-income side, it prefers bonds with low credit risk and maturities generally ranging from seven to 15 years.

Dreyfus

One of the giants—and legends—of the mutual fund industry, Dreyfus manages more than 150 funds.

Third-largest no-load family, Dreyfus boasts about 1.2 million shareholder accounts. Back in the 1950s, Dreyfus was the pre-eminent name in equity fund management. Its lion commercials became synonymous with growth. The venerable Dreyfus Fund, the group's flagship, has now gained 22,119% (including reinvested dividends and capital gains) since its inception in 1951.

But in recent decades Dreyfus seemed to have lost its way. Its growth fund heritage gave way to bonds, and Dreyfus recently has appealed primarily to income-oriented investors. In 1993, about 90% of the $80 billion that the firm then managed was in fixed-income or money market funds. Its equity funds produced mixed results.

In 1994 the Dreyfus Corporation was acquired by the Mellon Bank in a landmark transaction valued at $1.85 billion. Since the acquisition, Mellon has injected new life into Dreyfus. Equities now account for 23% of Dreyfus' $100 billion of assets. Furthermore, Dreyfus has strengthened its investment management capabilities. In 1996 and 1997 Dreyfus hired more than 25 mid-to senior-level investment professionals and introduced 28 new funds, of which 18 are equities. Moreover, overall performance has improved.

Like rival Fidelity, Dreyfus has opened 26 investor centers. Shareholders can visit and discuss their Dreyfus investments face-to-face. These shops are located in New York, Florida, California, Colorado, Connecticut, Georgia, Illinois, Maryland, Massachusetts, New Jersey, and Pennsylvania.

Fidelity

The General Motors of the mutual fund industry, Fidelity is a sprawling, privately-owned behemoth with about $600 billion in assets, 215 funds at last count, and a staggering 8 million retail customer accounts.

Like MacDonald's, Fidelity delights in reciting a litany of staggering statistics relating to the firm's preeminent size. For instance, it is estimated that Fidelity's trading desk accounts for 6%-8% of the trades on the New York Stock Exchange. Fidelity is the number one provider of 401(k) retirement plan services and the number three provider of 403(b) plans for non-profit institutions.

Even more impressive: as of June 1996, Fidelity shareholders owned 3% of the S&P 500, 2.8% of the entire U.S. stock market capitalization, and 1.3% of the world equities markets. Fidelity claims that these numbers are small enough to leave room for growth.

One hundred and two of Fidelity's stock, bond and money market retail funds are pure no-load, giving the company more than any other group. If you're looking for a fund—any type of fund—there's a good chance that Fidelity has it. However, Fidelity has placed sales charges on many of its most popular equity funds; in fact, only 39 stock funds are available retail—pure no-load. However, most of the loaded funds waive loads for certain tax-sheltered accounts, 401(k)s, 403(b)s and the like.

Fidelity's fame is due in part to its spectacular Magellan Fund. Through much of its life, Magellan was guided by Peter Lynch, possibly the most important mutual fund manager of all time. He and his staff helped to make Magellan a household name by turning in spectacular performance. Over the past 20 years, mostly as a result of Lynch's work through 1990, Magellan returned investors 8,246%. That's good enough to still rank Magellan number one for the two decades.

With its fame, Magellan's assets have grown. Now by far the largest mutual fund, with more assets than all but 19 *entire fund groups!*, Magellan's glory days clearly are over. And several other funds, notably Vanguard's Index 500, are fast gaining on Magellan in size.

Yet, Fidelity has plenty of other things going for it. As the leader in the the corporate retirement plan market, Fidelity is guaranteed a continuing gush of dollars into the company; Fidelity numbers a breathtaking 2.8 million retirement plan participants. And rising stars among its funds range from highly specific sector funds to broadly balanced stock, bond and money market funds. Beginning in 1989, Fidelity introduced a line of low cost Spartan funds. Now numbering 25 bond funds and four equity index funds, they provide long-term investors with no-load, low-operating-cost investments.

Fidelity is easily the most innovative and aggressive marketer in the mutual fund business. The company distributes pure no-load funds and low loads directly to investors. In addition, through its Fidelity Advisor subsidiary, the firm distributes funds with full loads through more than 820 banks, 2000 broker/dealers and 60 major insurance companies.

Fidelity sells funds to institutions, and also owns the nation's second largest discount brokerage company (with one million customers). Among other things, the brokerage house trades more than

3,400 load and no-load funds from more than 330 fund families. Fidelity has a publishing division that has co-published two winning investment books by Peter Lynch, and now publishes the monthly personal finance magazine, *Worth*. In 1995 it launched an Investment Information Center on the Internet.

Fidelity's customer service is unparalleled in the financial services industry—or, for that matter, in just about any industry. The firm pioneered 24-hour phone service to its retail customers, and its 24,000 employees now operate from operations centers located in its Boston headquarters, Covington, KY, Cincinnati, Dallas, Salt Lake City and Marlborough, MA. In order to serve shareholders directly, Fidelity has set up 81 Investor Centers around the country. The company has telecommunication services for the hearing impaired and offers a CD shopping service. It offers consolidated statements covering both its funds and brokerage accounts.

Behind the aggressive marketing is a highly individualized group of fund managers backed by a large array of analysts and traders. By industry standards they are on the young side. Tellingly, their performance often exceeds the market averages in both up and down markets.

As often happens with large corporations, Fidelity went into a funk around 1995. A number of seemingly small problems combined to suggest larger disorder. However, management was quick to address the problems, and the result has been massive reorganizations. In 1996, Fidelity realigned its equity division from four to eight groups so as to leverage research and management resources. They are: Capital appreciation, growth, income growth, asset allocation/income, international, specialized growth, quantitative and structured investments. Each group has it own leader. Whether the new organization helped, or whether if the market simply came Fidelity's way, the result is that Fidelity's fortunes have improved.

At press time Fidelity was planning to launch additional diversified funds. With its best performing funds all getting so large as to be unwieldy, this bodes well for Fidelity's future.

Founders

The Founders group of funds, based in Denver, traces its origins to the Founder Mutual Fund, which was formed in 1938.

By tradition, Founders is growth oriented, with eight of its eleven funds seeking various forms of conservative and speculative growth;

Founders offers only one balanced, one fixed-income fund and one money market fund.

The family, which is the 26th largest no-load company with $6.7 billion in assets, prefers an approach in which it first selects promising stocks, then looks at the overall state of the stock market. Founders does pay attention to the status of a stock's industry group, however, and several industries show up frequently in Founders portfolios. The group has moved away from its team approach to portfolio management; the lead manager is now more important.

Founders has a loyal following in its hometown area. But in recent years its top performing funds have enabled the company to gain more national recognition. One homey touch remains, though. At Founders, you can still call to make a purchase and then send in your money later.

As I am writing this, Founders is in the process of being acquired by Mellon Bank for $270 million. Mellon also owns the Dreyfus funds and in recent years had acquired the Laural and Boston Company funds. At least eight key Founders executives have signed agreements to continue with the merged firm. Thus, the sale should not result in dramatic changes among portfolio managers. After the merger, it may be possible to buy Founders funds through Dreyfus.

Gabelli

If you've never heard of Mario Gabelli, you certainly cannot call yourself a mutual fund enthusiast. With one of the largest egos in the investing business, and one of the most expansive styles, he has turned the fund group bearing his name into one of mutual fund investing's real success stories.

Mario formed the Gabelli Funds in 1986, capitalizing on his superb record as a private-account money manager. The group, headquartered one of New York City's northern suburbs, now has 22 funds with about $6 billion in assets. That's sufficient only to rank Gabelli 31st. However Gamco, the parent company, manages over $12 billion in all. This includes a joint venture with the Westwood funds, a five fund group that uses a top-down investing approach. Gabelli entered into that joint venture in 1994.

Gabelli has long specialized in certain market sectors, notably telecommunications, media and industrial equipment. He sometimes identifies key trends within those areas, then uncovers the companies most likely to benefit. His firm has broadened its research in these niches to a global perspective.

This equities-oriented fund family is divided into 18 no-loads, one load fund and three closed-ends. At one time, Gabelli had a habit of switching his funds back and forth between load, no-load and closed-end. This no longer seems to be the case.

Mario Gabelli's basic approach is to buy companies at a discount to private market value—what the operations would fetch based on their assets, cash flow or earnings. His funds emphasize the different aspects of this approach to varying degrees.

Although Gabelli is a value oriented shop, it does have one outstanding growth fund: Gabelli Growth. Originally managed by Elizabeth Bramwell, who left to start her own fund, it is now handled by Howard Ward, who came to Gabelli from Scudder.

Harbor

It's hard to characterize Harbor. Probably the thing casual investors find most notable is that several Harbor funds, which have excellent track records, are managed by mutual fund stars. Among these outsiders are William Gross, the best-known and one of the most successful bond managers in the U.S. (he manages the Harbor Bond Fund), and Hakan Castegren, who runs the Harbor International stock fund (now closed to new investors).

Ranked fifteenth among no-load families, Harbor Capital Advisors was formed in 1983 to manage equities for the Owens-Illinois pension fund. All nine of its no-load funds are managed by outside advisers who also run separate accounts for the pension fund.

The Harbor funds are based in Toledo. They are designed to provide different, non-overlapping risk and return characteristics, with something for everybody—conservative to aggressive, equities to bonds, investments in the U.S. as well as abroad.

The money managers are basically left alone. However, the group insists that managers must "add value"—in other words, beat appropriate market benchmarks with reasonable consistency. If they don't, they will be replaced. Among Harbor's tenets of value-added management, the funds hold a relatively limited number of securities and tend to stay fully invested.

A relative newcomer, Milwaukee-based Heartland Advisors was founded in 1982, and didn't launch its first fund until 1984. The group originally marketed its funds with loads. It became no-load in 1994.

Heartland

William Nasgovitz is the President and Founder of the firm. He began his career as a broker, then became president of the Milwaukee Company, an investment banking firm, before founding Heartland.

The group is value-oriented. In fact, four of its five equity funds have "value" in their names. The fifth fund, Small Cap Contrarian, represents a radical departure. While its small cap holdings are predominately value stocks, it also has a policy of maintaining sizeable short positions, around 25%, even in bull markets. In the event of a bear market, the firm plans to increase that percentage subtantially.

Heartland also runs four bond funds, including a Wisconsin-only muni fund. However, the group uses an independent money market fund.

Heartland ranks 36nd among no-load families.

Originally, Minneapolis-based Investment Advisers, Inc. served Midwestern clients. Founded in 1947, it was known until 1987 as North Star. And flagship IAI Regional still invests at least 80% of its assets in Midwestern companies.

IAI

Ranked forty-third among no-load companies, IAI has $16 billion under management, including $1.5 billion in 15 no-load funds (including an institutional bond fund). Now a subsidiary of Hill Samuel Group in London, IAI has developed alliances with major investment firms in key international markets, primarily Asia and western Europe.

IAI's equity funds generally are oriented towards earnings growth, emphasizing a bottom-up stock-selection approach. The bond funds invest top-down. Based on analysis of the economy, credit cycle and Federal Reserve policy, managers make judgments on interest-rate trends, bond sector and duration. The firm says it prefers a disciplined team management approach to a "star system."

IAA also has a Latin America Fund, which it does not actively market.

Invesco

Formerly the Financial Programs Funds, this Denver-based group changed its name to Invesco Funds in 1991 so as to establish a uniform global identity with its parent company, the British based INVESCO PLC. Thirteenth ranked, Invesco offers 38 no-load funds. Although once they were pure no-loads, the long-term funds now carry 12b-1 fees. Invesco manages approximately $17 billion.

You can purchase an Invesco fund with a $1,000 minimum investment; that's lower than with most other groups.

Invesco follows a rigid set of investment criteria in managing its funds. Their investment teams first determine the overall economic climate, then choose the industries and industry sectors that are most likely to benefit from that scenario. After that, managers scout for the best stocks within the chosen sectors.

Invesco's top-down approach reaches to its array of mutual funds as well as its fund management. With 11 sector funds, Invesco boasts the second-largest roster of sector funds in the mutual fund industry. Better still, they are the only ones without front- or back-end fees.

Investors who aren't hardy enough for the volatile sector funds can invest in Invesco's diversified equity, international, bond and money market funds.

Here's a curious fact. In 1997, Invesco merged with the AIM funds, a notable load-fund group. However, the two groups are run completely independently, Invesco remains a no-load family.

Invesco has two investor walk-in service centers, both in the Denver area.

Janus

Does it seem like the no-load capital of the universe is Denver? Of all the mutual fund families based there, powerhouse Janus Capital Corporation is the largest.

Founded in 1969 by Thomas Bailey, who remains at Janus' head, the family is the eighth-largest no-load group, serving as investment advisor to 35 mutual funds, 19 of them under the Janus label. Total assets under management: $67 billion.

Bailey oversees Janus's general investment philosophy and strategy—independent fundamental analysis, a bottom's up approach, and an aversion to risk. But the company has added portfolio managers and analysts to accommodate its resounding growth.

Janus looks for companies that are undergoing positive changes not yet recognized by Wall Street.

One very notable characteristic of Janus funds: unlike most other groups, its managers don't feel that they need to be fully invested at all times. When they buy, they buy aggressively. If they don't see values, though, Janus fund managers are content to hold cash. This frequently results in the anomaly of fairly volatile performance despite high cash positions, since the stocks they invest in are not, shall we say, your typical widows' and orphans' portfolio. With the company's propensity to maintain significant cash positions in its funds, Janus sometimes lags at the beginning of a new bull market. Over the long run, however, Janus funds have turned in very solid performances.

One major star who has developed in recent years is Helen Young Hayes. A perpetual darling of the financial press, she has presided over notable successes at the Janus Worldwide and Janus Overseas funds.

The family has had enormous growth in during the decade. In fact, it was one of the first groups to close a small cap fund, Venture. It also closed Janus Twenty, but subsequently reopened the fund.

While Janus is known as an equity specialist, it also manages four fixed-income funds and three money funds. In addition to its own funds, Janus manages Idex, a load fund group, as well as the Janus Aspen series, a group of funds offering variable annuity contracts.

Janus is now 83% owned by Kansas City Southern Industries, which also owns 80% of the Berger Funds. The railroad conglomerate has diversified into financial services.

Lexington

One of the oldest families in the no-load universe, Lexington was founded in 1938 as Templeton, Dobrow & Vance Management. The renowned Sir John Templeton was the company's initial leader.

In the late 60s, after Templeton moved to the Bahamas, some of the funds doing business under the Lexington name split off and formed their own group.

The fund family, located in Saddle Brook, New Jersey, considers itself value oriented. In fact, Lexington is a highly eclectic group of 12 equity funds with an emphasis on global investing and gold. In addition, Lexington has one money market fund and two bond funds. Including both individual and institutional clients, the firm now manages more than $3.5 billion, mostly in private accounts.

The Lexington funds tend to turn in middling performances. Once in a while one of Lexington's funds surprises the mutual fund world by turning in an outstanding performance. In the mid-90s, its World Emerging Markets Fund was a solid winner. In 1997, the Lexington Troika Dialog Russia Fund was the year's second best performing no-load.

Lexington investors beware, though. Two of the firm's equity funds—Strategic Silver and Strategic Investment—have loads. They came to Lexington through acquisition in 1991, after problems with prior management.

Lindner/Ryback

Kurt Lindner has at least two distinctions. He was one of the earliest and most successful no-load managers. And he groomed an able successor, Eric Ryback, who has been able to carry on the company's excellent tradition of superior performance.

The Lindner group began back in 1954 when Kurt Lindner launched his first fund, now called the Lindner Growth Fund. Twenty-two years later, feeling venturesome, he launched a second fund, Lindner Dividend. Both funds prospered with a conservative value strategy. Over its life, Lindner Dividend has had one of the best risk-adjusted performances of any fund.

In 1982 Lindner hired Eric Ryback, a young man just out of Idaho State college, whose main claim to fame was he the first person to complete backpacking's "triple crown" by hiking 8,000 miles over three summers along America's three great hiking routes: The Appalachian Trail, the Pacific Crest Trail, and the Continental Divide Trail.

When Linder retired in 1993 after years of poor health, he sold the group to Ryback, who at the time was managing Lindner Dividend. Ryback promptly began a long-overdue expansion program. The St. Louis based group now sports seven funds including a utility fund and Lindner Bulwark, a contrarian fund.

Lindner's first fund opened with $7,500 in assets. Today, 34th ranked Lindner/Ryback has $3.3 billion under management. Unlike most money managers, the company will not accept private accounts. When Ryback took over he got rid of them, saying "It's like having 60 more mutual funds."

The group takes an investment approach that's almost antithetical to that of most mutual fund managers. Its analysts and managers pick stocks by using a proprietory, numbers-driven formula. It was originally developed by Lindner. Not only do Lindner managers seldom visit companies, they aren't even on the phone with them very often.

Montgomery

Montgomery Asset Management is one of the new kids on the block, having been formed in 1990. So successful was the San Francisco-based company that in August 1997 Germany's Commerzbank bought the firm, which is now an independent affiliate of the bank.

Montgomery's original mission was to develop investment strategies for areas of the markets where investors were underserved, then recruit proven managers who could be expected to significantly outperform market averages. In return, the managers received considerable freedom and were offered an equity interest in Montgomery. However, as the group has grown, its newer funds, such as Growth and Equity Income, have been mainstream, garden variety funds.

Ranking 25th among no-load families, Montgomery has more than $10 billion under management. Of that, $5 billion is in its funds. According to Lipper Analytical, a statistical firm that serves the mutual fund industry, the Montgomery funds reached $1 billion under management faster than any other fund family in history.

Montgomery now has 21 no-load funds: six equity funds investing in the U.S., nine equity funds investing globally or internationally, including its Emerging Markets Fund, the first no-load of its type. All its overseas funds are managed from San Francisco. In addition, Montgomery has three bond and three money market funds.

In early 1998, Montgomery launched a load fund group called the Partner Series.

Neuberger-Berman

One of the most interesting no-load families, 12th ranked Neuberger-Berman attempts to find out-of-favor companies with low price-to-earnings ratios, good balance sheets, and understated assets—securities that have value now, not ones that may develop value in the future.

Long located in New York City, Neuberger-Berman manages approximately $18 billion in 13 mutual funds, and $53 billion overall. Neuberger-Berman is still headed by its founder, nonagenarian art patron Roy Neuberger, who still comes into the office to manage his own portfolio.

Neuberger-Berman is unusual in that the company has added funds by acquisition as well as by launching its own. It took over both its Partners and Manhattan funds from other advisers—and greatly improved them. It is one of the few major no-load firms to offer a socially responsive fund

Believing investors should own equity funds for growth and fixed-income funds for capital preservation, Neuberger-Berman emphasizes growth equity funds, fixed income funds that buy securities with short maturities, and money market funds. In 1988 Neuberger-Berman disposed of its only long-term bond fund, believing that bonds are riskier than investors believe—a prescient view considering the bond market debacle of 1994.

Nicholas

The Milwaukee-based Nicholas Company, which got its start with the Nicholas-Strong Fund in 1968, hit the big time in 1971 when the fund's performance was No. 1 in the mutual fund universe. But then the devastating 1973-1974 bear market raged, and Albert Nicholas and Richard Strong parted company. Strong went on to form his own fund group, described below.

Today, the six Nicholas funds are for the patient, long-term investor. The fund's primary manager is still Ab Nicholas, a former All-American basketball player at the University of Wisconsin. But his son, Dave, has now taken over two of the funds, Nicholas II and Limited Edition, and is also co-manager of the Nicholas Fund.

Nicholas is a value-oriented stock-picker who no longer aims for dizzying heights. Today he seeks low-priced, unrecognized companies with solid balance sheets and steady earnings. These criteria usually lead to smaller companies, but larger ones are not ruled out. Turnover in the portfolios is low.

This approach seldom launches a fund's NAV into the upper stratosphere. And in the speculative stages of a bull market, Nicholas funds aren't apt to set the world on fire. But over the long term, the funds generally offer outstanding growth and income.

The Nicholas funds do not attempt to forecast short-term swings in the market; instead their goal is to preserve gains and minimize losses through long-term fundamental investing. Sell disciplines are based primarily on fundamental and valuation considerations. The group, the 22nd largest no-load family, manages about $7.5 billion.

Pilgrim Baxter was founded in 1982 by Gary Pilgrim, Harold Baxter, Stephen Hoyt and W. George Greig, who had all worked together in the investment management department of the Philadelphia National Bank. Hoyt and Greig soon departed the new firm, but Pilgrim and Baxter carried on, growing PBGH into a powerhouse firm that manages more than $16 million and therefore is the 20th largest no-load family. The advisory firm is now called simply Pilgrim Baxter & Associates.

PBHG launched its first fund, PBHG Growth, in 1985. Emerging Growth followed in 1993. But since 1995 the firm has been on a tear, adding another eleven funds.

Pilgrim Baxter is a classic growth fund investor. Proponents of fundamental research, fund managers use a bottom-up approach to stock selection. Quantitative techniques are employed in the service of finding stocks with high and sustainable earnings growth that might exceed the expectations of the investment community. PBHG typically diversifies across 80-120 stocks with a maximum position of 3% in any single issue and 40% in any sector. One major exception: the PBHG Large Cap 20 Fund, a focus fund holding only 20 stocks.

PBHG funds are perfect for investors who love the thrills and spills of roller coaster volatility. For two years running, one of their funds was the top rated diversified no-load. (One was managed by Harold Baxter's then 27 year old daughter, Christine.) Then in 1997, three of their growth funds posted negative returns, and another four ecked out gains of 6.8% or less. This during a wondrous year for the U.S. stock markets in general.

In 1995, when it managed two funds with $5 billion of assets, Pilgrim Baxter became a wholly-owned automomous unit of United Asset Managment (UAM), a giant financial holding company that owns approximately 50 money management firms and has 32 funds listed in the papers under the UAM name. PBHG has made a commitment to future growth. In October 1997, it hired Paul Hondros, the President and CEO of Fidelity Investments Retail Group, to be responsible for its strategic operations.

PBHG

The T. Rowe Price funds, fifth largest of all no-load groups, are the legacy of Thomas Rowe Price, the group's founder, and one of Wall Street's legends. If there were a no-load Hall of Fame, he would be a charter member!

T. Rowe Price

Price developed the theory of growth stock investing that hinged on the consistency of a company's earnings, rather than on the phases of the business cycle. His first fund, the T. Rowe Price Growth Stock Fund, was organized in 1950.

Mr. Price retired in 1971. For a number of years after that, the family's funds turned in mediocre performances. However, a turnaround has occurred in recent years. Several of the Price funds have been industry pacesetters.

Price was also an early believer in small company investing. The Price New Horizons Fund is one of the oldest and largest small company funds.

The T. Rowe Price group still accents its growth stock orientation. But with 75 funds, it has become far larger and more diversified than Price probably could have imagined. For example, T. Rowe Price now offers one of the largest selections of fixed-income funds in the mutual fund industry, including funds for high-net-worth investors. The company has an innovative international division that manages more than $33 billion in 13 mutual funds and private accounts. It launched the first no-load international bond fund and the first no-load international small cap fund. In the past few years, Price has diversified further, offering a discount brokerage service and variable annuities.

T. Rowe Price is a leader in the growing 401(k) market which has made defined contribution plans so popular. It believes that investing for retirement is the core strategy that ties its products together. In that regard, Price offers a valuable retirement planning guide free, and retirement planning software for a small fee.

With $125 billion in assets under management overall, Price is one of the real forces in the no-load business. The company is headquartered in Baltimore, and also has offices in Los Angeles and Tampa, and an investor center in Washington, D.C.

Robertson Stephens

In 1969 Sanford Robertson launched a West Coast investment banking company to identify and invest in new companies. In 1978 he teamed with Paul Stephens to form the company we know today. For several years their firm sponsored venture capital funds, many of them investing in nearby Silicon Valley startups.

Not until 1987 did the firm introduce its first mutual fund, the Robertson Stephens Emerging Growth Fund. Today, Robertson

Stephens has 12 funds, more than $3 billion in assets under management, 85,000 shareholder accounts, and a rank of 39th place in the no-load world.

Robertson Stephens guides a particularly eclectic mix of funds. Unlike most groups of its size, all 12 funds invest in equities; there are no fixed-income or money funds. It has an emerging markets fund, but no regular international fund. On the other hand it does have three global funds. Among its specialty funds are an information age sector fund, and a contrarian fund.

Robertson Stephens has an unusually talented group of portfolio managers, most of them hired from the outside. For example, John Wallace, who runs Growth & Income and Diversified Growth, had compiled an outstanding record at Oppenheimer. James Callinan (Emerging Growth) came from Putnam. Ron Elija (Value + Growth and Information Age) was a Montgomery manager. These portfolio managers were attracted by an opportunity to work in a company where top managment considers themselves to be stock pickers first and foremost. Not administrators. Paul Stephens personally runs Contrarian. The Robertson Stephens managers typically make a significant personal investment in their own funds. In addition, Robertson Stephens boasts its own in-house geologist and several short sale specialists.

In October 1997, Robertson Stephens was acquired by the Bank of America. Acknowledging the capabilities of the portfolio managers in their new unit, the bank gave the Robertson Stephens managers responsibility for the combined asset management activities of both the funds and the bank.

Rushmore

Located in Bethesda, Maryland, the Rushmore funds chose the name of their firm as a tribute to the presidents on Mount Rushmore. (If they'd been in South Dakota, would they have called the company Chesapeake?).

Started in 1974 with the formation of the Fund For Government Investors, one of the nation's first government-only money market funds, the Rushmore funds added three other "Funds For" before inaugurating the Rushmore label in 1985.

In 1992, Rushmore launched a new group of equity funds, the Cappiello-Rushmore Funds. Those funds are managed by Frank

Cappiello, the well-known panelist and substitute host on Public Television's *Wall Street Week*. That group now has four funds.

Before the launch of the Capiello funds, Rushmore had offered several index funds, originally designed to appeal to market timers. However, frequent buying and selling made tracking the indexes difficult. So Rushmore has merged three of these funds into the Capiello-Rushmore group. One index fund remains; it specializes in natural gas stocks. The remaining Rushmore funds all invest in fixed-income securities.

Unlike some other small operations, Rushmore conducts its shareholder service and transfer agent operations in-house. Rushmore-Capiello has 10 funds with about $1 billion under management.

SAFECO

SAFECO has a conservative reputation, as befits a group of funds whose parent company is a property and casualty insurer. SAFECO has had generations of experience, having managed mutual funds since 1933. A medium-sized group with 19 funds and $28 billion under management, SAFECO ranks 32nd among no-load groups. About one-third of the firm's shareholders are on the West Coast.

The group pretty well covers the bases. Shareholders can choose from among all the important equity and fixed-income categories plus a fund that invests solely in companies located in the Pacific Northwest. Its sole international fund is subadvised by Bank of Ireland Asset Mngt.

SAFECO prides itself on its analysis and its customer service. Its investment research is done entirely in-house, generally using a value oriented, bottom-up approach. This paid off in 1997 when its Growth Fund was the top ranked diversified no-load fund. The $28 billion of assets under SAFECO's management is split 88%/12% between its parent company and the funds. So the funds benefit from the parent company's strength. And, unlike many other small and medium-sized groups, SAFECO is its own transfer agent, which means that the fund can often process its customers' account transactions faster—and more accurately—than other funds can.

In 1994, SAFECO launched a load fund group, SAFECO Advisors, consisting of eight funds. It didn't succeed, so now SAFE-CO has added "A" and "B" shares to its existing no-loads to be sold by brokers.

Charles Schwab, the country's largest discount broker, entered the mutual fund business in 1991 with the concept of bringing low cost, institutional-style investing to its economy-minded customers.

Charles Schwab

Initially, Schwab began with three money funds and the Schwab 1000 fund, an index fund that buys the 1000 largest companies. The group since has expanded into 30 funds with $58 billion under management. Schwab now offers thirteen equity funds, seven bond funds and ten money market funds. The firm has zoomed into seventh place among no-load families.

Schwab's equity funds fall into four categories: They have four index funds, including one that matches an international index. Schwab's four asset allocation funds have objectives that range from high growth to balanced. In addition, three fund-of-funds invest in some of the mutual funds that participate in Schwab's Mutual Fund OneSource service. In addition, there is one quantitative fund.

Schwab's index funds are offered in two classes: the Investor shares have a low $1,000 minimum investment; the Select shares, have a $50,000 minimum, but with lower expenses.

Their underlying theme: uncomplicated growth, high diversification and tax-efficiency. Schwab has refrained from developing high-performance funds, in part, because they would compete with many of the non-Schwab funds it sells in its huge mutual fund marketplace.

Scudder, Stevens & Clark

Scudder, Stevens & Clark is another of the mutual fund industry's real leaders. The firm has been in the investment counseling business since 1919, which gives Scudder considerably more experience in fund management than most of its competitors. Its Income fund, founded in 1928, is the oldest no-load fund.

In 1997 Scudder was bought by the Zurich Insurance Company, a leading international insurance and financial organization. Zurich also owns the Kemper funds. The combined assets for Scudder/Kemper now make it the fourth largest fund complex.

A true giant in its own right, Scudder offers 108 funds or portfolios and has over one million shareholder accounts. Overall, the company manages more than $90 billion, with $44 billion of it in no-load funds. Scudder's holdings include funds distributed directly to the public, as well as those it manages for other distributors. A notable example: the 15 funds it manages for the giant American Association of Retired People (AARP). Scudder also markets low-cost variable annuity funds.

The company has a major international presence. Seven of its eight closed-end funds are international. In fact, its 20 international and global funds account for 23% of Scudder's assets. A popular misconception among investors is that Sir John Templeton founded the concept of international investing with the funds that bear his name. Actually, Scudder's International fund is the oldest in that specialty. It was founded in 1953.

While Scudder manages such a range of funds that the family defies easy classification, most of its equity funds tend to be conservative. Income is a secondary consideration. The group also offers a huge array of bond funds, ranging from single state municipals to U.S. government zero-coupon bond funds. Fixed income now accounts for 36% of the assets that Scudder has under management.

Headquartered in New York, Scudder has nine walk-in mutual fund centers around the country. The other facilities are in Boca Raton, Boston, Chicago, Cincinnati, Los Angeles, Portland, San Diego, San Francisco, and Scottsdale.

Scudder has introduced a discount brokerage service that includes more than 1,000 funds from 150 other fund companies. Six hundred funds are available without a transaction fee.

Stein, Roe & Farnham

As even a casual reader of these profiles must have gathered by this point, the independently owned no-load mutual fund company is an endangered species.

Over the past few years, more and more of the firms have been gobbled up by large banks and insurance companies. Generally, this has not compromised the funds' status as no-loads. An exception is Chicago-based Stein, Roe & Farnham.

Now part of Liberty Financial, a subsidiary of Liberty Mutual Insurance Co., Stein, Roe finds itself a first cousin to several load-fund companies. In 1995, Liberty Financial acquired the Colonial and Newport groups. Thus, in 1997 Stein Roe closed its popular Growth Stock Fund to no-load investors so it could be distributed through Colonial with a load.

Stein, Roe is one of the older investment companies. It was founded during the depths of the Depression in 1932 to manage private client accounts. It offered its first mutual fund in 1949. Now a major no-load fund group, especially on its home turf in the Midwest, Stein, Roe ranks 21st among no-load families; it manages $7.2 billion in 18 no-load funds and overall has about $27 billion in assets under management.

The group, which is oriented to growth stock investing, prides itself on its research, the bulk of which is produced in-house.

The Stein Roe Young Investor Fund has proven itself attractive to children. The fund seeks long-term capital appreciation by investing in companies such as Walt Disney, McDonalds, and Toys 'R Us that affect the lives of children and teenagers. Stein Roe views the fund as an educational investment that will enable children to learn basic investment and economic principles. Young investors get an attractive wall poster, a certificate of enrollment and a welcome kit.

While Stein Roe manages a wide range of funds, its strengths seem to lie at opposite ends of the mutual fund spectrum. Stein Roe offers a wide selection of growth funds—and at the other extreme, an array of conservative fixed-income funds, taxable, tax-free and money market, but it has only two conservative equity funds.

Strong

Dick Strong started his own investment management firm to handle private accounts in 1974, after he and Albert Nicholas had parted company. In 1976 he teamed up with Bill Corneliuson, and their new firm offered its first mutual funds in 1981. Since then, the Strong Funds have become one of the most well-known in the industry, partly because of Dick Strong's expansive personality and ubiquitous marketing.

In 1992, co-founder Corneliuson retired from active management of the group. Although only 49, he had had enough of the 80-hour work weeks and constant traveling. His departure has not hurt the firm. However, the grueling pace at Strong exacts a toll.

Strong portfolio managers are constantly on the road sizing up companies whose stocks they own or are considering buying. Strong/Corneliuson now has 56 investment professionals, including a number of talented portfolio managers who were hired from the outside to rejuvenate the company after it had a couple of bad years in the early 90s. Included in this group are Dick Weiss, who runs the Common Stock fund, Ron Ognar at Growth and Mary Lisanti with Small Cap. Dick Strong has encouraged these managers to maintain their own distinct investing styles.

In addition, Strong entered into a marketing relationship with David Schafer, whose Value Fund has been a good long-term performer. In 1997, Schaeffer launched a Balanced fund for Strong.

As of year-end 1997, the firm managed about $28 billion of assets, of which $22 billion is in the Strong family of 40 no-load funds (including six that are vehicles for variable annuities). That puts Strong just out of the top 10 no-load families; it ranks eleventh. For a number of years, the group experimented with 1% and 2% loads on its equity funds. In 1992 all sales charges were dropped, and the family regained its status as a pure no-load fund manager.

Management of the fund group communicates well with its shareholders. The company sends out detailed information about its current outlook for the fund, its investments and its philosophy. Rare for a medium-sized firm, Strong's switchboard is open 24 hours a day.

U.S. Global Investors

Formerly, the United Services funds, the group changed its name to U.S. Global Investors in January 1997 to better reflect its world-wide orientation.

Founded in San Antonio in 1969 by Clark Aylsworth, U.S. Global began life with a nothing-special domestic growth fund. However, during the gold boom of the early 70s, the fund changed its orientation. Renamed Gold Shares, it invested exclusively in South African gold mining stocks, and three times was best-performing fund of the year. Today, the fund no longer invests exclusively in South Africa; it now owns senior mining companies around the world.

U.S. Global also has two other funds that hold gold stocks. One of these funds, Prospector, ran into trouble in 1984 because of some improper portfolio transactions in Canadian stocks. Partly as a result of this problem, Clark Aylsworth retired in 1989, and the firm was sold to the Frank E. Holmes organization. Holmes is a Canadian investment dealer who was instrumental in bringing the Prospector's troubles to light.

The group had begun a program of diversification several years earlier, and Holmes is continuing it. He wanted a complete range of funds for a wider array of investors. So Holmes added a number of new funds while liquidating others that didn't fit into his strategy; gold-oriented investments have been reduced from 51% to 20% of total assets. The group now offers fifteen funds. Eleven of them are actively managed equity funds, two are bond funds, and two are government money market funds that have been yield leaders.

Since 1994, the group entered into joint ventures with several well-known financial figures. Art Bonnel, formerly a portfolio manager at the MIM group, now manages the Bonnel Growth Fund under U.S. Global's sponsorship. Regent Pacific, a international advisory firm, runs an Eastern European fund. And investment newsletter publisher Steven Leeb's MegaTrends Fund is now under U.S. Global's umbrella.

United Services has some highly specialized—not to say exotic—funds. For example, the China Region Opportunity Fund invests predominately in China. (Most other China funds concentrate in Hong Kong, and most of the others are closed-end funds.)

United Services used to encourage switching. But now the company has instituted a modest fee for investors who buy and sell in six of the equity funds within 14 days. These half dozen funds had been highly favored by traders. Also noteworthy: a rarely found no-minimum check writing privilege on its U.S. Treasury Securities money fund.

USAA

Another San Antonio-based family, the USAA funds are a subsidiary of USAA, one of the country's largest low-cost, direct marketing insurance companies. The group offers 35 no-load funds with a wide array of objectives, including three that invest overseas. With over $20 billion in the funds, it ranks tenth among all no-load fund groups.

USAA is a value-oriented firm. So, its managers attempt to concentrate on companies that are not receiving heavy attention from the financial community. They do their research in-house, and don't rely on outside recommendations. With a wide variety of both equity and fixed-income funds, USAA is suitable for all phases of the business/economic cycle. The company also offers a discount brokerage service.

The USAA Growth & Tax Strategy Fund is unusual in that it is one of the few balanced funds that utilizes tax-free securities for the fixed-income portion of its portfolio.

In 1997, USAA launched the First Start Growth Fund, which is aimed at teenagers. It invests in stocks of companies whose products or services are likely to be familiar and recognizable to young investors. It avoids companies whose primary products or services are alcohol, tobacco or gambling activities. USAA also has an S&P Index fund which has, with expense waivers, an .18% expense ratio, slightly lower than Vanguard's.

Value Line

If you think of any group of funds when value investing comes to mind, surely that group would be Value Line.

The New York City company's famous stock-ranking system is one of the primary tools that Value Line's portfolio managers use in making their selections. The system is based partly on fundamental analysis, scrutinizing companies' balance sheet basics, and partly on more technical trend-following techniques, such as momentum and relative strength. The Value Line system tracks about 1,700 stocks.

Value Line's approach has been successful: the Value Line stock selection system is one of the most popular in the country. And the company's mutual fund arm has grown from one equity fund in 1949 to 15 today, spanning the gamut from aggressive growth to bond to money market. That includes two that are available only through variable annuity contracts.

Value Line has $6 billion under management, including $4 billion in the funds. It ranks 29th among no-load groups.

While the Value Line equity funds follow the Value Line system to greater or lesser extents, they haven't been world beaters in recent years. Perhaps it's easier to publish recommendations than to implement them. Note also, the Value Line system does not extend to fixed-income funds; those are managed conventionally.

Value Line's patrician founder, Arnold Bernhard, has passed away. But his daughter, Jean Bernhard Buttner, now Chairman and CEO, continues the company's traditional policies.

Vanguard

If you had said only a few years ago that another no-load company would soon be challenging industry behemouth Fidelity, probably the typical investor would have had two reactions. First: "I doubt it." Second: "Well, if anyone could, it would have to be Vanguard."

Challenge might be too strong a verb, if brute size is the only or main consideration. Fidelity is still almost twice as big as Vanguard. But if you take less tangible characteristics into account, Vanguard clearly is on the march.

For years one of the premiere fund companies, Vanguard has a lot going for it. Start with John Bogle, the firm's indomitable leader. He has been one of the most important voices in the mutual fund business for a generation. An old lion dedicated to integrity and to the customer, Bogle has ensured that Vanguard not only offers a trendy array of products (it was an early proponent of indexing, and is still a leader in that department) but also offers them at exceptionally low prices.

It's probably not too strong an endorsement for me to say that if, as a leading evangelist for no-loads, I were to design my perfect fund family, it would not look too different from Vanguard.

And now to some specifics.

Located in Valley Forge, Pennsylvania, outside of Philadelphia, Vanguard is the second largest no-load family, with 95 investment portfolios and $330 billion in assets under management. It has 7.5 million shareholder accounts. In recent years, Vanguard has been growing much faster than Fidelity.

Unique in the mutual fund industry, Vanguard's management company is responsible for administration, marketing and legal support. Consequently, the company is much more aggressive than the average mutual fund group in cutting management costs. Distribution expenses are furnished at cost to the funds, about half of which are run by outside managers (the remainder, primarily bond and index funds, are managed in-house).

More expense minded than performance oriented, Chairman Bogle decided in 1977 that all sales charges should be dropped. Better still, Vanguard funds boast exceptionally low expense ratios, making them ideal for long-term investors, particularly those interested in fixed-income investments. Among their lowest cost funds are their four Admiral funds, which have high $50,000 minimum investments. Vanguard is also looking to be a leader in offering tax-efficient funds; it now has three.

The family launched the first index fund for individuals and is now in the forefront with 20 low-cost index funds. These funds track stock, bond and real estate indexes. In addition, there's a quasi-index fund, the Growth & Income Portfolio, which attempts to improve on the S&P 500.

Vanguard was the first no-load group to offer mutual funds that invest in other funds in the family: the Star funds.

Vanguard prefers more conservative funds oriented toward long-term growth. The $11 billion Windsor Fund—closed to new investors since 1989 is a prime example. It produces above average long-term results. In addition, the group has several asset allocation funds. Vanguard has 25 general bond funds (plus seven other single state bond funds). Because of their low cost structure, they frequently are exceptional values. However, Vanguard tends to offer fewer aggressive funds, and those few have not been winners in recent years.

So, while you don't get exotic funds from Vanguard, it's most unlikely you'll get any nasty surprises in performance, either: the company aims for predictable long-term performance rather than short-term gains.

Consequently, Vanguard doesn't like market timers who jump in and out of funds. Do that and you'll receive a letter requesting you take your business elsewhere. In addition Vanguard does not participate in "no-fee" mutual fund marketplaces. Their cost structure is too low to pay the fees.

Vanguard also offers a discount brokerage service, and a low-cost variable annuity program with nine portfolios. It has entered the personal financial services busines.

And if you have plenty of money, Vanguard has a program for you. High-net-worth shareholders who are willing to commit $500,000 or more to Vanguard can qualify for a service called the Flagship Financial Service. It provides shareholders with a personal representative and free literature.

Warburg Pincus

It sounds like an ancient European investment banking firm. Warburg, Pincus. And that's not entirely false.

The mutual fund company, Warburg, Pincus Funds, is a subsidiary of a large investment management firm called Warburg, Pincus Counsellors. The firm is a subsidiary of E.M. Warburg, Pincus & Co., which was established in 1965 by Lionel Pincus and Eric Warburg, a descendant of the great German-American banking family. E. M. Warburg was a merchant bank founded in the 30s. In 1985, Warburg, Pincus Funds was begun.

Headquartered in New York City, Counsellors manages more than $22 billion, $10 billion of it in funds. Warburg, Pincus has 19 retail no-load funds, ranking it 17th among no-load groups.

Warburg, Pincus managers follow a "bottom-up" investment approach, taking a business owner's perspective and evaluation process. The company's portfolio managers favor internal research and on-site company visits, aiming to identify companies with strong management, innovative products and above-average earnings-growth potential.

The group's Growth & Income Fund was originally run by Anthony Orphanos in a highly eclectic fashion. Quite unlike the traditional growth and income fund, from time to time he had huge weightings in gold and technology stocks. This strategy eventually failed; Orphanos now runs the Warburg Pincus Strategic Value Fund, which has a contrarian objective. Since 1997, Growth & Income has been run in a more traditional manner by Brian Posner, formerly the well-regarded manager of the Fidelity Equity Income II Fund.

Other strengths of the group include its emerging-growth funds and its seven international funds which include one of the few actively managed country funds to focus on the EAFE countries (see Appendix A for a discussion of EAFE).

All of Warburg's money managers have been with their funds since inception and have an equity position in the firm. Some of the funds previously existed in partnership form.

CHAPTER 19

THE NO-LOAD FUND INVESTOR

Winning mutual fund strategies

Every year it seems we read that investors are living in uncertain times. That's certainly true this year—but then, when wasn't it? On the other hand, that's probably good news. The Wall Street axiom is that the stock market climbs a wall of worry. In fact, those rare years when the investment climate seemed the most favorable often turned out to be the most perilous. Thus, investment strategies are simply a way to enable you to deal with "uncertain times."

The simplest one—buying and holding—actually works quite well. If you have enough time before you need your investment dollars, you can wait out turbulent times. Keep in mind that as a historical average, stocks tend to rise about two and a half out of every three and a half years, and the proportions have risen during the post-World War II period.

A second strategy for coping with the inevitable peaks and valleys is market timing. That's the notion that you can get into stocks at the bottom, when prices are low, and then out at the top, when they are high. In theory, the strategy holds far greater potential than the buy/hold approach. That's the theory. The practice is another story. Market timing is exceedingly difficult to implement successfully.

Another approach is a strategy that I call the Flexible Funding Program. It is a way of switching between aggressive and conservative funds throughout the market cycle, staying largely or even fully invested all the while. This approach combines some of the best features of both buy-and-hold and market timing.

A look at stock market history provides a powerful argument in favor of staying largely invested at all times. Since 1975, when the current super bull market began, investors holding funds long-term have undoubtedly done better than market timers who flitted in and out of equities. Table 63 shows how investments in some top growth funds and those in the average fund have done over the past 23 years.

The merits of long-term investing

Table 63

Long-term winners

January 1975 - December 1997

Fund	What $1,000 grew to	Annualized rate %
Fidelity Magellan	$187,798	25.6%
Sequoia	112,629	22.8
American Century-20th Cent Growth	99,413	22.1
American Century-20th Cent Select	82,191	21.1
Royce Penn Mutual	81,844	21.1
Value Line Levgd Growth	80,066	21.0
Mutual Shares	73,193	20.5
Lindner Growth	71,696	20.4
Nicholas Fund	70,899	20.4
Acorn Fund	70,748	20.3
SteinRoe Special	60,511	19.5
SAFECO Growth	59,882	19.5
Fidelity Equity Income	59,162	19.4
Vangd Windsor	56,499	19.2
Columbia Growth	49,140	18.5
Scudder Development	48,858	18.4
Average Diversified	39,409	16.5

(from all funds followed by The No-Load Fund Investor)

If you made a $1,000 investment in a top performing fund, such as Twentieth Century Growth, at the beginning of 1975, your money would have grown to $99,413 by December 1997. That's an annual compounded growth rate of 22.1%. The sixteenth fund on the list, Scudder Development, increased over 48 times for an average growth of 18.4% per year. That's remarkable performance, considering that while most of the 23 years was a powerful bull market, three full-fledged bear markets plus several severe corrections daunted investors. Remember the 1,000 point decline in the Dow from August to December 1987?

Of course, you would have been hard pressed to know back in 1975 which funds would make the Top rankings. You would certainly have had an easier time picking an average fund. Any investor who had done that would have witnessed a breathtaking 39-fold rise in his investment, which works out to a satisfying 16.5% per year. (And, of course, today an index fund investment can guarantee you an average performance.)

These figures are impressive. But let me personalize them with an anecdote. On Tuesday, October 20, 1987—a panic day for many because the results of the Black Monday meltdown appeared in that day's paper—an elderly man called the Invesco Funds to find out what his investment in the Invesco Industrial Income Fund was worth.

"I've invested $10,000; how much have I lost?" he asked, his voice quavering.

The account service rep at Invesco called up the account on his computer and noted that the $10,000 investment had, in fact, been made in the early 1970s. "Your fund shares are now worth $164,000," he told the investor.

There was silence on the other end of the phone. The representative said he was sorry; he knew that the shares had been worth much more only a few weeks before. Still silence. "Is there anything else I can do for you?" Another pause. "No." As the representative was hanging up, he heard, faintly, "Yippee!"

Time is on your side

Of course, you might well argue that I picked a very favorable starting point to show this terrific long-term performance. And it's true that the period began one of the greatest bull markets of the twentieth century.

But that's a little beside the point. My argument: if you are making a long-term investment, just by sticking to your strategy, in good times and bad, you can limit your risk and get good results.

First of all, you have to realize that you need to take some risk. On average, stocks will provide you with two or three times the return of bonds in the long run.

Chart 64 shows that the S&P 500 has gained in 40 of the last 50 years, or eighty percent of the time. Thus, a buy/hold policy suggests that you will be okay in four out of five years, but will take your lumps the fifth year. This doesn't mean that the losing and gaining years rotate regularly.

While losses occur in one-fifth of all years, lengthening your holding period will dramatically diminish your chances of losing. If you hold a diversified portfolio of common stocks for five years, you have about a 96% chance of making a profit. If you hold for ten years, you are virtually guaranteed a profit.

Table 64

How time reduces risk

Total return on stocks, 50 years ending 1997
According to length of holding period

Holding period	# Gain years	# Loss years	% Gain years
1 Year	40	10	80%
Rolling 2 Years	45	4	92%
Rolling 5 Years	44	2	96%
Rolling 10 Years	41	0	100%

Source: Ibbotson, Roger G. and Rex A. Sinquefield.
Based on S&P 500 with distributions reinvested

Put another way, the last time stocks lost during a ten-year period, was the decade from 1929 to 1938. Never since has a ten-year period seen an overall loss. Longer periods are even safer. Since this data series began in 1926, there is no 15-year period in which an investment would have declined.

Your portfolio can go down substantially in any one day, month or year. But once you hold for even five years, it's almost impossible to lose much. The largest annualized loss over any five-year period since 1938: -2.3%.

Because time is on your side, long-term investment strategies are the easiest way to maximize your wealth. Too often young people in their twenties or even in their thirties see no hurry about starting an investment program. These people are throwing away one of the golden opportunities of their lives. Starting an investment program, particularly a tax-sheltered IRA, even a few years earlier can make a remarkable difference.

We all know the story of the tortoise and the hare. The slow, steady pace of the tortoise enables him to beat the far faster hare. Does it work that way in retirement planning?

How about if I modernize the fable. In my version, I have three

A modern fable

racers. I'll call the first one the resting hare. That's because this particular player starts an IRA at age 22, as soon as he begins his working life, putting in $2,000 a year for six years and then stopping. By that time, he has a family and needs all his income for current expenses. Thus, at age 28 he stops contributing and never puts another dime into his IRA.

The second racer does exactly the opposite: he parties away his 20s, and gives not a care to his future. By age 28, he has miraculously matured, and opens an IRA that he faithfully contributes $2,000 a year to until he is 65. Because he started late, he has to sprint to catch up. So, I'll call him the sprinting hare. He's the one in the pictogram with his ears laid back.

And then there's the tortoise. He starts early—at age 22—and faith-

Chart 65

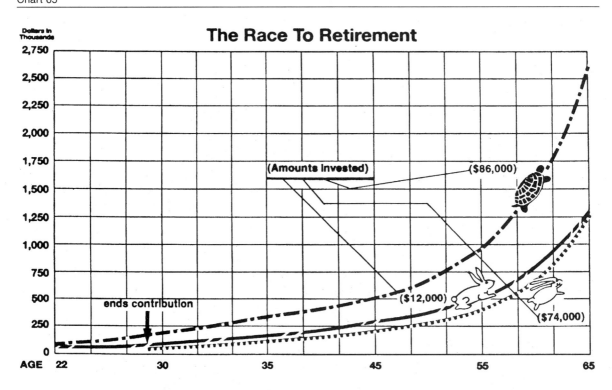

The Race To Retirement

fully makes his $2,000 yearly investment for the rest of his working life—to age 65.

Assume that all three IRA portfolios grow at the same 12% annual compounded rate of return.

Does the tortoise win? Of course. I wouldn't alter the famous fable. The $2,000 a year invested from age 22 to 65 grows to a fabulous $2,714,460. But more interesting is the fate of the two hares. *Incredibly, at age 65, both have about the same amount of money!* Even though the resting hare invested only $12,000, his nest egg is now worth $1,348,440, while the sprinting hare, who put in $74,000 after a later start, has $1,363,780. Starting early really pays!

I know that the vast majority of you (we're sorry to say) are too old to get optimal results by using this strategy for yourselves—but show this to your children and grandchildren. Make them start saving *now*. You can make their contribution for them for as great an amount as they earn up to $2,000. Starting young is by far the easiest way to build a very comfortable nest egg for old age.

Even if you didn't get out of the chute early, all is not lost. A late start is better than none at all. If the resting hare invested for the five years beginning at age 35 and the sprinting hare for the 20 years beginning at age 40, the results would again be about the same.

Back in 1929, Irving Fisher, a famous economist of his day, predicted that stocks had reached a "permanently high plateau." He was, of course, wrong. For, not many months later, the worst bear market in American history began.

The golden age of stocks?

With each sharp decline in the market, we hear renewed talk of another devastating bear market such as 1973-74, or even 1929-32. At the risk of being a modern-day Irving Fisher, I'd like to go on record predicting that the general trend will be up for years to come. So, for reasons I'll explain presently, don't get caught being too bearish.

Why? For one thing, bear markets don't last as long as they used to. Since the end of the 1981-82 bear market, there have been only three short-lived bear markets totalling 12.4 months. The first was a mild bear market from November 1983 to July 1984 in which the Dow lost 15%. That was followed by the 1987 and 1990 bear markets, both of which everyone still remembers. Thus, over the last 15 years, we suffered bear market conditions only 7% of the time. That's quite a contrast to previous decades. In the preceding 21.8 years—from 1960 through the 1981-82 bear market—there were eight bear markets which had a total duration of 114 months, or 44% of the time. The current long-running bull market even beats the halcyon days of the late 1940s and 1950s. Back then, 30% of that 13.5 year period was spent in bear markets.

Table 66

Period	No. years	Bear phase
Since 1982	15.3	7%
1960-1982	21.8	44%
1947-1960	13.5	30%

The last two bear markets, while about as deep as usual, have been short-lived. The worst was the crunching decline in 1987 that took the Dow Jones Industrial Average down 36%. But the decline itself lasted only 55 days. *Since 1982, no bear market has lasted for more than eight months!*

Table 67

Bear markets since 1982		
	Duration	**% decline**
1983-84	7.8 months	-15.6
1987	1.8 months	-36.1
1990	2.8 months	-21.2
Total	12.4 months	

In contrast, during the period 1960-1982, five of the eight bear markets lasted well over a year.

Table 68

Long-lasting bear markets	
1968-70	18 months
1973-74	22 months
1976-78	17 months
1978-80	19 months
1981-82	16 months

The flip side of a bear market is how long it takes to recoup the losses incurred. While it seems excruciatingly long while you're in the bear, in actuality the average time to recoup bear market losses is measured in months, not years. Looking at all market declines of 15% or more since 1953, it took, on average, only seven months for the S&P 500 to recoup three-fourths of its loss, and thirteen months to recoup the entire loss. The worst decline since the 1973-74 was in the fall of 1987. It took the S&P 500 Index 23 months to recover, while the average mutual fund came back in only 18 months.

What has changed? In brief, this remarkable long-run bull market has been driven by major structural changes:

■ The cold war is over, freeing up resources previously committed to national defense for other uses.

■ The computerization of America, and soon the world, has been a tremendous force for raising productivity.

■ Global trade is increasing, providing people all over the world with better goods and services at lower prices. Our corporations are now leaner and more profitable, so the market rejoices.

■ Worldwide competition and the demise of OPEC as a cartel has kept inflation low—always a boon for stocks

■ Economic cycles are not as severe as they used to be. This is due in part to the fact that a greater proportion of workers are in the more stable service industries, not manufacturing; computers are being used to better control inventory; and the Fed has better controls for managing the money supply, without creating sudden impact on financial markets.

And the good news will continue. We have changed from being a nation of savers to a nation of investors. About one-third of the population now invests in mutual funds. There has also been a sea-change in our pension plan system. Defined benefit plans, run by corporations, are on their way out. They're being replaced by defined contribution plans, such as 401(k)s, that are managed by the individual. Retirement plans now account for 35% of mutual fund assets and over half the assets of some large funds. Roughly two-thirds of mutual fund retirement assets are invested in equities.

The amount of money set aside for retirement will only grow in the future as more baby boomers enter their prime saving years. The new 20% capital gains tax increases after-tax profits.

All of this is fertile soil in which the financial markets should flourish. Here's a 120 year study showing how well stocks can do in periods of low inflation and price stability.

Table 69

Stocks total returns vs. inflation

1871-1991

Economic condition	Inflation rate	Annual real rate of return
Deflation	-0.2%	5.0%
Price Stability	0.2	19.0
Low Inflation	1.5	11.8
High Inflation	6.6	4.8

Because I see these favorable economic and political conditions continuing on well into the next decade, I believe the Dow Jones Industrial Average can attain *21,200 by the year 2010.*

If you think this forecast excessive, consider:

My prediction (made on December 31, 1997 with the Dow at 7908) assumes an 8.5% annual growth rate plus about 1.75% annually in dividends, for a total of 10.25%. Considering that the long-term performance of the stock market—not to mention its 17.5% annual growth since 1982—my prediction would seem to be on the conservative side.

There will, of course, still be bear markets along the way to Dow 21,200. At some point, valuations will get too high, or the Fed will tighten, or there will be some external shock (either political or economic), and this bull market will be history.

My guess is that in the near future, bear markets will continue to be short. They may be severe, but they will probably run less than a year, for two reasons: (1) professional money managers now control the market; (2) news and information travel so rapidly today.

Notwithstanding the forebodings about small investors panicking at the first sign of a downturn, it is now the professionals who trade precipitously. Corrections in 1996 and 1997 began and ended very quickly. Individuals, if they participated at all, were more likely to be found bottom fishing for bargains. I'm not unhappy about this. All things considered, I'd rather have a bear market that is short rather than long.

The principal drawback of a buy/hold strategy is that you need a long time horizon. If you must redeem your money in a few years, then a buy/hold strategy using equities may be too risky for you. Perhaps the safety of a money market fund is preferable.

You also need the psychological stamina to wait out bear markets or even sharp corrections during ongoing bull markets. In the decade of the 80s, on eight occasions mighty Magellan, the best fund in America during that period, dropped anywhere from 10 to 28 percent. After each major decline, some investors got out, and were later sorry that they did.

Thus, the buy/hold strategy is best suited for investors who have long time horizons and don't need to use their investment dollars to cover ordinary living expenses.

The disadvantages of buy/hold

While we have been in a long-running bull market, ups and downs occur along the way. To maximize your profits through them I have developed a moderate, easy to use approach I call *Flexible Funding*. It's an attractive alternative to both the passive strategy of buy/hold and the all-or-nothing approach that most market timers use. It's based on the premise that *you are better off using a theoretically inferior strategy that has a greater chance of success, than a theoretically superior strategy (such as calling market tops and bottoms) that has a far smaller chance of succeeding.*

It is a simple strategy that calls for buying aggressive growth funds when stocks are generally undervalued and the market is rising, then switching to conservative funds when the market reaches over-valuation levels. In other words taking more risk when the market is low, and less risk when the market is high. This can be much more profitable than being fully invested at all times in either type of fund. Moreover, when you are largely or fully invested in the market, you have a tremendous advantage because as we've just discussed, stocks rise most of the time.

I have implemented flexible funding in my newsletter's model portfolios throughout the 90s, with excellent results. Portfolio risk can be measured in many ways. I use betas because they are easily understandable. Table 70 shows how I have varied the risk level of my Master Wealth Builder Portfolio since 1991. At that time I was bullish. So I raised the risk level of portfolio to a beta of 1.10, in other words about

Flexible Funding— an effective middle course

10% riskier than the market. I then gradually brought the risk level down to .70 - .75 and kept it there during 1994, a poor year for the market. Sensing that 1995 and 1996 were going to be better years I raised the beta to about .90. I did not anticipate that 1997 was going to be a good year, so I once again lowered the beta, this time to about .75. That meant I was taking about one-fourth less risk than the market.

I adjusted risk mainly by changing my recommended allocations to the most aggressive funds. When I pushed the beta level down to .75, that meant eliminating those funds. Theoretically, my strategy permits cash to be held in the portfolio. But the Wealth Builder portfolio has been 100% invested in stocks since October 1990.

And here's the proof. The Wealth Builder portfolio, along with my Pre-Retirement and Retirement portfolios, were rated number one among all mutual fund newsletters on a risk-adjusted basis for the eight years ending September 1997 by the Hulbert Financial Digest, an independent rating service. Furthermore, the *Investor* was one of only two mutual fund newsletters to receive a grade of B or better in both up-and-down markets in the 1997 *Forbes* newsletter ratings.

Note that my judgement was off somewhat in 1997—I was too

Table 70

Wealth Builder Portfolio

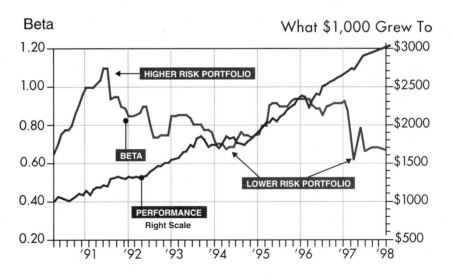

conservative. Nevertheless, my Wealth Builder portfolio gained 18.9% for the year. That's more than three times better than my results would have been if I had gone to cash. And don't forget I was buying insurance. If there had been a severe bear market in 1997, this portfolio would have had below-average losses.

In addition I am positioned for further gains in 1998. If I had gone to cash I would have to make a correct re-entry decision. Some investors who correctly exit a market, miss the early gains in the next bull market. These gains are generally substantial; missing them greatly reduces your long-run returns. For example, when the bear finally returned to his cave in 1975 following the disastrous 1973-4 market rout, 25% of the subsequent bull market gains were made in the first 45 days!

Some other advantages for the average investor:

■ Your temptation to stay with an aggressive growth fund too long is probably less than when the alternative is cash. Few investors sell at the top. However, you can switch to a growth or growth-income fund at any time, knowing you are still in the market and invested wisely.

■ Fully invested switching takes into account the fact that stocks can stay overvalued for years. Many considered stocks overvalued in early 1992 when the yield on the S&P 500 Index declined below 3%. That's when the Dow was at 3168! You just don't know how overvalued stocks will become or how long stocks will stay over-valued.

■ You eliminate the whipsaw that can occur if you sell and then have to get back into the market at higher prices. Whipsaws bedevil in-and-outers, particularly those making timing decisions based on moving averages.

■ In any type of market, some good funds always exist. While 1992 was a lackluster year for equities, the Oakmark Fund gained 48.9%. In 1994, a very trying year, PBHG Emerging Growth Fund was up 23.8%. You need to be in the market to be alert to this kind of opportunity.

■ It's a much more consistent approach.

■ You can use the plan with other strategies, such as dollar-cost-averaging.

While I describe flexible funding as an alternative to market timing, in another sense it is simply a way of keeping the risk of your fund investments at a level appropriate to current market conditions.

Guidelines for implementing a long-term strategy

■ Realize that even though that at some point there may be good reasons to be bearish, the odds are against you. So stay fully invested most of the time at a risk level you are comfortable with.

■ Don't worry about day-to-day news. Newspapers tend toward alarmist headlines when the Dow declines 100 points or more. But at today's lofty levels, large point changes mean very little. If the Dow declines 240 points when the index is at 8000, it sounds scary; but it is really only off 3%—not the end of the world.

■ Buy on dips. That's what most investors have been doing in recent years. It'll be the right decision most of the time.

■ If you do decide to time the market and are successful in selling before the next decline, do not stay out of the market more than about eight months. Go back in even if the new bull market hasn't yet started. Bull markets start suddenly and as we've said, a significant percentage of the gains come in the first few weeks. Don't miss them.

Dollar-cost averaging

Those familiar words refer to a long-term strategy that can be used in conjunction with the buy/hold or Flexible Funding strategies. It's an especially useful approach if you are making regular contributions to an investment portfolio that you expect to hold for a number of years. Dollar-cost averaging (DCA) can be an effective way to make market fluctuations work for you, rather than against you. You can cope successfully with stock market fluctuations without having to become a market timer.

If you make regular, periodic purchases, investing the same dollar amount each month, you'll be buying more shares of a fund when its price is low, fewer when it's high. You have effectively reduced the risk that you are putting your money into stocks at the top of the market.

No-load mutual funds are the ideal vehicle for employing the dollar-cost averaging strategy. You can easily invest just about any amount monthly—$100, $200 or more—and pay no commissions. In addition, every purchase represents a completely diversified investment. Equally important, mutual funds usually move with the market. However, don't lose sight of the fact that the profitability of dollar-cost averaging is wholly related to the fund's performance. If you are purchasing shares of speculative funds, you'll get different results than if you're buying conservative ones.

DCA probably got its start years ago when most investors bought individual stocks. But, dollar-cost averaging doesn't work as effectively with individual stocks as with funds. It is harder to invest equal dollar amounts, for one thing, and the commissions on stock transactions will seriously erode small investments. Unlike mutual funds, individual stocks don't always recover after a long decline, as investors who have averaged down sometimes discover to their sorrow.

Here's a specific example of how dollar-cost averaging can work. Assume that both the market and your fund decline, then return to their original levels. You've been investing $100 every month. In the first month, you bought ten shares at $10 each. The next month, the price declined to $9, so your $100 purchased 11.1 shares. In succeeding months, the price dipped still lower and your $100 bought even more shares. Then the market turned up. As the price gradually returned to $10, you were buying fewer and fewer shares. In seven months, you'd spent $700 and owned 81.5 shares. Your average cost: $8.59 a share. With the shares again worth $10, your profit was 16% (Chart 71).

Note that at any time, the value of the accumulated shares is determined by the current share price. In the above example, a loss occurred in some months.

In the previous illustration, the per share price declined $3 and came back. What if, instead, it went up steadily? Say the market is rising. The price starts at $10, then gradually climbs to $13 over the next six months (Chart 72). As the months pass, you are buying fewer and fewer shares because of the increasing price. Thus, your total profit is less than in the previous example—only 12%. Reason: there was less fluctuation in the period. Surprising as it may seem, fluctuations in price produce greater profits than long-term growth can by itself. Consequently, dollar-cost averaging is more profitable with aggressive growth funds than it is with less volatile growth or growth-income funds—although, of course, your exposure to risk is far greater.

In my first example, the fund declined from $10 to $7 and then returned to $10, providing a 16% profit. If the fund had been still more volatile, declining to $5 before coming back to $10, an investor who

Chart 71

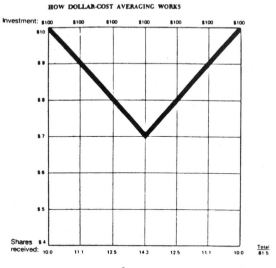

HOW DOLLAR-COST AVERAGING WORKS

Investment: $100 $100 $100 $100 $100 $100 $100

Shares received: 10.0 11.1 12.5 14.3 12.5 11.1 10.0   Total 81.5

Summary	Per share	Total
Cost	$ 8.59	$700.00
End value	$10.00	$815.08
Profit	$ 1.41	$115.08 or +16%

Chart 72

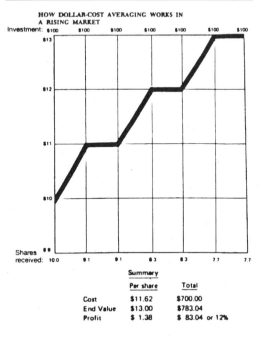

HOW DOLLAR-COST AVERAGING WORKS IN A RISING MARKET

Investment: $100 $100 $100 $100 $100 $100 $100

Shares received: 10.0 9.1 9.1 8.3 8.3 7.7 7.7

Summary	Per share	Total
Cost	$11.62	$700.00
End Value	$13.00	$783.04
Profit	$ 1.38	$ 83.04 or 12%

Chart 73

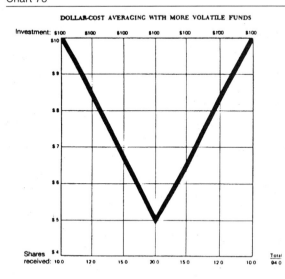

DOLLAR-COST AVERAGING WITH MORE VOLATILE FUNDS

Investment: $100 $100 $100 $100 $100 $100 $100

Shares received: 10.0 12.0 15.0 20.0 15.0 12.0 10.0   Total 94.0

Summary	Per share	Total
Cost	$ 7.45	$700.00
End value	$10.00	$939.96
Profit	$ 2.55	$239.96 or +34%

Chart 74

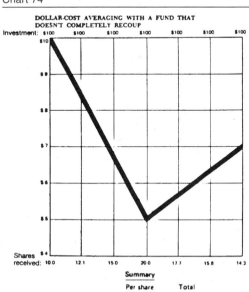

DOLLAR-COST AVERAGING WITH A FUND THAT DOESN'T COMPLETELY RECOUP

Investment: $100 $100 $100 $100 $100 $100 $100

Shares received: 10.0 12.1 15.0 20.0 17.7 15.8 14.3

Summary	Per share	Total
Cost	$6.68	$700.00
End value	$7.00	$733.24
Profit	$0.32	$ 33.24 or +5%

had conscientiously bought at regular intervals, would have had a substantially greater gain, 34%. The average price would have been $7.45, not $8.59 (Chart 73).

Even with aggressive growth funds that recoup very slowly after bear markets, dollar-cost averaging can make sense. If, for example, you began your investment program when an aggressive growth fund was selling for $10 per share, then kept putting in equal dollar commitments as it sank to $5, and came back to only $7, your profit would still be 5% (Chart 74).

For dollar-cost averaging to work, you have to stick with your program, continuing to buy, especially when the market is at its lowest. If you stop investing during market downturns, you've defeated the purpose of the strategy. Moreover, for the approach to be successful you need to have time on your side. You cannot stick with the program for a year or two and then abandon it. You need to invest over many, many years, which is why practically speaking dollar-cost averaging works best for people who are automatically contributing each year to a retirement plan or profit-sharing program.

Like most strategies, dollar-cost averaging has its advantages and disadvantages. It's not a panacea. Perhaps its greatest benefit is that it can force you to save regularly—and *make you buy some shares when prices are low*. Too often, investors are perverse. People will buy more of almost any product or service when its price is low than when it is high. Except stocks! Buyer enthusiasm increases as stock prices rise, and decreases when stock prices fall. It's been said that a bull market is when you look in the paper every morning to find out how much your stocks went up the day before. And a bear market is when you don't check the financial pages at all.

The value of DCA fades away with time. The strategy doesn't work as well over the long term because of inflation and also because of the overall growth in the stock markets. If the same amount is invested each month, its inflation-adjusted value decreases over the years. Investments of $100 a month, for example, may have made sense 20 years ago, but are truly inadequate today.

One solution is to increase the amount invested each year. I recommend that an investor boost the monthly amount by at least 10% a year, if possible. That's not always feasible. Funding an IRA is an important application of DCA, but obviously you can't increase your annual invest-

Pitfalls of dollar-cost averaging

ments beyond $2,000. Therefore, you need to supplement the IRA with other regular investments.

DCA doesn't offer any guidance on selling. The ultimate value of the investments you accumulate through regular investing depends greatly on the end value. One study showed that dollar-cost averaging over the ten years ending in 1974 actually produced a 28.1% loss. The best solution: use averaging in reverse after your accumulation period has ended. A regular withdrawal plan at a fund group would accomplish this objective, making your ending point less critical.

It might even be prudent to completely abandon averaging once you have accumulated a large sum. As the years go by, each additional investment becomes less significant. If you have built up an account to, say, $20,000, the next $100 is of little consequence. You should be more worried about protecting principal than rejoicing when a major decline provides you with the opportunity to pick up a few more shares at bargain prices.

It's hard to invest significant amounts at bargain prices. While dollar-cost averaging forces you to make at least some investments during bear markets, when prices are low, that's not sufficient in itself. Bull markets traditionally last much longer than bear markets, meaning that the bulk of your periodic purchases will be made when prices are high. One antidote: double up your purchases during bear markets, when prices are low.

You have less money working for you than if you invested a lump sum. One DCA study found that $12,000 invested over a ten-year period ending in 1988 grew to $21,810. In contrast, if the $12,000 had been invested lump sum at the beginning of the period, it would have grown to $36,747, 68% more. That's because you would have had only half as much money working for you, on average, when investing steadily over the ten years. Of course, if you didn't have the lump sum at the beginning, then investing regularly is your only alternative. But if, say, you receive an inheritance, or a lump-sum distribution from your company's pension or profit-sharing plan, then you need to compare the strategies.

Averaging versus lump sum purchases

People often ask me what time frame to use to dollar-cost-average a large sum of money into the market. You should realize that that's really a market-timing question. No one answer is correct. If the market is going to rise, then the best strategy is to plunge every penny in immediately. On the other hand, if the market is about to decline, you'd obviously be better off waiting to invest. The less money you invest in a falling market, the less you lose.

Since I'm predicting that future bear markets will be short and that the long-run trend is up, if you come into a large sum of money, invest it all at once, rather than dribbling it into the market. However, here's a compromise: invest 50% or more of a lump sum right away into conservative equity and growth-income funds; then dollar-cost-average the balance in over three to eight months.

The BJ Group, our subsidiary that actively manages client portfolios, follows that strategy. A client once sent us $100,000 to invest. We invested $50,000 immediately, and planned to invest the remaining $50,000 over the next few months, or during any buying opportunity a correction might provide. A week later the client called asking when the remaining money would be invested. I explained the strategy. "I'm 82" he exploded. "I'm too old to dollar-cost average! Dump it in." Moral of the story: you don't have to be 82 for that strategy to make sense.

Over the years, analysts have searched for ways to enhance the effectiveness of dollar-cost averaging. One variation that makes sense is to substantially increase the amount you invest when the market declines, and decrease the amount that you invest when the market is high. Various formulas have been developed to implement this.

Value Averaging, a 1991 book by Harvard business professor Michael Edleson (International Publishing Corp.) developed some variations that have potential. The main one, value averaging, calls for the value of your holdings to increase by $100 (or some other set amount) each month. If the market goes down the previous month, you will have to invest more than $100 to meet your goal. If the market increases, a lesser amount would be invested. Under the basic version of the strategy, you would find yourself selling some shares in those months when the market made striking gains in order to limit your portfolio's growth to $100 that month. In an alternative version, you wouldn't sell (which might mean capital gains taxes) but simply wait until your portfolio's actual value was less than the required value before you resumed buying. Edleson's studies found that value averaging was potentially more profitable than straight dollar-cost averaging.

Dollar-cost averaging variations

I think the idea is a good one because it enables you to focus more clearly on your goals. With standard dollar-cost averaging, you don't know how much money you will have at retirement. With value averaging you will know. It's similar to the difference between defined contribution and defined benefit retirement plans. With value averaging you can work back to determine how much money you need to put aside each period to meet your long-range goals. One caution: the correct implementation of value averaging is not as straight-forward as the above description. It pays to buy the book if you are going to try to employ the professor's strategies.

How even the worst losers can make money

Let's say your timing is terrible. You had an auto accident the week after you dropped your collision insurance. You bought a beach house just before the hurricane struck. And when it comes to investing, you invariably buy in at the market's highest points. If you sell when the market is substantially lower, that is, of course, a guaranteed way to lose money. But what if you don't sell low? Studies show that even the worst timing need not be fatal for the long-term investor.

T. Rowe Price has calculated the hypothetical performance of annual investments made in the S&P 500 stock index on the *worst day of each year* for the last 24 years. This calculation is similar to a typical dollar-cost averaging program, but with one significant difference. Instead of investing at regular intervals so that at least some shares are purchased at below-average prices, the example deliberately showed purchases chronically being made at the worst time possible, the day the market made its high for the year. In this calculation, an investor deposited a $2,000 lump sum on the day the market peaked each year. Not withstanding this major impediment, the results over the long run are still spectacular.

The period includes the horrendous 1973-74 bear market. So, it was very rocky going for a few years. But when the bull markets of the late 70s and 80s began, the investments began to bear fruit. By the 90s, the investments were growing at geometric rates. The gain in 1995 alone was $79,553. By December 1996, the $48,000 invested over the years was now worth $357,763!

Similar studies have been done using individual funds. Their results all show that if the market is in a long uptrend, it doesn't mat-

Table 75

	Buying at the worst time of the year		
	S & P 500 (with dividends reinvested)		
Investment date (S&P high)	**Cumulative investment**	**Value at year end**	**Cumulative profit/loss**
01/11/73	$ 2,000	$ 1,676	$ (324)
01/03/74	4,000	2,675	(1,325)
07/15/75	6,000	5,596	(404)
09/21/76	8,000	8,962	962
01/03/77	10,000	10,182	182
09/12/78	12,000	12,690	690
10/05/79	14,000	17,006	3,006
11/28/80	16,000	24,478	8,478
01/06/81	18,000	25,154	7,154
11/09/82	20,000	32,553	12,553
11/10/83	22,000	41,795	19,795
11/16/84	24,000	46,381	22,381
12/16/85	26,000	63,069	37,069
12/12/86	28,000	76,733	48,733
08/25/87	30,000	82,198	52,198
10/21/88	32,000	97,734	65,734
10/09/89	34,000	130,588	96,588
07/16/90	36,000	128,338	92,338
12/31/91	38,000	169,377	131,377
12/31/92	40,000	184,252	144,252
12/31/93	42,000	204,734	162,734
02/02/94	44,000	209,951	165,951
12/13/95	46,000	289,504	243,804
11/30/96	48,000	357,763	309,763

ter how egregious your mistakes; the market can still bail you out. Your patience and tenacity will be richly rewarded.

Let's turn the study upside down. Surprisingly, even picking the best days to invest doesn't dramatically alter the outcome in the long run. A 30-year study reported in May 1996 found that if a person had invested each year at the annual market low, he'd have gotten an 11.6% annual return. On the other hand, if he had invested once a year at the market's annual high, his annual return would be 10.7%. The former figure is, of course, better. But not as much better as you might think. And as a practical matter, it's totally unachievable. The point is: If you invest regularly in stocks, you will make enough purchases at low prices to do just fine in the long run.

While these results are truly startling, I don't think they mean you can abdicate all judgment. If you are going to invest in stocks you must have an informed opinion about long-term trends. Stocks aren't always in a long-term uptrend. They declined between 1968 and 1974. In the Great Depression, stocks lost 90% of their value—and took 15 years (even with dividends included) to come back. And that period certainly exceeds our preferred time horizons.

A speculative way to make big bucks

Psst. Wanna hear how you could do over four times was well as investing in the average equity fund?

At the end of each year, buy that year's top-ranked diversified no-load equity fund. Hold it for one more year. Then switch to the new top-ranked fund.

A study by *The No-Load Fund Investor* newsletter found that if you had actually implemented such an approach from 1975 to 1997, an investment of $1,000 would have grown to $95,566. At the same time, an investment in the average diversified domestic stock fund grew to only $22,587. My methodology was simple. I reviewed the list of top no-load funds until I found the best diversified equity fund available for sale. Since the performances of specialized gold and sector funds are notoriously inconsistent, I excluded them from the study.

I then examined each fund's performance in the year following its #1 ranking and compared this performance to the average no-load fund.

For example, 44 Wall was the top rated fund in 1975 with a gain of 184.1%. For the purpose of this study, let's say that I bought it on Jan. 1, 1976 and held the fund for one year. In 1976 Forty-four Wall gained 46.5%, as compared to a 27.6% gain for the average equity fund. That's the approach I used for the entire 19 years.

The results: If you had simply bought each year's top performing no-load diversified domestic equity fund on January 1 of the following year, held it until December 31, and then switched into the new No. 1 fund, you would have had an average (uncompounded) gain of 23.0% per year since 1976. By way of comparison, the average equity fund gained 15.2% per year. The top funds outperformed the average fund in 15 of the 22 years. In one year it was a tie. There were only two years with losses, and one year with gains while the average fund declined.

Caution: while this strategy produced remarkable results in the measured period, it is a high-risk approach. In two of the four bear market years, the top-rated fund seriously underperformed the averages. So don't bet the farm on my thesis.

Table 76

How the top diversified domestic no-load equity funds fared

Year	No-load fund	Gain in record year	Gain following year	Average diversified no-load fund
1975	44 Wall Street	184.1	46.5	27.6
1976	Sequoia	70.8	19.9	3.5
1977	Value Line Leveraged Growth	51.1	27.6	11.6
1978	Twentieth Century Gr (3)	47.2	74.2	28.6
1979	Able Associates (3)	79.1	56.7	33.6
1980	Hartwell Leverage	93.9	-13.2	-1.0
1981	Lindner	34.8	27.1	23.7
1982	Tudor (6)	44.5	28.0	21.2
1983	Strong Investment (2)	44.7	9.7	-0.6
1984	Vanguard High Yield Stock	25.2	30.1	27.1
1985	Fidelity OTC (2)	69.0	11.4	13.9
1986	Strong Opportunity (7)	59.9	11.8	0.4
1987	Mathers (11)	26.9	13.7	15.6
1988	Kaufmann	58.6	46.8	22.9
1989	Twentieth Century Vista (5)	52.2	-15.7	-5.8
1990	Founders Discovery (11)	13.1	62.5	33.2
1991	Montgomery Small Cap (3)	98.7	9.6	9.6
1992	Oakmark (2)	48.9	30.5	14.7
1993	PBHG Growth (26)	46.5	4.8	-0.7
1994	PBHG Emerging Growth (2)	23.8	48.4	1.5
1995	Wasatch Mid-Cap (4)	58.8	3.6	18.6
1996	Robertson Stephens Partners (7)	43.3	18.1	22.6
1997	SAFECO Growth (6)	50.0		
	Average gain	54.9%	23.0%	15.2%
	What $1,000 grew to:		$95,566	$22,587

The numbers in parentheses show the rank among all funds.

In December 1992, *The Wall Street Journal* did a similar study using the Lipper data base. Its analysis presumed that three investors each bought the top 25% of diversified stock funds (load and no-load). The first investor "bought" the top funds based on the latest one-year performances, the second "bought" on the basis of the previous five-years, the third on the basis of the previous ten-year performances. All three investors then held the funds for an additional five years. To determine which one did best, 19 rolling five-year time periods were evaluated, beginning with 1970-1974. The winner: the investor who bought on the basis of the previous one-year performance.

Wall Street Journal study

Table 77

No. years top quartile funds beat average fund		
Out of 19 five-year time periods		
Previous performance base:	**No. years**	**Avg 5 yr gain**
One year	12	95.6%
Five years	6	80.7%
Ten years	8	82.6%
Average fund		84.0%

Source: The Wall Street Journal

Why did the investor who made purchases on the basis of the latest one-year performance fare best? The *Journal* suggests that the answer relates to investment cycles. There are major cycles in equities: small caps versus large, growth versus value. Both rotate in long, multi-year cycles. A great many funds specialize in one of these categories. As a result, if you buy one type of fund after it has been ascendent for, say, five years, you are likely to be buying it at or near the end of the cycle for its kind of stocks. In contrast, buying a fund based on the most recent year's performance gives you a better chance of riding its cycle to completion.

Vanguard's Jack Bogle, in his book, *Bogle on Mutual Funds*, undertook a similar study. He took the top 20 funds each year for a decade and calculated their second year results. Averaging all ten years together, he found that the top 20 funds returned 17.6% the following year, substantially better than the all-fund average of 13.5%.

Shorting funds

I'm frequently asked by investors who are unfamiliar with mutual funds whether it's possible to sell them short. That's the name of a strategy, which you can easily use with individual stocks, in which you "borrow" the stock and sell it. Your expectation is that the stock will drop in price, so that you can buy it more cheaply sometime in the future, replace it in the account you borrowed the shares from, and make money on the stock's drop in value. Short selling is not universally available with mutual funds. But it can be done.

You can short all Fidelity Select Funds. In order to sell short you will need to open a margin account with Fidelity Brokerage. Of course, you will need to meet various margin and collateral requirements. And, be aware that you can't margin an IRA or other qualified account. Commissions are the same as for stock transactions.

Jack White, the discount brokerage firm, also offers a service for short sellers. Subject to availability, White will permit customers to sell short 40 to 50 no-load funds including funds in the Babson, Dreyfus, Evergreen, Founders, Gabelli, Janus, Lexington, Neuberger-Berman, Rushmore, Scudder, Strong, Price, and United Services groups.

Another way to make money on the downside would be to short a closed-end investment company, which is traded on an exchange. A disadvantage of shorting closed-ends is their relative illiquidity. For some of them, the average daily trading volume is low. If a fund doesn't trade many shares each day, selling short would be a more ponderous proposition. A sophisticated investor who was going to execute this strategy would have to plan his short sales well in advance. And, such an investor would find equity substitutes, such as index options, more effective vehicles for short sales.

Better still, why not use the two bear market funds that we mentioned in Chapter 12. Those two are wholly or largely short the market.

In December, 1997, Lipper Analytical Services, Salomon Brothers, and the CBOE (Chicago Board Options Exchange) introduced two index option contracts based on the performance of two new indexes of mutual fund performance: Lipper/Salomon Growth Mutual Fund Index and the Lipper/Salomon Growth and Income Mutual Fund Index. The first tracks the performance of the 30 largest growth mutual funds; the latter the 30 largest growth-income funds. An option is the right (but not the obligation) to buy or sell a security at a specified price within a certain time period.

Investors, including mutual fund investors, have long been able to hedge their holdings, improve their timing, and enhance their tax situation by using options based on passive indexes such as the S&P 500. The Growth Fund index offers a more accurate proxy for the typical growth fund portfolio than the S&P 500; the Growth and Income Fund Index is only a slightly better proxy for growth-income portfolios than the 500. The Growth Index has a .93 correlation with the average fund in the index as compared to a .88 correlation for the S&P 500. For Growth-Income, the advantage is .94 vs. .92 for the S&P. Not surprising; that's why we've always categorized S&P 500

Index options for mutual fund investors

funds as growth-income. But that's only part of the story. These fund indexes are less volatile than market indexes, and since volatility is an important factor in pricing options, they can be cheaper.

Here are some ways to use these indexes:

■ If you become less bullish or bearish, you can modify your portfolio's risk level by purchasing put options.

■ You can lock in profits. Gains can be shifted from one year to the next, thus deferring taxes.

■ It gives you the potential to establish a long or short position in a basket of mutual funds during the day. For example, on October 28, 1997, the day after the 554 point drop in the Dow, the market initially traded lower, before ultimately recovering 337 points that day. You could have bought index option calls in the morning and profited from the subsequent rise. Investors who buy funds directly receive the 4 PM price.

■ The options can be used as fund substitutes. Options can give you the opportunity to profit this year, while limiting your risk to the price of the options.

The ticker symbol for the Growth Index is LGO, for the Growth-Income Index, LIO. At this writing, the price on the Growth Index is 185; for the Growth-Income Index, 312. Since there is a $100 multiplier, one contract would be $18,500 and $31,200 respectively.

These options may help fund managers more than individuals since the repeal of the short-short rule is expected to facilitate mutual fund option strategies. Managers can buy options to stay 100% invested within their discipline, while still keeping some cash on hand to meet redemptions.

You can place limit orders at American Century

In 1990, the Benham group began a practice of accepting open or limit orders for mutual funds. Investors can specify in advance the prices at which they will buy and sell. Since the merger with Twentieth Century, the privilege has been extended to all the American Century variable priced funds. Shareholders in an American Century money fund who want to buy one of the group's stock or bond funds simply specify any price lower than the current one and the amount to be invested. If the fund falls to that price, the shares are bought automatically with money from the money fund, just as it would be in a stock brokerage account. Similarly, shareholders in a variable-priced fund can choose to sell automatically whenever the price goes up to a pre-determined level. (They cannot place a sell order *below* the market.) The proceeds go into a money fund. Both buy and sell orders expire if the fund does not reach the specified price within 90 days. They can be renewed, cancelled or amended to a new price or changed at any time within the 90 days. The service is free.

Upgrading, the process of replacing average to below-average funds with higher-ranked funds, is a perfectly acceptable investing strategy. I myself do it from time to time when a fund's performance falters. Some other advisers use a mechanical approach.

Upgrading mutual funds

You should beware, though, of a few advisers who carry the concept to extremes. They may advise selling a fund if it drops out of the top 5, the top 10 or some such, and replacing the fund with a current winner. That's too much. All mutual fund performance is time-period specific. These advisers seldom think through the period of time on which to rank funds, and how far out of their magic ranking a fund needs to drop before it is replaced.

As a general rule, as long as the market is rising and the fund is performing reasonably well, stick with it. Fund performance is too erratic for you to sensibly move around often to get just a small edge. It doesn't pay, particularly on an after-tax basis.

Understanding the time value of money is essential to good investing. Which of these two investors obtained the best return? Miss A's fund gained 20% in one year; Mr. B's gained 20% in two years. Obviously, Miss A gets our Shrewd Investor Award. Poor old B's fund grew at an annualized rate of less than 10% a year. Practically speaking, Miss A could have switched into a money market fund after one year, protecting her lead and tacking on additional gains.

The time value of money

This homely example suggests that investors should think clearly about the measurements of investments. Yet, there is an interesting dichotomy in the conventions of calculating investment returns. When discussing stocks and growth stock funds, returns under a year are almost always computed directly, without taking into account the length of time the investment has been held. Even multi-year periods are annualized only part of the time. Fixed income investments such as bank savings accounts, CD's, Treasury bills and money market funds, however, typically are quoted on the basis of annualized returns. When you buy a six-month CD paying a 5% return, the actual return over its life is only 2.5%.

The lesson: always adjust your returns for the length of time you've had the investment. That way you can put the profits from different investments on an equal footing. Similarly, you should reduce multi-year performance data to annualized figures.

This advice is even more urgent for commodity investments. Such things as gold, silver, raw land and art do not pay dividends. A common mistake with land, for example, is to buy too early. If a rise in value is many years in coming, your average annual return may be quite poor, even though your margin of profit is respectable. Similarly, the great auction houses like Sotheby's and Christie's love to publicize the multi-million prices paid for great paintings. But if you adjust them for time, it's another story. For example, in November 1994 Sotheby's sold a Claude Monet painting for $1.8 million. It had been purchased in 1916 for $5,000. The average annual gain over the 78 years: just 7.1%. Stocks did better! (O.K., so hanging your stock certificate on the wall isn't the same.)

Here are some other guidelines: When you are switching between equity and money market funds you should time-weight your returns. If you make a 20% gain in an equity fund over three months, that's an 80% gain annualized. You could spend the next nine months in a money fund and still have a super return for the full year. There is a date attached to every investment you make. The longer your money is invested, the more it has to earn for the return to be competitive.

Because the market can decline very fast, even a small gain on a short sale can, on occasion, be quite profitable.

Some state lotteries award "multi-million dollar" prizes, but actually pay $50,000 a year per million for 20 years. Is this the same? Not by a long shot. Taxes are withheld each year before payment. Depending on interest rates, taxes and inflation, the value of the yearly check dwindles over time.

If one million dollars were paid at once, it could be invested to throw off $100,000 or more a year, with the principal still in the winner's hands. Four states—Arizona, Colorado, Ohio, and Oregan—actually allow winners a lump sum option. But these states aren't fools. If the winners choose the lump sum, the states pay them only 40% to 50% of the full jackpot amount. Still, the winners are well advised to take it. By taking a lump sum today of $300,000 ($500,000 less 40% in taxes) and investing it wisely at 10%, they would have $2.4 million at the end of 20 years, and could live off the returns forever.

A 30-year mortgage isn't cheaper than a 15-year mortgage. It only looks that way. (Actually, it's much more expensive in terms of the interest you pay over the long haul.) Similarly, second-to-die life insurance policies (which take longer to pay off) aren't cheaper than individual policies when you take the time value of money into account.

Take advantage of the float. That's another perfect illustration of the time value of money. When you write a check on a money market fund, you hope the recipient will take forever to cash it. Each day of delay puts additional interest in your pocket. Conversely, deposit checks you receive as quickly as possible. And don't retain unused traveler's checks. Why give American Express unnecessary interest income for using your money?

To reduce this discussion to our favorite subject, when you examine a fund's "mountain" (see page 153), be sure to take into account the number of years that have gone into obtaining that performance.

At various times during the last two decades, investors' expectations have become, shall we say, greatly inflated. Many people, even today, think that earning 15% to 20% per year is normal, even conservative. That's simply not true over the long run. A far more realistic goal with my conservative switching strategy: 12% to 13% per year over a great many years. It's hard not to be influenced by the unrealistic expectations of others. Make sure *your* expectations are realistic.

Inflated expectations can damage your fiscal health

Seattle money manager Paul Merriman tells the following story: Speaking before an investment seminar in Costa Mesa, CA, he asked the audience, "How many of you are looking for a 12% or greater compounded rate of return?" Almost every one of the 150 or so people in the audience raised a hand. So he asked: "How many of you are willing to lose 50% of your investment in one year in attempting to achieve a 12% return?" No hands went up. "How about a 40% loss?" Again, no hands went up. "Thirty percent?" Three people raised their hands. "Twenty percent?" A couple of dozen hands went up. "Ten percent?" Finally, 40 to 50 hands were raised. Stunningly, more than 30% of this group were unwilling to lose *any* money in pursuit of a 12% plus rate of return. Needless to say, Merriman concluded that the group's expectations were unrealistic.

A summary: rules for successful investing in the 90s

Throughout this book, I have talked about these precepts. Here is a synopsis of my advice:

■ *Invest early and often.* This is the real secret to investment success. Make the magic of compounding work for you. Successful entrepreneurs may be able to accumulate vast fortunes in no time. But passive investors in other people's businesses, which is what you are as a stock investor, don't have such ripe opportunities. For you, what counts is the slow steady accumulation of wealth over the long haul.

■ *Make common stocks your core investment.* Your potential return is always greater if you own a business or property—or even a small sliver of them—than if you lend money. Thus equities (stocks or real estate) will outperform debt (bonds).

Stocks gained 15.3% annually during the period from 1933 to 1994. But an investor who was out of stocks on the market's ten best days during all that time gained only 9.7% annually. As the New York State Lottery is fond of saying, you gotta be in it to win it.

■ *Don't take needless risks.* A rational investor is risk averse. You should avoid specific-company risk by diversifying. That's what mutual fund investing is all about. Avoid market risk by diversifying among various markets—stocks, bonds, cash, real estate. Even within the equity category you should diversify. When appropriate, I suggest you consider both large and small growth funds, value funds that buy large and small companies, natural resource funds, and international funds. Generally speaking, you should be cautious about increasing your risk by borrowing.

■ *Understand how much risk you are taking.* There is no wealth without risk. When an adviser or newsletter tells you that they can obtain superior rewards without taking risks, you are well advised to run as fast as you can—in the opposite direction. If you are young, you can probably afford to take chances, and you should. When you are older, you will undoubtedly want to guard against losing dollars that you may not be able to replace.

■ *Speculate only with money that you can afford to lose.* I would define that as a sum that, if you lost it, wouldn't change your life-style or standard of living. You can't be taking chances that could force you to put off a major expenditure that you had planned to make, buying a car or house, for instance, or financing your children's education. Never put more than 25% of your financial assets in the most speculative aggressive growth funds. Don't speculate past your "sleep at night" level. Diversify. Don't forget real estate, particularly home ownership. Don't borrow money to play the market. And that includes not only margin but also such risky endeavors as taking out a home equity loan.

■ *Reduce your equity risk by holding long-term.* While equities are risky in the short run, your risk is substantially reduced by lengthening your holding period.

■ *Be optimistic.* Bears make the headlines, but it's the bulls that make the money. Never forget that the long-term trend of the market is up!

■ *Avoid making emotionally-based financial decisions.* Don't panic and sell at the bottom of a crash. Take your time in making important financial decisions, particularly after a major life change such as divorce, job loss, or death in the family.

■ If you're married or have a long-term partner, try to *manage your finances in a joint and comprehensive fashion.* Set aside time periodically to discuss financial goals, issues, and concerns. Be accepting of your partner's "money personality." Your spouse is an economic partner.

■ *Avoid zero sum games.* Options, futures, gambling are all zero sum games where there is a loser for every winner. They may be fun, but they're not for making money. If you want to make money, invest in stocks; they are a positive sum game, meaning that any number of players can win. And where does that positive sum come from? From the growth of the economy itself, whose fruits accrue to corporate owners—in other words, equity investors—as well as all consumers.

■ *Understand that there are no gurus.* No one can predict the future. There is no perfection in calling the markets—or in any kind of forecasting, even my own. Make your core investments in ways that don't depend on predictions. My Flexible Funding Program is one such approach.

■ *Invest only in what you understand.* Restrict your investments to no-load funds, mostly diversified, that you can grasp. Don't invest in complicated limited partnerships that come with 100+ page prospectuses you'll never read. Avoid coins, stamps and other collectibles, unless you are willing to take the time to become expert in them. Heed the wisdom of Fidelity's Peter Lynch, who says he shuns high-tech stocks because he doesn't understand them, and that of superinvestor, Warren Buffett, who says, "We don't buy things we don't understand." Similarly, the mighty Mario Gabelli believes in "kicking the tires." He doesn't buy international stocks. If John Deere were located in Manheim instead of Moline, or if Pepsico were in Paris instead of Purchase (NY), presumably he wouldn't invest in those companies.

■ *Avoid commission-based financial advisers.* Their advice comes with an inherent conflict of interest. Avoid full-service brokers. If you need a broker, use a discount firm that provides executions only. If you absolutely need advice, try this method of working with full-service brokers. Tell them that you'll call them when you need them, and that under no circumstances are they to call you with recommendations, suggestions, tips, research reports, etc. Needless to say, never give a broker discretionary authority or sign an options agreement. Finally, if you need investment advice, get it from an investment adviser. Lawyers and accountants are seldom qualified investment advisers.

Use fee-only financial planners. Similarly, patronize money managers whose fees are based solely on assets under management. Be wary when buying insurance products. Their benefit projections can be misleading.

Primarily the naive are taken advantage of. If you know the ropes, it's relatively unlikely that a broker will try to sell you an unsuitable product because it provides him or her with a high commission. On the other hand, it is, unfortunately, not at all uncommon for them to fatten their incomes at the expense of the ignorant. "Takes time to become knowledgeable," you say. You put in the time and effort when you buy a new car or house or take an expensive vacation. It's your money. And needless to say, if you've gotten this far in my book, you're definitely committed to investing enough effort to become knowledgable.

■ *Pay yourself first.* Before your paycheck is entirely spent, make sure you have put aside some money for your savings. Many mutu-al funds have arrangements by which they can instruct your bank to automatically deduct a specific sum each month from your checking account. That way, you never see the money in the first place.

■ *Save and invest at least 10% of your income.* These savings should be in a tax-deferred account where possible. One of the best wealth accumulation devices ever invented is the thrift, profit-shar-ing or 401(k) plan that many companies offer their employees. Invest as much as you can in this sort of plan, whether your employer matches your money or not. As a participant in a tax-qualified plan, as your account begins to grow, you have the satis-faction of managing an ever-larger portfolio. With a bit of self-dis-cipline, you can eventually control a substantial amount of money. An early start and a systematic plan can lead to a small fortune. In any case, you should be able to accumulate a nest egg sizeable enough to bring you financial peace of mind.

■ *Keep your costs down.* That's the essential reason for no-load fund investing.

CHAPTER 20

THE NO-LOAD FUND INVESTOR

When to sell your fund

Everybody loves buying. Selling, that's another story. Psychologically, it's always more traumatic to jettison a mutual fund than it is to purchase shares.

Yet, knowing when to sell a fund is if anything more important than knowing when to buy one. But that critical subject receives much less attention than it deserves, for several reasons:

■ The fund industry has no interest in discussing the issue.

■ Most investors' normal inclination is to buy, not to sell.

■ The bulk of the press and independent advisers are similarly oriented to the happier activity of buying.

Magazines, newspapers, and broadcast outlets, in particular, virtually never offer sell advice, or even follow up their previous recommendations. Financial newsletters, which carry continuously monitored model portfolios, typically do offer sell advice. But even here, sell recommendations may sometimes be in the context of market timing.

I also think less is said about selling because the decision making process is simply harder than it is with buying. And ironically, you might be better off *not* selling in certain circumstances. For example, if you have a modestly underperforming fund in a taxable account, you might better hang onto it than generate a capital gains tax by selling in order to upgrade to a better fund.

Because buying is more fun for everyone involved, the industry and its salesmen offer simple advice about the best time to buy: Now. Any time is a good time to buy mutual funds, so the rationale goes, because in the long run you are almost certain to make money.

Indeed, if you'll recall, I myself observed in the last chapter that if you hold funds for at least five years, you have a high probability of making money; if you can hold for 15 years, you are almost certain to be ahead. While it's true that staying in equities for the long haul is likely to be a winning decision, you are nevertheless much better off if you evaluate your specific funds periodically as you would any investment—and switch or sell, when necessary.

The ability to sell at an opportune moment distinguishes professional money managers from amateurs. The pros understand that paper losses are very real and that it is best to take them while they are small.

By contrast, amateurs are inclined to nurture the often unrealistic hope that their sinking funds will surge sooner or later. Optimism, inertia or both prevent amateurs from taking decisive action. Brokerage commissions and taxes also deter some people from selling. Having difficulty facing up to a mistake is an even more potent psychological roadblock.

Every investor should try to emulate the professionals, especially in terms of dealing with mistakes quickly and effectively. A good example is the way money managers who run emerging market funds reacted in the wake of the sudden Mexican peso crisis in December 1994 and January 1995. Almost uniformly, they were quick to reduce their Mexican stock positions. In contrast, individuals are more likely to sell toward the tail end of declines, often about the time the professionals are getting ready to repurchase.

Unburdened of the load

Mutual funds eliminate most of the reasons that handicap stock buyers. Selling mutual funds is an impersonal process. You don't need to explain to a broker. You simply talk to a stranger on the phone for a few seconds or, less commonly, send a brief business letter to the fund or its custodial bank. It's easier to sell mutual funds in anticipation of a downturn, since it's a virtual certainty that diversified funds will track the market. (With individual stocks, you always have the hope that the stock you hold will buck the market trend. That's a negative because it seldom does.)

While the sales commission on load funds can be a real deterrent, selling no-loads costs you nothing. With no-loads, the most you'll ever pay is a nominal redemption fee.

Sell for personal reasons

Mutual funds are generally thought of as a nestegg for retirement. And with a great many investors, retirement may be the only reason to sell.

But many other circumstances may compel you to cash in your stash: buying a house, facing unexpected medical bills, putting your children through college, even taking an expensive vacation. While you certainly may decide to hold onto your mutual funds the long term, you have to accept the likelihood that circumstances might compel you to sell long before you originally anticipated.

Moreover, your objectives may change. A person owning an aggressive growth fund may want to switch to a growth or a growth-income fund at retirement. On the other hand, an investor who had been unduly timid might want to exchange some income funds for more aggressive growth-oriented holdings. That could occur because your financial situation improved dramatically. For example, what if you received an inheritance, got a better job, or your kids became self-supporting? Under those circumstances, you might want more exposure to speculative funds.

No-load funds, of course, readily accommodate selling decisions for such personal reasons.

Sell when performance lags

Standing pat is no guarantee of a winning hand. Even if your circumstances or objectives have not changed, you will want to switch funds from time to time, so as to stay in top-performing investments. So everybody's advice is: sell when performance lags.

However, advisors seldom explain just what performance they are referring to. A month's? A quarter's? A year's? Two years'? The press and investors look for simple answers, but the truth is there aren't any.

When I'm asked the question, my first response is to say, "let's try to find out the reason for the underperformance." Only then can I give meaningful advice as when to sell.

Check the fund's annual report for the reason

In some cases the quickest way to discover the cause of poor performance is to simply read the president's letter in the latest fund report. Responsible fund groups will not try to cover it up.

The normally superior Strong funds turned in awful performances in 1989. In a February 1990 report to shareholders, the managers explained that the primary problem had been heavy investments in junk bonds. While these speculative securities had been winners for the funds for several years, they were a disaster in 1989. In its report, Strong management announced a change in policy. Henceforth, the Strong funds would limit junk bond holdings to 5% of each fund's assets. The funds have had relatively good years since then.

Similarly, the Vanguard funds are generally candid in discussing any of their fund's shortcomings. The usually top-performing Windsor Fund did terribly in 1990. In its annual report, Vanguard Chairman Bogle laid it on the line as these excerpts from his letter attest: "The Fund provided a distinctly poor return to its investors during the fiscal year...While the stock market environment was unfavorable...the Fund's stunning decline was far larger than that of stocks as a group, and of most competitive funds." Bogle then went on at great length to spell out the details of how they went wrong.

If the fund's reports don't provide the answer, here are some other factors to check before you arrive at a sell decision:

If you were a Green Bay Packers fan, and quarterback Brett Favre decided to retire, would you worry that the team's streak of Super Bowl appearances was at an end? When the Florida Marlins, after their 1997 World Series victory disbanded their team, did their rooters wonder what was in store for them?

Here's a still more instructive example. When the legendary Michael Jordan decided to retire—as he did at the end of the 1992-1993 season—how concerned do you think Chicago Bulls fans were about the team's performance? Very, no doubt. And sure enough, in the years following the departure of his Airness, the Bulls were a far cry from the team that won three straight national Basketball Association Championships. Then when he returned, the team was propelled to a magical place seldom enjoyed by any group working toward a common goal.

Sports teams have anywhere from five to dozens of starting players, not to mention a collection of sometimes stellar subs. The mutual fund world is quite different. Often, a fund's success is the expression of one or two exceptionally savvy managers. So, when a manager leaves, the impact can be as dramatic as the departure of a genius like Michael Jordan.

In 1989, Andrew Massie, the portfolio manager for the Scudder

A change in advisers is a reason to sell—sometimes

Capital Growth Fund and the AARP Capital Growth Fund, moved on to another fund group. The funds performance deteriorated for several years after that. The same situation prevailed at the Primary Trend Fund. President James R. Arnold, Sr. died suddenly on November 2, 1989. After that the group fell on hard times.

In January 1996, Garrett Van Wagoner left the helm of the Govett Smaller Companies Fund to launch his own fund group. The Govett fund had been number 2 among all funds under Van Wagoner. But after he left, the Govett Smaller Company Fund fared poorly. The new manager had a 10.6% *loss* in his first year.

As in sports, you need to evaluate each significant change in a mutual fund on its own merits. On February 12, 1988, Max Heine, the 77-year-old founder and chairman of the board of the Mutual Series Funds, was killed in an auto accident. Investors who had taken the trouble to acquaint themselves with the group's management knew that a top-notch, well-qualified replacement was already on hand. Michael Price had joined the Heine organization in 1975 and had already earned a reputation as a savvy fund manager and heir apparent. The Mutual Series funds under Price's leadership have done as well as they could have with Heine.

In May 1990, the fund industry witnessed its most significant management change in years. The great Peter Lynch—the Michael Jordan of mutual funds—left Fidelity Magellan. A wizard who had compiled probably the best management record in the history of the business, left the gargantuan fund in the hands of Morris Smith, who previously had done an excellent job of managing the Fidelity OTC Fund. Without question, the greatest part of Magellan's impressive gains had been achieved when the fund was smaller. Still, Lynch had done a very creditable job even after the fund grew huge. In this regard, he was lucky that small company stocks were doing well when the fund was small and large company stocks excelled when the fund was large.

Almost all the Magellan shareholders elected to remain with Morris Smith—and, at the time, I counseled my newsletter subscribers to take a wait-and-see attitude. Then in April 1991, I advised newsletter subscribers to switch to other Fidelity growth funds. In subsequent months the fund did, indeed, underperform its logical alternatives in up markets. (There have been two managers since then. They too have underperformed Peter Lynch, but that's mostly due to the fund's unwieldy size. Fidelity finally closed the fund in 1997 at $62 billion, though that was something of a farce, as I noted earlier in this book, since millions of investors are still regularly putting money into Magellan through their retirement plans.) The decision to sell after Lynch left was a correct one, particularly when a simple phone call would switch you into a better Fidelity performer.

In December 1995, John Neff retired after 31 years running the Vanguard Windsor Fund. Neff's reputation in the fund industry was second only to Peter Lynch, so a number of experts counseled selling. But Neff was succeeded by Charles Freeman, who had been his long-time assistant. Under Freeman the fund has done very well.

Every year some personnel changes are important—and some aren't. Here's a general guideline: The larger the advisory organization, the less likely it is that a departure will cause significant problems. The portfolio manager is not as crucial in a larger organization as in a smaller one, since it is far easier for a larger organization to replace a departing portfolio manager with someone equally skilled.

Be patient with larger groups

With larger fund groups you can almost always adopt a wait and see attitude. I documented this point in Chapter 14 when I examined the turnover of portfolio managers at Fidelity, finding that their frequent turnover didn't seem to have any effect on the performance of Fidelity's funds. (See table 42 on page 160).

This conclusion was also confirmed by a special study undertaken by the *Fidelity Monitor* newsletter. The *Monitor* found that Fidelity funds that had only one manager over the five-year period ending December 31, 1996 performed only fractionally better than funds with several managers. In fact, given the small amount of performance difference and the limited number of funds in the sample, I doubt if manager turnover had any impact on performance at all.

One explanation for these results is that Fidelity managers are supported by a group of 231 analysts and researchers who have a vested interest in the quality of their recommendations. Fund managers often do research as a team, such as questioning company managers during face-to-face meetings. Findings are well documented and shared internally so every manager at Fidelity can benefit. This is also true at several other large complexes. All else being equal, that's a good reason to prefer these large fund companies.

Table 78

Performance vs. manager turnover at Fidelity
Annual return for the five years ending 12/31/96

# Managers	# Funds	Avg. return over 5 yrs
One	5	17.2%
Two	17	16.1%
Three	18	17.1%
Four	12	16.7%
Five	5	16.7%

Source: Fidelity Monitor, Feb. 1997. The study encompassed Fidelity's domestic funds (growth, growth & income and Selects except Electronics) that were at least five years old. Select Electronics was excluded from the study because it had an unusually high return for the period. (It had five managers.)

Watch manager changes in small groups

Smaller organizations lack this depth of management. The worst problem is when the owner/star of a small group leaves because of death or incapacitation. (They can't get fired or would quit because they own the management company.) For example, if such stars as Don Yacktman or Ron Baron were no longer on the scene at their eponymous fund groups, I would be quick to sell.

Smaller organizations lack this depth of management. In business, the big usually get bigger and for good reason. What should this mean to you as an investor? If two funds have similar performances, one belonging to a small group and the other to a large fund family, the odds favor selecting the latter. You'll probably get more consistently good performance. Your account will probably also get better service and administration. And if the fund at the larger group falters, it's a lot simpler to switch to another excellent investment. When a fund in a small organization veers off the road, you may well have to go through a time-consuming redemption/reinvestment process.

In any case, you are wise to be alert to the possible downside when management changes. Fund management is a people business; the person or group managing a fund is key. If you learn about a management change, investigate the replacement. If you don't feel that the new manager is worthy, or if the fund's performance begins to deteriorate, you should sell.

Each year about 7%-10% of funds get new managers. In most cases, performance will not be affected, but there will always be some cases where a manager's departure does make a difference. You need to be aware of those cases.

Since nobody buys a diversified fund with a poor performance record, the problem is always, "why did the fund's performance deteriorate after I bought it?" The answer is that the fund was just waiting for your money before heading south. Just kidding.

In a surprising number of cases, the culprit is a change in market leadership. You own a growth fund, only to find it lagging funds that invest in value-oriented stocks. Or vice-versa. You own a value fund, then suddenly find that growth stock funds are doing better. That's because growth and value move in cycles. And typically you purchase a fund well into the cycle. Similarly, leadership between small cap and large cap funds changes from time to time, as I explained in Chapter 5.

What to do? Frankly a case can be made for doing nothing. Since these cycles are often unpredictable, it makes sense to diversify among both growth and value funds, and among large and small cap funds. That way something will always be working. Furthermore, if you bought good management, sooner or later the

Watch out for shifts in market leadership

Table 79

T. Rowe Price New Horizons Fund

Long-term performance cycles

	Duration	NHF	S&P 500	Spread
06/60 - 10/64	4.3 years	0.8	71.4	-70.6
10/64 - 12/68	4.2 years	298.6	39.9	258.7
12/68 - 06/70	1.5 years	-38.3	-26.3	-12.0
06/70 - 05/72	1.9 years	162.3	60.2	102.1
05/72 - 10/76	4.4 years	-51.1	11.2	-62.3
10/76 - 06/83	6.7 years	388.8	131.0	257.8
06/83 - 10/90	7.3 years	-1.0	138.3	-139.3
10/90 - 05/96	5.6 years	341.9	158.6	183.3
05/96 - 10/97	1.4 years	18.5	48.5	-30.0

Source: T. Rowe Price

laggard style will come back into fashion, and the fund will once again regain its luster.

These cycles are notoriously irregular. Table 79 on page 295 shows the T. Rowe Price New Horizons Fund, a proxy for small cap investing, has performed relative to a large cap index, the S&P 500, over the years. Note that the cycles varied from 1.4 to 7.3 years.

On the other hand, if economic forces favor one style or another for extended periods of time, then it makes sense to switch from the laggard to the leading style.

For example, small cap funds frequently do better when the dollar is strong, and worse when the dollar is weak. That's because small companies are less dependent on overseas economies than the large multi-national corporations. Thus, they don't suffer currency losses when these dollars are repatriated back to America.

Chart 80

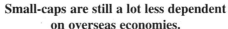

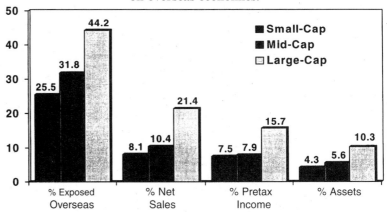

Data are five years average from 1992-96.
Source: Prudential Securities

Consider selling if a fund's investing style drifts

A successful small cap fund may grow too large, for example, and be forced to add mid-cap stocks. Or, a fund may find that its usual strategy (say, contrarianism) isn't working, and the fund shifts to a more trendy approach. The ploy may work. But keep in mind that that was not what initially attracted you to the fund. When a fund changes its style, it can wreck your portfolio diversification.

With so many funds angling for the investor's dollar, fund marketeers are always looking for new niches to exploit. Several trendy examples have occurred in recent years. They seemed good when announced and their sponsors gave logical reasons for expecting them to succeed. But success was illusive.

Global asset allocation funds are a good example. What could be a brighter idea than having professional managers deploying your dollars around the world and all over the asset spectrum in order to give you the finest returns? Great idea, but hard to successfully implement. Granted, the funds' performance was hurt by the unexpectedly poor showing of gold, and to a lesser extent international stocks and bonds. But the point is that reality didn't come close to meeting expectations.

Global short-term income funds are another example. They were hurt by unexpected changes in currency rates. Their hedging didn't provide the degree of protection that they had expected. And thus, they frequently underperformed comparable short-term funds that invest domestically.

Another example of a new concept that was hurt by an unforeseen risk: funds that invest in adjustable-rate mortgages.

All these concepts—and many more over the years—held some initial promise. You can't succeed without taking some chances. But if the concept turns sour, don't hesitate to move on to something better.

Sell when a new concept doesn't pan out

If you believe the market is about to nosedive and your fund is fully invested—let alone leveraged—disagree with the fund's management by selling. Conversely, if you are bullish but your fund has a high cash position, switch to another fund that is fully invested in stocks, for instance, an index fund.

Sell when the cash position is inappropriate

If other investors are bailing out in droves, that's almost always symptomatic of serious problems at that fund.

If a star leaves, so may other shareholders. When Garrett Van Wagoner left Govett Smaller Companies, shareholders who had purchased Govett were hit with investment losses to meet redemptions caused by his departure.

Mutual fund supermarkets (discussed in detail in Chapter 22), such as Charles Schwab Mutual Fund Marketplace, now oversee a huge amount of assets and are changing the character of fund mar-

Sell when a fund is in net redemptions

keting. Funds that have a high percentage of their assets at these supermarkets are far more likely to be liquidated in the event of a bear market than assets held directly at the fund. Heavy redemptions, particularly among small-cap funds, are likely to impair performance.

For example, the Montgomery funds issued a proxy statement in 1997 in connection with their sale to Commerzbank AG. The following table shows the percent of each Montgomery stock and bond funds' shares held in Schwab omnibus accounts.

I cite the Montgomery funds here because the data were readily available. I don't mean to single Montgomery out unfairly; many other fund groups have similar percentages. If a high percentage of a fund's assets are held at a brokerage supermarket, you should be quicker to sell when necessary.

Table 81

% of Montgomery funds' assets held by Schwab	
Emerging Markets	45%
Equity Income	44%
Global Communications	42%
International Small Cap	40%
Global Opportunities	39%
Micro Cap	36%
Growth	36%
Small Cap Opportunities	36%
Asset Allocation	34%
Short Duration Gov. Bond	30%
CA Tax Free Inter Bond	29%
Select 50	26%
Emerging Asia	22%
International Growth	17%
Small Cap	15%
Global Asset Allocation	5%

Sell erratic performers

Non-diversified and industry funds often perform erratically. Even diversified funds can show occasional brilliance if they hit it big with a trendy industry group. When the group cools, performance returns to normal.

Sell tax-inefficient funds

It's nice to know that your fund is doing well. But more important, how well are you doing? If a fund realizes a lot of short-term capital gains, there's going to be a great disparity between its performance and yours, because it does not pay the taxman—you do! To spot such funds, check previous distribution amounts and portfolio turnover.

Many new readers will discover that they own 12b-1 funds (see Chapter 2 for details) with as much as 1% taken off the top annually to pay for "distribution" expenses. It's costly to redeem these funds prematurely since you may well have to pay a contingent deferred sales charge that can cost you 5-6% of your assets in the first year. What's the best way to get out of this bad situation?

Sell 12b-1 funds

   If the fund turns out to be a poor performer, there is no good way. You simply have to gulp hard and take your lumps. If the fund is a good performer, it probably pays to wait until the CDSC is reduced (it usually drops to zero within five years). Then switch to a more cost-effective alternative.

Never feel that you are locked into a fund—not even a load fund. You paid a sales commission to buy a car, but that doesn't stop you from selling it when it no longer performs. Similarly, you should sell a fund—load or no-load—that gives you the wrong kind of ride.

Don't be deterred by a load

When you need a tax deduction, selling a losing fund can be a good way to get it. The money can easily be switched to another fund, and the government will share your loss with you. Under current law, capital losses can be used to offset capital gains. Moreover, you can deduct up to $3,000 from your earned income. And if you wait as little as 31 days, you can return to the same fund you originally sold without running afoul of IRS's wash-sale rules.

Sell to realize a tax loss

   Although I have been primarily discussing stock funds, the same principles are even more applicable to bond funds. You should swap or sell them to establish a tax loss. Since the government is primarily responsible for bond losses, it's only proper that Uncle Sam share these losses, particularly since there are no transaction costs to reduce the tax loss benefits. This is one of the funds' great advantages over individual bonds. When selling small lots of individual bonds, the brokerage fees can be killers. And worst of all, they are largely hidden expenses.

Sell small holdings

Perhaps you inherited a small holding, or maybe it came to you as a birthday present. If a particular fund position is worth less than $1,000 or represents less than 1% of your financial assets, it's just cluttering up your portfolio. Simplify your life.

Sell to rectify a mistake

You may have bought a fund because it qualified under all the guidelines I've given you. Yet, unaccountably, it may fail to live up to your expectations. Investing is an imperfect science. Sell.

Sell poorly performing aggressive growth funds quickly

Aggressive funds take great risks in seeking large profits, and sometimes wind up with substantial losses. So making a long-term commitment can be foolhardy.

The American Heritage Fund was a high-flyer for three years. Then in February 1994, disaster struck. The fund was off 7.9%—as a result of declines in its outsized investment in Spectrum Technologies, a small computer company. This was a classic case where immediate selling was imperative. And many shareholders did. Redemptions were immediate, and that threw fund manager Heiko Thieme off balance. The fund ended 1994 off 35.4% in a year when the average equity fund declined 1.8%.

Conversely, managers of the growth and growth-income funds don't promise to make money overnight. They are selling on the basis of long-term performance. As an investor, you should be prepared to make a correspondingly long-term commitment. So, don't sell if your growth or growth-income fund does poorly over a short period. But don't "marry" your fund. You may love your investments, but they won't love you back. Remember, you can easily switch to a better-performing fund with the same objective.

Aggressive growth funds take a beating in bear markets

The most volatile funds lack defensive capabilities. The speculative stocks they hold can take terrible drubbings, and most aggressive growth funds view that as simply the cost of doing their kind of business.

During the devastating bear markets of 1969-70 and 1973-74, the average high-performance fund declined by about half! Aggressive funds were also the hardest hit in the October 1987 meltdown, plunging 26% on average, versus a 13% decline for conservative income funds. Hopefully, no bears quite that grizzly are lurking around a near corner. But obviously we can't be sure. Certainly the markets will experience corrections from time to time. From July 16, 1990 to October 31, 1990, for instance, the average diversified equity fund declined 18.3%, while the average aggressive growth fund plunged by 24.4% on average. Bull & Bear Special Equities was at the ursine extreme, off 50.1%. Funds like CGM Capital Development, Columbia Special, Price New Horizons, SteinRoe Capital Opportunities, Twentieth Century Giftrust and Vista and USAA Aggressive Growth—outstanding investments in better markets—declined 30% or more. The S&P 500 was down 14.6% during this period. Even in the relatively mild 1994 downturn, at least 100 load and no-load funds plummeted from 15% to 50%.

If you could accurately predict a bear market, clearly you would't hold aggressive growth funds through it. Alas, most investors make very poor forecasters, and are worse still at acting on their instincts. So I recommend my Flexible Funding Program strategy (explained in the last chapter) as a sound way to minimize your bear market losses.

What if your fund is merged

On rare occasions you may find yourself receiving a proxy statement announcing that management wishes to merge your fund into another one. What should you do? In most cases there isn't too much to worry about because the general rule in the fund business is that losers are merged into winners, rarely the other way around.

The acquiring fund will usually have a better performance record than the fund being acquired. The merged fund's record disappears into oblivion, never again to deter a potential investor.

Sometimes there are other reasons. In 1989, the Liberty Fund, a small high-yield bond fund managed by Neuberger-Berman, was merged into the T. Rowe Price High Yield Bond Fund because at that time, Neuberger-Berman felt that junk bonds were an inappropriate investment for its shareholders.

Here's a question: because a merger will almost always be approved no matter how you vote, should you retain any shares in the new fund? Or should you sell? Consider these factors. Generally speaking a merger entails no tax consequences. But do read the fine print in the prospectus, and possibly consult a tax advisor to make certain. On the other hand, if you sell, potentially, you could have a tax liability.

Steadman funds — the all-time worst!

You wouldn't think that constant, unmitigated disastrous performance was possible, would you? Just by the law of averages, you'd figure that lousy money managers would find some success, wouldn't you?

Well, you'd be wrong. Undoubtedly the all-time champion *underperformer* is Washington DC-based Steadman Funds. So stinky are they that one mutual fund publication actually names its annual prize for worst fund manager the "Steadman." Three of the group's four funds rank dead last for the twenty years ending with 1996. Steadman Technology and Growth declined 80.1%, American Industry was down 61.7%, and Steadman Investment declined 19.5%, all in the midst of a great bull market! The fourth Steadman fund, Associated, gained 87.6% over the twenty years to rank fifth from last. How is it even possible to do so poorly? One major reason is the group's sky high expense ratios—around 20%. Nobody can make money with that overhead!

Notwithstanding this abominable performance, as of year-end 1997, the Steadman funds still had 16,757 shareholders. Who, in their right mind, would stay with this group? *Barron's*, the weekly financial newspaper, attempted to answer that question, and reported their findings in the Jan. 9, 1995 edition. They failed to locate a single shareholder. I was asked to aid in the quest, but I flippantly replied, "They're mostly dead or near the end," which of course became the opening quote in the story. It turned out I was partly right. Under the terms of a legal settlement, shares representing 7%-22% of assets have been turned over to the District of Columbia under the Disposition of Unclaimed Property Act.

With an average account holding of $530, it's quite likely that the balance of the accounts are for all practical purposes lost. Some might be long-forgotten custodial accounts set up for children, or the accounts of elderly people who are in nursing homes. Consider this a lesson. Redeem small accounts before you forget about them. All you need to do is move a couple times, and you, too, can be a lost account.

Epilogue: On December 4, 1997 the fund's 83-year old founder, Charles Steadman, passed away. The new management is trying to merge the group—now with $6 million in assets—into one fund to reduce expenses. But it's going to be a struggle. With so many lost shareholders they may never get a quorum to vote on the proposal.

Next, look at the acquiring fund as if it were a new purchase. Is its objective the same as that of the about-to-be-merged fund? If not, is its objective compatible with your investment goals? Does the fund buy the same types of stocks to achieve the objective? Will the same manager continue to guide the surviving fund? If not, the performance record of the acquiring fund will not mean as much. Is its expense ratio acceptable? Does the new fund have more high-dividend stocks (which can increase ordinary income taxes)? If these factors present no problems, you probably should stay with the new fund.

You should also be alert to potential paperwork problems. Make sure that you are being credited with the proper number of shares in the new fund. When you get your first statement, look closely at your number of shares. They will have been adjusted to account for the fact that the surviving fund has a different NAV from the merged fund. Also, double check to make sure that you have all your confirmation slips for your original purchases and reinvestments. Years after the merger, they could be impossible to obtain from the fund.

Here's a situation that doesn't happen very often, but one to be aware of. In February 1995, Gabelli Asset Management proposed that its Gabelli Convertible Securities Fund, at that time a no-load, be converted to a closed-end fund. In my newsletter I strongly recommended that shareholders oppose the conversion, and switch out of the fund when the anticipated approval occurred. The reason, fully explained in the proxy statement (thanks to the SEC), was the strong possibility that as a closed-end, the fund would trade on an exchange for less than its net asset value, giving shareholders an unwanted loss. Sure enough, a few weeks later 75% of the shares were voted in favor of the proposal, proof again that shareholders will approve almost anything management asks for. There was little to lose by selling, and a lot to lose by not.

When not to sell

Size is not sufficient reason to sell aggressive growth funds. Although I have cautioned against buying such a fund once it gets too large, some large funds continue to turn in good performances, particularly if the market is favoring large capitalization stocks. So wait for a fund's performance to falter before you sell.

Don't sell funds for which you've paid front-end loads so long as they continue to perform. (You've already paid the commission.) If they are not performing well, you might first try to move to a better performing fund within the same family, which would not cost you any additional commission.

Don't sell a mutual fund for the same reason that you might sell a stock. Many investors believe quite logically that if a stock achieves a certain goal—for instance, doubling or tripling in price—they should sell it. This may be a good rule with stocks. Individual companies seldom go through more than one period of sustained rapid growth. Once they have passed this phase, future growth probably won't exceed that of the economy. The stock then becomes cyclical, moving in harmony with the rhythms of the economy. At this point, most investors who want spectacular growth sell the stock.

Funds are different. A fund is a constantly changing, managed portfolio of stocks and bonds. As long as the manager is performing well and the stock market is gaining, the fund should continue growing. It can never become "fully priced" in the sense that a stock can. Therefore, a fund need never be sold because it has hit some anticipated growth target. Moreover, don't hesitate to buy a fund because its per-share price has risen substantially. In a long-term bull market, it can continue to grow indefinitely.

A word of caution: don't sell after a big plunge. The dramatic stock market meltdown on October 19th, 1887 understandably spooked many investors. Yet, those who hung onto their funds were rewarded; for most funds, less than two years was required to regain the ground lost that October.

Despite what has sometimes been written, there were no massive liquidations of holdings by stock fund managers or shareholders on October 19th. The ICI reports that on that date, only two percent of stock fund assets were redeemed by shareholders, and two-thirds of the redemptions were handled from existing cash positions.

Sometimes after dramatic news, such as the injury or sickness of a major world leader, stocks will sell off. More often than not, this news has no economic consequences. You will be selling at a low if you panic. So, hold on. Eventually the market will rebound.

It's not a good idea to sell a fund with a large unrealized capital loss, if that loss is due to a general market decline. The tax consequences down the road may be less costly than they'd be with an alternative investment, which has no losses to offset against future gains.

Don't sell to raise money for charity

If you have a large unrealized capital gain in a fund, don't sell the shares and use the cash for a charitable donation. A far better way is to give the shares directly to the charity. That way you avoid any tax on the appreciation in addition to getting a deduction for the gift. You can do this directly on your own, but there is another way that provides far greater flexibility, particularly if you're looking for a year-end charitable deduction, and haven't found a charity to your liking.

In that case, consider setting up an account at the Fidelity Charitable Gift Fund. You get a current-year income tax deduction, and you can make your contributions to the non-profit organizations of your choice at any time in the future. If you give appreciated securities, you can avoid the capital gains taxes you would incur if you sold the securities outright and made a gift of cash.

The Gift Fund is not a mutual fund per se. Rather, it consists of four asset pools into which charitable contributions may be invested. You can make donations of cash or securities, including appreciated stock, into these pools. The donations are irrevocable, and you may not receive a life income or interest. Since the IRS has approved the fund as a tax-exempt public charity, you may claim a tax deduction for the contribution based on fair market value, and the assets will grow tax-free until you decide to distribute them. Minimum initial investment is $10,000; minimum subsequent investment is $1,000, and the minimum distribution is $250. Distributions to non-profit organizations can be made at any time, in your name or anonymously. Any IRS approved charity is eligible for the payouts.

You can make your contribution into a Growth Pool, currently invested in Fidelity Fund, New Millennium, Magellan, Growth Co., Latin America, Southeast Asia, and Overseas; an Equity Income Pool, invested in Dividend Growth, Value, Equity Income, Growth & Income, and Int'l Growth & Income; an Interest Income Pool, currently invested in Intermediate Bond, Spartan Limited Maturity Government, and Short-Term Bond; and a Money Market Pool. Fidelity selects and apportions the investments in each pool on a discretionary basis. You can switch between pools twice per calendar year.

All sales loads are waived for the portfolio funds, but there is an annual 1% administrative fee for record keeping, distributions and tax reporting, plus the ongoing fees and expenses of the underlying portfolio funds. Call 800-682-4438 for further details.

In updating this chapter for the *Guide*, I was struck by how much it has become the conventional wisdom. This wasn't always the case. The advice in this chapter has survived pretty much intact for more than two decades, since I gave it in my first book, *Put Money In Your Pocket*, back in 1974. When that book was published, this chapter on selling caused something of a sensation in the investing world. A

An editorial aside

number of reviewers commented on it. *Money* magazine reprinted the entire chapter. Until this was written, nobody had ever challenged the then conventional mutual fund wisdom: buy and hold forever. Times certainly have changed!

CHAPTER 21

Understanding the *Investor's* recommendations

Chapters one through 20 are designed not only to enable you to choose mutual funds on your own, but also to understand the specific no-load fund recommendations that I offer monthly in my companion publication, *The No-Load Fund Investor* newsletter.

The newsletter recommends funds, provides up-to-the-minute performance data, investment strategies and fund news. Since I don't have room in the *Investor* for detailed instructions on how to interpret its recommendations, the following guide explains the general rationales for my recommendations. There are, of course, exceptions, which I endeavor to spell out in the newsletter if they aren't covered below.

Unlike the measures of past performance discussed in Chapter 17 (top ten lists, etc.), the *Investor* recommends those funds that its editors believe most likely will achieve superior performance in the future. Recommendations are based on the analysis of fund performance over both the long and the short term. I do not use a mechanical system to recommend funds. I go beyond the quintile rankings and utilize the judgement that years of experience have accumulated. I look at size, betas, cash positions, and my personal knowledge of management and its history of performance. Some fund groups deliver good performance over the long haul. I try to be patient with these groups if their funds are temporarily out of favor. Conversely, other funds have a long history of mediocrity. Every now and then one of these funds rockets in the standings. I will generally ascribe that performance to luck, and will ignore it until it is proven otherwise. I usually avoid recommending funds with unusually high expenses or 12b-1 fees.

With some exceptions (sometimes when a fund is first in a new niche or when the manager is very experienced), it is my general policy not to recommend a new fund until I have followed it for several months.

While the *Investor* newsletter follows a number of low-loads, primarily at Fidelity, I do not recommend them as a matter of principle. I make an exception to this rule for funds that charge a .5%-1% load payable to the *fund*, not to management. I highlight these funds with a dagger symbol to make sure that you are aware of the charge. But for all practical purposes they are pure no-loads, and I feel free to recommend them.

The *Investor* features two categories of recommended funds. The first can be found in the tabular performance tables where I bold face recommended funds that I believe are the best in their peer group, usually the objective category. However, in the case of fixed-income and international funds my recommendations refer to sub-categories. I bold face what I regard as the best of the short, intermediate, and long-term government and corporate bond funds, the best of the high yield, investment grade, and single state tax-free bond funds for those states that are covered by three or more funds. Sometimes these funds are not overall winners. Similarly, I compare international equity funds separately by region.

Funds that are closed or are available both with or without a load may be asterisked. These funds can be held. A Fidelity low-load fund with an asterisk can be bought no-load in many tax-sheltered accounts.

These recommendations are competitive. Sometimes I remove a recommendation simply because many other funds are doing better. However, on occasion I continue to recommend funds with below-average quintiles. The reason is that funds do not perform consistently. If a fund has good management and has performed well in the past, I quite often stick with that fund. The fund's performance may have dropped because the stocks it holds are temporarily out of favor or its cash position is inappropriate. Of course, if the stocks remain out of favor and the fund sticks with them, I will eventually drop my recommendation.

In the equity area I sometimes have standing recommendations on a few funds that tend to maintain high cash positions. These funds do well in down markets, but are usually weak performers in strong upmarkets.

Recommendations in the statistical tables do not imply market forecasts. By this I mean, for example, that while the recommendations for aggressive growth funds essentially apply to rising markets, I don't withdraw them during bear markets. That's because I want to give you time to pre-select the best aggressive growth funds for subsequent bull markets. Or it may not be obvious whether the market is a bull or bear.

The "Best Buys" list of recommendations on the last three pages of the newsletter are my prime recommendations. They do take into account my market forecast (and, thus, may include a cash position). A deletion from Best Buys does not necessarily mean you should sell the fund unless it is no longer shown in bold face in the tables. A deletion frequently means that I have found other funds in the same category that have somewhat higher potential, and that I want new subscribers to start with the best available selections. Funds not bold-faced in the tables are OK to sell. If I think a fund should be sold immediately, I will make that very clear in the text.

Each newsletter features five sets of Best Buys portfolios each month. There are lifestyle model portfolios for two major fund groups: Vanguard and T. Rowe Price; two for discount brokers Charles Schwab and Fidelity; and my Master Portfolio. The Master Portfolio is composed of the best no-load funds available anywhere.

The Schwab and Fidelity Brokerage portfolios are limited to NTF funds. That means that the Schwab Portfolio will *not* include any Fidelity, Vanguard, or Price funds. The Fidelity Brokerage Portfolio will not include the last two. However, these large-group funds are available through both discount brokers if you pay a modest transaction fee. If you don't mind these small fees, then you should consider the Fidelity, Vanguard, or Rowe Price funds that are recommended in the Master Portfolio or buy them directly from the fund group. Additionally, if any of the choices available for the Vanguard or Price single-family portfolios are borderline, I may add alternative selections from other fund groups.

Mostly for lack of space, I do not have a portfolio of exclusively Fidelity funds. Rather, it is combined with a Fidelity Brokerage NTF Portfolio. This way, all worthy Fidelity no-loads are available as well as no-loads from more than 100 other families. When possible the Fidelity NTF Portfolio will emphasize Fidelity funds. If you have—or want to start—a single-family portfolio at Fidelity, I recommend you open a brokerage account and use the Fidelity NTF Portfolio. See page 320 in the next chapter for details of the Schwab and Fidelity NTF service.

In theory, the principal advantages of the single-family and NTF portfolios are the reduction of paperwork and the ability to switch without delay. The Master Portfolio—which can select any no-load fund regardless of family—should turn in the best performances over the long run.

However, given the vagaries of fund selection, there will probably be periods when a single-family portfolio will lead. I think it would be a mistake to rush from one fund group or discount broker to another based on what may be short-term advantages. All organizations have great strengths that will probably endure over the years. Conservative investors should lean toward Vanguard; growth investors can take their pick. Most investors who want to limit themselves to a single-family or discount broker should pick one and stay there.

Within each set of "Best Buys" model portfolios, there are three model portfolios, each oriented for a different life style objective. They're discussed in detail in Chapter 17, page 208. Each portfolio is a complete investment program.

The portfolios should be tailored to meet your individual needs by adjusting for specific risk preferences and time horizons. Similar funds that are bold-faced in the tables can be substituted for model portfolio recommendations. (This is a must if a recommended fund is unavailable in your state.) Investors with sizeable assets should use additional funds for greater diversification, providing that the total doesn't exceed my recommended percent distributions in each category. The model portfolios typically contain taxable funds. If you're in a high tax bracket, substitute munis for any taxable bond funds. If, by some chance, the reverse is the case, substitute taxable bond funds if you're in a low bracket.

Our model portfolios are investment portfolios which do not take into account cash on hand in money funds or savings accounts for day-to-day living expenses, emergencies, and large consumer purchases such as cars. Make sure that you have adequate amounts of money for these purposes.

Finally, note that write-ups in Fund News are *not* recommendations.

On the bottom of page three of every issue of *The No-Load Fund Investor* is an explanation of the symbols and data used in the tables. Since some of us aren't seeing as well as we used to, here's the boilerplate data in normal type size:

Page 3 boilerplate

Explanation of symbols and data — Funds in bold face are recommended in appropriate market climate. ℭ telephone switch funds. † fund has a low load; as a matter of principle these funds are not bold faced. †† Fidelity low-load waiving fee for certain retirement accounts. ‡ Fund is not selling shares or has restricted its sale to certain investors. * after restricted sale or low-load fund indicates a hold or recommended on a no-load basis. (r) redemption fee. SC Small company funds. X Stock fund with an expense ratio 2%+, bond fund, 1.5%+ **C** indicates a change in recommendation from previous month. NAV is the fund's price. f previous day's price. Total return is % change with distributions reinvested for measured period. Periods over 1 yr are shown compounded annually. Superscript numbers next to performance figures indicate each fund's quintile rank within objective. "1" top 20% of all aggr grth funds rated, "2" next 20%, to "5" the bottom 20%, same for other objective categories except fixed which is ranked within S, I, L. Yield is latest 12 months dividends divided by current NAV. Cash % is the % of a fund's portfolio in cash or cash equivalents, generally at month-end. Parentheses indicate fund is leveraged. Betas and std. deviations are computed for the 3 yrs ending previous quarter. See the *Guide,* Chapter 21, and the *Handbook,* Chapter 3, for further explanation, addresses and phone numbers.

PART IV

The Pragmatic Side of Investing in No-Load Funds

CHAPTER 22

**THE
NO-LOAD
FUND INVESTOR**

Dealing with
your no-load

Knowing the best procedures for buying, selling, keeping records and using the services offered by a no-load mutual can save you time and aggravation—and make you money.

You purchase no-load fund shares directly from the fund, ordinarily bypassing a broker. The exceptions generally involve money market funds. You can buy Merrill Lynch Ready Assets Trust through any Merrill Lynch broker, for instance, or PaineWebber Cashfund through a PaineWebber broker. These transactions and balances are often listed on your regular brokerage statement.

**How to buy
fund shares**

You can always buy shares through the mail, and some twenty groups permit that to be initiated by phone. However, if you are allowed to buy by phone, SEC regulations require that you settle the purchase within three days. This essentially means you can't use first class U.S. mail to pay for fund purchases. You will need to use more costly alternatives: Express Mail, a private overnight service, or a bank or fed wire. If the money does not arrive on time, the order will be cancelled and you will become liable for any loss on the trade. There is some flexibility, however; SEC regulations allow for an automatic two-day extension.

The introduction of toll-free calls has revolutionized fund marketing. Almost all no-loads have 800 numbers, enabling you to deal directly with the fund, or the fund's transfer agent, at no charge and with a minimum of fuss and bother. That gives no-loads a human voice to handle many of the duties once taken care of by fund salesmen. (Fidelity, Vanguard, T. Rowe Price and others also use their 800 facilities to provide discount brokerage services for stock transactions.)

Funds are supposed to send you a prospectus before they accept your purchase. Those that take telephone orders usually will ask you if you have received the prospectus. If you tell them that you haven't, you may not be able to buy shares on that day. If you say that you have, there's a very good chance that the representative will take your order, particularly if you already have an account in another fund at the group, and are paying via exchange from the group's money fund. Usually the group will then send you a prospectus, automatically, a few days later. If not, you can always call again to request it.

If the fund doesn't accept phone orders or you don't want to wait for the prospectus to arrive, send the following letter:

Dear Sirs:

Please purchase as many shares as the enclosed check for $_____ will buy. Register the shares under *(name and address)*. My social security number is _____. Please reinvest all distributions.

Sincerely,

_____

Enclose your check with the letter. A few funds will return your check accompanied by a prospectus, but others will take the order, and then send the prospectus back with the confirmation. In any case, make sure that your order meets the fund's minimum initial investment requirements.

Note that funds are beginning to restrict the use of third-party checks. For example, Neuberger-Berman will no longer accept any check not made payable to Neuberger-Berman. Fidelity accepts second party checks, but not third party checks. That means that you can endorse over to Fidelity a check that has been written to you. But you cannot endorse to Fidelity a check that has been endorsed over to you by someone else. I would check with a fund before mailing them a third-party check.

Forget price per share

With mutual funds, price is virtually irrelevant. It is never a consideration in either the purchase or sale of a fund. You buy funds in dollar amounts, not a specific number of shares. Funds issue fractional shares to round out your purchases to the exact dollar amount you ordered.

Mutual fund returns are almost always analyzed in terms of percent changes, not in the change in the price of a share—i.e., the fund went from $7 to $10. That's because a discussion of growth in terms of price per share can be misleading if there has been a distribution, which lowers the apparent price. In this case, it would be similar to comparing the price of a stock after a split with the pre-split price. In evaluating a fund, the percent increase *with distributions included* is the only important consideration.

Unlike stocks, the per share price is not an indication of quality. There is no difference between a fund selling at $1.05 per share and one selling at $50 per share. Incidentally banks, which often will lend money against quality stocks but not against very low-priced stocks, occasionally apply the same policy to mutual funds. That's because they just don't understand how mutual fund pricing works. Surprisingly, two discount brokers that permit mutual fund trading— Jack White and Waterhouse Securities—also discriminate. They won't allow investors to borrow on margin against funds with NAVs under approximately $5.

Like stocks, funds sometimes split their shares—often for the same reasons. Funds split their shares to broaden their market by bringing the price down. This sometimes happens when a fund that has been marketed to institutions at a high per share NAV is now being marketed to individuals. Psychologically, it's comforting to some investors to have more shares at a lower price.

Moreover, a lower NAV means smaller daily cents per share fluctuations, which is also psychologically reassuring. When the Blanchard Short-Term Global Income Fund was launched, the sponsor put a low $1.97 price on it. A few months later the similar Scudder Short-Term Global Income Fund was launched at a $12 price. Since the shareholders of both funds prefer a stable price, the Blanchard Fund's pricing policy gave it a distinct edge. Minor price fluctuations are less likely to produce a one cent price change than in the case of the Scudder fund with its higher NAV.

Establishing relations with a fund family

If you plan to work extensively with a particular fund group, I recommend that you start by getting prospectuses for all of that company's funds that you think you might use. Be sure to include the group's money funds. Do this ahead of the time when you plan to make your purchases.

I suggest that you establish your first account in the money fund by making the minimum investment. Set up wiring instructions, check writing, telephone switch to other funds and all the other features you might conceivably use.

You'd be surprised how long it can take if any problems arise. For example, if the money fund account is in your name and your bank checking account is in a joint name, this might cause a delay. Corporations and trusts may have special problems. Once everything is set up and in good working order, deposit the full amount that you intend to invest into the money fund. At that point it can be left there or easily switched to the stock or bond funds of your choice.

It's not a bad idea to test all these services. Switch a small amount. Wire some money back to your bank to see that the fund group has the bank's correct ABA routing number and to find out exactly how long the wiring process takes.

By making a trial run immediately, you minimize the chance of a costly disappointment later on. I know of an investor who was an astute market timer but careless in keeping his fund account in per-

fect order. With all his money in the group's stock fund, he was carefully tracking the market. On October 16, 1987, this investor's indi-
cators gave him a sell signal. He immediately called the group and
told them to switch everything to their money market fund. He was
told they couldn't do it; the telephone switch privilege had to be set
up in advance—and he hadn't done it! By the time this fellow got his
account in order, and received the appropriate forms, it was too late.
Black Monday intervened.

Nowadays, switching privileges are generally—but not invariably—automatic. You still should read the application form carefully.
I know of another case where it took one week to wire money from a
money market fund to a bank the first time the shareholder tried it.

Active investors should consider buying and selling no-load mutual
funds through a discount brokerage firm. The fee is nominal. And if
you plan to switch sizable sums between fund groups, or simply want
to diversify among a number of fund groups, the convenience of dealing with one broker is well worth the cost. The brokerage firm provides you with regular statements. All your fund holdings are consolidated on one piece of paper, and at the end of the year, you receive
just one 1099-DIV for all your funds.

Using discount brokers

You can execute overnight switching between fund groups using
their extended-hours telephone service. This means you no longer have
to wait for a redemption check or wire from one fund group before you
can invest in another. That always causes a loss of interest on your
money, and frequently lost profits, as well. In addition, the major discount brokers have branch offices throughout the U.S., so you can hand
carry checks or paperwork to them when time is of the essence. These
conveniences are particularly valuable for IRA accounts, where the
paperwork involved in switching among several groups is more onerous.

On the other hand, the infrequent trader or smaller investor who is
committed to one fund group can obtain better service by dealing directly with the fund. In many cases, that avoids transaction and 12b-1 fees.

Over 40 discount brokers now trade mutual funds, but by far the
most important are Charles Schwab, Fidelity and Jack White. Schwab
will let you invest in about 2,500 funds; Fidelity, about 3,300; White,
about 5,500. The fees are generally modest and in many cases, "free."

As an illustration of how important the discount brokers have become in distributing mutual funds, particularly for smaller fund families, note the experience of the new Baron Small Cap Fund, which ended its initial one-month subscription period on October 1, 1997. The fund raised $108 million during the subscription period, very good for a fund without a major national presence. Of that total, $74.5 million was raised by Schwab's Mutual Fund OneSource program. Without Schwab, it is doubtful that the Baron group on its own could have raised even $50 million in that short a period.

Trading funds without paying transaction fees

Most discount brokers now trade many no-load funds on a no-transaction-fee basis. They are able to do this by having the no-load funds, rather than the investor, pay the commissions. The amounts vary somewhat but range from 0.25% to 0.35%. In the case of 12b-1 funds, the broker's commission is paid out of the 12b-1 fee. For pure no-loads, about 10-15 basis points comes from transfer agent savings, the balance from the manager.

The funds like this approach because they can add investor accounts without having to pay any marketing costs. So the fund realizes offsetting savings. When Schwab first began the program back in 1996 few if any charges were passed onto investors. As the programs have developed, some of the costs are being passed on, but even now they are far less than the usual commissions. As an example of what is happening, see the listings for Neuberger-Berman in the newspapers. There is a listing called Neuberger-Berman funds and directly below it another set of listings called Neuberger-Berman Trust. Most of the fund names are the same. The explanation is that the Trust series was set up for the Fidelity NTF (no-transaction-fee) program. If you buy the fund through Fidelity, you'll pay an extra 10 basis points per year (0.1%). I think that's an acceptable charge for the convenience.

At press time, Charles Schwab was offering more than 800 no-load funds from 121 families fee-free; Fidelity, over 800 from more than 100 families; Jack White, 1,200 from 190 families. (More funds are being constantly added.)

You can buy almost any fund worth owning, fee-free, with the following exceptions: Neither Vanguard nor T. Rowe Price is available NTF from any of the supermarkets (except their own). They are available for a commission. American Century and Scudder are available NTF through Schwab, but not Fidelity. Fidelity, Value Line and Lindner are not available through Schwab. Our companion *Handbook* has the details, as do the representatives at each supermarket.

This program is not a gold mine for frequent switchers. They still have to pay the usual commissions. If you think you may be in this category, call each brokerage firm for its exact definition. (It's also in our *Handbook.*)

In selecting a discount broker, you are better off dealing with Fidelity Brokerage if you plan to move in and out of Fidelity funds, since that's the only way to get those funds without paying transaction costs. Charles Schwab, the innovator, provides excellent all-around service. Jack White, the third major player, is somewhat cheaper.

Mutual funds are organized and operated under federal laws. But, in addition, they must be registered in accordance with the laws of the states where they conduct business. Before 1996, it was expensive and time-consuming to obtain registrations in all states because each state could mandate its own rules. For example, each state could make a fund add certain language to the prospectus. And since it wasn't feasible to write a prospectus for each state, either the lowest common denominator prevailed or the fund decided not to sell its shares in that state. Many funds failed to register in all 50 states.

Not all funds are available everywhere

This is now changing. In 1996, Congress passed the National Securities Markets Improvement Act, which now gives the SEC exclusive registration authority over the funds. The states can still charge their fees, but can no longer meddle. Consequently, funds are now going into states they had previously avoided.

If you try to buy shares of a fund that's not registered in your state, don't be surprised if your money is returned. The reason some funds are cautious is the possibility of recissions; investors holding fund shares sold improperly can, in some circumstances, demand that the sale be rescinded. In this case, the investor gets back the same amount he paid for the shares, plus interest—regardless of the shares' current value. That's pretty tempting if the value of the fund's shares has dropped. The laws and practices governing rescissions are complex, and vary from state to state. The decisions resulting from a few court cases have not been clear-cut. So fund policies differ.

If you want a particular fund and it isn't qualified in your state, you may want to try anyway, particularly if you're in no hurry. Our annual *Handbook* lists states qualified. If it's a new fund, they may have added your state recently. The funds should tell you their policy over the phone.

Telephone switching

Modern no-load fund investors can now take advantage of telephone switching offered by practically every fund family. With a simple phone call, mutual fund investors can buy and sell funds as easily as they can stocks. The only requirement is that they move their money around within one fund family or, in a few instances, back and forth to an independent money fund. Groups can offer this flexibility because of their in-house money market funds. Before money funds, fund managers used to discourage selling because they derived their income solely from management fees, which disappear when you redeem your fund shares. But that is not the case when an investor switches from a stock fund to a money market fund within the same group. The adviser still collects his management fee.

Telephone switching is a very good way to sell fund shares. Traditionally, selling mutual fund shares was a problem; the procedure was made intentionally cumbersome by the fund groups. To redeem your shares you first had to read the prospectus to find out the fund's specific procedures. Usually, you'd then need to write a letter. And invariably you'd then have to get your signature guaranteed at your bank or brokerage firm. Then you'd have to settle in for a wait until your letter was received by the fund or its custodian bank. The fund has seven days to mail the proceeds out. Funds usually take somewhat less. But the whole process can easily consume a couple of weeks from the time you decide to sell until you get your money. Now, one telephone call accomplishes your primary purpose—to get out of equities! In the October 1987 meltdown, more than 80% of the money redeemed from stock funds was switched into money market or bond funds.

Caveat: Switching from one fund to another, whether by phone or in writing, is considered by the IRS to be like any other sale. The transaction must be reported as a capital gain or loss on Schedule D.

When you buy, sell or switch by phone you should keep a record of the transaction. Major groups like Fidelity will give you a confirmation number at the end of the transaction. Keep it until the confirmation arrives. If you don't get a number, get the name of the representative you spoke to and the time and date of the conversation.

Most funds permit unlimited switching. But because it is difficult to manage a fund when large amounts of money are moving in and out, a number of major fund families discourage short-term market timers by placing limitations on the switching privilege. Scudder and SteinRoe limit switching to four round trips per year, American Century to six. Funds limit switching to protect their managers against potential disruptions in the portfolio which can result from too frequent in and out activity by market timers. For this reason, a few funds refuse to provide telephone switch privileges. A few others won't join the discount broker services that facilitate trading by phone. On the other hand, most of the bigger groups don't care how frequently small investors trade. Instead, they monitor large investors and professional money managers using funds closely.

Switching has become very popular. In 1987, a traumatic year, more than one-quarter of fund assets were switched. In recent years, about one-eighth of fund assets move from one fund to another each year.

How telephone switching began

In the early seventies, Fundpack, a Florida multifund, conducted studies which led to the hypothesis that using a stop-loss strategy would produce returns superior to a buy-hold strategy. Fundpack selected a rigid 10% guidepost based on its hypothetical studies. It would sell any funds in its portfolio that declined more than 10% from any point, and would buy back after a 10% rise or an unusually positive news development.

Fundpack's strategy turned out to be the loser. In a mid-1973 special report to shareholders, the firm noted: "But in the neurotic current market decline, Fundpack's prices declined 26% before Fundpack solidified itself. What happened?" The firm went on to explain that, "in whipsaw actions of the market, some of our buybacks declined a second and even a third 10%." Consequently, Fundpack discontinued its strategy in 1975. After adding a money market fund, it became the first fund group to offer telephone switching, thus leaving any stop-loss strategies to the discretion of its shareholders.

Almost all mutual funds are priced—the net asset value is computed—at the close of the business day—4 PM Eastern time. As a result, any investor buying or selling a mutual fund gets this end-of-day price, no matter what time the mail or phone call arrives.

This pricing policy has important implications for investors purchasing fund shares by telephone who are looking for that extra tim-

The only time of day to buy

ing edge, or who just want all the information humanly possible before making a buy or sell decision. The fact that you can only get the 4 PM Eastern time price can sometimes make or save money for you. But it can also lose you money.

Guideline: When buying or selling by telephone, make your decision shortly before the market's close.

Sometimes the market surges upward at the opening bell because some important news occurred the previous evening after the market had closed or just because traders feel the market may have reached a turning point. If you're buying funds, do nothing! The surge may last only a few hours and be inconsequential. You lose nothing by waiting. There was no way you could have gotten an earlier price.

Another situation: It is not uncommon for sharp moves that occur in the last hour or two to continue in the same direction the following morning. If the market is down considerably at 3:30 PM it may be advantageous to wait a day before buying.

The lone exception to the end-of-day pricing practice is at Fidelity, which prices its Select sector funds *hourly*. Select investors can buy in or sell out at any time of the day, and they can day-trade (buying and selling the same day). As is always the case, the funds are forward priced. That means you get the price at the top of the next hour. The only investors getting the end-of-the-day price are those who buy between 3 PM and 4 PM If you bought at the 9:30 AM opening, you will get the 10 AM price and you can call Fidelity back at about 10:15 AM to find out how much you paid. Hourly pricing can give sophisticated investors an additional edge; but it's not essential—and could be dangerous—for laymen who don't follow their investments closely.

Another way to buy and sell mutual fund shares throughout the day is to trade the two CBOE option contracts, the Lipper/Salomon Growth Mutual Fund Index and the Growth & Income Index. They're discussed in detail in in Chapter 19.

Fair value pricing

End of the day pricing can sometimes give you a greater edge when you're buying international funds. Most overseas markets are already closed by 4 PM Eastern Time. Once in a while, late news and developments subsequent to the foreign market's closing can virtually assure arbitraging profits for traders. In late 1997, Fidelity and some other fund groups moved to limit this practice. Called "fair-value" pricing, these funds have repriced overseas stocks based on latest information, to deprive traders of these arbitraging profits.

For example, on October 28, 1997, the Hong Kong market closed at 3 AM Eastern time, down 13.7%. But after the market had closed, trading in certain securities listed on the Hong Kong exchange continued in other markets around the world. In this "after-hours" trading, the prices of these securities rebounded significantly by the time Fidelity needed to price its funds at the close of the U.S. market. Rather than value Hong Kong stocks at prices that were 13 hours old, Fidelity took the later trading into account and priced them up about 10% on average. Fidelity was vindicated when the Hong Kong market reopened for trading a few hours later. Equities were up about 14%. Fidelity thus protected its long-term shareholders by preventing traders from making virtually guaranteed arbitrage profits by selling a day later. Also if any Fidelity shareholders sold on the 29th, they received fair value, not an artificially depressed price.

The SEC has given its blessing to this practice. A fund must state in its prospectus that it may "fair-value" price.

Redeeming your shares

If you've invested in a stock or bond fund that is part of a group with a money fund, you'll probably find it easier to first switch to the money fund and then write a check for your money.

If you need the money instantly you may want it transferred to your bank by wire. Major groups permit redemptions by telephone; a few only by mail. Each fund spells out its redemption procedures in its prospectus. You'll get your money more easily if you follow the directions exactly. If you can't find the prospectus, call the fund on its 800 number and ask for instructions. A sample redemption letter appears on the following page.

It is also helpful to enclose a blank copy of a subsequent investment form. It will have the exact account name and number on it. Send the redemption letter to either the fund or its transfer agent, as described in the prospectus. For large sums, register the letter, requesting a return receipt. It costs more, but you will have a record of the date the fund actually received your request. Your shares should be sold at the closing price on that date.

Dear Sirs:

Please redeem all shares (or *number* shares) of XYZ Fund. My account number is _____. Please send proceeds to the address of record as soon as possible.

Sincerely,

_____

When redeeming, be sure to find out whether you need a signature guarantee. Mutual funds commonly require that your signature on the redemption letter be guaranteed by a commercial bank or brokerage firm. Having it notarized is not acceptable.

If you want your redemption to be made as fast as possible, you should write your redemption letter now, leaving the amount blank if you plan to make only a partial redemption. Take it to the bank and have your signature guaranteed. Then file it with your other records. When the time comes to redeem, send it by overnight mail. This way you will be assured of next-day redemption.

According to SEC regulations, payment for shares redeemed must be made within seven days after the letter of redemption has been received or after issued shares have been deposited with the fund. While checks are usually sent out promptly, it is not unknown for a custodial bank to hold up payment for the full seven days and sometimes longer. Considering weekends and slow mail, it may take as much as two weeks for your check to arrive. So, if you are planning to redeem to meet a specific financial need and have a deadline, allow two weeks between writing your letter of redemption and getting a check back.

Purchases and redemptions during panics

Monday, October 19, 1987, when the Dow Jones Industrial average plummeted 508 points (22.6%), was a disaster for most mutual fund investors. If they hadn't sold the previous week, they were, with one exception, locked in for the full loss. But as it turned out, investors who sold out that Monday were actually worse off than those who didn't. There was a 289 point rally over the next two days, which made Wednesday the optimum point to exit the market until the shocks of the aftermath were over. Sometimes, the inability to sell in a panic works to the investor's advantage.

Ever since "Black Monday" investors have tended to view such crashes as buying opportunities. And so far they've been right. Ten years later, on Monday October 27, 1997, the market plunged 554 points. (Of course, in percentage terms, that drop was less than one-third as much as the 1987 decline.) This time there was virtually no panic on the part of individual investors.

In fact, it was seen as a an excellent buying opportunity. If anything, there was a *buying* panic the following day. The market regained 337 points on the extraordinary volume of almost 1.2 billion shares. (That volume was 74% higher than the second busiest day.) Even though over the intervening decade funds had beefed up their 800 telephone number capacity, there were still some busy signals, particularly at dis-

---

Why you need a signature guarantee

You may wonder why that is necessary; why you can't have your signature notarized instead. The answer is that a notary public merely certifies the identity of the person signing the document. The purpose of the signature guarantee is to protect against improper transfer of property interest—in this instance the ownership of mutual fund shares. The guarantor warrants that not only is the signature genuine, but also that the person is an appropriate person to endorse and has the legal capacity to sign. The ultimate effect of the signature guarantee is to transfer liability to the guarantor. This protects the funds from the costs of fraudulent transactions.

Since such improprieties are rare, the signature guarantee may not be necessary for small amounts.

count brokers, when investors attempted to take advantage of the lower prices.

Here are some tips for reaching your fund in times of unusual market activity:

■ Start dialing the fund's 800 number early in the day. Don't wait till just before closing.

■ Try the fund's regular (non-toll-free) number.

■ Send purchase or redemption letters by fax.

■ Join the three million investors trading on the Internet.

■ Get through a day later using overnight mail.

■ Walk over to the fund's or discount broker's local office, if it has one.

If 1987 does repeat

On October 19 and 20, 1987, some fund groups decided to take the full seven days allowed before mailing out checks. Fidelity was one, but by the 21st, had resumed regular daily payment procedures. When the purpose of a redemption is to avoid dropping stock prices, it is not so important if there's a few days' delay in receiving your check.

By law (the Investment Company Act of 1940) all mutual funds must redeem shares at a price based on the current NAV per share that the fund next computes after receipt of a redemption order. However, under certain unusual conditions the right of redemption can be temporarily suspended. One is when the New York Stock Exchange closes (for other than regular holidays). That's because funds simply can't price their portfolios when the market is closed. The Investment Company Act also permits the SEC to declare an emergency during which mutual funds can suspend redemptions. The SEC has exercised its authority under this section when, for example, major snowstorms have paralyzed the Northeast corridor. In addition, funds may suspend both sales and redemptions during customary local holidays (such as Patriot's Day in Boston), provided adequate disclosure of the holiday closing schedule is given to investors in the fund's prospectus.

Theoretically, funds can also redeem in kind. This means you receive a proportionate share of the fund's portfolio securities. Redeeming in kind is virtually unheard of in the industry. A few years ago, the ICI conducted a survey of its larger members and found only one redemption in kind. And that was an unusual case in which a shareholder request was being honored. It's not difficult for a fund to redeem in cash. The fund is required to have at least 85% of its portfolio invested in liquid securities, i.e., readily saleable securities.

In addition, funds keep cash reserves, usually have some new money flowing in, if only from dividends, and frequently have credit lines with banks. In September 1997, *The Wall Street Journal* reported that the funds had $20 billion in credit lines to meet redemptions. The Oakmark funds' credit line was $187 million. Taking another tack, giant Fidelity received authorization from the SEC in 1990 to lend money between funds to meet redemptions.

Incidentally, when you redeem a fund account completely, most funds do not immediately remove the account from their shareholder records. Therefore, you may be able to reinvest in the same account at a later date, a simpler procedure than having to open a new account. Most funds purge their inactive subscriber records about once a year.

Communicating with your fund group

A few years ago, the funds were publicly criticized for providing account information or accepting buy and sell orders over the phone without properly identifying each caller. While I doubt that this practice caused significant harm, most fund groups now require that callers properly identify themselves. Thus, when you call a fund about your account, it's also a good idea to have your Social Security or tax ID number and your account number close at hand before you call. For security reasons many groups have deleted Social Security numbers from periodic statements and confirmations, in case they fall into the wrong hands. That way, you don't have to worry that somebody will be able to switch your money from an equity-income to an aggressive growth fund without your permission.

Mutual fund distributions

One of the most confusing aspects of mutual fund investing is the manner in which distributions are made. Like operating companies, funds declare dividends. But since they are investment companies, they also declare capital gains distributions, resulting from the gains realized when stocks or bonds in the fund's portfolio are sold at a profit.

Federal regulations require that mutual funds distribute at least 98% of their ordinary income and net realized capital gains for the calendar year within that same calendar year. Failure to do so results in a 4% excise tax on the excess not distributed. These distributions must be declared prior to December 31 of each year and paid prior to January 31 of the following year. The distributions are considered as taxable income to investors in the year in which they are declared, even if paid the following January.

Prior to 1986, funds commonly made their distributions in January for the prior year's income. These so-called spillover dividends gave shareholders a full year before they had to pay taxes on the profits. Unfortunately, this great loophole has long since been closed.

Distribution options

Mutual funds commonly offer three distribution options: All income and capital gains distributions are automatically reinvested in additional shares, income distributions are paid in cash while capital gains distributions are reinvested in additional shares, or both income and capital gains distributions can be paid in cash.

For most investors, the first option—reinvestment of all distributions—is best. Your investment compounds and in a rising market will grow faster. Reinvesting dividends is actually a form of dollar-cost averaging.

The logic behind the second option is that you are gaining immediate benefits from the income dividend distributions, but are not eating into your capital. It is important to maintain your capital in real (inflation adjusted) terms. In the case of equity funds, reinvesting capital gains will generally accomplish this purpose. Secondly, while there is no real distinction between dividend income and capital gains, as a practical matter an investor looking for steady income might prefer the second option so he or she does not receive occasional, large distributions that would only have to be reinvested. (Dividends and capital gains are said to be of the same nature because a corporation has the option of reinvesting its profits for further growth, rather than paying dividends. What is the logic of utilities paying out millions in dividends, and then turning around and borrowing or selling more stock or bonds for expansion?) I recommend this option for most retired investors living on their income.

If you take the third option, you receive all distributions in cash. This option can be used to restrict the size of your investment without incurring possible gains by selling. The distributions can then be reallocated to other investments. This option is a good one to consider if you have a sizeable capital gain from a long-term investment in a fund that is no longer performing as it used to.

Don't overlook your bond funds; when interest rates are rising, take their distributions in cash. This option will also simplify your accounting when the time comes to sell. If your purchases were in one lump sum and you didn't reinvest distributions, you will have only one cost basis; you'll save a few minutes when you are preparing Schedule D of your tax return.

In addition, be aware that a number of the larger groups offer another option that can be highly desirable. Fidelity, Dreyfus, Vanguard and T. Rowe Price, for example, will direct the distributions from one fund in the group to another fund for reinvestment. You can implement option three by having the cash distributions from a stock or a bond fund reinvested in the group's money fund. This is a convenient way of maximizing your returns until you actually need the money.

As with individuals, mutual funds can have realized or unrealized gains on their portfolios, or realized or unrealized losses. These gains and losses have investment implications.

As I noted earlier, net realized gains will be distributed to shareholders of record at the time of the distribution. Old shareholders will rightfully pay taxes on these distributions since they received the growth. New shareholders receive no benefit, only the tax liability. If the gain is unrealized there is no immediate tax liability, but certainly a potential one. After several bull market years, many funds will have unrealized appreciation. If they sell appreciated stocks, perhaps anticipating a bear market, the gains will become realized and the tax collector will receive his due. (Of course, that's assuming that an investor holds the fund shares in a non-tax-qualified account.)

Conversely, realized losses offer opportunities for tax deferral. In a bear market, smart mutual fund managers often realize their losses as they sell losing positions. But, unlike gains, the resulting tax loss benefits are not passed through immediately to the shareholders. The fund doesn't distribute capital gains profits until its losses are fully offset. And because the Internal Revenue Service permits funds to

Gains—both realized and unrealized—affect you

carry these losses forward for five years, shareholders can enjoy a considerable grace period while the fund is accruing new gains. In this situation, there is no tax liability until the shareholder sells the shares at a profit.

While other criteria are more important, don't ignore this valuable plus when you are considering buying a fund. The prospectus or quarterly reports will provide information on gains or losses. During a long bull market, few funds have capital loss carry forwards. But when the bear comes out of hibernation, or if the fund has catastrophic losses, it's another story. For example, as of May 1997, the American Heritage Fund had net capital loss carryforwards of approximately $31.5 million expiring in 2003 through 2005, and net operating loss carryforwards of approximately $2.0 million, which begin to expire in 1998 through 2013. At the time of the report, the fund's total net assets were only $17.5 million, so it's obvious this fund will not have a year-end capital gains distribution in the near future. If ever.

Reducing the tax burden

Novice fund investors rejoice when they receive a dividend. More experienced investors aren't always so glad. Here's why.

Let's assume your fund has accumulated profits and plans to distribute them to its shareholders. The fund now has an NAV of $12 per share and plans to distribute $1 per share in income. The fund goes ex-dividend. (That's when the dividends to be paid are segregated from the rest of the fund's assets. The day that happens the daily papers put an "x" next to the fund.) The per share price immediately drops $1 to $11 since funds are always priced at net asset value. A shareholder will soon receive $1 per share in dividends or have the $1 reinvested in additional shares of the fund. Either way, the shareholder still has a total equity of $12 per share. If he takes the distribution in cash, he has fund shares worth $11 per share plus a dollar in his pocket. If he reinvests the shares his total equity—number of shares times per share price—is still the same. He has not benefited from the distribution, only incurred a tax liability. That's assuming the investor's account is not an IRA, Keogh or other tax-qualified plan. This is true even if the distribution is reinvested!

After several bull market years, gains can be sizeable. In December, 1996, the Blanchard Precious Metals Fund had a capital gains distribution amounting to a whopping 40% of assets. Incidentally, in the wonderful world of accounting, it is possible for the capital gains distribution to be greater than a fund's total return in the same year. In May of 1996, Fidelity Magellan paid a distribution amounting to 16.6% of assets and followed with a second distribution in December of 0.7% of assets. However, the fund gained only 11.7% in 1996. The explanation was that Magellan's then manager, Jeff Vinik, sold a number of long-term stock holdings, resulting in large realized gains.

You can minimize your tax liability by carefully timing your purchases. Take the case of a fund that distributes once a year, in December. If you buy just before the distribution, you immediately incur a tax liability. You have acquired a share of the other stockholders' profits. On the other hand, if you wait until after the distribution, the NAV will be lower by the amount of the distribution. You will be able to buy more shares for your money, and have no tax liability until you sell or until the fund declares its next annual distribution.

Many funds will give you the exact dates of their distributions a few days or weeks before they are made if you phone them. When you call, make sure to find out the precise ex-dividend date and the record date (not the date the distribution actually gets paid—often a week or so later). Go by the ex date, usually the day after the record date.

Here's another situation where careful timing made a difference. A fund makes a distribution of $2.17 consisting of $1.20 in short-term gains and $0.97 in long-term gains. Investor "A" buys the fund before the distribution at a price of $22.17. Investor "B" waits until after the distribution and buys the fund for $20.00 (assumes no price fluctuation). Both investors sell a month later for $21.00. Investor "B" has $1 in short-term gains he pays taxes on at his ordinary income rate. "A" sold his shares at a loss of $1.17 per share ($21.00 - $22.17) which when combined with his $1.20 short-term gain distribution results in a short-term gain of $0.03 and a long-term gain from the distribution of $0.97. "A" pays taxes on the ordinary income rate on only $0.03. The other $0.97 will be taxed at the lower capital gains rate.

Money market funds and most bond funds declare dividends daily. In the case of these funds, the advice offered in the preceding paragraphs does not apply since there is no chance for the interest income to build up. Their NAVs are unaffected by the daily distribution of interest income.

As this discussion makes clear, you need to be careful about your purchases, but less so with your sales. In general, it makes no difference whether you sell just before or just after a distribution is made. By selling just prior to a distribution, you will receive a higher price, potentially giving you a larger gain. If you sell afterwards, the price, and your capital gains liability, will be lower; but you'll also be taxed on the fund's capital distribution. Exception: if the distribution is an income or short-term capital gains distribution, it is fully taxable. On the other hand, if selling prior to the distribution enables you to obtain a long-term capital gain, you will benefit if you are in a high tax bracket.

Don't over-worry about December distributions

Most funds now make major distributions in November or December. If you're a long-term holder of the fund, you'll be paying tax on the profits you've accrued over time. But if you buy a fund for the first time in November or December, you may be paying tax on someone else's profits.

Along with the financial press in general, the *Investor* has been bringing this fact to investors' attention for several years now. Just as this advice has helped many investors reduce taxes, it's also succeeded in scaring other investors away from all funds the last couple months of the year. Consequently, year-end distributions need to be put into perspective.

While some funds make huge year-end capital gains distributions, they are the exception. In 1996, the average capital gain paid out by equity funds amounted to only 6% of assets. That meant that if you are in a 28% or a 31% tax bracket, the capital gains tax would be about 2% of your market value. So, if the market gained another 3% or more between the time you bought the fund and the end of the year, you could be ahead by not waiting for the distribution before buying. Also, from a longer-term perspective, each capital gains distribution reduces net asset value per share, which means that you will take less capital gain when you ultimately sell your shares. The bottom line is that all you have lost is the time value of the money you pay Uncle Sam.

Don't forego all fund purchases in November and December.

Rather take the time to get an estimate of the annual capital gains distributions. Most groups have estimates by late November or early December. You will find that some funds have already paid their distributions or do not plan to pay any. You can buy them, along with funds that have indicated they will pay out distributions of less than 6%-8% of assets. (To calculate, just divide the dollar amount of the distribution by the NAV.)

Finally, don't forget these caveats concern taxable accounts only. There are no tax implications for funds in tax-sheltered retirement plans.

When a fund reinvests your dividend and capital gains distributions, these sums become part of your cost basis. For tax purposes, it's as if the fund had sent you checks and you'd then used the money to buy additional shares. And, of course, you paid taxes on each distribution the year it was declared. Here, for example, are the final tax consequences of a ten-year gain through December 1996 on a $10,000 investment in the T. Rowe Price International Stock Fund.

Know your cost basis

Value of shares initially purchased 12/31/86	$17,585
Value of shares acquired by reinvestment of dividends	656
Value of shares acquired by reinvestment of capital gains	26,993
Total value of investment after 10 Years	$45,234

While the only money the investor actually paid to the fund during the 10 years was the initial $10,000, if he or she sold the shares on December 31, 1996, the cost basis would be:

Initial investment —	
Dec. 31, 1986	$10,000
Dividends used to	
purchase shares	340
Capital gains distributions	
used to purchase shares	<u>19,625</u>
Total Cost Basis	$29,965

Thus, although the original investment of $10,000 is now larger by $35,234, the capital gain reported for tax purposes is only $15,269 (the difference between $45,234 and $29,965). The investor already paid taxes on the balance of the gains. Always save the distribution statements that the fund sends you so that you can provide the IRS with the proper cost basis if and when the time comes.

When you sell fund shares, you can use any of several methods for determining your cost basis. The differences can be important if you are making a partial liquidation.

1. You can sell *specific shares*. It is best to do this by letter, specifically identifying by number and purchase date the shares you want to sell. Keep a copy of the letter; the fund's confirmation statement will be of no help.

2. *First in, first out (FIFO)*. If you don't instruct otherwise, the shares bought first will be deemed to have been sold first. If these were bought at the lowest cost, the tax bill will be higher.

3. *Average cost per share*. You take the total cost of your shares and divide by the total number of shares to get the average. You must make a special election with the IRS to use this method. Some funds are now providing their shareholders with average cost per share data.

4. *Double category method*. You can figure one average cost for long-term holdings and another for short-term holdings. This method is important if you're in a high tax bracket, substantially above long-term capital gains rates.

The "wash sale" trap

If you have set up your fund account for dividend reinvestment, don't fall into this tax trap. Mutual funds, like any other securities, can be sold to establish a tax loss. If you sell a security at a loss, you can't buy back your shares until more than 30 days have passed or the IRS will disallow the loss for tax purposes as a wash sale. This potential problem can occur with any fund, but it can really catch you unawares if you make a partial liquidation of a bond fund that pays monthly dividends. That's because any dividend reinvestment is a purchase that offsets your sale. You can avoid this complication, either by making a complete, rather than a partial, liquidation, by switching from a reinvestment to a cash distribution account for at least 31 days, or by specifying which shares you are selling. This tax problem is also a good reason for not establishing a check redemption feature in bond funds with variable NAVs.

As a mutual fund shareowner you will receive many types of reports from your fund. You should save some, usually for tax purposes. Read and discard others.

Read and retain: The *prospectus*. This provides basic information you need to know about the fund. Save the current prospectus.

Reports of transactions: Every time you make a purchase or redemption, or the fund declares a distribution, you should receive a confirmation. These confirmations note how many shares you bought and sold and at what price. Funds send individual confirmations, statements that recapitulate previous transactions, usually for the calendar year, or both. In the case of cumulative statements, save only the most recent. These confirmations and statements must be saved for tax purposes until you sell your shares, then for as long as you retain tax records, generally for three years after the date you file your returns. If you are missing a statement, the fund can usually provide you with a duplicate, in some cases at a nominal charge.

It also helps to keep a simple ledger for each fund you own. That ledger should list the date, dollar value and number of shares of each transaction (including automatic dividend distributions), and a running total of shares owned. This ledger will prove to be invaluable when filing taxes after the fund is sold.

You get a form 1099 from the fund each year (usually in January) after it makes its income or capital gains distributions. Put it with your other tax records. Note that the IRS requires that funds treat distributions of short-term capital gains as "ordinary income." The two categories are combined on the 1099, even though they are generally shown separately on the fund's transaction confirmations.

Record keeping

Another form you should retain is the "explanation of tax information" that sometimes accompanies the 1099. It lists the classifications of distributions for your income tax returns. The form explains how the information should be reported. Municipal bond funds usually enclose a form listing dividends by state. You can deduct that percentage of the dividend payment that originates in your own state when paying state taxes.

Sign and return: proxy statements. Do the fund a favor. It needs a quorum of the shares so the annual meeting can be held. Usually it is sufficient to read the front page only. Quite often it says only that the directors and accounting firm will be continued. Sometimes you will be asked to vote for an increase in the management fee or a 12b-1 fee. If you disagree you can vote no. In any case, send it back. If you do disagree with the direction that the fund's management is taking, your best recourse, as with most public corporations, is to sell.

Note: some funds are organized as Massachusetts Business Trusts. By doing so they are able to issue an unlimited number of shares without specific shareholder approval and thus avoid the requirement that they hold annual shareholder meetings. The latter is no big loss, since few shareholders ever attend. All other shareholder rights remain intact.

Read: quarterly and annual reports. If you want to refer to the composition of the fund's portfolio, save these reports until later ones arrive. You can read and discard informational material, such as letters from the president and fund newsletters.

How safe are mutual funds

Since investing in a mutual fund generally entails sending money somewhere out of sight, it's only natural that investors frequently raise questions about the safety of money in mutual funds.

Rest easy. While the price of your fund shares rises or falls with moves in the markets, there is little cause for concern in terms of a fund company going bankrupt or defrauding shareholders. Safeguards were imposed on the industry as long ago as the Investment Company Act of 1940. Some provisions that protect you: the act prevents

■ insiders from manipulating the companies to their own benefit and to the detriment of public investors;

■ issuance of securities that have inequitable or discriminatory provisions;

■ management of investment companies by irresponsible persons.

■ the use of unsound or misleading methods of computing earnings and asset value;

■ changes in the character of investment companies without the consent of investors; and

■ excessive leveraging on the part of investment companies.

The act also ensures the disclosure of full and accurate information about companies and their sponsors.

Mutual funds are organized as wholly separate companies with their assets held by a separate custodian. No creditor has recourse against the assets of your mutual fund to meet the obligations of an investment advisor or underwriter. The funds' assets are held by separate custodians. The advisor's officers and key employees are bonded, and auditing is done by outside firms.

Why a fund can't go broke

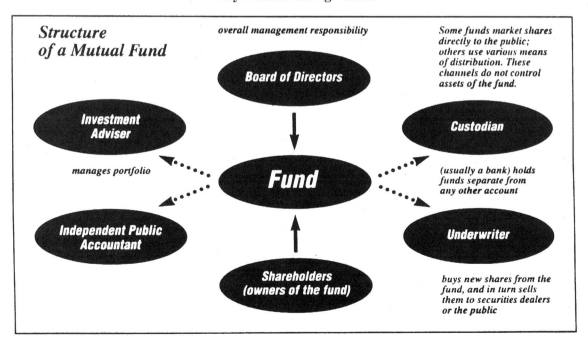

Do I want a stock certificate?

Funds prefer not to issue stock certificates, and will do so only if you request one. T. Rowe Price has eliminated certificates entirely.

In any case, as a general rule it's better to leave your shares on deposit with the mutual fund company. That's safer and facilitates selling. If you have certificated shares they must be sent, properly signed, to the fund's transfer agent for redemption. However, there is one possible reason for obtaining the certificates: to use as collateral for a loan. Incidentally, if you lose your certificates (fund or corporate stock), you will have to put down 2%-3% of the value of the shares as a deposit before the shares will be reissued. The deposit is basically for insurance to the fund company against the possibility that someone will try to sell the original certificates.

What to do when your fund fouls up completely

Has your fund lost your account? It's happened. Have you failed to get a dividend check? That's happened, too. And have you had trouble getting the matter straightened out? If you're in such a fix, here are some suggestions that may help.

You can always complain to the Securities and Exchange Commission (SEC), of course. But the SEC recommends that you first attempt to contact the senior fund official responsible for shareholder or customer relations. When you have located this person, explain your problem as clearly and concisely as possible. Describe the background of the problem, including the details of any transactions, in chronological order. Then mention the present status of the matter and the adjustment that you feel is necessary. Always follow up with a letter spelling out what you stated on the phone. Some funds won't consider a complaint serious unless you commit it to writing.

If this doesn't get satisfaction, then try contacting the Securities and Exchange Commission Office of Consumer Affairs and Information Services, 450 5th St., N.W., Washington, D.C., 20549 (telephone 202-942-7040, e-mail: help@sec.gov) or one of its branch offices. The SEC staff will respond to all investor complaints and inquiries, answer questions and where appropriate, contact the fund for its response.

When writing to the SEC, include the name and address of the fund advisor, the name of the particular fund, your account number, a brief description of the problem, copies of related documents (for example, confirmations of transactions and monthly account statements) and/or copies of any correspondence regarding the matter. Also include a daytime telephone number where the SEC staff can reach you if they have questions. If you are simultaneously furnishing other individuals and/or securities industry organizations with information copies of your complaint, mention that so there's no duplication of efforts.

Here's a list of the Regional and District SEC offices. The states that each one covers are listed in parentheses.

Northeast Regional Office, 7 World Trade Center, Suite 1300, New York, NY 10048, 212-748-8000, e-mail: newyork@sec.gov (CT, DE, DC, ME, MD, MA, NH, NJ, NY, PA, RI, VT, VA, WV)

Boston District Office, 73 Tremont Street, Suite 600, Boston, MA 02108-3912, 617-424-5900, e-mail: boston@sec.gov

Philadelphia District Office, The Curtis Center, Suite 1005 E., 601 Walnut Street, Philadelphia, PA 19106-3322, 215-597-3100, e-mail: philadelphia@sec.gov

Southeast Regional Office, 1401 Brickell Avenue, Suite 200, Miami, FL 33131, 305-536-4700, e-mail: miami@sec.gov (AL, FL, GA, LA, MS, NC, Puerto Rico, SC, TN, Virgin Islands)

Atlanta District Office, 3475 Lenox Road, N.E., Suite 1000, Atlanta, GA 30326-1232, 404-842-7600, e-mail: atlanta@sec.gov

Midwest Regional Office, Citicorp Center, 500 West Madison Street, Suite 1400, Chicago, IL 60661-2511, 312-353-7390, e-mail: chicago@sec.gov (IL, IN, IA, KY, MI, MN, MO, OH, WI)

Central Regional Office, 1801 California Street, Suite 4800, Denver, CO, 80202-2648, 303-844-1000, e-mail: denver@sec.gov (AR, CO, KS, NE, NM, ND, OK, SD, TX, UT, WY).

Fort Worth District Office, 801 Cherry Street, 19th Floor, Fort Worth, TX 76102, 817-978-3821, e-mail: dfw@sec.gov

Salt Lake District Office, 500 Key Bank Tower, 50 S. Main Street, Suite 500, Box 79, Salt Lake City, UT, 84144-0402, 801-524-5796, e-mail: saltlake@sec.gov

Pacific Regional Office, 5760 Wilshire Boulevard, 11th Floor, Los Angeles, CA 90036-3648, 213-965-3998, e-mail: losangeles@sec.gov (AK, AZ, CA, Guam, HI, ID, MT, NV, OR, WA)

San Francisco District Office, 44 Montgomery Street, Suite 1100, San Francisco, CA 94104, 415-705-2500, e-mail: sanfrancisco@sec.gov

Transferring IRAs

You may have IRA accounts at several different financial institutions. If so, the paperwork is no doubt beginning to mount up and there may be annual IRA fees. A solution: transfer all of your IRAs under one roof.

The best roofs: discount brokerage firms specializing in no-loads, or a no-load mutual fund company. That way you can diversify your investments while making record-keeping simple. Some fund groups now lower or eliminate the IRA fees for large accounts.

You can transfer your IRAs between institutions in one of two ways. Either do it yourself, once a year, through what is called a "60-day rollover." That means that you can take possession of your tax-qualified money for up to 60 days with no tax or penalty, so long as by the 60th day it is back under the shelter of an IRA custodian. Or you can authorize the institutions involved—one surrendering your money, one accepting it—handle the process directly, through what's called a custodian-to-custodian transfer. With that approach, you can move money from one fund family to another as often as you want.

Custodian-to-custodian transfers have gotten simpler. The paperwork doesn't take as long as it used to. Some funds have specialists to advise you on IRAs and other tax-sheltered plans. It's a good idea to review the details with them, particularly when you are dealing with an IRA rollover. Current law makes it almost mandatory to do a custodian-to-custodian transfer of a rollover, at least at the time you receive the distribution from your company.

Withdrawal plans

A mutual fund withdrawal program is a systematic means of obtaining regular monthly payments from dividends and invested principal. It is a logical outgrowth of the fund's capabilities and a highly convenient service. These plans are flexible. You can change the amount of the payout at any time, terminate it at will or withdraw lump sums when you need to. Checks can be sent directly to you, to your bank for deposit or to any third person.

You can, of course, take out any amount. However, I generally recommend that you try to stay at 6% or less of your invested capital each year. If the fund is well managed, its dividends and capital appreciation will be more than enough to cover these monthly payments.

If you want a monthly fixed income, the simplicity of a withdrawal plan gives mutual funds a tremendous advantage over stocks. Since most stock dividends are paid quarterly, you would have to own three stocks paying dividends in different months of each quarter in order to approximate the monthly payout principle of a fund withdrawal program. And with stocks, there's no easy way to take out your principal regularly. Moreover, you'd have to pay a commission if you sold stock.

Most fund families offer withdrawal plans; however, they seldom publicize them. If you're interested in setting one up, ask the fund's representative for details. Funds generally require that you have a minimum invested before you can set up a systematic withdrawal program; $10,000 is a common minimum. A few funds will set up a plan if you have as little as $5,000 invested, but then generally permit only quarterly, rather than monthly, withdrawals. This is logical; too small a check makes the plan hardly worthwhile.

Some ways withdrawal plans can be used

Although mutual fund withdrawal plans are most commonly associated with payouts to the widowed and the retired, they can serve other objectives equally well. They can be used to:

■ Care for dependents.

■ Pay for school or college expenses. A program can be set up in which the principal is depleted over a specific period, such as four years.

■ Make alimony payments.

■ Pay any regular monthly bill such as rent or mortgage payments.

The major difficulty with withdrawal plans is that shares of your fund undoubtedly will have to be sold in order to make up the required distribution. These sales, like all others, are taxable events. If your income from Social Security and a pension is sufficient to cover your basic living expenses, you are better off not using a systematic withdrawal plan. It will simplify your life—and your record keeping—if you satisfy your needs simply by taking the fund's income distributions in cash. If that's not sufficient, then take capital gains distributions in cash, and if you need to make occasional redemptions to pay large bills. If that's still not enough, then use a withdrawal plan. Obviously, you maximize your assets by refraining from dipping into your principal except when you really need to.

When not to use withdrawal plans

Since a common reason for a withdrawal plan is to supply retirement income, often for an extended period of years, it follows that investors will be better off using a conservative growth or growth-income fund as the vehicle. These funds are less volatile when investing for the long haul. Theoretically, there is no reason why you cannot use an aggressive growth fund. But if it loses 30% in a year, in addition to your with-

Which funds are appropriate for withdrawal plans?

drawals, you may not sleep very well. Or, more likely, you will feel constrained to abandon the withdrawal program while the fund is dropping, and that would undoubtedly be aggravating.

The major variables guiding your selection should be your other income and your life expectancy. Couples retiring at age 60, have an average life expectancy of 30 more years, and they may well be depending upon their funds to provide income throughout their lives. Obviously, taking a long-term view is advisable. So, you should invest a portion in a growth fund, where the opportunity for capital appreciation is greater.

On the other hand, a couple at 75 has a joint life expectancy of 16 years (meaning that one or the other is likely to live to 91). Since these older folks don't need as much inflation protection, they can concentrate more on investments paying high interest or dividend income.

Table 82

| | **Years in retirement** | |
| | **Life expectancy** | |
Expected retirement age	**For individual**	**For couple same age**
55	28 years	34 years
60	24	30
65	20	25
70	16	21
75	12	16

Source: Based on IRS life expectancy tables

What if you withdraw money faster than the fund is growing?

If you take your money out at the rate of 6% a year, and your fund grows at a higher rate, which decent-performing mutual funds certainly should over the long haul, your capital will never be depleted. You can live forever and not run out of money.

However, some elderly investors, especially those whose nestegg isn't too large, may find 6% inadequate to meet their current expenses. They need more, even if they have to deplete their capital to an extent. If that's you, my best advice is: be careful. To determine the maximum at which you can safely withdraw money, look at the triangular Table (83), which gives the "financial life expectancy" of an investment where the rate of withdrawal from principal is higher than the rate of growth.

Suppose you have $100,000 which is growing at 9% a year, and you withdraw at a 12% annual rate—$12,000 a year or $1,000 a month. Looking at the box where these two percentages intersect shows you that your principal will last for 16 years. On the other hand, if you withdraw at the rate of 11%, it will last 19 years, and at 10%, 26 years. Use the chart in conjunction with standard mortality tables to determine the number of years you'll need a payout. You can also read in the other direction. Assume you need withdrawals of 8% a year for 20 years. Then the right side of the chart shows that you need an investment that pays only 5% a year. Since a wise investor is "risk averse," the money should be conservatively invested. If the fund's rate of return exceeds your withdrawal rate (below the table's base line), then your assets will increase, and you will make your children very happy.

Table 83

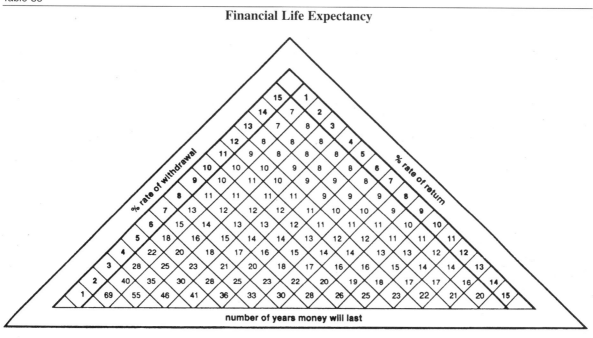

Financial Life Expectancy

CHAPTER 23

THE
NO-LOAD
FUND INVESTOR

The mutual fund prospectus

If you buy a mutual fund you are bound to get a prospectus, if not before the purchase, then after. If you're at all typical, the odds that you'll read it thoroughly are nil, and the chances of you even glancing at it aren't very good, either. Yet you know it's important, that you should read it. The reason you don't is that prospectuses read like lawyers' briefs.

In fact, that's how they began. They were first mandated by the Securities Act of 1933 in the aftermath of the '29 crash. The act specified that whenever a corporation issued new stock, its terms of sale had to be detailed in a prospectus. Now most corporations only need a prospectus once in their life—at the time of the initial underwriting. (Less frequently, prospectuses are needed for secondary stock offerings.) These operating company prospectuses are written by the underwriter's trained security analysts and lawyers, and are meant to be read by other professionals. After the initial issue, stocks trade among investors without any further disclosure documents.

Unfortunately, mutual funds never really fit into this regulatory scheme. Mutual funds, which are investment companies, are quite unlike operating companies. By law, mutual funds are considered to be in continuous registration because when you buy their shares you buy directly from the fund, not from another investor.

The fund industry, knowing that the readers of their prospectuses were overwhelmingly individual investors, has tried over the years to turn the prospectus into more of a marketing brochure than a legal document. And it looks like they have finally succeeded. In 1996, at the instigation of SEC Chairman Arthur Levitt, the "profile" prospectus was devised. It's a simple three to six page pamphlet covering just 11 items in a set order:

1. The fund's objectives and goals;
2. Its investment strategies;
3. Its risks;
4. The kind of investors for whom the fund might be an appropriate or inappropriate investment;
5. A table showing fees and expenses of the fund;
6. A graphic depiction of the variability of the fund's performance over time in the form of a bar chart presenting the fund's total return in each of the last 10 years;
7. The name of the fund's investment advisor;
8. How to purchase shares, and minimum investment requirements;
9. How to redeem shares;
10. When and how distributions are made;
11. Other services offered to investors.

Profile prospectuses were approved by the SEC on March 10, 1998 for implementation after June 1, 1998. The SEC also ordered funds to use "plain English" prospectus for new offerings after December 1, 1998 and a year after that for existing funds. I think this is a step forward for the industry and for investors.

So let's talk about the current prospectus, which federal law requires that you get when you buy a fund. You really need to read at least portions of it, and in this chapter I'll tell you which. In any case, always save it. Even if you don't read it right away, you may need to refer to it later.

The primary purpose of a prospectus is to provide "full and fair disclosure" of all relevant investment information. The document is valuable for this reason alone. Occasionally it provides facts that some funds would just as soon leave unsaid. For example: whether a fund is being sued, how experienced—or inexperienced—management is and whether management's fee is abnormally high. These are facts you won't get when you buy stock that was previously issued, or when you select an investment counselor or a broker. Most important, the prospectus generally gives you a clear, detailed explanation of the fund's objectives, not the one- or two-word short-hand descriptions that most advisory services use.

What the prospectus does *not* tell you is how the fund stacks up against others. The SEC prohibits such comparisons.

What you need to read

Even in the era of "prospectus lite," reading through one can be a chore. So let's zoom in on the most important sections first, helping you to glean most of the information you need. Later in the chapter I will cover information of lesser importance.

Investment objectives, policies and types of investments. This is one of the most valuable sections in the prospectus. Mutual fund guides and directories usually provide one word descriptions, or at most short extracts of the objective, and are even less likely to describe a fund's policies. These are vital facts and you really should read the prospectus section about them in full. They generally run only a few paragraphs.

A fund's objective—growth, income, etc.—is different from its policy. Its policies are the means it proposes to use to achieve its objective. The fund may have a policy of buying dividend-paying common stocks or of buying bonds to achieve an income objective, for example.

A fund's policy spells out what is permitted. For example, it will describe investment techniques such as borrowing money, selling stocks short, buying warrants or put and call options, writing options, or investing in restricted securities. Not that the fund is using the techniques at any given time, only that it can. Lately, funds have had the tendency to list everything they might possibly use—just in case. This gives them far more latitude but makes this section of the prospectus less valuable.

The SEC does ask that emphasis be given to current policies. A fund does not have to disclose policies which it is authorized to follow if it hasn't within the past year and has no intention of doing so. Also, if a policy doesn't put more than 5% of the fund's assets at risk, the policy need only be identified; such as, "the fund may buy options."

If a fund concentrates more than 25% of its assets in any one industry, the prospectus will say so. If a fund provides high income by investing in lower rated bonds, that will be noted.

You should also check the summary or cover page (usually the first page of the prospectus) for warnings or special risk factors. These paragraphs should be read carefully. In 1988, I perused the prospectus of the Renaissance Fund, a new no-load, closed-end, market timing, index fund (it's not worth explaining how that's possible). Under Risk Factors I found the following statement: "There will be no continuous offering of shares of the fund. AS A PRACTICAL MATTER AFTER THE OFFERING MADE BY THIS PROSPECTUS, THERE MAY BE NO MARKET FOR FUND SHARES TO BE TRADED." I investigated and found out that, sure enough, there was no market. If you invested, there'd be *no* practical way for you to sell your shares!

The prospectus for the Strong Growth Funds notes in solid caps that "THE FUNDS MAY ENGAGE IN SUBSTANTIAL SHORT-TERM TRADING, WHICH MAY INCREASE A FUND'S EXPENSES. EACH FUND MAY INVEST A SIGNIFICANT PORTION OF ITS ASSETS IN RESTRICTED SECURITIES. THESE INVESTMENT POLICIES INVOLVE SUBSTANTIAL RISK AND MAY BE CONSIDERED SPECULATIVE."

There will also be a notation if the fund's expenses are unusually high.

No-loads generally proclaim their status on the cover page, which will also provide the date of the prospectus. Make sure you are reading a current one, no more than a year old.

All prospectuses must include a **Fee table**, which discloses all the costs associated with buying and owning mutual fund shares. *If you don't look at anything else in the prospectus, look at the fee table.*

The fee table breaks out separately non-recurring expenses such as front- and back-end sales charges, as well as recurring expenses such as management and 12b-1 fees. You can generally find that table on page two or three of the prospectus. Fee tables are in a section titled "Fee Table" or "Summary of Fund Expenses" or "Shareholder and Fund Expenses" or "Expense Information" or "Fee information." Checking this table is a must.

Here's the Fee Table for the Partners Fund. This is exactly the sort of fee table you are looking for. It's ideal.

Neuberger & Berman Partners Fund:
Expense Information

Shareholder Transaction Expenses

Sales Load Imposed on Purchases	None
Sales Load Imposed on Reinvested Dividends	None
Deferred Sales Load	None
Redemption Fees	None
Exchange Fees	None

Restated Annual Fund Operating Expenses
Net of Expense Reimbursement
(As a percentage of average net assets)

Management fee	0.72%
12b-1 fees	None
Other Expenses	0.09%
Total operating expenses after expense reimbursement	0.81%

Contrast that with an example on the next page of a typical Fee Table from a load fund, which you would obviously be better off avoiding. The Merrill Lynch Emerging Tigers Fund has both A shares (front-end load), B shares (back end load), C shares (level load), and D shares (frankly, I'm not sure what they are).

Pay particular attention to the **Per Share Income and Capital Changes** table, which tracks the value of a share throughout the year. This table may also be labeled "Financial Highlights" or "Selected Per Share Data and Ratios. It is placed toward the front of the document because of its importance. The data must be shown for the latest 10 years or for the life of the fund. Using this table, you can review the fund's historical results in per-share amounts, which offer you the most revealing perspective on the fund's investment results. Skip to the bottom of this table where, ironically, the most important information is. That's where you will find two important ratios: expenses to average net assets—the expense ratio—and the portfolio turnover rate. These important data are illustrated in Table 84 for the Warburg Pincus Int'l Equity Fund.

Ratio of expenses to average net assets, popularly known as the **expense ratio,** is of critical importance. Also found in the fee table (where it may be a projection), this information is presented as a tabulation of all the fund's on-going expenses divided by the fund's total assets. These expenses include the adviser's fee, which generally

Merrill Lynch Emerging Tigers Fund
Fee Table

	Class A(a)	Class B(b)	Class C	Class D
Shareholder Transaction Expenses:				
Maximum Sales Charge Imposed on Purchases (as a percentage of offering price)	5.25%(c)	None	None	5.25%(c)
Sales Charge Imposed on Dividend Reinvestments	None	None	None	None
Deferred Sales Charge (as a percentage of original purchase price or redemption proceeds, whichever is lower)	None(d)	4.0% during the first year decreasing 1.0% annually thereafter to 0.0% after the fourth year(e)	1.0% for one year(f)	None(d)
Exchange Fee	None	None	None	None
Annual Fund Operating Expenses (as a percentage of average net assets)(e):				
Investment Advisory Fees(g)	1.00%	1.00%	1.00%	1.00%
Rule 12b-1 Fees(h):				
Account Maintenance Fees	None	0.25%	0.25%	0.25%
Distribution Fees	None	0.75%	0.75%	None
		(Class B shares convert to Class D shares automatically after approximately eight years and cease being subject to distribution fees)		
Other Expenses:				
Custodial Fees	.16%	.16%	.16%	.16%
Shareholder Servicing Costs(i)	.08%	.20%	.21%	.14%
Other	.12%	.31%	.31%	.33%
Total Other Expenses	.36%	.67%	.68%	.63%
Total Fund Operating Expenses	1.36%	2.67%	2.68%	1.88%

covers the cost of providing investment advice—office space, book-keeping, statistical and clerical expenses, executive salaries and promotional expenses incurred in connection with the distribution of fund shares. The 12b-1 distribution fee, and expenses paid directly by the fund—printing and mailing costs for shareholder material and prospectuses, legal and auditing fees, expenses of independent directors (sometimes reimbursed by the adviser) and custodian and transfer agent fees. (One huge bill not included in the expense ratio is the brokerage charge for buying and selling securities. It's considered a capital expenditure. The cost is simply deducted from the value of the holdings, as would be the case if you were buying a stock or bond as an individual investor.)

The total is what's important. Some funds with modest 12b-1 fees have lower overall expense ratios than other funds that don't levy these marketing fees. That's why you shouldn't automatically exclude funds with 12b-1 fees. The goal is to find funds with low expenses. In Chapter 14 I discussed ways you can properly evaluate the expense ratio.

Portfolio turnover rate. Turnover is the annual rate at which the fund buys and sells its holdings. For example, a turnover factor of 100% would be the equivalent of all the fund's securities being sold and replaced during the year. A 200% turnover indicates that stocks were held on average only six months. The rate is calculated by dividing the lesser of purchases or sales of portfolio securities for the year by the monthly average value of the portfolio. Government securities, both short and long-term, and all other securities including options that mature or expire in one year or less, are excluded from the calculation.

Table 84

Warburg Pincus International Equity Fund

Financial Highlights

(For a Common Share of the Fund Outstanding Through Each Period)

	For the Year Ended October 31,				
	1997	1996	1995	1994	1993
Net Asset Value, Beginning of Period	$20.69	$19.30	$20.51	$17.00	$12.22
Income from Investment Operations:					
Net Investment Income (Loss)	0.04	0.22	0.12	0.09	0.09
Net Gain (Loss) from Securities and Foreign Currency Related Items (both realized and unrealized)	0.88	1.73	(0.67)	3.51	4.84
Total from Investment Operations	0.92	1.95	(0.55)	3.60	4.93
Less Distributions:					
Dividends from Net Investment Income	(0.11)	(0.56)	(0.13)	(0.04)	(0.02)
Distributions in Excess of Net Investment Income	0.00	0.00	0.00	(0.01)	0.00
Distributions from Realized Gains	(0.74)	0.00	(0.53)	(0.04)	(0.13)
Total Distributions	(0.85)	(0.56)	(0.66)	(0.09)	(0.15)
Net Asset Value, End of Period	$20.76	$20.69	$19.30	$20.51	$17.00
Total Return	4.54%	10.35%	(2.55%)	21.22%	40.68%
Ratios/Supplemental Data:					
Net Assets, End of Period (000s)	$2,312,042	$2,885,453	$2,068,207	$1,533,872	$378,661
Ratios to average daily net assets:					
Operating expenses	1.33%@	1.38%@	1.39%	1.44%	1.48%
Net investment income	.56%	.62%	.69%	.19%	.38%
Portfolio Turnover Rate	61.80%	32.49%	39.24%	17.02%	22.60%
Average Commission Rate #	$0.0169	$0.0170	—	—	—

Studies of portfolio turnover generally have not found any particular correlation between turnover and performance. Some funds with a very high turnover rate do very well, some badly. And vice-versa: as many funds with low turnover perform badly as do well.

Interestingly, though, a 1994 study by Value Line evaluated the performance of 531 funds during a five-year period, looking closely at their volatility. That analysis found that among the most volatile funds, high turnover is a predictor of superior performance. But among the least volatile funds, the reverse is true: high turnover correlates with poor performance.

One thing is certain. In a bull market, high turnover will increase realized profits, and they will generally be short-term gains rather than long-term. That means that investors must pay taxes on their profits at ordinary-income rates, rather than receiving the more favorable capital gains rate. A fund's policy towards portfolio turnover may be covered in the objective or policies section. New funds may estimate what their rate will be.

If you do nothing else, check the above sections in the prospectus. That will help you make informed judgements about your fund.

Of lesser importance

A wealth of additional information is contained in the prospectus. It can be helpful to you, but is not as momentous as the above.

Note the **Ratio of net income to average net assets** which shows the same data as a percentage. When this figure is positive, the dividend and interest is covering the fund's expenses. When the figure is negative, the fund will have to dip into capital to meet expenses.

The section labeled Distributions is the amount paid out to shareholders in dividends and realized capital gains. The sum of these two sections when added to the beginning NAV (top line) equals the ending NAV. Next, the total return for the period is shown separately.

The section called **Management of the fund** describes the fund's adviser (i.e., the management company), and provides a summary of its experience and compensation. This section has become more important because the SEC now requires that the name of the portfolio manager and his or her experience be detailed.

Unfortunately, the SEC exempted money funds and those funds run by committee from this requirement. Unhappily, the number of funds run by committee has increased dramatically since this requirement was adopted—or so the funds would have us believe. If there isn't a section called "Management," keep looking. Fidelity, for example, places this information in a section titled "Charter."

The prospectus will also note instances in which the adviser is controlled by a parent company and whether it employs a sub-adviser. It's not uncommon for a management company to hire another firm to run the portfolio. Dreyfus, for instance, employs Fayez Sarofim to manage the Dreyfus Appreciation Fund. Dreyfus benefits from Sarofim's expertise while retaining the administrative and marketing functions. This is especially true with international funds. Many mutual fund families that lack expertise overseas employ a sub-advisor to manage their international funds.

This section usually includes details of the manager's fee. How big is it? Is it scaled down as the fund increases in size? Are there any incentive features? What portion of the fund's expenses are paid by the adviser out of the management fee? What portion is borne directly by the fund? The management fee used to be 0.5% of total net assets per year, and for many large funds it still is. Small funds can't exist at that level, however, and its very common to see managers' fees in the 0.75% to 1.00% range, particularly for aggressive growth funds. One fund charges 2% of the first $2 million in assets. Many funds with fees based on asset size now list an effective management fee based on the fund's actual size in the prospectus.

Over 80 funds have incentive, or performance, fees. They include 31 Fidelity Funds and 18 Vanguard Funds.

Using the Vanguard International Value Portfolio as an illustration, let me explain how this works. This fund's management fee is 0.475% of the first $50 million of assets, declining to 0.11% of assets over $1 billion. This basic fee may then be increased or decreased by as much as 50% by applying a performance fee adjustment based on the fund's performance relative to the MSCI-EAFE Index measured over a 36-month period.

The vast majority of fund managers don't install incentive fees because they are not a win-win situation. If the fund underperforms the benchmark, the fee must be cut. For example, the management fee for Fidelity Magellan's fiscal year 1997 was .45% compared to .75% in the 1995 fiscal year. In this great bull market, incentive fees haven't been needed as a marketing tool. Thus, very few funds take the risk.

In the cases above, the incentive fee goes to the adviser, thus directly affecting fund results. However, many fund groups pay their portfolio managers incentives and bonuses for superior performance. Such payments have no direct impact on the fund's management fees.

You will also find the names of the transfer and dividend paying agent in the prospectus. Many funds have you deal directly with the transfer agent when you are buying or selling shares. Some transfer agents represent many funds. Some are inept at administering your account, and you'd like to avoid them. But if the fund you are considering investing in has an excellent track record, you may not want to skip it just because the fund's administrative side annoys you.

Since the point of the prospectus is to get you to buy, one section will tell you how to **purchase and redeem shares.** Included are minimum purchase amounts, wire or telephone privileges, sales charges, distribution fees and valuation of shares.

Sometimes funds raise their minimum investment requirement as a way to cut costs by allowing the fund to deal with fewer and larger accounts. At other times, funds will lower the minimum in order to stimulate sales. You can open an account at the Muhlenkamp Fund if you have as little as $200 in your jeans. Minimum subsequent investments are often in range of $50 to $100.

Generally, you invest in a no-load mutual fund by filling out the application form that accompanies the prospectus and attaching your check. The application requests such information as your Social Security or tax I.D. number, the name and address under which you want your shares to be registered, and whether dividends and/or capital gains should be reinvested or sent to you. The application tells where it is to be sent and to whom your check should be made payable.

The prospectus also describes any special purchase or accumulation plans, exchange services and the procedures for redeeming your shares. Always check this section before you redeem. It will save you time and aggravation.

There will be a section that tells you when and how often the fund distributes **dividends and capital gains.**

Once in a while you will find a section called **Pending legal proceedings.** If the fund is involved in any significant lawsuits, they must be disclosed here. Such disclosures won't usually affect your investment, but you should be aware of them, because occasionally the fund's shareholders have to pay some of the costs of litigation.

Note: A fund can use the same prospectus for a year before it must be updated. Therefore, the fund's latest quarterly or annual report may furnish more up-to-date financial and portfolio data than its prospectus.

Umbrella funds

Often you may find that several funds are included in one prospectus. This arrangement has become popular because it cuts down on registration and distribution expenses. Instead of printing different prospectuses for each fund and going to the trouble of registering each in all 50 states, the fund company can gain economies of scale by including a handful of funds in the same prospectus.

It's important to realize, though, that each fund contained in such an umbrella prospectus is separate and distinct. In some cases the portfolios have a common objective. The Vanguard Municipal Bond Fund, for instance, has seven portfolios, each providing tax-free income. The portfolios are distinguished primarily by the varying maturities of the bonds they hold. On the other hand Weitz Series Fund's four portfolios—Value, Hickory, Fixed-income, and Government Money Market—have nothing in common but their advisor. And the Fidelity Select Fund, with 38 widely disparate portfolios, contains a dazzling array of different investments.

The good news for investors is that these omnibus prospectuses often have drastically lower administrative expenses, and these savings can be passed on to shareholders. But since they are separate entities, switching between portfolios, just like switching between funds, is a taxable event. Capital gains or losses may be realized.

What's in a name?

For your protection, the SEC will not allow a fund to use a name or title that may be deceptive or misleading. If a fund's name implies that its distributions are exempt from federal income taxation—for example, XYZ Muni Bond Fund—then under normal conditions at least 80% of the fund's assets must be invested in securities that will produce tax-exempt income. Similarly if the name indicates a money fund, the fund had better be investing in money market instruments.

Since 1988, the SEC has made bond funds use the word "Municipal" in their titles if a significant percentage of the municipal bonds held by these funds are subject to the alternative minimum tax. Formerly, the word "Tax-Free" could be used virtually inter-changably in their titles. Now, if the fund says it's "Tax-Free," it can't present you with an AMT problem.

You will recall in Chapter 8 that I noted how two global asset allocation funds had changed their charters to permit greater flexibility in their allocations. A third global asset allocation fund, the Permanent Portfolio Fund, has not made any changes. It has a problem that the other funds didn't have—its name. The SEC took the position that the word Permanent in the name meant just that. There will be no changes in its objective, even though the fund and its share-holders want them.

Still, it always pays to look beyond the name. There was a time when several Fidelity funds didn't invest in the type of stocks one could assume from the fund's name. At one time half the stocks in the Fidelity Dividend Growth Fund paid no dividends. Contrafund didn't really follow a contrarian strategy. Primarily because of complaints from professional managers and retirement plan administrators, Fidelity now requires their funds to hew closer to their charters.

Statement of Additional Information

In addition to the prospectus, funds are also required to provide another document, even drearier than the prospectus, called the Statement of Additional Information (SAI). It provides more infor-mation of even less importance. If you're a potential investor in the fund, it must send you this Statement at no charge if you ask for it. If you don't ask for it, you won't get it. Basically, don't ask for it. (In fact, so few SAIs are requested, many fund groups don't even bother to typset them.)

The Statement of Additional Information may contain sections that virtually duplicate ones in the prospectus as well as some infor-mation considered to be too detailed to put into the prospectus. Sometimes you will find a list of investment restrictions in the SAI but not in the prospectus. These are techniques that the fund has agreed not to use. Most funds agree not to buy commodities and real estate, for example. Just as with the statements of objective and poli-cies, these restrictions cannot be changed without shareholder approval. Similarly, officers and directors, while sometimes listed in the prospectus, must be named in the SAI.

If details of the advisory service contract and the 12b-1 distribution fee are not in the prospectus, they will be listed here. Sometimes this information in the prospectus is so abbreviated that this is one instance where it pays to look further in the SAI.

In addition the SAI has information regarding how the fund allocates the brokerage commissions incurred when buying and selling stocks. If the fund is managed by a brokerage firm or affiliate of such a firm, the prospectus will explain the relationship between the fund and its parent broker, and the percent of the brokerage fees given to the broker-parent company.

Custodian, Transfer and Dividend Disbursing Agent, Counsel and Auditors are organizations who provide administrative and technical assistance. Mutual funds have custodial banks that hold the fund's securities and cash. This is an important safeguard against fraud or embezzlement by the adviser or one of its employees. The transfer agent maintains shareholder records. Sometimes one organization performs both the custodial and transfer functions, but more frequently these duties are performed by separate organizations.

Annual reports

The prospectus isn't the only literature you will receive from your fund. They're required by law to send annual and semi-annual reports. Many funds do it quarterly. These periodic reports are also important to look at. Think of it this way: the prospectus tells you what the fund is *allowed* to do. The annual reports tell you what the fund is *actually doing*.

A philosopher once remarked that a pat on the back is a great incentive to success—if delivered early enough, hard enough and low enough. So, dear dedicated investor, because you have taken the time and effort to complete this intricate journey with us, please consider this book a pat on the back.

You've gotten it early enough (because it's never too late to make money with no-load funds), you've gotten it hard enough (I've pulled no punches in stating the principles of successful no-load investing), and you will have gotten it low enough, if this *Guide* will make you get off your seat and start working on an intelligently conceived and carefully monitored no-load investment program.

Remember, the potential rewards and personal satisfactions are both great. Good luck—and good fortune.

A pat on the back

APPENDIX A

How to use stock market indexes

I've always thought that the best way to evaluate a mutual fund is to compare its performance to the average fund in its peer group. I also believe that comparing a fund's performance with stock market indexes, as the popular press generally does and as the SEC requires of the funds, is of limited value.

Funds are entirely different from indexes. Their portfolios are often composed of stocks from various exchanges. Most also contain cash, at a minimum to provide liquidity for shareholder redemptions. And many also have bonds in their portfolios.

Moreover, a fund's performance is reduced by the costs of buying and selling stocks, by management fees and by the expenses of serving shareholders. For example, an index won't reinvest dividends for you. It won't wire you money. Depending on the amount of trading a fund does and its other expenses, costs can amount to 1%-3% of a fund's assets each year.

By contrast, the stock market indexes have no expenses, no transaction costs, and for the most part include just stocks and only from one exchange. They are weighted differently than fund portfolios. The fact that funds in general over- or under-perform an index by a few points doesn't mean much, particularly if the comparison is to a universe of stocks such as the Dow Jones 30 Industrials or the S&P 500, which primarily measure large, blue chip stocks. You will find that in years when large cap stocks do well, the funds will typically lag these indexes. In years when small cap stocks do well, funds will generally outperform the well-known indexes. There is no perfect bogey. So, you should use the stock market averages only to give you a general gauge of market direction.

The money fund average provides a different, more relevant comparison. Money funds are an alternative to stock or bond investments. So, they measure the correctness of your asset allocation decisions. In some years you would have done better investing in the money funds than you would have in almost any diversified stock fund. In other years, virtually every stock fund fares better than a money fund. So if you owned a stock fund that did significantly better than a money fund, how important is a fund's performance against some arbitrary index?

Nevertheless, since mutual fund performance is constantly being compared to stock market indexes, you should understand them—the math behind them, how they differ and how and whether to use them.

The granddaddy is, of course, the **Dow Jones Industrial Average**— commonly called the Dow (though there are three other Dow averages). It is composed of 30 blue chip stocks, a roster that is altered periodically. While the Dow stocks are few in number, they include many of our largest companies. The DJIA accounts for 14.6% of the market value of all U.S. equities. While outmoded by the broader indexes, it continues to dominate the news and investors' thoughts because of its historical importance and the fact it is sponsored by Dow Jones, publishers of *The Wall Street Journal*. The Dow has been a shorthand for the stock market in the minds of most people for so long that it would be impossible to eradicate.

Benchmarks for every purpose

Perhaps you have wondered how the average of 30 stocks can be as high as it is, and how it can change more than 500 points in a single day. When the Dow was first constructed by Charles Dow in the last century, it was calculated by simply adding up the prices of the stocks then in the index and dividing by the total number of stocks. But soon there were problems. If a stock worth, say, $60 a share was split, it might be worth only $30 after the split. Some way had to be found to account for the split. Otherwise the index would show a totally artificial decline since splitting a stock doesn't decrease its value, and in fact, frequently results in gains. The solution was to change the divisor to compensate for the split. Over the years there have been numerous splits and each time the denominator has been lowered. In early 1998, the divisor for the 30 Dow stocks was not 30 but .25089! The divisor has become a multiplier. With the denominator so low, if each stock in the index moves just one dollar, the index will gain or lose 119.57 points. To get a 554 point drop—as happened in October 1997—each Dow stock would have to decline $4.63.

Another peculiarity of the index is that the Dow is price-weighted. The high-priced stocks count for more in the average than the low-priced stocks. There's no reason why this should be so; it was just the simplest way to do things in the pre-computer age.

The Dow can be used to compare conservative stock funds which emphasize the large blue chip companies in their portfolios.

The various **NYSE** and **Standard & Poor's** indexes are weighted by capitalization. In computing the index, the price of each stock is multiplied by the number of its shares outstanding. Then all shares are averaged. As a result, these indexes measure market value rather than simply price. This method eliminates the Dow's need to adjust for stock splits. In addition it has the more important result of giving greater weight to larger companies. The S&P 500 Index companies account for almost two-thirds of U.S. equity valuations including 36 large NASDAQ stocks. But that's misleading. The ten S&P 500 stocks with the biggest market value account for 19% of the index's value and movement, the biggest 50 stocks account for about half of the weighting and the bottom 100 only 2.3%. So as is the case with the Dow, a fairly small number of stocks represent the "market."

Similarly, the 2,834 stocks in the New York Stock Exchange Composite Index account for 82% of U.S. equity valuations. Here again, a few large companies have a disproportionate influence on the index.

Because a handful of large capitalization stocks dominate these indexes, they sometimes fail to represent the average stock. In 1994, more than 80% of 7,363 actively traded stocks, were down more than 10% from their 52-week highs; more than 58% of them were down more than 20%; and more than 40% were down 30% or more. Putting the broad market indexes on a comparable basis, the Dow Jones Industrial Average and the S&P 500 declined only 3.6% and 4.7% from their 1994 high points.

If you are going to use these market indexes that are skewed to favor a few large companies as benchmarks for mutual fund performance, I suggest that you take a close look at the number of stocks that are rising or falling.

The S&P and NYSE indexes provide a good yardstick for comparing a typical growth or growth-income fund buying large cap stocks. But don't be concerned if your fund lags the Index, particularly when these indexes don't reflect the average stock.

One of the best indexes for mutual fund comparisons is **NAS-DAQ,** the National Association of Securities Dealers Automated Quotation system. It is a market-value weighted average of what used to be called over-the-counter stocks.

Unlike the organized exchanges, NASDAQ has no centralized floor. Instead it is an elaborate network of market makers and broker-dealers connected by a phone and computer system. There are about 5,500 NASDAQ stocks accounting for 17.7% of U.S. equity valuations. The volume of trading on NASDAQ is enormous; in terms of shares, it's greater than that of the NYSE. In addition it leads all other U.S. markets in listings of new public companies; about 85% choose NASDAQ.

There's a perception abroad in the land that all NASDAQ companies are small, but that's not true. Such giants as Microsoft, Intel, and MCI Communications are traded on NASDAQ. The index is heavily weighted toward technology stocks. Thirteen of the 15 largest NASDAQ stocks are computer, telecommunication or biotech companies. In fact, these technology stocks make up 50% of the value of the Composite Index. Microsoft alone accounts for 9.7% of the index. NASDAQ's Composite Index is the most important one to watch, but there are a number of sub-indexes for specialized purposes.

An index coming into increasing prominence is the **Wilshire 5000 Equity Index.** This index, which is computed by Wilshire Associates of Santa Monica, CA, measures the performance of all U.S. common equity securities with readily available daily price data. The moniker is an anomalie. While Wilshire continues to call it the 5,000, actually the index now is composed of about 7,325 stocks. It is capitalization weighted, with about 81% of its capitalization on the NYSE, 1% Amex and 18% NASDAQ. Wilshire also recomputes the index with equal weighting, but you are unlikely to run across this version. In addition the company computes a sub-index called the Wilshire 4,500, which deletes the S&P 500 stocks. We think this broad measure is a good one for mutual fund comparisons.

The **Value Line Index** provides another useful comparison for mutual fund investors. It consists of 1,674 stocks—1,497 industrials, 168 utilities, and 9 rails. Every stock has the same value since equal changes are treated equally whether the companies are big or small. Few mutual fund give larger companies a greater weighting in their portfolios simply because they have more shares outstanding, so the Value Line Index is more relevant to growth funds than are the other indexes. An emerging growth fund, for example, may invest about equally in large numbers of small companies. There are actually two Value Line Indexes. The more common one uses a geometric average, the newer one, an arithmetic average. Over time, the geometric average will produce lower results.

The **Amex Market Value Index** is a volatile index that's useful as a benchmark for aggressive funds. The Index has heavy weightings in the securities of consumer goods, service, financial, high technology, and capital goods stocks. Since the volume of trading on the AMEX is slight compared to NYSE and NASDAQ, the performance of this index is less important.

You should at least be aware of several specialized indexes. The **Russell Indexes** have come to the attention of mutual fund investors because one of them, the Russell 2000, is the basis for Vanguard's Small Capitalization Stock Fund, an index fund.

There are three Russell indexes. The Russell 3000 Index consists of the 3000 largest publicly traded stocks in the US, as determined by market capitalization. This index represents about 98% of the investable US equity market. The Russell 2000 Index consists of the 2000 smallest stocks in the 3000 index. It represents approximately 10% of US equities, with an median market cap of $395 million. Finally the Russell 1000 tracks the largest 1000 stocks. Unfortunately, all three are market-value indexes. From the point of view of a fund investor, it would be better if they were unweighted.

Standard & Poor's unveiled the **S&P MidCap 400 Index** in June 1991 as a result of increasing interest in mid-size stocks. The index covers 400 companies with market capitalizations generally ranging from $56 million to $9.6 billion. The median cap is approximately $1.1 billion. The Index is capitalization weighted, which means the 50 largest companies account for one-third of the Index. Of the companies, 73% are listed on the NYSE, 25% on NASDAQ, and 2% on the AMEX. This mid-cap index combined with the S&P 500 Index will together account for 85% of the market value of all traded U.S. stocks.

The most popular benchmark for comparing international funds is the **EAFE Index.** This is the Morgan Stanley Capital International Europe, Australia, Far East Index. It's a market-capitalization-weighted index containing 1,075 companies representing approximately 60% of market capitalization of 20 developed countries. Two-thirds of the assets are in Europe, one-third in the Far East. Three years ago, Japan accounted for 42% of the Index. With its market going nowhere in recent years, its weighting has declined to 28.7%. But Japan is still the largest component of the EAFE Index. Next largest representation is the United Kingdom with 21%. This is followed by Germany, 9.2%; Switzerland, 7.3%; Netherlands, 5.6%; and Italy, 3.7%. Most international funds allocate their investments by referencing this index. When an international fund manager says he is underweighting or overweighting a country, he means compared to the EAFE Index.

Morgan Stanley also has an Emerging Markets Index covering markets in 26 developing countries. The largest weighting is in Brazil, 14.8%; next South Africa, 11.6%; and third Mexico, 11.1%. Vanguard's Emerging Market Index Fund is a sub-set of the MSCI Index, consisting of 14 countries.

APPENDIX B

THE NO-LOAD FUND INVESTOR

Glossary of mutual fund terms

Account: Used in such terms as mutual fund account or open account. It denotes an investor's business arrangement or record of his investments, together with reinvestments or distributions and/or withdrawals and charges; an open account is open to further investment.

Acquisition Cost: The load, or sales commission, charged.

Adjustable Rate Mortgage Fund: A fund that invests in adjustable rate mortgage (ARM) securities issued guaranteed by the U.S. government or its agencies. The funds are designed for conservative, income-oriented investors who are willing to accept minimal fluctuations in the funds' share prices. ARMs generally have lower yields which vary frequently since their dividends rates are reset every six to 12 months. (See ARMS.)

Adjustable Rate Preferred: A bond or preferred stock whose dividends are adjusted periodically to maintain a yield within some designated range of a benchmark Treasury security. The dividend is also fixed between floor and ceiling yields, and the stock can be redeemed before maturity.

Adviser: The organization employed by a mutual fund to give professional advice on its investments and management of its assets.

Aggressive Growth Fund: A mutual fund which seeks maximum capital appreciation through the use of investment techniques involving greater than ordinary risk, including such techniques as borrowing money in order to provide leverage, short selling, hedging, options and warrants.

All-Weather Fund: A fund that long-term investors can hold safely throughout a complete market cycle. Market timing, low volatility, and asset allocation funds may be all-weather.

Alpha: A statistical measure representing the difference between the actual and expected performance of a fund given its characteristic volatility. A positive alpha is often considered a measure of management's ability.

Alternative Minimum Tax (AMT): A substitute computation of tax, which ensures that those taxpayers with substantial deductions and credits, pay at least some income tax.

American Stock Exchange (AMEX): The second largest securities exchange in the U.S., located in New York City.

Appreciation: Increase in the value of an asset such as a stock, bond, or real estate.

Arbitrage: The purchase of an asset in one market accompanied by a simultaneous sale of the same (or a similar) asset in a different market to take advantage of the difference in price. For example, buying gold in New York and selling at a higher price in London.

ARMS: Adjustable rate mortgages. The index rate on the loan is periodically reset relative to a base rate. Most follow either a short Treasury index or COFI, which is the 11th District Cost of Funds Index, as determined by the 11th District Federal Home Loan Bank (predominately California). Also see Adjustable-rate mortgage funds.

Asked or Offering Price: The price at which a mutual fund's shares can be purchased. The asked or offering price means the current net asset value per share plus sales charge, if any.

Asset Allocation Fund: A broadly diversified fund that varies its holdings between U.S. stocks, bonds and money market instruments depending on market conditions in order to obtain satisfactory performances in both up and down markets. These funds are sometimes known as Flexibly diversified funds. Asset allocation funds that also invest internationally and in gold are defined as Global Asset Allocation Funds.

Asset Class: A group of securities that share a common systematic risk element. U.S. stocks, foreign stocks, bonds, etc. are all considered asset classes.

Asset-based sales charge: A sales charge deducted from the net assets of a mutual fund under the terms of a 12b-1 plan.

Asset Value: Either total or per share. Total net assets of a fund are made up of market value of holdings plus any other resources such as cash, minus liabilities. Per share is determined by dividing the total by the number of shares outstanding.

Automatic Reinvestment: The option available to mutual fund shareholders whereby fund income dividends and capital gains distributions are automatically put back into the fund to buy new shares and thereby build up holdings.

Back-end Load: A fee paid when withdrawing money from a fund. In the case of a 12b-1 fund, it is designed to recoup sales expenses not collected by the periodic 12b-1 fee, due to premature withdrawal.

Back-testing: The process of testing a trading strategy on historical data.

Balanced Fund: A mutual fund that has an investment policy of always balancing its portfolio, generally by including relatively fixed portions of bonds, preferred stocks and common stocks.

Bankers' Acceptances: Short-term credit arrangements designed to enable businesses to obtain funds to finance commercial transactions. Generally, an acceptance is a time draft drawn on a bank by an exporter or an importer to obtain a stated amount of funds to pay for specific merchandise. The draft is then "accepted" by a bank that, in effect, unconditionally guarantees to pay the face value of the instrument on its maturity date.

Basis Point: A unit used to measure changes in interest rates and bond yields. One basis point equals .01% (or 1/100 of 1%).

Bear Market: A market climate in which stock prices are generally falling.

Beta: A coefficient that measures a fund's volatility relative to the total market, usually as represented by the S&P 500. It is the percentage performance of a fund which has historically accompanied a 1.00% move up or down in the S&P 500. High beta funds have price fluctuations greater than the broad market; low beta funds fluctuate less than the market as a whole. Funds with high betas are consequently riskier than the market, those with low betas are less risky.

Bid or Redemption Price: The price at which a mutual fund's shares are redeemed (bought back) by the fund. The bid or redemption price usually means the current net asset value per share.

Big Board: Another name for the New York Stock Exchange.

Blue Chip: The common stock of well-established companies with a stable record of earnings and dividends.

Blue Sky Laws: Rules and regulations of the various states governing the securities business, including mutual funds, broker/dealers and salesmen.

Bond Fund: A mutual fund whose portfolio consists primarily of fixed-income securities. The emphasis of such funds is normally on income rather than growth.

Bookshares: A share-recording system that gives the fund shareowner a record of his holdings. Used in lieu of share certificates.

Broker: A person who makes securities transactions for others for a commission.

Broker-Dealer (or Dealer): A firm which retails mutual fund shares and other securities to the public.

Bull Market: A market climate in which stock prices are generally rising.

Call Option: The right to buy 100 shares of a particular stock or stock index at a predetermined price before a preset deadline, in exchange for a premium. Options permit a profit from a smaller investment than it would take to buy the underlying stock.

Capital Gain or Loss: Profit or loss resulting from the sale of property or securities. Long-term gains or losses result from the sale of assets held one year or eighteen months or more; short-term - less than one year.

Capital Gains Distributions: Payments to mutual fund shareholders of gains realized on sales within the fund's portfolio securities. These amounts are paid at least once a year if realized.

Capital Growth: The increase in the market value of securities held, which is the prime short or long term objective of many funds. A gain is called unrealized until a security is actually sold.

Cash Equivalent: Receivables, short-term bonds and notes.

Cash Position: Cash plus cash equivalents minus current liabilities.

Certificate: Printed evidence of ownership of securities including mutual fund shares.

Certificates of Deposit: Negotiable certificates of indebtedness issue by a commercial bank to repay funds deposited with it for a definite period of time (usually from 14 days to one year) at a stated or variable interest rate. Money funds generally buy jumbo CDs ($100,000 or more) that are not FDIC insured. They are backed only by the creditworthiness of the bank.

Closed-end Investment Company: Unlike mutual funds (known as open-end funds), closed-end companies issue only a limited number of shares and do not redeem them (buy them back). Instead, closed-end shares are traded in the securities markets, with supply and demand determining the price. Also called *publicly traded* funds.

CMO: A security where a group of mortgage pass-through securities have been put together, and the cash flows are paid out in a specific order or preference to different buyers in order to give structure to the uncertain cash flows of mortgage pass-through securities.

Commercial Paper: Unsecured short-term notes issued in bearer form by large well known corporation and finance companies and certain governmental bodies. Maturities on commercial paper range from a few days to nine months. Regular money funds usually hold large amounts of commercial paper.

Commission: A fee paid to a broker or mutual fund salesmen for the buying or selling of securities.

Common Stock: A security representing ownership in a corporation's assets.

Common Stock Fund: A mutual fund whose portfolio consists primarily of common stocks. The emphasis of such funds is usually on growth.

Compounding: The process that occurs through the reinvestment of interest, dividends, or profits. Growth thus occurs at the same rate that the investment itself earns, allowing the reinvested money to multiply, rather than simply adding to the investment.

Conduit: The nature of a fund, which permits it to channel investment dividend income or capital gains to fund shareholders for tax liability, rather than being taxed within the fund.

Contingent Deferred Sales Charge: A sales fee payable when the shareholder redeems shares, rather than when shares are purchased, and which is frequently reduced each year that the shares are held. For example, if shares are redeemed less than one year after purchase, a fee of 5% of N.A.V. might be charged; if redeemed in more than one but less than two years, 4%, etc. Also called a contingent deferred sales load.

Contractual Plan: A program for the accumulation of mutual fund shares in which the investor agrees to invest a fixed amount on a regular basis for a specified number of years. A substantial portion of the sales charge applicable to the total investment is usually deducted from early payments.

Contrarian: An investor who does the opposite of what most investors are doing at a particular time. A contrarian fund generally invests in out-of-favor securities, whose price/earnings ratio is lower than the rest of the market or industry.

Convertible Securities: A preferred stock or bond providing the right for the owner to exchange it for another security, such as common stock, under specified or unspecified conditions of time, price and/or number of shares.

Corporate Obligations: Bonds and notes issued by corporations and other business organizations, including business trusts, in order to finance their long-term credit needs.

CUSIP: The Committee on Uniform Securities Identification Procedures—it assigns identifying numbers and codes to all securities. These CUSIP numbers are used when recording all buy and sell orders. Each fund has a CUSIP number.

Custodian: The organization (usually a bank) that holds in custody and safekeeping the securities and other assets of a mutual fund.

Cycle: A pattern of swings and reversals in a trend that recurs on a regular time schedule.

Daily Dividend Fund: A fund that declares its income dividends daily. The fund usually reinvests or distributes them daily or monthly.

Date of Record: That date on which declared distributions are set aside (held separate, for payment to shareholders at a later date) and deducted from total net assets.

Deflation: A fall in the general price level.

Derivatives: Securities whose returns are linked to, or derived from, some underlying stock, bond, commodity, or other asset. There are two basic types: options and forward type derivatives, which include forwards, futures and swaps. They may be listed on exchanges or negotiated privately between two parties, usually institutions.

Direct Marketed Fund: A no-load or low-load fund whose shares can be bought directly, without going through a dealer, thus avoiding all or most of the sales commission. Investors purchase fund shares through the mail or by telephone in response to advertising or publicity. Also called *direct purchase fund.*

Discount: The percentage below asset value at which an investment company sells in the open market.

Disinflation: A slowdown in the rate of inflation without turning into deflation.

Distributions: The payments of dividends or realized capital gains that a fund determines to pass along to shareholders, who can take them in cash or in additional shares, sometimes in fractions thereof.

Distributor: An organization that purchases mutual fund shares directly from the issuer for resale to other parties.

Diversification: The mutual fund policy of spreading its investments among a number of different securities to reduce the risks inherent in investing.

Diversified Investment Company: A fund complying with statutory requirements under the Federal Investment Company Act of 1940, which specifies that such a fund have at least 75% of its assets represented by cash, government securities, securities of other investment companies, and other securities limited in respect to any one issuer in the amount of not greater than 5% of a fund's assets and not more than 10% of the voting securities of a single issuer.

Dividend: As distinct from a capital gain distribution, represents dividends from investment income.

Dollar-Cost Averaging: Investing equal amounts of money at regular intervals regardless of whether the stock market is moving upward or downward. This reduces average share costs to the investor who acquired more shares in periods of lower securities prices and fewer shares in periods of higher prices.

Dual-Purpose Fund: It differs from other closed-end funds in that leverage is provided by issuing two separate classes of shares. One class, the *income* shares, receives all income from the entire portfolio but none of the capital gain. The other, *capital* shares, receives all the capital gain but none of the income. As a closed-end fund, shares may be purchased or sold only on the open market, subject to a premium or discount from asset value. At present, there are no dual-purpose funds in existence.

EAFE Index: An abbreviation for the Morgan Stanley Capital International Europe, Australia, Far East Index. It's a market-capitalization-weighted index representing approximately 60% of market capitalizations of 20 countries. Japanese stocks have the heaviest weighting in the index. Most international funds allocate their investments by referencing this index. When an international fund manager says he is underweighting or overweighting a country, he means compared to the EAFE Index.

Economics: The study of how people use limited resources—personal, commercial, national or international—to achieve maximum well-being.

Efficient Market: Theory that market prices reflect the knowledge and expectations of all investors. Believers of the theory hold that any new development is quickly reflected in a company's stock price, making it impossible for an investor to beat the market over the long run.

Elliott Wave Theory: A pattern recognition technique published by Ralph N. Elliott in 1939, which holds that the stock market follows a rhythm or pattern of five waves up with three waves down in a bull market, and five waves down with three waves up in a bear market to form a complete cycle of eight waves.

Equity: In investments, an ownership interest by shareholders of a corporation. Stock is equity, as opposed to bonds, which are debt.

Equity Fund: A common stock mutual fund.

Eurodollar CDs: Certificates of deposit issued by a foreign branch (usually London) of a domestic bank, and as such, the credit is deemed to be that of the domestic bank.

Exchange Fund: An investment company that allows persons holding individual securities to exchange these securities for fund shares without paying a capital gains tax.

Exchange Privilege: Enables a mutual fund shareholder to transfer his investment from one fund to another within the same fund group if his needs or objectives change. The term is sometimes used by funds, which do not offer telephone switch, to indicate an exchange by mail.

Ex-Dividend: For mutual funds (but not for securities listed on a stock exchange), that date on which declared distributions are deducted from total net assets. On the day a fund goes ex-dividend, its closing net asset value per share is computed minus the distribution.

Expense Ratio: Annual expenses (not including interest and income taxes paid) divided by average net assets.

Family of funds: A group of mutual funds under the same management. Fund families frequently provide convenient telephone switching between funds.

FANNIE MAE: Nickname for the Federal National Mortgage Association.

Fed: Nickname for the Federal Reserve System.

Fedwire: High speed computerized communications network connecting the Federal Reserve banks, their branches and other governmental agencies. It enables banks to transfer funds for immediate available credit.

Fiduciary: A person vested with legal power to be used for benefit of another person.

Fixed Income Fund: A mutual fund investing all or a major portion of its assets (normally 75% or more) in fixed income securities.

Fixed Income Security: A debt security such as a bond and a preferred stock with a stated return in percentage or dollars.

Flexibly Diversified: In contrast to a balanced fund whose portfolio at all times must be diversified among a generally stated minimum or maximum percentage of bonds/preferred/common stocks—flexible diversification means that management, at its discretion, may allot the percentage for each type of security.

Float: The period between the writing of a check and the debiting of an account for that amount. Money fund shareholders can earn interest on the float when they write checks on their accounts.

FREDDIE MAC: Nickname for the Federal Home Loan Mortgage Corporation, and also the mortgage-backed securities it issues.

Front-end Load: Sales charge applied to an investment at the time of initial purchase.

Fully-Managed Fund: A term generally used when a fund's prospectus permits assets to be converted to debt securities or all cash at management's discretion, for timing purchases and sales.

Fundamental Analysis: Analysis of corporate balance sheets, income statements, management, sales, products and markets in order to forecast future stock price movements.

Futures Contracts: Standard forward agreements traded on exchanges. They are obligations to buy or deliver a quantity of the underlying commodity or financial instrument at the agreed-upon price by a certain date. Most contracts are simply nullified by an opposite trade before they come due.

General Obligation Securities: The obligations of an issuer with taxing power that are payable from the issuer's general, unrestricted revenues. These securities are backed by the full faith, credit and taxing power of the issuer for the payment of principal and interest; they are not limited to repayment from any particular fund or revenue source.

Global Asset Allocation Fund: A broadly diversified fund that typically invests across a number of markets to provide a hedge against declines in the U.S. stock market. Their holdings may include U.S. stocks; international stocks; U.S. bonds, often governments; international bonds; gold or gold mining shares; cash equivalents, and sometimes real estate securities. They seek satisfactory performances in almost all foreseeable economic climates - inflation, deflation, stability. Also see Asset Allocation Fund.

Global Fund: A fund that invests in the securities of the U.S. as well as those of foreign countries.

GNMA Fund: A fund investing in GNMA securities issued by the Government National Mortgage Association, a corporation that helps finance mortgages.

Growth Fund: A mutual fund whose primary investment objective is long-term growth of capital. It invests principally in common stocks with growth potential.

Growth-Income Fund: A mutual fund whose aim is to provide for a degree of both income and long-term growth.

Hedge: To offset. To safeguard oneself from loss on a risk by making compensatory arrangements on the other side. For example, to hedge one's long positions with short sales, so that if the market declines the loss on long positions will be offset by profit on the short positions.

Hedge Fund: A flexible investment fund for rich people and institutions. The minimum investment is typically $1 million, and since they are restricted to less than 100 investors, they do not come under the same regulations as mutual funds. Hedge funds can use aggressive strategies that are unavailable to mutual funds. Historically, they were simply funds that had a policy of hedging long positions with short positions. In the 1960s the term was used to describe any aggressive fund.

Illiquid: According to SEC regulations, open-end investment companies (mutual funds) can invest no more than 15 percent of their capital in illiquid investments. This rule is aimed at assuring that the funds will be able to redeem their shares on demand. Real estate restricted issues, letter stock-securities requiring registration before they can be sold, are considered illiquid. (See Liquidity.)

Incentive Compensation: The fee paid to a fund manager based upon performance in relation to a market index such as the Dow Jones Industrial Average.

Income Dividends: Payments to mutual fund shareholders of dividends, interest and short-term capital gains earned on the fund's portfolio securities after deduction of operating expenses.

Income Fund: A mutual fund whose primary investment objective is current income rather than growth of capital. It usually invests in stocks and bonds that normally pay higher dividends and interest.

Incubator Fund: A fund that is run on a small scale in-house for a period of time, and then is publicly offered to investors if its private record has been good.

Index Fund: A mutual fund whose investment objective is to match the composite investment performance of a large group of publicly-traded common stocks represented in a stock market index.

Individual Retirement Account (IRA): A retirement program for working individuals. An individual may contribute and deduct from his or her income tax an amount up to $2,000 per year. An Individual Retirement Account may be funded with mutual fund shares.

Institutional Investor: A bank, insurance company, mutual or pension fund that invests other people's money on their behalf. It typically trades securities in larger volume than individuals.

Interval fund: A hybrid between an open-end and closed-end fund that only accepts redemptions on a specific time schedule, say once a month or quarter.

Industry Group Index: The grouping of stocks comprising a specific industry group such as the Oil and Gas and Computer Technology Indexes listed on the AMEX.

Investment Advisor: See Advisor.

Investment Company: A corporation, trust or partnership in which investors pool their money to obtain professional management and diversification of their investments. Mutual funds are the most popular type of investment company.

Investment Company Act of 1940: The federal law governing the registration and regulation of funds.

Investment Objective: The goal—e.g., long-term capital growth, current income, etc.—which an investor or a mutual fund pursues.

Junk Bonds: Low-quality, high-risk bonds that typically offer above average yields.

Keogh Plan: A retirement program for self-employed individuals and their employees based on tax-saving provisions. A Keogh plan may be funded with mutual fund shares. Named after former New York Congressman, Eugene J. Keogh. (Also known as H.R. 10 Plans.)

Legal List: A list published by a state government authority, enumerating or setting standards for securities proper for money held in trust.

Letter Stock: A form of restricted security so-called because it is generally accompanied by a letter stating that the stock has been purchased only for investment and will not be offered to the public until registered. See Restricted Security.

Leverage: The use of borrowed money, primarily to increase volatility.

Liquidity: The ease of converting an asset to cash and/or the minimal effect on price that such liquidation incurs. (See Illiquid.)

Liquid Asset Fund: A money market fund.

Load: The sales charge or commission for buying into a mutual fund.

Load Fund: A fund whose shares are sold by a broker or salesmen with a sales charge. Generally refers to funds with a sales charge greater than 3% as load funds (see Low-load mutual funds).

Long Position: That part of a fund's portfolio which represents securities purchased for price appreciation in a rising market.

Long-term Funds: An industry designation for all funds other than short-term funds (money market and short-term municipal bond). The two broad categories of long-term funds are equity and bond and income funds.

Low-load Mutual Fund: A fund with a front-end load of approximately 3% or less.

Management Company: The entity which manages a fund, as distinct from the fund itself. Officials of both, and even of a company distributing shares or acting as a broker may be the same persons.

Management Fee: The amount paid by a mutual fund to the investment adviser for its services. Industry-wide, fees generally range from 0.5%-1.0% a year of a fund's assets.

Market Timer: An investor who attempts to time the market so that shares are sold before they decrease in value and bought when they are about to increase in value. Sometimes the strategy calls for frequent buy and sell decisions.

Master/feeder fund: A fund structure that achieves operating efficiencies by consolidating portfolio management in a "master" fund while maintaining separate "feeder" funds with different distribution and servicing structures. For example, one feeder fund may be no-load, a second institutional, with the assets commingled in a master fund.

Money managers: Professionals employed by mutual fund companies to invest the pool of money in accordance with the fund's investment objectives. Also called portfolio managers.

Money Market Fund: Also called a liquid asset or cash fund, it is a mutual fund whose primary objective is to make higher interest securities available to the average investor who wants safety of principle, liquidity, and current income. This is accomplished through the purchase of short-term money market instruments such as U.S. Government securities, bank securities, bank certificates of deposit and commercial paper.

Money Market Instruments: Include the following types of short term investments: U.S. Government securities, certificates of deposit, time deposits, bankers acceptances, commercial paper and other corporate obligations; also included within such term are short-term repurchase agreements backed by any of the foregoing instruments.

Mortgage-backed Securities: *Passthrough* securities created from pools of mortgages that are packaged together and sold as bonds. The monthly payments of interest and principal on the underlying mortgage debt are passed through to investors.

Moving Average: A mathematical transform which is the sum of the current value plus (n-1) previous values divided by n. The result smooths fluctuations in the raw data.

Municipal Bond Fund: A mutual fund which invests in a broad range of tax-exempt bonds issued by states, cities and other local governments. The interest obtained from these bonds is passed through to shareowners free of federal tax. The fund's primary objective is current tax-free income.

Municipal Securities: Include a wide variety of debt obligations issued for public purposes by or on behalf of the States, territories and possessions of the United States, their political subdivisions, the District of Columbia, and the duly constituted authorities, agencies, public corporations and other instrumentalities of these juris-dictions. Municipal Securities may be used for numerous public purposes, including construction of public facilities, such as airports, bridges, highways, housing, hospi-tals, mass transportation, schools, streets, water and sewer works, and gas and elec-tric utilities. Municipal Securities may also be used to obtain funds to lend to other public institutions and to certain private borrowers. Municipal Securities are gener-ally classified as either the general obligation, revenue, or industrial development type.

Mutual Fund: An investment company that pools investors' money and is managed by a professional advisor. It ordinarily stands ready to buy back (redeem) its shares at their current net asset value; the value of the shares depends on the market value of the fund's portfolio securities at the time. Most mutual funds continuously offer new shares to investors.

NASDAQ: An automated information network which provides brokers and dealers with price quotations on securities traded over-the-counter. NASDAQ is an acronym for National Association of Securities Dealers Automated Quotations.

National Association of Securities Dealers, Inc. (NASD): The trade association charged by federal law with policing the SEC regulations applying to mutual funds and over-the-counter securities, but not those traded on stock exchanges.

Nest Egg: Assets put aside to provide for a secure standard of living after one's retirement.

Net Assets: A fund's total assets less current liabilities such as taxes and other oper-ating expenses.

Net Asset Value Per Share: A fund's total assets—securities, cash and any accrued earnings—after deduction of liabilities, divided by the number of shares outstanding. It is synonymous with the bid price, and in the case of no-loads also the offering or mar-ket price.

Net Investment Income per Share: Dividends and interest earned during an accounting period (such as a year) on a fund's portfolio, less operating expenses, divid-ed by number of shares outstanding.

Net Realized Capital Gains per Share: The amount of capital gain realized on sale of a fund's portfolio holdings during an accounting period (such as a year), less losses realized on such transactions, divided by number of shares outstanding.

No-Load Fund: A mutual fund selling its shares at net asset value, without the addi-tion of front-end or back-end sales charges. The fund may have a redemption fee or a 12b-1 fee of no more than .25%.

No-Load Fund, "pure": A mutual fund selling its shares at net asset value without the addition of low sales charges, long-lived redemption or 12b-1 fees.

Non-Diversified Investment Company: A fund whose portfolio does not meet the requirements of the Investment Company Act of 1940 to qualify as a diversified invest-ment company. For example, a fund which (as to 50% of its assets) may invest up to 25% in the securities of one company.

Off-the-page Advertising: A way to permit no-loads to sell shares directly from a print advertisement without first sending a prospectus.

Offering Price: Same as asked price, which is net asset value per share plus any applicable sales commission.

Open-end Investment Company: The more formal name for a mutual fund, indicating that it stands ready to redeem its shares (buy them back) on demand.

Options: Give purchasers the right, but not the obligation, to buy or sell a fixed amount of a given asset at a specific price within a certain time period. Buyers pay a premium to acquire them. While the buyer can never lose more than the premium paid, the seller's potential losses are unlimited.

Option Income Fund: The investment objective of these funds is to seek a high current return by investing primarily in dividend-paying common stocks on which call options are traded on national securities exchanges. Current return generally consists of dividends, premiums from expired call options, net short-term gains from sales of portfolio securities on exercises of options or otherwise, and any profits from closing purchase transactions.

Over-the-Counter Market: A trading network composed of dealers nation-wide who trade issues off the regular stock exchanges. Now generally called NASDAQ.

Passively Managed Fund: Similar to an index fund, it invests long-term in a universe of stocks that do not necessarily correspond to a recognized index.

Payment Date: The day on which a distribution is mailed to shareholders. Usually is later than the declaration date, which is the day the distribution is announced by the board of directors; and also usually follows the date of record, which is the date the distribution goes ex-dividend. Only shareholders as of the date of record are entitled to the payment.

Performance: The percentage change in a fund's per share value over a specified period of time. As used in the mutual fund industry, it generally includes the value of the income and capital gains dividends distributed during the specified period.

Portfolio: The group name for securities owned by a fund.

Portfolio Managers: See *Money Managers.*

Portfolio Turnover: Generally given in percentage of total assets in a year; 80% of the dollar value of a portfolio's holdings, for example, were changed in a year. See Turnover Ratio.

Preferred Stock: An equity security generally carrying a fixed return in percentage or dollars, which must be paid before common stock can share in earnings or assets.

Premium: The percentage above asset value at which an investment company sells in the open market. Applies generally only to closed-end funds whose shares must be purchased or sold only through a broker and not through the fund.

Prepayment risk: A danger to investors in mortgage-backed mutual funds, such as GNMA funds. When interest rates fall, many homeowners will refinance their mortgages. When the older mortgages are paid off early, the fund will have to reinvest the money in lower yielding securities.

Prospectus: The official booklet which describes the mutual fund and offers its shares for sale. It contains information as required by the Securities and Exchange Commission on such subjects as the fund's investment objectives and policies, services, investment restrictions, officers and directors, how shares can be bought and redeemed, its charges and its financial statements. A more detailed document known as "Part B" of the prospectus or the *Statement of Additional Information* is available upon request. A *Profile Prospectus* is a short summary document.

Proxy: Enables shareholders not attending a fund meeting to transfer their voting power to another person, usually fund management, to vote on fund business at the meeting.

Prudent Man Rule: The rule which enables a trustee to use his own judgement in making investments as long as he acts conservatively. The rule comes from an 1830 court decision.

Publicly Traded Investment Company: A closed-end fund.

Qualified Dividend Funds: are offered to corporations that want to take advantage of a provision in the tax code that allows U.S. corporations to exclude a percentage of the dividends they receive from federal taxation. Funds invest in high-yielding common and preferred stock.

Qualified For Sale: Qualified by reason of registration with the SEC or in accordance with state's regulations.

Real Estate Fund: A mutual fund owning REITs and/or real estate operating companies.

Real Estate Investment Trust: (REIT). An investment company that specializes in real estate holdings. Cannot be a mutual fund because investments are considered illiquid (see *Illiquid*).

Redemption Fee: The charge levied by a few funds when shares are redeemed.

Redemption Price: The amount per share the mutual fund shareholder receives when he cashes in his shares. The value of the shares depends on the market value of the fund's portfolio securities at the time and any redemption fees.

Red Herring: A preliminary prospectus.

Registrar: The organization, usually a bank, that maintains a registry of the share owners of a mutual fund, and the number of shares which they hold.

Regulated investment company: A fund that meets the income and diversification criteria required under law to avoid corporation income taxation.

Reinvestment Privilege: A service provided by most mutual funds for the automatic reinvestment of a shareholder's income dividends and capital gains distributions in additional shares.

Repos: A short term for repurchase agreements.

Repurchase Agreements: A sale of securities with the concurrent agreement of the seller to repurchase the securities at the same price plus an amount equal to interest at an agreed-upon rate, within a specified time, usually less than one week, but, on occasion, at a later time.

Restricted Security: One which requires registration with the SEC before it may be sold to the public. Because of this restriction, the security may not be considered a liquid asset and therefore may be priced at a substantial discount from market value.

Revenue Securities: Securities repayable only from revenues derived from a particular facility, local agency, special tax, facility user or other specific revenue source; certain revenue issues may also be backed by a reserve fund or specific collateral.

Revenue Anticipation Notes: Issued by governmental entities in anticipation of specific future non-tax revenue, such as Federal revenues available under the Federal Revenue Sharing Programs. Some such notes are general obligations of the issuer and others are payable only from specific future revenues.

Reverse Repurchase Agreements: Ordinary repurchase agreements in which a Fund is the seller of, rather than the investor in, securities, and agrees to repurchase them at an agreed-upon time and price. Use of reverse repurchase agreements may be preferable to a regular sale and later repurchase of the securities.

Risk-free rate: The rate on a short-term, default-free security, usually a Treasury bill.

Roth IRA: Named for the Delaware senator who sponsored them in the 1997 Tax Act. With a Roth IRA you pay your income tax going in; there are no taxes upon distributions from the account.

Sales Charge: An amount charged to purchase shares in a mutual fund. The charge can range from 1.0% to 8.5% of the initial investment. The charge is added to the net asset value per share in the determination of the offering price. Also, now known as a *front-end sales charge.* See *Contingent Deferred Sales Charge* and *12b-1 Plan.*

Sales Force Marketing: A method of distribution whereby funds sell their shares to the public through brokers, financial planners, and insurance agents. Some fund organizations sell shares through a captive sales force-salesmen employed by the fund organization to market only the shares of its associated funds.

Sector: Particular group of stocks, usually found in one industry.

Sector Funds: A number of separate industry portfolios grouped under the umbrella of one fund. Adviser usually provides easy switching by phone between portfolios and a related money fund.

Securities and Exchange Commission (S.E.C.): The agency of the U.S. government which administers Federal securities laws.

Senior Securities: Notes, bonds, debentures or preferred stocks, which have a prior (senior) claim ahead of common stock to assets and earnings.

Service fee: A payment by a fund to brokers, financial planners, and money managers for personal service to shareholders and/or the maintenance of shareholders accounts. Transfer agent, custodian and similar fees are not considered service fees. Also see *Trailing Commission.*

Short Sale: The sale of a security which is not owned, in the hope that the price will go down so that it can be repurchased at a profit. The person making a short sale borrows stock in order to make delivery to the buyer and must eventually purchase the stock for return to the lender.

Short-term Funds: An industry designation for money market and short-term municipal bond funds.

Single-state Funds: These funds invest in the tax-exempt securities issued by governmental organizations of a single state. Investors receive earnings free from both federal and state taxes. Single-state funds can be both short- and long-term.

Social Conscience Fund: A fund that invests in the securities of companies that do not conflict with certain social priorities. Some social conscience funds do not invest in tobacco, liquor or defense stocks.

Specialized Mutual Fund: A mutual fund specializing in the securities of certain industries, special types of securities or in regional investments. Gold funds and sector funds are examples.

Split Funding: A program which combines the purchase of mutual fund shares with the purchase of life insurance contracts or other products.

Stability: Relative volatility in a declining market. For example, a fund rated above-average for stability, is one that declines relatively the least.

Standard Deviation: The variations in performance from a long-term average. Standard deviation differs from beta in that it measures variability within a fund, while beta measures it in relation to an outside index.

Stock-index Options: Options give holders the right, but not the obligation, to buy (a call) or sell (a put) a specified amount of an underlying investment by a certain date at a preset price, known as the strike price. For stock indexes, the underlying investment may be a stock-index futures contract or the cash value of a stock index. For example, there are options on the S&P 500 futures contract and on the S&P 100 index.

Target Fund: A fixed income fund whose portfolio matures within a given year. Generally structured as a series fund with each series maturing in a different year.

Tax Anticipation Notes: Issued by governmental entities in anticipation of specific future tax revenue, such as property, income, sales, use, and business taxes. Some such notes are general obligations of the issuer, and others are payable only from specific future taxes.

Technical Analysis: Research into the supply and demand for securities based on trading volume and price studies. Technical analysis uses charts or computer programs to identify price trends in order to foretell future price movements. Unlike fundamental analysts, technical analysts do not concern themselves with the financial position of a company, such as earnings, etc.

Telephone Switching: Process of selling one mutual fund and buying another at the same time by telephone. Switching is often between stock, bond, or money market funds within the same fund family.

Total Return: A comprehensive measure of a mutual fund's performance, including price changes, realized capital gains and dividend distributions. See Performance.

Total Return Fund: A fund whose objective is to obtain the highest possible total return, i.e. a combination of ordinary income and capital gains. Funds usually invest in a combination of dividend paying stocks and bonds. Similar to a balanced fund.

Trailing Commission: Also called a trail, it is a small commission periodically paid to a broker or a financial planner to service an existing shareholder as long as money remains in the fund. A typical trail might be .25% per year. It is often paid out of the 12b-1 fee. Also see *Service Fee.*

Transfer Agent: The organization which is employed by a mutual fund to prepare and maintain records relating to the accounts of its shareholders.

Treasury Bills: Marketable U. S. Government securities with an original maturity of up to one year.

Treasury Bonds: Marketable U. S. Government securities with an original maturity of ten years or more.

Treasury Notes: Marketable U. S. Government securities with an original maturity of from two to ten years.

Turnover Ratio: The extent to which an investment company's portfolio is turned over during the course of a year. Calculated by dividing the lesser of purchases or sales of portfolio securities for the fiscal year by the monthly average of the value the portfolio securities owned by the mutual fund during the fiscal year. Excluded from the numerator and denominator all U.S. Government securities and all other securities whose maturities at the time of acquisition were one year or less.

12b-1 Plan: Allows the fund to pay a percentage of its assets to cover the distributor's sales and marketing costs. Also, see *asset-based sales charges.*

Underwriter or Principal Underwriter: The organization which acts as the distributor of a mutual fund's shares to broker-dealers and the public.

Unit Trust: An investment company with an unmanaged portfolio that is liquidated after a specified, limited life span. In the U.K. the term refers to an investment company very much like American mutual funds.

Unrealized Appreciation or Depreciation: The amount by which the market value of a security or a portfolio of securities, at a given time, is above (appreciation) or below (depreciation) the cost price.

U.S. Government Obligations: Debt securities (including bills, notes, and bonds) issued by the U.S. Treasury or issued by an agency or instrumentality of the U.S. government which is established under the authority of an act of Congress. Such agencies or instrumentalities include, but are not limited to, the Federal National Mortgage Association, the Federal Farm Credit Bank, and the Federal Home Loan Bank. Although all obligations of agencies and instrumentalities are not direct obligations of the U.S. Treasury, payment of the interest and principal on these obligations is generally backed directly or indirectly by the U.S. government. This support can range from the backing of the full faith and credit of the United States, to U.S. government guarantees, or to the backing solely of the issuing instrumentality itself. In the latter case of securities not backed by the full faith and credit of the United States, the investor must look principally to the agency issuing or guaranteeing the obligation for ultimate repayment, and may not be able to assert claim against the United States itself in the event the agency or instrumentality does not meet its commitments.

Volatility: The relative rate at which a fund share tends to move up or down in price as compared to the change in price of a stock market index or a mutual fund average. For example, a highly volatile fund is one that usually rises or declines far more than the average fund.

Voluntary Plan: A flexible accumulation plan in which there is no definite time period or total amount to be invested.

Whipsaw: Losing money on both sides of a price swing.

Withdrawal Plans: Many mutual funds offer withdrawal programs whereby shareholders receive payments from their investments at regular intervals. These payments typically are drawn from the fund's dividends and capital gains distributions, if any, and from principal, to the extent necessary.

Yield: Income received from investments, usually expressed as a percentage of market price; also referred to as current yield. Usually computed on the basis of one year's income.

Yield to Maturity: The yield earned on a bond over its full life. Includes capital gains if the bond was bought at a discount from its face value.

Zero-coupon bond: A bond that is bought at a price below par with no coupons. Your return is the difference between the purchase and sale price, or par if held to maturity. Zeros accumulate and compound interest at the same rate that prevailed when the bond was bought.

INDEX
THE NO-LOAD FUND INVESTOR

How You Can Save $51 While Earning More Mutual Fund Profits!

Please see the SPECIAL NO-RISK OFFER on the opposite side of this tear-off Order Form for:

- 12-month subscription to *The No-Load Fund Investor* newsletter

- *The Handbook for No-Load Fund Investors*

SPECIAL OFFER: $129 FOR BOTH!
($51 savings over regular price of each separately.)

▼ Detach along perforation and mail

FROM

_____

_____

_____

THE **NO-LOAD** FUND INVESTOR, INC.
PO Box 318
Irvington-on-Hudson, NY 10533-0318